Reducing Inequalities
A Sustainable Development Challenge

Rémi Genevey
Executive Director, Head of Strategy, AFD (Agence française de développement), Paris, France

Rajendra K. Pachauri
Director General, TERI (The Energy and Resources Institute), TERI University, New Delhi, India

Laurence Tubiana
Director, IDDRI (Institute for Sustainable Development and International Relations), Paris, France

CONTENTS

■ **Agence Française de Développement (AFD)** is a public development finance institution that has been working to fight poverty and foster economic growth in developing countries and the French Overseas Communities for seventy years. It executes the policy defined by the French Government. AFD is present on four continents where it has an international network of seventy agencies and representation offices, including nine in the French Overseas Communities and one in Brussels. It finances and supports projects that improve people's living conditions, promote economic growth and protect the planet, such as schooling for children, maternal health, support for farmers and small businesses, water supply, tropical forest preservation, and the fight against climate change.

In 2011, AFD approved nearly €6.9 billion to finance activities in developing countries and the French Overseas Communities. The funds will help get 4 million children into primary school and 2 million into secondary school; they will also improve drinking water supply for 1.53 million people. Energy efficiency projects financed by AFD in 2011 will save nearly 3.8 million tons of carbon dioxide emissions annually. More information and publications available at www.afd.fr

■ **The Institute for Sustainable Development and International Relations (IDDRI)** is a non-profit policy research institute. Its objective is to determine and share the keys for analyzing and understanding strategic issues linked to sustainable development from a global perspective. As an independent institute, IDDRI helps stakeholders in deliberating on global governance of the major issues of common interest: action to attenuate climate change, to protect biodiversity, to enhance food security and to manage urbanisation. IDDRI also takes part in efforts to reframe development pathways. Through its partnership with Sciences Po in Paris, France, IDDRI is also involved in teaching and participates in the development of research programmes with support from the Sustainable Development Centre of Sciences Po. More information and publications available at www.iddri.org

■ **The Energy and Resources Institute (TERI)** was set up in 1974 to deal inter alia with issues relating to sustainable development, the environment, energy efficiency and the sustainable use of natural resources. Its goal is to develop innovative solutions for achieving sustainable development. Its activities range from the formulation of local and national strategies, to proposals for global solutions, to energy and environment-related issues. TERI is based in New Delhi, and also present in many other regions of India. It has over 900 employees and is headed by Rajendra K. Pachauri who is also the Chairman of the Intergovernmental Panel on Climate Change (IPCC), which was awarded the 2007 Nobel Prize. More information and publications available at www.teriin.org

Reducing Inequalities: A sustainable Development Challenge
Rémi Genevey, Rajendra K. Pachauri and Laurence Tubiana (Editors)
Delhi: TERI, 2013
ISBN 978-81-7993-530-9
© 2013, AFD, IDDRI
© 2013, TERI

Editors. Rémi Genevey, Executiv Director, Head of Strategy, French Development Agency (AFD); Rajendra K. Pachauri, Director General of The Energy and Resources Institute (TERI) and Chairman of the Intergovernmental Panel on Climate Change (IPCC), which was awarded a Nobel Prize in 2007; and Laurence Tubiana, Director of the Institute for Sustainable Development and International Relations (IDDRI) and the Sustainable Development Centre at Sciences Po.

Associate Editors: Raphaël Jozan (AFD), Tancrède Voituriez (IDDRI), Sanjivi Sundar (TERI University).

Editorial coordinators: Raphaël Jozan (AFD) and Isabelle Biagiotti (Courrier de la planète).

Translation and adaptation from French: Jim and Katell Johnson.

Text- and copy-editing: Jim and Katell Johnson. Foreword and Introduction translated by Suzan Nolan and Leila Whittemore (BlueSky International)

Print-Production: TERI Press

Maps and figures: Légendes Cartographie, SARL.

Graphic design: Alain Chevallier, design and cover.

Photo credits: Cover: Getty Images

Rémi Genevey
Executive Director, Head of Strategy, AFD (Agence française de développement), Paris, France

Rajendra K. Pachauri
Director General, TERI (The Energy and Resources Institute), TERI University, New Delhi, India

Laurence Tubiana
Director, IDDRI (Institute for Sustainable Development and International Relations), Paris, France

Foreword

Already a key component of sustainable development policies, the alleviation of inequalities within and between countries also stands as a policy goal, one with high economic, social and environmental stakes.

We have dedicated this 2013 edition of *A Planet for Life* to inequality reduction, in light of significant recent works that reframe debate on sustainable development. Such works suggest that equity effectively supports long-term economic growth and increases resilience within economies[1]. Scholars have recently demonstrated a strong empirical correlation between an increase in inequality and a decrease in biodiversity[2]. In addition, others have argued that greater inequality has toxic effects on society, lowering life expectancy, undermining trust in government and eroding social cohesion[3].

More importantly, since the 2008 global economic crisis, inequalities have regained centre stage as major public and policy concerns. Since 2008, many events have

1. Bourguignon F., 2012, La mondialisation de l'inégalité, Seuil. Stiglitz, J., The price of inequalities: How Today's Divided Society Endangers our Future. .

2. Mikkelson G. M., et al., 2007, Economic Inequality Predicts Biodiversity Loss. Public Library of Science (PLoS) ONE 2.e444.

3. Wilkinson R.G. and Pickett, K.E., 2009, The Spirit Level: Why More Equal Societies Almost Always Do Better. Penguin, New York, NY.

highlighted the unequal excesses arising from previous economic policies and their inattention to equality. These events include social movements and electoral campaigns, along with outrage at outsized compensation for the finance sector – the chief culprits of the crisis – and protests against governmental austerity policies. Most development professionals have seized upon these excesses, fueling debate through published reports and their own expanded views of sectoral and topical themes: society, the economy and the environment.

This volume, *Reducing Inequalities: A Sustainable Development Challenge,* represents a unique international initiative: it collects the works of many experts, researchers and development professionals who do not usually interact, bringing them together for this year's *A Planet for Life,* a series focused on sustainable development issues. The authors have grounded their work on conceptual and strategic thinking, and – most importantly – empirical experiments, conducted on five continents and touching on multiple realities. The authors draw on this fieldwork to analyse and evaluate inequalities and the policy actions that aim to reduce them. This unprecedented collection proposes a solid empirical approach, rather than an ideological one, to inform future debate.

We must all realize that inequality reduction does not occur by decree; neither does it automatically arise through economic growth, nor through policies that equalize incomes downward via ill conceived fiscal policies. Inequality reduction involves a collaborative effort that must motivate all concerned parties, one that constitutes a genuine political and social innovation, and one that often runs counter to prevailing political and economic forces.

The case studies collected in this volume demonstrate the complexity of the new systems required to accommodate each country's specific economic, political and cultural realities. These systems combine technical, financial, legal, fiscal and organizational elements with a great deal of applied expertise, and must be connected within a clear, well-understood, growth- and job-generating development strategy. Their durability depends on their ability to inspire collaboration among stakeholders who frequently hold antagonistic interests, values and rationales.

In the international realm, inclusive economic growth, improved well-being and conservation of public goods – especially environmental ones – require that all countries reduce inequalities and promote common rules. Such efforts depend on the establishment of rules that are fair and applicable to all

The publication of this 2013 edition of *A Planet for Life* coincides with the acceleration of "post-2015" negotiations and the design of Sustainable Development Goals, agreed during the Rio+20 Summit in 2012. Among those goals, inequality reduction deserves to take centre stage. This volume is an important contribution for enhancing a shared understanding of inequalities. Its insights will provide valuable guidance for AFD, IDDRI and TERI in their relationships with partners. We hope this volume will also receive recognition during current and future international negotiations and that it will bolster collective action to alleviate inequality wherever it arises. ∎

Raphaël Jozan
AFD (Agence française de développement), Paris, France

Sanjivi Sundar
TERI University, Delhi, India

Tancrède Voituriez
IDDRI (Institute for Sustainable Development and International Relations), France

Reducing Inequalties: A Sustainable Development Challenge

What is the state of inequalities worldwide?

s the world increasingly unequal? Are the rich getting richer and the poor poorer? Inequalities mobilize citizens more today than they did twenty years ago, fuelling protests by activist groups such as Occupy, the 99%, or the Indignant, to cite just a few. Such critics oppose and rebel against an unfair distribution of globalization's costs and benefits – especially as the lion's share of the latter goes first and foremost to the richest.

To truly understand how inequalities have evolved, we must first distinguish between gaps in living standards *among* countries and those *within* a country. Both inequality types have seen great reversals that mark a historic change for humanity (**Pedro Ramos Pinto, Chapter 1**). The first is the reversal of a secular trend that fostered ever-larger *regional* income gaps, which had reached extremely high levels at the end of the twentieth century. The new geography of growth has displaced the world's economic centre of gravity from the West to the East, ending what the head of the World Bank's research department, Branko Milanovic, calls the "great divergence"[1]. The spectacular growth of emerging countries has reduced, on average, income inequality between countries. In addition, a significant reduction in absolute poverty has accompanied this growth. Twenty years ago, people lived twenty times better in Western Europe than in China; that

1. Milanovic, B., 2009, "Global inequality and the global inequality extraction ratio: the story of the past two centuries." World Bank Policy Research Working Paper Series, no. 5061.

gap has been halved. During the same period, more than 500 million people have escaped poverty. These trends fuel a guarded optimism, especially about Africa; many observers view the emergence of a middle class in Africa as a lever for inclusive and democratic development[2].

At the same time, a second reversal saw a major breakdown in developed countries, with inequalities increasing *within* many countries. In Europe and North America, a very long period of contraction in income inequality certainly helped maintain the illusion that societies had automatically moved toward reduced inequality. However, Europe has entered a protracted phase in which inequalities have increased because of slack economic growth; this greatly favours inherited capital, raising the spectre of a resurgence of a rentier society some thought had vanished (**Piketty, Chapter 2**). This problem has arisen in developed countries as diverse as France, the United Kingdom, Japan and Germany. An implacable arithmetic tallies the increases in income inequality as the rate of return on capital exceeds the pace of economic growth, threatening all European countries, even the most egalitarian ones, such as Sweden. In the United States, income inequality has reached heights not seen in a century.

Does globalization drive the inexorable rise of inequalities worldwide? A historical comparison of inter-country and intra-country inequalities shows a far more complex relationship between inequalities and globalization, one at odds with the overly-simplistic view of a world that is increasingly unequal. The entrance of nearly one billion unskilled Chinese and Indian workers into the global labour market has certainly led to changes in pay scales and the shift of production units to Asia. In addition, technological advances, growth of corporations, and the structural changes in value-chains have principally benefited capital, not labour, increasing and concentrating profits. That said, over the last ten years globalization has also helped reduce inequality levels at the international level, driving the convergence of countries' average income (**Bourguignon, Chapter 4**). This convergence remains fragile and unequal, particularly among the least-developed countries.

Inequality and unsustainable development trajectories

Inequalities have never achieved a central place in development cooperation strategies, despite pressure from some countries, particularly France (**Tomasi, Radar 4**). Poverty alleviation and human development have taken priority since the turn of the century. Can inequalities take centre stage in the development agenda today? And why consider inequalities a collective-action problem whose solution requires cooperation within and between countries?

First of all, despite the reduction in national income gaps worldwide – particularly between emerging and developed countries – large gaps remain; growth rates will not easily erase these gaps for several decades. Taken globally, the measurable

---

2. See, for example, a 2009 report published by the African Development Bank: *The Middle of the Pyramid: Dynamics of the Middle Class in Africa*. Tunis: AfDB.

decrease in inequalities between countries, and their increase within countries, stems from China's population share and the high concentration of wealth among its rich (**Pinto, Chapter 1**). Much of humanity remains trapped in poverty. Emerging countries have become more unequal over time. Brazil and Indonesia have escaped this trend, but their levels of inequality nevertheless remain very high, as do those in China (**Cook and Dong, Radar 11**), in India (**Bouver, Radar 12**) and South Africa (**Giordano, Radar 10**). Countering the oft-expressed enthusiasm about the African middle class, Pierre Jacquemot's meta-analysis on studies on sub-Saharan Africa (**Radar 9**) notes that social inequalities generally deepen despite the emergence of middle classes; traditional social ties disintegrate without public action to reshape or "modernize" them.

Second, a growing number of economists and institutions also see a positive link between reducing inequalities and increasing the capacity for sustained and stable long-term growth. Equality may well be an important ingredient in promoting and sustaining growth, particularly over the medium and long term, making economies more resilient (**Berg, Ostry, Radar 4bis**). By contrast, the growth of inequalities contributes to economic crises; two economists from the International Monetary Fund, Andrew Berg and Jonathan Ostry (**Radar 4bis**) highlight the role that American inequalities played in igniting the global financial crisis five years ago[3]. We now see social cohesion emerging as a critical objective for governments, as expressed in the *2012 OECD World Development Perspective: Social Cohesion in a Shifting World* report. In and of themselves, improvements to living standards, health and education do not necessarily translate into greater satisfaction among the populace. The 2010 anti-government protests in Thailand and the 2011 overthrow of Ben Ali in Tunisia demanded more fairness, and not just income distribution. Unequal access to productive resources, education, credit, justice, employment and policy making play a critical role, combining and reinforcing each other, segregating social groups and regions.

Inequalities and development: a changing paradigm

In **Chapter 4**, François Bourguignon, former World Bank chief economist and a major scholar of the relationship between growth and equality, describes how in academic circles from the 1950s to present, debates about inequality, growth and poverty and their interconnections have shaped national policies and development organization strategies. His history of economic ideas reveals that the growth paradigm has changed over the past twenty years, with a progressively greater focus on a key issue for sustainable growth: how can the most disadvantaged accumulate productive assets. The World Bank's 2006 *World Development Report* proved a crucial turning point; it established inequality's impact on growth as development's central problem,

---

3. In recent decades, the growth of inequalities in the United States resembles that of the 1920s, marked then as now by a boom in the financial sector, heavy borrowing by the poor and relatively insolvent, and the devastating financial crisis that followed.

thus bridging the divide between the academic sphere and the operational world of development.

This report signalled the acceptance of a multidimensional approach to inequalities, based in part on Amartya Sen's concept of "capacity"[4]. The report draws on the major breakthroughs made by scholars in the 1990s who empirically demonstrated that high levels of inequality interfere with the allocation of investment capital; only entrepreneurs holding collateral or investible cash can complete projects using loans, even if their projects perform at a suboptimal level. Meanwhile, more potentially profitable entrepreneurs and investment projects are sidelined (**Bourguignon, Chapter 4**).

Since the middle of the 2000s – in the wake of these studies and the 2006 World Bank report – we have seen a certain proliferation of econometric analyses exploring the impact of inequalities on other aspects of development, particularly environmental conservation and human health. In 2007, Gregory Mikkelson (**Chapter 5**) demonstrated a strong positive empirical relationship between increased inequality and decreasing biodiversity: his key findings are presented in this volume. In 2009, Richard Wilkinson and Kate Pickett published their groundbreaking book, *The Sprit Level: Why More Equal Societies Almost Always Do Better*, shedding light on correlations between equality and health; Sridhar Venkatapuram discusses that book's conclusions (**Chapter 6**). In all these ways, inequalities impact on the three pillars of sustainable development: economic, social and environmental.

The recognition of a positive relationship between sustainable development and inequality reduction has imbued public and development policies. Serge Tomasi (**Radar 4**) recalls how a multidimensional view of inequalities and poverty gradually gained a foothold in international organizations, as seen through the refinements of their programmes, measurements and indicators. Vincent Bonnecase (**Chapter 3**) and Benoît Martin (**Radar 3**) analyse the history of this current of thought.

François Bourguignon (**Chapter 4**) also finds that governments have changed their attitude toward inequality. Tellingly, for example, the Chinese government currently recognizes that their large inequality problem threatens the viability of their growth model: Chinese households' excessive savings rate may be due, in part, to the uncertain and limited nature of health insurance and pension coverage. Previously, a country's growth was measured by its GDP growth rate; today, governments and international organizations analyse GDP growth along with the pattern of income growth distribution. Many chapters and varied case studies in the book illustrate how governments strive to ensure more equitable access to productive resources, health care, education, credit, justice, natural resources and public policy.

---

4. Sen, A., 1985, *Commodities and Capabilities*. New York: Oxford University Press.

Inequality reduction, a collaborative and innovative process

Authors in this volume share their analyses of national experiments, such as the collective management of natural resources in Namibia (**Radar 5**), health insurance systems in Cambodia (**Radar 6**), social policies in Brazil (**Chapter 10**), inequality reduction policies in municipalities in low- and medium-income countries (**Chapter 7**), carbon tax implementations in Sweden (**Radar 8**) and France (**Chapter 8**), and so-called bottom-of-the-pyramid initiatives of private companies (**Chapter 11**).

It is no simple matter to implement effective inequality reduction policies. **Chapter 10** illustrates this particularly well in its analysis of social policy systems in Brazil, one of the only emerging countries to achieve inequality reductions in the last ten years: the country serves as a real-life "laboratory." The authors Barbosa and Oliveira, note that multiple technical, institutional, organizational, financial, fiscal and legal elements must coexist to stimulate a virtuous circle of inequality reduction. This virtuous circle also needs clear, socially accepted rules that will foster individual responsibility; equally, it requires capable human resource managers who can train competent civil servants. All the stakeholders – policymakers, development professionals, academics and other actors like local communities and the private sector – must work together synergistically and horizontally to address the problem of inequality. The natural resource management programmes in Namibia (**Lapeyre, Corbier-Barthaux, Radar 5**) and health care services in Cambodia (**Radar 6**) are other good examples of collaboration between stakeholders.

These networks and systems do not get established overnight or in a linear fashion. Trial and error is inevitable. Reading through these chapters, we see that many emerging and developing economies strive to strengthen their institutional capacities through decentralization and stronger local tax collection and disbursement. However, these efforts frequently disappoint. South Africa provides a good example (**Giordano, Radar 11**). Typically, the central government may give impetus to socially inclusive programmes, but corruption and conflicts of interest could undermine the programmes and service quality, as could local governments stymied by a lack of capacity and resources.

Inequality reduction involves real social and policy innovation that often collides with vested interests and with political and economic forces. In Cambodia (**Radar 6**), organizations setting up a universal health insurance system are required to work alongside a for-profit private sector over which they have no control. The challenge for Cambodia and other governments lies in making suitable arrangements with the private sector and moving unregulated, informal activities into the formal and regulated market. The system's sustainability (in the sense of duration) will depend on maintaining a coalition of actors even though they may have different (sometimes contradictory) interests and values.

Some of the national experiments described in the book display a naive vision of economic growth or of fiscal policies leading by themselves to a reduction of inequalities. Brazilian authors **Barbosa and Oliveira** argue that, on the contrary, a social security system must be articulated within a clear, well-understood, growth- and job-generating development strategy (**Chapter 10**). Fiscal policy may then finance the system, but only if it does not call for "equalizing down" incomes to achieve absolute equality. Even if it still seems possible, on paper, to redistribute wealth and prevent inequalities from worsening, we must recognize that redistribution comes with economic costs and political constraints that cannot be ignored (**Bourguignon 2012**). The state must explain its goals and promote the public good; this means expressing a vision and involving stakeholders. We saw this process work in Sweden; everyone understood that the carbon tax would go together with a wealth-and-job-generating industrial policy, and adopted it (**Sterner, Focus 7**). The episode of the Sarkozy carbon tax in France is a perfect example to the contrary (**Hourcade, Chapter 8**).

Charismatic political leaders, deeply committed to equality and social justice, work at various levels to reduce inequality: Nelson Mandela (**Giordano, Radar 10**), Lula da Silva (**Chapter 10**), some leaders of informal urban settlements (**Satterthwaite, Chapter 7**), and social activist groups, like Ekta Parishad in India (**Bouver, Radar 12**) are inspiring examples. These steel-willed social entrepreneurs orchestrate collective action through a legitimacy earned by changing citizens' daily lives and their relationship to the political, economic, social and even natural environment.

Measurement promotes collaboration

"Comparing nobles to commoners foreshadows the night of 4 August;[5] comparing Blacks to Whites calls for the abolition of slavery; comparing men to women calls for truly universal suffrage, one that includes women," Alain Derosières writes in his book, *The Politics of Large Numbers*, cited in **Chapter 3**. He explains that measuring things is as much a technical as a political act: measuring changes the world.

The emergence of new measurement tools underpins the change in governmental attitudes toward inequalities and their interest in combining GDP growth with the pattern of income distribution. Governments analyse trends in so-called "growth incidence curves" to see how much different income levels have increased over time. These measures have come into wide use (**Chapter 4**) because approaches to development and public affairs management are now more multidimensional, and especially because a "statistical revolution" (and the widening accessibility of computers) has now made the data available for analysis. This statistical revolution occurred in the 1980s and 1990s in a few pioneering countries, followed by others as USAID, the World Bank and the United Nations Development Program funded universities and national or local statistical agencies to conduct large-scale household surveys. Statisticians must transform the surveys and databases to "capture poverty" – to measure it in a granular fashion. This allows information to escape the confines

---

5. In France, during the night of 4 August 1789, members of the National Constituent Assembly, formed from the National Assembly during the first stage of French Revolution, vowed to end feudalism and abandon their privileges.

of administrative statistics that are "structured by the formal sector, when poverty and hunger most affect families living outside the formal system" (**Chapter 10**). This re-working of household surveys and other new data allows decision-makers to go beyond the formal versus informal dichotomy – too often used in some countries to justify the difficulty if not the impossibility of implementing social policies.

Moreover, this new knowledge promotes platforms for collaboration between actors who do not a priori share the same interests and values. Cambodia's health insurance initiative best illustrates this point (**Radar 6**). Insurers cannot set premiums or carry out actuarial analyses in the absence of reliable data and risk analyses. A similar situation occurs in the field of natural resources management (**Radar 5**), or in the field of GHG emission reduction initiatives (**Radar 8**).

Historically, researchers have been the first to undertake the risky business of quantifying inequalities, as **Chapter 2** clearly points out. Thomas Piketty reminds us how often researchers have preceded institutions and politicians, furnishing the latter with the conceptual apparatus and statistics needed to comprehend the problem and devise solutions. For example, the World Top Incomes database contributes to scientific initiatives with policy implications: President Obama cited two of its authors in his 2009 inauguration speech, paying homage to science and showing gratitude for the researchers' statistical work. Availability of data by itself is not adequate. Data must be intelligently used by governments to reduce inequalities. Since the advent of databases like the World Top Incomes, many governments have agreed to take inequalities firmly into account and have changed their measurement procedures accordingly (**Martin, Radar 3**). Other, more hermetic governments have not used the information; these countries show the highest levels of inequalities.

Given the new certainties found in empirical measures, it is striking to see how many issues remain poorly understood. The authors of **Radar 6** suggest this is true for micro-insurance: insurance system impact studies remain scarce, especially in developing countries. In 2007, the French development agency AFD, Domrei Research and Consulting, and the University of California, Berkeley conducted the first rigorous evaluation of micro-insurance in Cambodia. This highlights how many solutions for some international problems rest on incomplete empirical bases.

Policy challenges to reduce inequalities

Various chapters of this volume highlight the increase in inequalities within countries. Without minimizing the problem of unequal living standards and access to opportunities between countries, we find that internal inequality presents the primary obstacle to even-handed, sustainable environmental, social and economic development. This raises a question: can such an apparently common problem find a jointly developed solution, one based on consensus and shared efforts between countries? Several sections of this volume, especially **Radars 1 and 4**, demonstrate the usefulness of international collective action in reducing (for instance) economic inequalities. Addressing unequal pay and the (low) share of wages compared to profits in an economy may boost employment and growth, and skirt the non-negligible risk of "free riders". The first challenge, an enormous one, lies in coordinating fiscal and social policies.

Creating a political consensus to address inequalities worldwide poses an equally large challenge. Are all governments ready to follow the recommendation of the International Labour Organisation presented in **Radar 4**. Are they all committed to reducing inequalities within their own countries? Inequality reduction, as such, does not seem to hold universal appeal within all countries – indeed, inequalities continue to grow within many. In his contribution to this volume (**Chapter 9**), Peter Utting stresses that the game is not over yet; changes in power relations between countries affect collective action paradigms, forcing them to evolve. A real opportunity exists to restructure cooperation, in the broadest sense of the word, through shared analysis of the underlying causes of capitalism's current crisis.

What about inequality between countries? The international community regularly includes inequality in its negotiating agenda, so often that inequality has become a refrain; countries seem to pay little attention to it, because they are not politically committed to reducing inequalities. The international community constantly seems pulled in two directions: toward creating effective but ultimately unfair agreements, or producing fair but probably ineffective ones. We might recall that the United Nation's principle of common but differentiated responsibility grants developing countries the privilege of exoneration from absolute and quantifiable reductions in greenhouse gas emissions, given that these countries have emitted fewer greenhouse gases than developed countries have since 1950. The Kyoto Protocol and the United Nations Framework Convention on Climate Change may be considered equitable from this perspective, although some countries may argue this is at the cost of efficiency.

It seems, however, that the United Nations Millennium Development Goals (MDGs) have aimed to circumvent such trade-offs between fairness and effectiveness. Building on successes on the MDG front, the United Nations has begun to extend them to Sustainable Development Goals (SDGs) in all countries. Mark Halle notes that this aim remains programme-based (**Radar 13**); fast-forwarding to 2015 – the official MDGs end-date, announced in 2000 – Halle predicts a bout of international self-congratulation, although "it would be an exaggeration to think that China's and India's relative success results from measures taken to respond to the MDGs". Furthermore, the lack or near-absence of substantive decisions in Rio in 2012 on the twentieth anniversary of the Earth Summit highlights how little appetite countries have for negotiations. Might the international community successfully negotiate SDGs in the next two years? That was the question asked in Rio.

The last chapter of this volume is dedicated to the SDGs and their universal reach and specific targets for each country (**Chapter 13**). Such a tailored approach to inequalities has real merit. Serge Tomasi (**Radar 4**) believes it necessary to define goals and indicators that go beyond general goals and comparable measures for all countries. His proposals include national goals in indicators, to follow each country's progress vis-à-vis its specific situation. Sustainable development rests on trial and error more than on a conceptualization or a prescription; the SDGs may help guide and measure the effects of these experiments in each country.

The SDGs borrow important characteristics from the MDGs, even while offering distinct ones. Like the MDGs, the SDGs must be simple to state, measurable and attainable. However, their underlying concept differs. The MDGs answered a demand for results and remobilized exhausted donors. They provided goals related to a world we know is possible – a world free of its greatest scourges, poverty first and foremost among them. The SDGs are transformative..

As the international community prepares the SDGs, it must capitalize on the experience of various countries and regions. As **David Satterthwaite and Diana Mitlin (Chapter 7)** emphasize, the international community must also be receptive to social innovations; these must take centre stage in political discussions to increase their visibility and impact, according to **Bruno Frère (Chapter 12)**. Capitalizing on experience also requires increasing experimentation; this is the focus of the Sustainable Development Solution Network, presented in the last chapter of this volume (**Chapter 13**).

Sustainable development continues to be a collective experiment, composed of trials and errors. To what extent do these experiments require inequality reductions in order to succeed and be replicated? This is the key political question that has to be addressed in the pursuit of a sustainable development agenda. The various chapters in this volume, written by eminent authors from across the world, offer some guidance. ■

It is easier to recognize the problems caused by unequal resource allocation than it is to understand what causes them. Comprehending the causes requires an analysis of the conditions that produce differential access to resources; it also requires an understanding of the criteria that categorize people into differential social groups. A historical view of inequality shows the durability of these social categorizations; it also shows opportunities for altering them and transforming society.

Why inequalities matter

A concern for inequality has long been central to the field of development, whose aim for some time has been to see a narrowing of the gaps between the "developing" and the "developed" world. In recent years, however, changes in the way inequalities express themselves across the world have drawn our attention to differences in income, opportunities and life-chances within nations (BOURGUIGNON, 2012). This transformation of stratification has implications for the sustainability of development in human and environmental terms. Understanding it requires thinking beyond economic structures and taking seriously the role of social factors and historical trajectories.

Pedro Ramos Pinto,
University of Manchester, Manchester, United Kingdom

After a long period of contraction in income inequality in Western European and North American countries, in recent decades these regions have seen the gap between the rich, the poor and the not-so-rich increase. At the same time as rich nations became more unequal, new studies and sources of data have become available which show that inequalities are associated to a variety of other differences in more important quality of life dimensions: in comparison to more equal nations, more unequal countries tend to be less healthy, have lower life-expectancy, experience more crime and a range of other negative social outcomes (WILKINSON AND PICKETT, 2009).

This renewed interest in issues of distribution in rich countries has had the knock-on effect of returning the issue of inequality in global development to the forefront of policy and political debates. Since the start of the era of "development" following the break-up of empires in the second half of the twentieth century, the dominant modes of thought in the fields of economics and development have seen inequality as a lamentable, but ultimately transient side-effect of economic maturation. Drawing on the historical experience of the first industrialized nations, the economist Simon Kuznets proposed that inequality accompanied economic development in a bell-shaped curve: so that it would be expected to grow as leading economic sectors in each country forged ahead of traditional modes of production, widening the gap between the incomes of say, family-based farming, and those of skilled workers and investors in modern industrial production. This pattern, extrapolated from the history of the United States and Great Britain from the eighteenth to the early twentieth century, suggested a happy ending: urbanization, modernization, industrial diffusion, and the political pressure exerted by a widening waged workforce would lead to the creation of welfare systems and redistributive policies that would bring equalization at a greater plateau of wealth for all, completing the second half of Kuznets' bell curve. Kuznets' economic view of modernization as ultimately equalizing had a counterpart in political science and sociology with the equally influential work of T.H. Marshall on the evolution of citizenship, which saw societies evolving systems of civic, political and ultimately social rights which would eventually produce equalizing institutions not dissimilar to the welfare states created in post-war Europe (KUZNETS, 1955; MARSHALL, 1955). Over time, Kuznets' and Marshall's hypotheses on modernization became solid certainties for development experts and rising inequality in industrializing countries was not only a matter that warranted little concern, but could even be taken for a sign that a country was on the "right" path.

Scales of inequality

INEQUALITY OVER TIME. Evidence for the trajectories of inequality in longitudinal and international perspectives is difficult to come by (for an overview and critique see Clarke (2011); Ortiz and Cummins (2011)), but recent efforts in data collection and standardization have allowed more solidly based comparisons to be made; and these have failed to give Kuznets' hypothesis strong support. As Ferreira and Rosanvallon note in their review, economic growth seems as likely to reduce inequality as to increase it (FERREIRA and ROSANVALLON, 2009; ACEMOGLU and ROBINSON, 2002). This is clearly the case in many high-income countries where, despite continued economic growth (at least until the financial crisis of 2008), inequality has increased again since the late 1970s.

Looking more broadly, a global view reveals a varied and complex picture that escapes a single-factor explanation, or even straightforward description – there is not one, but several distinct trends in levels of inequality between, and within, countries. Historically, the clearest and best known shift in inequality is what has been called "the great divergence": at around 1500 AD, differences in wealth and standards of living across the world were not extreme (See Box 1). While within societies there were large differences in status, power and wealth between aristocracies and the mass of the population, these did not vary widely across the more fertile and populous parts of the world: around this time the livelihood of a Chinese peasant under the Ming Dynasty would not be very different to that of a peasant living under Emperor Charles V in Europe.

FIGURE 1 **A recent divergence of income levels**

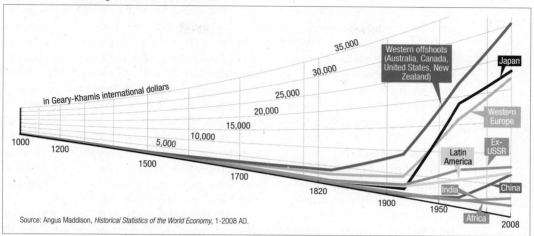

Source: Angus Maddison, *Historical Statistics of the World Economy*, 1-2008 AD.

Until 1500, it is estimated that incomes were relatively similar in all regions of the world. Since the mid-nineteenth century, the average standard of living is more reliably predicted by the place where one lives, compared to one's social position within a given society.

Between then and the end of the twentieth century, Western Europe as a region multiplied its economic capacity at a much faster rate than the rest of the world. Over time other regions, including colonial territories in North America and Oceania, but also pockets of industrial productivity such as Japan, joined what became a powerful club of rich nations. The disparity in wealth and standards of living between the "West and the rest" became particularly marked from the middle of the nineteenth century onwards, creating a club of very rich nations which are home to a small fraction of the world's population (MADDISON, 2001). The result of this decoupling of the fortunes of different parts of the world was that, when considered in a global perspective (taking each individual in the world as a unit) inequality went from being largely accounted for by each individual's position in the income ladder in their own country, to being largely the result of where in the world each individual was born, or managed to move to, in the case of migrants (MILANOVIC, 2012). Milanovic has calculated that the great divergence in national incomes between industrializing nations and the Global South stretched inequality between individual incomes, expressed in a near doubling of the global Gini coefficient between 1820 and 2002 (MILANOVIC, 2009)[1].

HISTORY AND THE GREAT DIVERGENCE. What were the historical causes of the so-called "great divergence"? This has been a foundational problem of Western social science and economics. While the constraints of this chapter do not allow for a detailed survey of the most vibrant areas of research in economic history, it is possible to draw an

---

1. See Milanovic (2009), Table 2, which gives a global Gini coefficient in 1820 of 43, rising to 70.7 in 2002. Using the Theil index, the change is between 58 in 1820 and 104.8 in 2002.

outline of these debates. Early accounts of the transformations that led to Western global dominance focused on specificities of European societies that were said to promote economic growth, contrasting them to supposed impediments in Eastern and Southern economies. While some followed Marx in arguing for the importance of the bourgeois revolutions in ushering in a productive capitalist mode of production, over the supposed resilience of feudal systems elsewhere, followers of Max Weber suggested that again supposedly European legal, cultural and ideological institutions (such as the "Protestant work ethic") were endogenous factors that promoted an economic take-off. Whilst they all looked to different factors as causes, these classic accounts of European economic growth shared an outlook that contrasted an assumed European political and social "appropriateness" to economic growth, with an often badly informed orientalist view of non-European societies as closed, backward and economically stagnant, views which pervaded (and often pervade still) the attitudes of Western policy-makers to non-Western societies (ESCOBAR, 2012 [1995]).

Over time the debate has come to include other factors, from the role of Western imperialism and colonialism both bolstering economic dominance and constraining opportunities for development elsewhere (WALLERSTEIN, 1974) – a proposition that continues to feed intense argument – to current research that relativizes Western "take-off", pointing to the fact that until at least the late eighteenth century, if not later, many non-European regions possessed a commercial and institutional environment no less conducive to investment than Europe (BIN WONG, 1997; POMMERANZ, 2000). Just as Kuznet's theory has been challenged by recent research, so new perspectives on the "Great Divergence" are beginning to show that the Western path to economic growth, and the conditions and technological breakthroughs that potentiated it, are more contingent and less generalizable than previously thought. Similarly, the recent economic growth of nations which, as recently as the mid-twentieth century, seemed locked in a situation of arrested development, has emphasized the fact that historically, the institutional underpinnings of development are more varied than Eurocentric accounts have credited (CHANG, 2011; POMMERANZ, 2002)[2]. The problem, as the Indian economic historian Tirthankar Roy points out, is that theories focused on explaining why the "Third World" was poor, become useless once substantial parts of it begin to get richer (ROY, 2012).

THE LIMITS OF CONVERGENCE. During the course of the last two decades, economic growth in what have been called the "rising powers" of the global economy, led by China, India and Brazil, has been indeed spectacular. Remarkably, there seems to be a reversal in the secular trend of the "Great Divergence" between rich, mostly Western, nations and the other countries in the world, and a shift towards a new era of convergence in levels of national wealth, and therefore a reduction in inequalities between countries in that dimension. Significantly, this has also brought with it important reductions in absolute poverty and improvements in standards of living, as

2. For a review of the "Great Divergence" debate over the last few decades see O'Brien (2010).

measured by the Human Development Index.

However, while much is made of the progress and challenge to Western economic dominance on the basis of continued double-digit growth in some middle-income countries, a measure of caution is necessary. The gaps in income and power between the richest countries are still large and are likely to remain so for some time: the scale of the economies of the rich world means that just to keep up with modest rates of growth in the rich countries and to maintain the distance, emerging economies need to achieve rates of growth that are very hard to sustain (MILANOVIC, 2011). In addition, there are no guarantees that this trend will continue – particularly as the consequences of the current financial crisis spread from the developed to the developing world, and questions remain about who will be the ultimate losers of the global economic shakedown. The sustainability of the growth experienced by many emerging econo-mies in these new economic conditions, particu-larly as a result of the retraction in consumption in rich nations, is a critical question.

FIGURE 2 Rising national inequalities

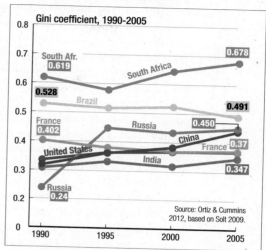

Source: Ortiz & Cummins 2012, based on Solt 2009.

Although emerging countries are presently catching up to the incomes of the West, this has not resulted in a uniform enrichment of their populations. In South Africa, Russia and China, amongst others, inequalities are persisting or even getting worse, alongside the general increase in living conditions.

The issue of sustainability is also relevant if we focus on a second, and increas-ingly noticeable trend in inequality. Inequality between individuals (considered both globally and within countries), as opposed to inequality between nations, is increasing. Just as this is happening in rich nations, so is inequality growing (and rapidly), amongst the strongest performing economies that are driving the conver-gence between the West and the rest. It is becoming increasingly clear that conver-gence in national incomes has not been translated into a significant levelling of incomes of the world's population, taken as a whole (MILANOVIC, 2009a; CLARK, 2011; HUNG and KUCINSKAS, 2011). In short, the proceeds of growth are not evenly distributed and two of the key emerging economies – India but especially China – have witnessed significant rises in inequality, even if Brazil has seen a slight reduc-tion in its traditionally extreme levels of inequality.

Clark has estimated that over the last 20 years, it is only in Africa that the incomes of the poorest quarter of the population have risen faster than those of the richest quarter. Elsewhere, but particularly in Asia and Eastern Europe, the incomes of the top quartile rose significantly faster than those of the bottom quartile – even where the absolute incomes of the poorest grew most strongly (CLARK, 2011). Just as much of the decline in (population-weighted) between-country inequality is the result of China's rates of growth (due to its large share of the world's total population), so is this the cause of the rise in within-country inequality globally considered, due to the growth in incomes of the top quartile of the Chinese population having been a lot faster than that experienced by those of the lowest (CLARK, 2011). The result is growing inequality within countries, as the very richest capture the lion's share of aggregate rises in income, particularly at the expense of the very poorest. This issue is coming increasingly to the attention of the development community (GOESLING 2001; CORNIA, ADDISON and KIISKI, 2004; FERREIRA and RAVALLION, 2008; PALMA, 2011). There is also mounting evidence that inequality - not only absolute poverty - matters for a number of social outcomes in low- and middle-income countries, just as they do in wealthier nations. A growing distance between rich and poor is likely to have significant negative externalities: firstly an increasing polarization of wealth in society makes it more difficult for the poor to bridge the gap towards a median standard of living, increasing the costs for the poor to achieve a minimum to participate fully in society (FERREIRA and RAVALLION, 2008). Income inequality is also likely to have important mediating effects on how development affects other important human functionings, not least health: surveying the interaction between GDP, inequality and a range of health outcomes in Latin American countries between 1960 and 2007, Biggs and colleagues found that "Wealthier is indeed healthier, but how much healthier depends on how increases in wealth are distributed" (BIGGS et al., 2010). Other reviews have noted how low relative returns to labour are likely to affect productivity; and, perhaps most importantly, a concentration of wealth reinforces the capacity of elites to capture power and engage in rent-seeking behaviour to the detriment of other sectors of society (VOITCHOVSKY, 2009; ECHEVERRI-GENT, 2009).

The causes and contexts of inequality

The realization that inequality per se matters for human development outcomes, points to a renewed challenge for the development community in understanding and addressing within-country inequalities. But recognizing the issue is easier than understanding its causes. Within economic and development circles, causes of inequality have been understood primarily within the parameters of countries' differential positions within the world market (the effect of globalization) or whether technological change has affected labour markets (the role of human capital stocks). These factors are, without a doubt, relevant in providing prima facie hypotheses on the causes of income inequality within and across nations. They are, however, limited in accounting for a more diverse range of experiences of inequality (of gender, ethnicity, age, etc.) and accounting for how individuals and groups find themselves in differentiated positions vis-à-vis markets, politics and society. Looking simply at two dimensions of inequality, gender and income, Figure 3 shows how diverse inequalities can be, even across such a limited range of examples. While the Gini figure on the left represents the degree of income inequality between individuals or households (methods of assessment differ) regardless of gender, the Gender Inequality index on the right measures the differences between men and women across a range of indicators, including access to labour markets, health, education and political representation. Despite having similar levels of income inequality, China and India reveal markedly distinct patterns of gender inequality, with women enjoying greater parity with men in China. Even South Africa and Brazil, which have some of the highest income disparities in the world, evidence lower inequality gaps between men and women than India (UNDP, 2011).

I have chosen these four countries to illustrate this point as they are often grouped together as the "rising powers" of the world economy and treated uniformly, despite their significant political, social and economic differences. What then, makes us so blind to the diversity of experiences and causes of inequality? To a large degree, such limitations stem from the way inequality is most often considered. As the Indian sociologist André Betteille noted, the study of inequality is usually approached from one of two different perspectives: the distributional and the relational (BETTEILLE, 2003). The former focuses on how valued qualities or assets (land, knowledge, capital) are distributed among a population, while the latter looks to social exchange between individuals and groups to explain unequal outcomes. A distributive account is essential, particularly in identifying which resources become the fulcrum of different systems of inequality. Seen in this light, we can for instance show how the critical resources for economic differentiation has changed from the possession of slaves in classical antiquity, to land-ownership, to access to moveable capital and, more recently, to knowledge and information.

Nonetheless, the distributive account cannot tell us (a) how individuals gain differentiated access to these resources; (b) how and why the value of resources changes across time and social contexts; and (c) how groups and societies manage, maintain and transform the systems that allocate such resources. These questions have to be addressed in an essentially relational and historical manner: by looking at the context of how individuals interact, exchange, cooperate and compete. Such contexts are influenced and conditioned by history to the extent that the relationships, ways of seeing the world and concepts that people and groups use in such interactions have been constructed and evolved over time. In what follows I give a brief and schematic overview of how a sociological and contextually grounded approach to inequalities can help address these questions, before turning more specifically to how a historical perspective, or sensitivity to the role of history in shaping inequality, can aid us in promoting sustainable development.

FROM MEASUREMENT TO EXPLANATION. The example of the role of human capital in determining inequalities illustrates the above-noted difference between

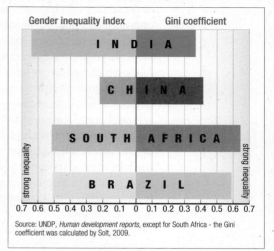

FIGURE 3 **The unequal inequality against women**

Gender inequality index   Gini coefficient

I N D I A

C H I N A

S O U T H   A F R I C A

B R A Z I L

0.7 0.6 0.5 0.4 0.3 0.2 0.1 0 0.1 0.2 0.3 0.4 0.5 0.6 0.7

strong inequality (left)   strong inequality (right)

Source: UNDP, *Human development reports*, except for South Africa - the Gini coefficient was calculated by Solt, 2009.

Inequalities suffered by women around the world do not only depend on the overall standard of living in the country in which they live. Indeed, the rules of distribution of goods are the result of principles that are much more complex than just scarcity.

distributional and relational accounts of inequality. In both rich and developing nations, research has demonstrated how in the latest phase of globalization, individuals with access to particular types of knowledge (for instance, high-level proficiency in IT) have seen their incomes rise quickly, while those of lower-skilled workers have stagnated or even declined in real terms. While this is important in identifying which resources have become critical in differentiating workers, it does little to illuminate the root causes of inequality, to the extent that it leaves two central questions unanswered.

First, what determines which individuals are able to gain access to the education that provides them with such skills? Answering this question requires an exploration of how a much broader set of social processes condition access to skills: are opportunities in education equally available to all members of society, regardless of race, class, gender or religion, or are there explicit and implicit obstacles that mean access is differentiated? All societies have systems that manage the allocation of resources, and the conditions of access to them: institutions, broadly speaking, also influence the shape of inequality. Political systems influence levels of taxation and redistribution, but also of investment in education, healthcare and other goods (ESPING-ANDERSEN, 1990; PIERSON, 2004). Legal systems influence ownership of assets, such as land or intellectual property, or police the enforcement of rights to opportunities and resources. Social systems, including social attitudes, religion, and beliefs about status, and the way in which societies enforce conformity with them, are particularly important in determining the social value of roles and qualities, and how these are inscribed in political and legal institutions.

Second, how and why do some qualities and assets become valued differentially from others? On the face of it, the issue of value of different types of human capital (say, technical knowledge and management knowledge) may seem to be determined by the basic economic mechanism of supply and demand. But the closer we look into this, the more complicated the relationship becomes. Take, for instance, current debates about executive remuneration in rich economies, an issue that is closely related to the growing share of national income accruing to the so-called 1%, and therefore the shape of inequality in those countries. To what extent do such immensely unequal rewards reflect the underlying "value" or performance of top executives, as opposed to, say roles such as teaching, housework or low-skill but high risk industrial employment?

Looking at inequality in a relational way highlights that income and educational inequalities are only one facet of difference and hierarchies in society. The emphasis on incomes may seem apt in increasingly commodified contemporary post-industrial societies (SANDEL, 2012) but in reality the experience of inequality is not solely, or perhaps even primarily connected to income. Inequalities express themselves in levels and access to education, in health and well-being, in rights and in freedoms. As Amartya Sen notes, inequality is a multi-dimensional concept which depends largely on the field on which distribution is being evaluated: of rights, resources, talents, characteristics or, ultimately, capabilities and social opportunity (SEN, 1992).

BOX 1 HISTORICAL CATEGORIZATION PROCESSES CAN SHAPE REGIONAL WITHIN-COUNTRY INEQUALITIES

■ Regional disparities in income, health and other social indicators are critical to understanding the dynamics of inequality within three of the key emerging giants, India, Brazil and China. Taking a historical perspective on all three reveals how diversity between regions has distinct historical roots in each country. In all three, however, the creation of categorical distinctions over time has produced groups with differential resources and assets with which to engage in a globalizing economy, leading to a reinforcement of existing inequalities.

In Brazil, Barbara Weinstein showed how São Paulo's planter elites in the 1920s used the political, cultural and financial resources that accrued to them during the coffee boom to develop a distinction between the Paulista – hailed as enterprising, risk taking and hard-working people – and the people of rural areas of northeastern Brazil, who in contrast were portrayed as uniformly backward, lazy and culturally underdeveloped. This categorization was used to justify channelling subsidies and support to industrial development in São Paulo, and for the political prominence of its elites in national government, to the exclusion of the northeast. That region was instead characterized and planned for as if it were a "disaster area": public funds to the northeast were more often than not channelled to emergency relief and resettlement programmes that brought workers to the south, rather than to the kinds of investment that would work towards a convergence between the two regions (WEINSTEIN, 2008).

Indian regional development trajectories evidence different aspects of inequality generation: the integration of India into Britain's imperial economy in the mid-nineteenth century ushered in a period of large-scale de-industrialization in many areas of the country, while focusing industrialization in concentrated pockets which were more closely embedded in an emerging world economy (ROY, 2012). This process was aided not only by legislation restricting competition between Indian manufacture and British industry, but also by the construction of sharper boundaries between Europeans and Indians by emphasizing rurality, tradition and tribalism as the "real India", masking over equally "typical" cosmopolitan, literate and urban aspects of Indian society. Such a process not only reinforced inequalities between colonizer and colonized, but also shaped the state's attitude to economic development and integration in a way that contributed to exacerbating regional inequalities (LUDDEN, 2002).

Over the last century China has seen its patterns of inequality undergo significant and dramatic changes. The establishment of State Socialism in Communist China brought in a period of equalization of incomes and social outcomes (particularly between genders), although to a very low level and involving tremendous human suffering. Since economic reforms began gathering pace in the 1980s, inequality between regions has increased substantially. Wang and Wang link the divergence between Chinese regions to formal and informal institutions and bounded categories created under socialism. The state's ambition for rapid industrialization was seen to require an unequal allocation of resources to the benefit of key regions and key personnel (skilled labour, technicians and planners), a goal which clashed with its own commitment to equality but which was skirted around through the institution of different categories of workers and different categories of citizenship (WANG and WANG, 2003). One key feature of this has been the hukou system of household registration created in 1958, which divides citizens into "rural" or "urban", with differentiated entitlements to welfare services, benefits, housing, education and employment, in favour of urban citizens. Movement between these categories is difficult and since the 1980s, a third "grey" category has emerged, which consists of millions of migrant workers in China's cities who find themselves with no or limited entitlement to certain goods and opportunities (SOLINGER, 1999). Over time, differentiated access to housing, welfare, education and employment in high-skilled and administrative jobs has reinforced the advantages accrued by those living in cities, which in turn has made them better able to capitalize on the opening of the economy to competition and to global trade, which again served to underscore patterns of regional and inter-personal inequality. In addition, the categorical distinction between groups has filtered through to attitudes on equality of rights, with fewer urban residents than migrants supporting a removal of the institutional barriers created by the hukou system (WANG, 2007).

CATEGORICAL INEQUALITIES. If inequalities are multidimensional, is it possible to develop an account of how they are created, reproduced and transformed that is usable as a tool in promoting development? Recent interdisciplinary approaches in the human sciences offer a way forward by suggesting ways of integrating the role of institutions, culture, and of social norms in shaping inequality and its reproduction in ways that help us understand its diversity and changing character. Contributions from these disciplines suggest that the common denominator in the production of inequalities does not lie primarily with individuals" stock of resources (physical, cognitive and social forms of capital) or opportunities, but in the social relationships that condition their entitlement to such resources and opportunities. An emerging approach to understanding inequality focuses on the process through which people are categorized into social groups; how such categories carry with them norms regulating entitlement to resources and positions, generating inequalities in status, assets and opportunities; and how the boundaries that circumscribe those categories are maintained and reproduced in ways that lock in differential rewards (TILLY, 1999; SCHWALBE et al., 2000; SCHWALBE, 2008).

Social categorization is a relational process through which individuals are assigned to a group according to certain criteria – a ubiquitous process in social relationships. Some of these categories are near-universal, such as gender (male-female), age (old, middle-aged, child, teenager) or citizenship (citizen/non-citizen), others are more context-specific, such as grouping individuals according to ethnic, racial or social belonging, or by religious belief. These categories become the central inequality-producing mechanism when they go hand-in-hand with the ascription of differential capacities and entitlements that justify differential access to goods, status and opportunities.

The creation of social groups often entails the ascription of qualities (or the lack thereof) to the members of these groups. It is a well established fact in the social sciences that groups tend to attribute themselves positive qualities such as intelligence, ability, trustworthiness and other traits, and regard non-group members as lacking in these traits (for a foundational perspective, see Tajfel (1981); for a recent survey of the field see Hornsey (2008)). These qualities can then be used to justify excluding access to goods, status or opportunities, or their unequal allocation[3]. Such justifications are transformed into actual inequalities by the exercise of social norms that prescribe entitlements to individuals according to a certain category (e.g. woman, man, indigenous, non-citizen, etc.)[4]. Social norms in various guises, ranging from explicit legal codes to informal traditions and including religious law, often prescribe differential

---

3. Tilly calls these twin processes "opportunity hoarding" and "exploitation" (TILLY, 1999).

4. Sen defines entitlements as "the set of alternative commodity bundles that a person can command in a society using the totality of rights and opportunities that he or she faces" (SEN 1984, p.497), but circumscribes its interpretation to (mostly) material commodities and legally defined rights. The concept of entitlement can be useful in articulating the relationship between categories and social norms that produce inequality, but to do so I propose extending the concept by (a) including a wider range of "commodity bundles" that encompasses not only material resources, but status, cultural, social and human capital, access to social roles and positions; and (b) going beyond legal rights to include all formal and informal social norms that define the person's ability to command such commodity bundles.

entitlements to goods, opportunities and positions according to group membership: age can, for instance, regulate access to political power by having minimum age limits for voting or holding office, as can, in well-known historical cases, race, sex, education or property. Such norms often prescribe differential entitlements to resources: pay-differentials, rations or access to food or education across categories are regulated by a range of formal and informal arrangements, including the differential inputs and rewards within the household economy, which for instance, demand higher inputs and allocate lower rewards to women (SEN, 1990; RADCLIFFE, 2004; for a richly textured historical example see Ogilvie (2003)). Ascribed categories can also restrict access to jobs where they attribute qualities that supposedly make members of those categories "unsuitable" for those roles – these can be driven by beliefs about competency, fears of pollution, or even of the effects of the role on the individual (e.g. "no job for a lady"). Alternatively, categories and norms combine to give a particular group exclusive access to a certain position or resource because only the bearers of certain characteristics are said to be entitled to them – with, for instance, birth regulating exclusive access sovereignty monarchies, or to particular professions in caste societies.

Both the distribution of entitlements and of individuals across such social categories is policed by social values and norms that enforce compliance in multiple ways. Many of these may be coercive to the extent that they involve a direct threat to those who seek to transgress boundaries or violate norms, but to a large extent they rely on the (at least) outward consent of those that are subject to their rules, through processes of value-assimilation or "naturalization", or at the very least adaptation to conditions (TILLY, 1999; SCHWALBE, 2000; LUKES, 2004).

The link between social category and inequality is not, however, a feature restricted to other times or "developing" societies. Wealthier nations and their welfare regimes also have to deal with this problem: as an emerging body of literature shows, public support for welfare and redistribution is eroded when the sense of community that underpins it is challenged by social categories that emphasize difference, whether they are focused on multiculturalism or a distinction between "deserving" and "undeserving" poor (KYMLICKA and BANTING, 2007).

EXPLORING INSTITUTIONAL ORIGINS AND CHANGE. Seeing the roots of inequalities through such processes of categorization and the normative entitlements that they regulate both within and across categories is a good way to begin addressing the three questions outlined above. Firstly, this helps us better analyse the full range of causes of inequality by looking upstream from the market allocation mechanisms to questioning both the acquisition of resources with which individuals enter into market relationships; and the extent to which those very market relationships are embedded in broader systems of social and cultural distinction. Categories and entitlements condition access to resources and positions that are translated into aggregated statistics as inequalities of income, health or political participation[5].

---

5. For an overview of how such social and cultural factors influence health, see Hall and Lamont (2009).

Secondly, the focus on social norms allows us to explore issues of changing social value, and to explain and compare differential rewards both within societies, between societies and across time – for instance exploring the social norms behind why Japanese firms reveal much lower pay inequalities between executives and other workers compared to US ones (WILKINSON and PICKETT, 2009)[6]. Finally, it also draws attention to the variety of institutions, both formal and informal, that regulate access and reward and the ways in which they are constructed and maintained, such as: educational systems and beliefs about different types of education, for who and to what purpose; welfare and tax structures, as well as debates about deserving and non-deserving recipients; property and inheritance systems, and who is entitled to it; and political systems, along with discourses on rights, values and citizenship.

Inequality, history and sustainable development

Seen in this way, it is clear that history matters for understanding inequality in general, and the specificities of how and why inequalities are expressed differently across time and across the world. Rao, Szreter and Woolcok (2011) have proposed three key ways in which history and a historical understanding can make a contribution to development practice and policy: it can help development practice learn about itself and question its own role in the construction of categorical boundaries and difference, or how past interventions affected locally rooted systems of inequality; it can serve to uncover trajectories and provide a long-term comparative perspective, addressing the question of "how did we arrive at this point?"; and finally, it can serve development practice by exploring the historicity of the categories and entitlement systems that structure inequalities across different contexts. This last aspect can prove particularly valuable in understanding the diversity of ways of being unequal encountered across different contexts, to the extent that it can highlight ways in which locally-specific histories and cultures intersect with global processes and inequality, which creates mechanisms that produce diverse outcomes.

DEVELOPMENT HAS A HISTORY. In the first instance then, a historical perspective can provide a "critical and reflexive stance on the nature of development, knowledge and practice", showing for instance, how assumptions about the role of inequality in development based on a narrow reading of the historical evidence have served to hide the effects and experience of inequality, not least (until recently) by not developing measures and indicators that made it a quantifiable issue. Along these lines we can also see how different ideas from international organizations on what "development" is, and how it is achieved, have contributed to the reinforcement of inequalities, or to the shaping of new ones that are structured around categories such as colonizer vs. colonized, modern vs. backward, or by framing women's

---

6. However, there are also signs that while wage inequality for long-term contracted employees has remained low, there is rising inequalities of pay and benefits between long-term employment and irregular or short-term forms of employment, which recruit particularly certain categories, namely women (JONES, 2007).

BOX 2 HISTORIES AND INSTITUTIONS: UNEQUAL WELFARE IN SOUTHERN EUROPE

■ Formal institutions, including constitutions, welfare regimes or other government policy structures are important factors in the constitution of inequality to the extent that they reinforce categorical boundaries and distribute access and resources unequally according to them. Institutions are also the product of historical trajectories and their development can be to a great extent conditioned by their past (PIERSON, 2011). One example of how institutional origins continue to influence the shape of inequality in the present is the case of Southern European welfare regimes – welfare regimes are systems of redistribution of income and access to services, but as Esping-Andersen (1999) notes, that distribution need not be from rich to poor, nor particularly equitable, and systems vary extensively on how they do so.

Southern European countries such as Portugal, Spain and Greece share, despite their differences in many other domains, levels of inequality significantly above the average for European Union countries[1]. Their experience of inequality has been explained on the basis of the divisions on the terms of inclusion in the labour market and access to welfare services, including pensions and unemployment insurance. Employees in a minority of sectors, both public and private can access generously subsidized contribution-defined pensions and unemployment benefits, whilst the majority of the population has to rely on very limited general benefits, reinforcing inside-outside divisions. Rather than being universalistic, these regimes are both fragmented and segmented, contributing to the reproduction of inequalities (GARCIA and KARAKATSANIS, 2006). But why are there such distinct rewards, and how did that situation come about? Historians increasingly argue that these differences are to a significant extent derived from these countries' authoritarian past and its legacies. In particular they have pointed to how Southern European welfare regimes reinforce inequality through inequitable redistribution, a legacy of their authoritarian origins (ESPUELAS, 2012).

Southern European welfare regimes began their developments in the early to mid-twentieth century, when these countries found themselves ruled by conservative authoritarian (or semi-authoritarian) regimes – Franco in Spain between 1939 and 1975, Salazar in Portugal between 1928 and 1974, and to some extent Greece even before military rule between 1967 and 1974[2]. These welfare systems were designed and implemented as tools of social engineering, looking to reinforce certain categorical distinctions between citizens as a way of shaping society along conservative and corporatist lines. The aim of these systems was to enshrine what these regimes considered "natural" inequalities and hierarchies in society through unequal benefits and entitlements, as well as the preservation of tradition, religion, and male authority over the family. This was done by targeting benefits according to class origins and gender – forms of categorical distinction – so that workers would be tied to tiered and sector-specific insurance systems (such as insurance for agricultural workers); by ensuring that such benefits were set distinctly according to ideological pre-defined needs; and that they flowed through the male head of household and were therefore rarely accessible to women (e.g. RAMOS PINTO, 2012; MOLINERO, 2005).

Despite democratization in the 1970s, these regimes left enduring legacies that have hindered the equalizing reforms of welfare systems. As well as inheriting the structural inequalities created and maintained by authoritarian systems, new democratic regimes were faced with the daunting task of addressing entrenched interests in welfare systems. While this was possible in the creation of universal health systems, southern European states have been less successful at enacting reforms that would entail breaking the privileges of entrenched groups who benefit from such inequitable systems (e.g. FERREIRA, 2008).

---

1. Using 2005 data for 24 European countries, the average EU Gini score is 29.7. Spain's stands at 31.6, Greece's at 33.4 and Portugal's at 37.

2. Greece's post-civil war regime up until the military coup of 1967, although subject to regular elections, was a conservative-dominated "guided democracy" that mirrored in many ways the corporatist ideals of other Southern European regimes (Mouzelis and Pagoulatos, 2005).

role in development in ways that reinforced their subaltern status (COPPER and RANDALL, 1998; KOTHARI, 2005; EASTERLY, 2006; PEPPIN-VAUGHAN, 2010). Other recent work explores how humanitarian practice developed particular political and social contexts, both in wealthy nations (e.g. DAVEY, 2011; DAVIS and TAITHE, 2011), but also rediscovering the history and tradition of non-Western humanitarianism (e.g. FULLER, 2013; DAVEY, 2012).

HISTORICAL CONTEXTS AND INEQUALITY. Equally relevant in providing development practice with a sharper focus on the causes and dynamics of inequality is the use of history to understand local contexts that produce and structure inequalities, and how these change over time. Different social and cultural historical legacies shape the types of inequalities that are created. Figure 1 synthesizes some historical perspectives which explore three different contexts through which some within-country inequalities were created in China, India and Brazil, revealing very different elements at play: inter-regional competition in the case of Brazil, colonial administration in the case of India, and the communist state's transforming agenda in China. All three histories create different implications to tackling those inequalities.

While Western European nations are relatively equal societies, especially when compared with extremes of polarisation in some low- and middle-income countries, there are also considerable variations between the more egalitarian Scandinavian nations and other parts of the continent. While these differences are often attributed to recent economic performance, its political and institutional history is also critical in understanding how such societies function. Box 2 looks at the origins of Southern European welfare regimes since the mid-twentieth century, particularly at how their development under authoritarianism created social policies that not only were less redistributive than elsewhere, but they actively reinforced inequalities and power along categorical distinctions. The historical experience of the development of "authoritarian welfare" in conditioning present-day inequalities is an under-explored but urgent consideration, especially as we come to see that globally, non-democratic regimes have been primarily responsible for the creation of social policies that can continue to shape inequalities long into the future (MARES and CARNES, 2009).

But a historical perspective on inequality emphasizes not only its durability, but also how it changes and adapts. Social systems are not stable, but constantly challenged by changing circumstances, and human action consists of adapting and innovating on existing ways of understanding and operating with the world at such critical junctures. In doing so, the nature and structure of inequality may be transformed or extended. Before concluding, I would like to briefly highlight some of the ways in which we can see this happening historically. As Tilly noted, one of the key factors in the production of inequality is the process of inscriptions of categories and systems of entitlement from one context to another: this can happen as much on a local level – with say employers translating racial categories and their ascriptions into lower pay and little advancement for members of a given racial group – to processes on a global scale, such as when Portuguese and Spanish colonizers transferred to their conquests in Latin America and Africa categorical systems that had been developed to manage (and control) the multi-religious populations of Iberia, including Christians, Muslims and Jews (BETHENCOURT and PEARCE, 2012).

CHALLENGING CATEGORIES, CHALLENGING INEQUALITIES. Inequalities are not static because any translation or application of one frame to a new context requires adaptation and transformation, particularly in the context of globalization and technological change. As such, durable forms of social categorization and values can be adapted to new circumstances by merging them with social categories and values from elsewhere, creating "hybrid" forms of categorical inequality. In India, for instance, the structures that underpinned key aspects of gender inequality were profoundly altered by the combination of British rule and law, and Indian legal and social practice. As India gained independence and formed its own body of law, these were combined to create a system which reinforced patriarchal control over the assets and labour of family members, particularly women, transforming, yet reinforcing, structures of inequality (NEWBIGIN, 2010). Looking into the way in which different nations and social contexts have constructed and adapted inequality-producing social structures in different ways is an essential first step.

Yet, the transformation and adaptation of structures of inequality to new conditions can also open up the opportunities for challenges that aim to equalize relations or recast the content of categories. In China, the very categorization used by the state to ensure differences between types of citizen has been used to contest the management of inequality and demand interventions that force equalization, what has been called "rightful resistance" (O'BRIEN and LI, 2006). Other scholars point to similar forms of action that both use and challenge categories to the benefit of the poor (CHATTERJEE, 2004; HOLSTON, 2008).

Yet, the historical perspective also shows how, even within nations, the social structures that shape inequality are changeable and contingent. The long view on the development of democracy (which to be sustainable must entail substantial equality across its various dimensions) shows that it can arrive by both exogenous and endogenous change, and there have been multiple paths towards democratization, as well as away from it (TILLY, 2004). In European history, the incorporation of larger swathes of the population into the market as waged workers also brought with it the conditions for challenging long-standing inequalities through the collective mobilization of new political actors (ZIBLATT, 2010). Such mobilization, however, was made possible not only by sheer numbers, but also by the way in which beliefs, ideas, and values were shaped by the interaction between popular traditions and radical critiques of liberal capitalism from both right and left, leading to new ways of conceptualizing social justice, the role of markets and the position of individuals within them. These challenged the dominant idea that inequality was a "natural" outcome of market relations, and therefore either fair or unchangeable, providing a frame for political movements and coalitions to mobilize and shape the reform of states and markets in the twentieth century (BEVIR, 2000; BIAGINI and REID, 1991; STEDMAN-JONES, 2004).

In key moments of change in Europe, such as after each of the World Wars, tremendous exogenous shocks contributed to a realignment of categories and social relationships that shaped inequality. But those shocks only produced such results because once they destabilized entrenched ways of seeing the world, there were social actors – parties, movements, opinion-makers – that were well positioned to offer alternative ideas and conceptualizations. Crisis meant change because political action can itself provide a way of challenging and transforming categories (CLEMENS, 1998).

Conclusion

In this short overview I have tried to highlight how inequalities, or ways of thinking and seeing unequally, are embedded in social relations and as a result are pervasive and durable. Taking a historical perspective on the causes of inequality offers up a paradox: whilst it helps to frame and understand the dynamics of contemporary inequalities and finds cross-cutting elements that recur in the creation of multiple forms of injustice, on the other hand it also emphasizes the point that there are many ways of being unequal, because of the variation in contexts and histories that intersect to make inequality in say, the United States, something different to what it is in Brazil.

As a result, inequality and the obstacles it poses for truly sustainable human development pose a tremendous challenge. Redistribution, or even "predistribution" (HACKER, 2012), and legislation on equality of opportunities are only one way to address these issues – the roots of inequality lie deeper and further upstream, and have to be understood in their own historical, cultural and political context. That deep embeddedness of social categories also raises the difficult question of the clash between deeply held values and a quest for equality, which is a problem that must be faced not just in relation to those who profit from inequality, but also to those who suffer from it.

Yet, I have also tried to show how historians account for social and political change, and in the process highlight how inequalities are liable to change. Inequality is the product of human action, not of an abstract and anonymous economic machine. As such they can, and are, challenged and transformed by human action. Which brings us back to the point I made above: because of its roots in the interaction of global processes and local cultures and societies, sustainable development towards a more equal (and sustainable) future will depend as much as on the actions of social actors within countries – parties, civil society and others – as it will on international organizations and transnational actors. How both can combine and interact productively is, therefore, a key question. ∎

REFERENCES

ACEMOGLU D. and ROBINSON J. A., 2002, "The political economy of the Kuznets curve." Review of Development Economics 6.2: 183-203

BEVIR M., 2000, "Socialism, Civil Society, and the State in Modern Britain" in Frank Trentmann (ed.) Paradoxes of Civil Society: New Perspectives on Modern German and British History, Berghan Books.

BETTEILLE A., 2003, "The Idea of Natural Inequality" in The Idea of Natural Inequality and Other Essays, Oxford University Press.

BETHENCOURT F. and PEARCE A. (eds.), 2012, Racism and ethnic relations in the portuguese-speaking world, Oxford University Press

BIAGINI E. and REID A. (eds.), 1991, Currents of Radicalism: Popular Radicalism, Organised Labour and Party Politics in Britain, 1850-1914, Cambridge University Press.

BIGGS B. et al., "Is wealthier always healthier? The impact of national income level, inequality, and poverty on public health in Latin America." Social Science & Medicine 71.2 (2010): 266.

BIN WONG R., 1997, China Transformed: Historical Change and the Limits of European Experience, Ithaca, NY.

BOURGUIGNON F., 2012, La Mondialisation de l'inégalite, Seuil.

CHANG H.-J., 2011, 23 things they don't tell you about capitalism. Bloomsbury Press.

CHATTERJEE P., 2004, The politics of the governed: reflections on popular politics in most of the world. Columbia University Press.

CLARK R., 2011, "World Income Inequality in the Global Era: New Estimates, 1990-2008", Social Problems, 58, 4: 565-592

CLEMENS E. S., 1998, "To Move Mountains: Collective Action and the Possibility of Institutional Change." In From Contention to Democracy, edited by Marco G. Giugni, Doug McAdam and Charles Tilly. Rowman & Littlefield.

COOPER F. and PACKARD R. (eds.), 1998, International development and the social sciences: Essays on the history and politics of knowledge. University of California Press.

CORNIA G. A., ADDISON T. and KIISKI S., 2004, "Income Distribution Changes and Their Impact in the Post-Second World War Period." In Cornia, G.A. (ed.) Inequality, Growth, and Poverty in an Era of Liberalisation and Globalization. Oxford University Press.

DAVEY E., 2012, "New players through old lenses: Why history matters in engaging with Southern actors."

Overseas Development Institute – HPG Policy Brief 48, http://www.odi.org.uk/publications/6692-history-humanitarian-action-aid-ngos

DAVEY E., 2011, "Famine, Aid, and Ideology: The Political Activism of Médecins sans Frontières in the 1980s." French Historical Studies 34.3: 529-558.

DAVIS A. J. and TAITHE B., 2011, "From the Purse and the Heart: Exploring Charity, Humanitarianism, and Human Rights in France." French Historical Studies 34.3: 413-432.

EASTERLY W., 2006, The White Man's Burden: Why the West's Efforts to Aid the Rest Have Done So Much Ill and So Little Good, Penguin.

ESCOBAR A., 2012 [1995], Encountering Development: the Making and Unmaking of the Third World. Princeton

ESPUELAS S., 2012, "Are Dictatorships Less Redistributive? A Comparative Analysis of Social Spending in Europe, 1950-1980" European Review of Economic History, 16, 2: 211-232.

FERREIRA F. and RAVALLION M., 2008, "Global poverty and inequality: a review of the evidence." World Bank Policy Research Working Paper Series, no. 4623

FERREIRA L. V., 2008, "Persistent poverty: Portugal and the Southern European welfare regime." European Societies 10.1 (2008): 49-71.

GARCÍA M. and KARAKATSANIS N., 2006, "Social Policy, Democracy, and Citizenship in Southern Europe." In Gunther, Richard, Diamandouros, P. N., and Sotiropoulos D. A. eds. Democracy and the State in the New Southern Europe, Oxford University Press.

GOESLING B., 2001, "Changing Income Inequalities Within and Between Nations: New Evidence." American Sociological Review 66:745–61.

HOLSTON J., 2008, Insurgent citizenship: disjunctions of democracy and modernity in Brazil. Princeton University Press.

ESCOBAR A., 2012 [1995], Encountering Development: the Making and Unmaking of the Third World. Princeton

ESPING-ANDERSEN G., 1990, The Three Worlds of Welfare Capitalism. Cambridge: Polity Press.

FULLER P., 2013, "North China Famine Revisited: Unsung Native Relief in the Warlord Era, 1920–1921". Modern Asian Studies, forthcoming.

HACKER J. S., 2012, "The Institutional Foundations of Middle-Class Democracy", Policy Network.

HUNG H.-F. and KUCINSKAS J., 2011, "Globalization and Global Inequality: Assessing the Impact of the Rise of China and India, 1980–20051." American Journal of Sociology 116.5: 1478-1513.

JONES R. S., 2007, "Income Inequality, Poverty and Social Spending in Japan", OECD Economics Department Working Papers, No. 556, OECD publishing

KYMLICKA W. and BANTING K. (eds.), 2007, Multiculturalism and the welfare state: recognition and redistribution in contemporary democracies. Oxford University Press.

KOTHARI U. (ed.), 2005, A radical history of development studies: Individuals, institutions and ideologies. Zed Books.

KUZNETS S., 1955, "Economic Growth and Income Inequality." American Economic Review 45(1):1–28.

LUDDEN D., 2002, "Modern Inequality and Early Modernity: A Comment for the AHR on Articles by R. Bin Wong and Kenneth Pomeranz." The American Historical Review 107.2 (2002): 470-480.

LUKES S., 2005, Power: A Radical View (2nd Edition), Palgrave Macmillan.

MADDISON A., 2006, The World Economy – A Millenial Perspective and Historical Statistics (2 Volume Edition), Development Centre Studies, OECD

MARES I. and MATTHEW C. E., 2009, "Social policy in developing countries." Annual Review of Political Science, 12: 93-113.

MARSHALL T. H., 1964, Class, Citizenship and Social Development. Garden City: Doubleday & Co.

MILANOVIC B., 2009, "Global inequality and the global inequality extraction ratio: the story of the past two centuries." World Bank Policy Research Working Paper Series, no. 5044.

MILANOVIC B., 2009a, "Global inequality recalculated: The effect of new 2005 PPP estimates on global inequality." World Bank Policy Research Working Paper Series, no. 5061.

MILANOVIC B., 2011, The Haves and the Have-Nots: a brief and idiosyncratic history of global inequality. Basic Books.

MILANOVIC B., 2012, "Global Inequality: From Class to Location, from Proletarians to Migrants." Global Policy 3.2: 125-134.

MOLINERO C., 2005, La Captación De Las Masas: Política Social y Propaganda En El Régimen Franquista. Cátedra.

MOUZELIS N. and PAGOULATOS G., 2005, "Civil society and citizenship in post-war Greece" in Birtek, Farouk and Dragonas, Thalia, eds. Citizenship and the Nation-State in Greece and Turkey, Routledge.

NEWBIGIN E., 2010, "A post-colonial patriarchy? Representing family in the Indian nation-state." Modern Asian Studies 44, 1: 121-144.

O'BRIEN P., 2010, "Ten Years of Debate on the Origins of the Great Divergence", Reviews in History (review no. 1008) http://www.history.ac.uk/reviews/review/1008

OGILVIE S., 2003, A bitter living: women, markets, and social capital in early modern Germany. Oxford University Press.

ORTIZ I. and CUMMINS M., 2011, "Global Inequality: Beyond the bottom billion–A rapid review of income distribution in 141 countries." UNICEF Working Paper.

PALMA J. G., 2011. "Homogeneous Middles vs. Heterogeneous Tails, and the End of the "Inverted-U': It's All About the Share of the Rich." Development and Change 42.1 (2011): 87-153.

PEPPIN VAUGHAN R., 2010, "Girls' and women's education within Unesco and the World Bank, 1945–2000." Compare 40.4: 405-423.

PIERSON P., 2011, Politics in time: History, institutions, and social analysis. Princeton University Press

POMERANZ K., 2000, The Great Divergence. China, Europe and the Making of the Modern World Economy, Princeton.

RADCLIFFE S. A., 2004, "Geography of Development: development, civil society and inequality - social capital is (almost) dead?" Progress in Human Geography 28 (4):517-27

RAMOS PINTO P., 2012, "Everyday Citizenship under Authoritarianism: the cases of Spain and Portugal", in Cavatorta, Francesco, ed. Civil Society Activism under Authoritarian Rule: A Comparative Perspective. Routledge.

ROY T., 2012, "Beyond Divergence: Rethinking the Economic History of India." Economic History of Developing Regions 27.sup1 (2012): 57-65.

SANDEL M. J., 2012, What money can't buy: the moral limits of markets. Farrar, Straus and Giroux.

SEN A. K., 1990, "Gender and Cooperative Conflicts". In Persistent Inequalities: Women and World Development, edited by Irene Tinker. Oxford University Press.

SEN A. K., 1992, Inequality reexamined. Clarendon Press

SOLINGER D. J., 1999, Contesting Citizenship in Urban China: Peasant Migrants, the State and the Logic of the Market. Berkley: University of California Press.

STEDMAN-JONES G., 2004 An End to Poverty? A Historical Debate, Profile Books.

TAJFEL H., 1981, Human Groups and Social Categories - Studies in Social Psychology. Cambridge University Press.

TILLY C., 1999, Durable inequality. University of California Press.

TILLY C., 2004, Contention & Democracy in Europe, 1945-2000. Cambridge University Press.

UNDP, 2011, Human Development Report 2011 – Sustainability and Equity: A Better Future for All.

WALLERSTEIN I., 1974, The modern world system. Capitalist agriculture and the European world economy in the sixteenth century. Academic Press.

WANG F. and WANG T., 2003, "Bringing Categories Back In: Institutional Factors of Income Inequality in Urban China." Centre for the Study of Democracy Working Papers, UC Irvine.

WANG F., 2007, "Boundaries of Inequality: Perceptions of Distributive Justice Among Urbanites, Migrants, and Peasants", Centre for the Study of Democracy Working Papers, UC Irvine, http://escholarship.org/uc/item/1v62q8pw

WILKINSON R. and PICKETT K., 2009, The spirit level: Why greater equality makes societies stronger. Bloomsbury Press.

WOOLCOCK M., SZRETER S. and VIJAYENDRA R., 2011, "How and why does history matter for development policy?" The Journal of Development Studies, 47 (1), 70-96.

The shapes and causes of inequality

Dean Baker and David Rosnick Center for Economic and Policy Research, Washington, United States of America

n December 2011 the Organization for Economic Cooperation and Development (OECD) published a volume, *Divided We Stand: Why Inequality Keeps Rising*, that examined trends in inequality in the OECD countries in the years since 1980 (OECD, 2011). The OECD's analysis found that growing inequality was a common trend among the OECD countries. It attributed this growth in part to institutional changes that had the effect of raising wage inequality, most notably declining labour tax rates and weaker employment protection legislation. It noted increases in secondary education were an important factor reducing inequality, along with increased labour force participation among women. And it argued that technology was the dominant force leading to higher wage inequality over this period. While the volume contained much useful analysis and data, its analysis of the dimensions and causes of inequality is incomplete.

There were three main ways in which the OECD analysis was inadequate. First, it relied heavily on the change in the ratio of the earnings of workers at the 90th percentile to the earnings of workers at the 10th percentile. This only captures part of the story. Workers at the 10th percentile of the earnings distribution were indeed losers over the last three decades in many OECD countries; however workers at the 90th percentile were not really winners. In most countries their wages just kept even with average wage growth in the economy, meaning that they were not the beneficiaries of any upward redistribution. The upward redistribution went to individuals further up on the income ladder.

The second inadequacy was the brevity of the discussion on the financial sector. Many of those who receive the highest incomes are located in the financial sector. Recent research also shows that a bloated financial sector can be a drag on growth by pulling resources away from productive sectors of the economy (Cecchetti and Kharroubbi, 2012). It is likely that the financial sector played an important role in the rise in inequality over the last three decades.

Finally, the OECD analysis was too quick to claim that technology was a major cause of the rise in inequality over this period. It actually found that a measure of the improvement trend in technology was not associated with a rise in inequality. Only a cyclical measure of technology was correlated with inequality; and cyclical changes in spending on technology cannot explain a decades-long trend of rising inequality.

We examine each of these issues in more detail below.

Figure 1a shows the difference between wage growth at each decile cut-off and average wage growth in the economy for six OECD countries. As shown, the lower eight deciles of the wage distribution all saw wage increases that were less than the average, with the biggest losses for those near the bottom of the distribution. Clearly those at the middle and the bottom of the wage distribution were not getting their share of the gains from growth over this period. However, workers at the 90th percentile of the wage distribution certainly were not big winners. In Australia – where the 90th percentile grew fastest relative to the mean – that wage only rose 0.27 percentage points faster than the average rate of wage growth over this period. This means that the OECD's analysis focused largely on the losers in this story of redistribution. The winners were further up on the income distribution.

Figure 2 shows average income growth at the 90th, 95th, 99th, 99.5th, 99.9th and (except Australia) 99.99th percentiles in comparison to the average rate of income growth from the World Top Incomes database (note that this series includes non-wage income, so these numbers are not strictly comparable to those in Figure 1). As can be seen, the incomes for the very highest income groups substantially outpaced the average rate of income growth over this period, with the difference being greater the closer you get to the top of the income distribution.

FIGURE 1 Unequal income growth

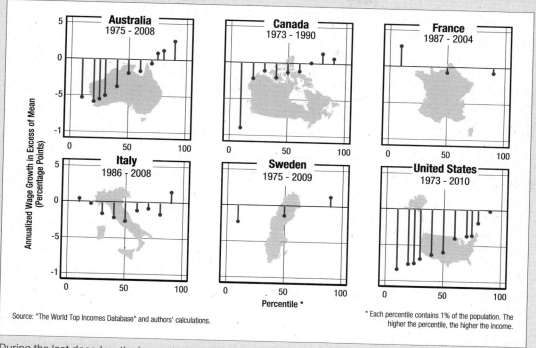

Source: "The World Top Incomes Database" and authors' calculations.

* Each percentile contains 1% of the population. The higher the percentile, the higher the income.

During the last decades, the lowest incomes in all OECD countries have grown less rapidly than average – with the notable exception of France. In some cases, as in the United States, only the highest salaries, representing only 10% of the population, did not decline. National redistribution devices have not played their role in protecting the lower and middle classes.

This point is important. The redistribution did not go from the middle and bottom of the distribution to those who were merely better off workers. It went primarily to those who were at or near the very top of the income distribution. This fact hugely influences how we should think about this upward redistribution and possible remedies.

The second inadequacy of the OECD analysis, its exclusion of finance from the discussion, is also a significant issue. We know that the financial sector has expanded hugely as a share of the economy in many OECD countries, especially in countries like the United States and United Kingdom which have seen some of the largest rises in inequality. In our analysis of the OECD data we find a strong association between the share of financial compensation in GDP and the ratio of wages for workers at the 90th percentile to workers at the 10th percentile.

While this analysis is far from conclusive, there are good reasons for believing that the financial sector has been a major contributor to the growth of inequality over this period. First and most importantly many of the highest incomes originate in the financial sector (PHILIPPON and RESHEF, 2009). The most successful managers of hedge funds can earn hundreds of millions or even billions of dollars a year. Even less successful but experienced traders often earn paychecks that are well into the millions, fifty or a hundred times the pay of a typical worker. By contrast, in 2010 the wage of the 90th percentile earner in the United States stood at only 2.37 times that of the 50th.

The earnings from the financial sector must come from somewhere. If the financial sector led to a more

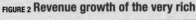

FIGURE 2 **Revenue growth of the very rich**

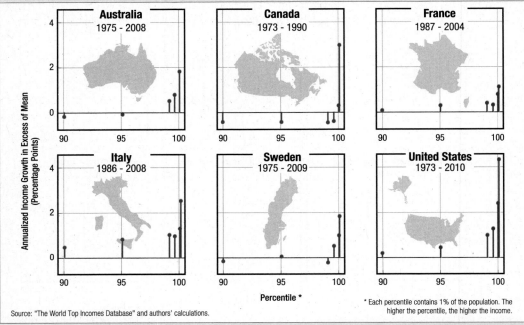

Source: "The World Top Incomes Database" and authors' calculations.

* Each percentile contains 1% of the population. The higher the percentile, the higher the income.

If we consider the total income of inhabitants of OECD countries, we note first that the income evolution is part of a broader trend. The most affluent employees, representing less than 5% of the population, have seen their incomes grow significantly above the national averages.

productive economy, then these high earners may be generating wealth comparable to their compensation. A recent study by Stephan Cecchetti and Enisse Kharroubbi, two researchers at the Bank of International Settlements suggests that a large financial sector does not contribute to growth, but rather is a drain on the economy. The paper examined the growth of 50 countries over the period from 1980 to 2009. It found a U-shaped relationship between the size of the financial sector and economic growth. The implication is that an underdeveloped financial sector impedes economic growth presumably because economies are not effectively allocating resources between sectors. However after the financial sector reaches a certain size relative to the overall economy, further expansion of the sector slows economic growth.

The paper then sought to examine how the financial sector could have this negative effect. It looked at the rate of productivity growth in 15 manufacturing industries in 30 wealthy countries. It found that a larger financial sector was associated with slower productivity growth in industries with large amounts of research and development spending. This would be consistent with a story where the financial sector was responsible for pulling people with highly developed mathematics skills away from other sectors; people who could have been developing computers and clean energy, for example, are instead developing algorithms to be one up on the competition.

Their study also found that a larger financial sector is associated with slower productivity growth in industries that are heavily dependent on external capital. This would be consistent with a scenario in which a larger financial sector ties up more capital in financial speculation, thereby making it harder for new firms to raise the necessary funds for investment.

A fuller analysis of inequality has to examine the role of the financial sector more closely. There is good circumstantial evidence to suggest that it is a major culprit, but more work needs to be done before the case can be closed[1].

The report's final inadequacy, the rapidity at which the OECD accepted the argument that technology is an important factor in the rise in inequality over this period, is an issue because the evidence suggests otherwise. On this point there is an extensive literature, largely focused on the United States, which tries to blame technology for the rise in inequality over the last three decades (e.g. GOLDIN and KATZ, 2008; AUTOR et al., 2005).

While many of the world's most prominent labour economists argue that this has been the case, there are a number of basic facts about the pattern of wage inequality that call this conclusion into question (e.g. GOLDIN and KATZ, 2008).

First, the sharpest rise in the gap between the wages of college educated and non-college educated workers was in the early 1980s. This was well before computers and other information age technologies were having any major role in transforming the workplace or increasing productivity. Second, inequality has continued to rise in the years since 2000 even though college educated workers did not see real wage gains over this period. By education level, it has only been workers with advanced degrees who have seen real wage gains in the years since 2000. If technology is the one of the main forces that explain wage inequality thean the workers who are beneficiaries are consistently changing and now seem to comprise a very narrow group.

In the case of the OECD data, it is very hard to come up with a story whereby technology provides much of the explanation. While the OECD's simulation finds that technology explains two-thirds of the rise in inequality over this period, it is difficult to reconcile this conclusion with either their analysis or that of the authors of this paper. The OECD uses a measure of spending on research and development as a share of GDP as a proxy for technology. They find a cyclical relationship between this variable and the ratio of wages for workers at the 90th percentile and workers at the 10th percentile. This seems quite plausible. At a cyclical spending peak, workers with substantial technical skills, who are likely to be near the 90th percentile of the wage distribution will be in short supply. Therefore their wages will be bid up.

However, the OECD and the authors of this paper find no relationship between spending on technology over the longer term and the ratio of wages for workers at the 90th percentile to wages for workers at the 10th percentile. This result can be readily explained by a rising trend in the number of workers with technical skills. There is no obvious reason that the supply of such workers should not keep pace with the demand.

With no trend relationship between technology and inequality as measured by the 90/10 ratio, we find that technology explains none of the rise in inequality over the last 30 years. Whatever impact the cyclical component might have in raising inequality during the upturn of a technology cycle is offset by the opposite impact it has in the downturn, leaving zero net effect.

The technology point is important because it focuses on whether the rise in inequality was a part of the natural development of the economyendogenous development of the market over the last three decades or whether it was due to policy changes that more directly affect distribution. If we assume that technology is the culprit, thean inequality is a natural development that we may as a matter of policy decide to alleviate to a greater or lesser extent.

Figure 3 shows our calculations of the factors contributing to inequality as measured by the ratio of the wages of the 90th percentile worker to the 10th percentile worker.

While we find no role for technology, like the OECD we find that education, as measured by the share of the workforce with a secondary degree, has a substantial positive effect in reducing inequality. This is readily explained by the fact that the more educated workers there are, the less their wages will rise relative to those of less educated workers. Like the OECD, we also find that a change in institutional structures has been a major factor contributing to inequality. Among these institutional factors, employment protection legislation appears to be an important factor in the reduction of inequality. Some

---

1. For example, we found an association between the ratio of wages for workers at the 90th percentile to the wages of workers at the 10th percentile and the portion of the economy dedicated to financial sector compensation (See BAKER and ROSNICK, 2012).

FIGURE 3 The causes of income inequality

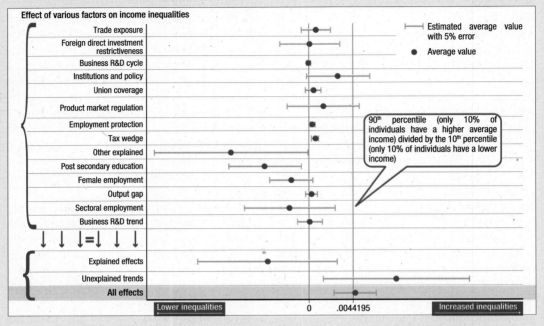

The development of inequality within OECD countries is difficult to explain. Factors such as education have indeed tended to reduce the widening inequalities while some institutional choices have increased it. There remains much to be done, however, to definitively identify the most influential factors.

regressions found that greater labour union density lowers inequality, as does a higher minimum wage, however these results are not robust, while in the latter case reliable data is only available for a small subset of countries (the results of these regressions are available from the authors on request). It also appears that a lower tax rate on labour income is a factor that has increased inequality. While there is more work to be done on how these sorts of institutional factors may affect inequality, the OECD's research suggests that changes in institutional factors played an important role in the rise in inequality over the last three decades.

This analysis still leaves the rise in inequality over this period largely unexplained. While the weakening of institutional support for workers has led to more inequality, this was almost exactly offset by an increase in the number of educated workers. The net effect of these two developments on the ratio of wages for workers at the 90th percentile to the wages of workers at the 10th percentile was close to zero.

We believe that the causes of the rise in inequality are likely to be found elsewhere, most probably in the factors that have led to the sharp rises in income for those in the top five percent, and especially the top one percent of the income distribution. As noted above, it is likely that the financial sector is a big part of the picture, as the high incomes of those in the financial sector must come from elsewhere in the economy. If will be important to determine more precisely the extent to which the growth of the financial sector has come at the expense of the wages of those at the middle and bottom of the wage distribution. In effect, excessive income for the sector can be seen as a tax imposed on the rest of the economy, reducing real incomes for workers outside of the sector.

There are also other factors that are likely to lead to large economic rents for those at the top of the income distribution. Recent research on the pay of top executives at U.S. corporations has found little relationship between pay and any standard measure of performance (BEBCHUK and FRIED, 2004). Top executives in the United States receive compensation packages that are far above those of top executives in other countries or what CEOs in the United States earned 30 or 40 years ago. Insofar as this higher pay is not tied to productivity, it must be coming at the expense of others. Further research is necessary to determine the extent to which excessive pay for top corporate executives has contributed to inequality.

Finally, stronger patent protection is likely to have played a role in increasing inequality[2]. Patent rents have taken up an increasing share of GDP over the last three decades. This is especially true in the United States where spending on prescription drugs alone accounts for close to two percent of GDP. The vast majority of this spending is due to patent monopolies, since most drugs would be available at little cost in a free market.

To sum up, while the OECD report advances our knowledge about trends in inequality in wealthy countries over the last three decades, it leaves much unexplained. A substantial portion of the rise in inequality is clearly attributable to government policies such as weakened employment protection legislation and reduced tax rates on labour income. However much of the rise is still unexplained. Further research is required to determine the extent to which the rise in inequality is due to the development of technology and other processes that are largely endogenous to the economy, as opposed to conscious policy interventions that have had the effect of redistributing income upward. ■

REFERENCES

AUTOR D. A., KATZ L. F., and KEARNEY M. S., 2005, "Trends in U.S. Wage Inequality: Re-Assessing the Revisionists" National Bureau of Economic Research, Working Paper # 11627.

BEBCHUK L. A. AND FRIED J. M., 2004, *Pay Without Performance: The Unfilled Promise of Executive Remuneration*, Cambridge, MA: Harvard University Press.

CECCHETTI S. and KHAROUBBI E., 2012, "Reassessing the Impact of Finance on Growth," Bank of International Settlements, Working Paper #318.

GOLDIN C. and KATZ L. F., 2008, *The Race Between Education and Technology*. Cambridge, MA: Belknap Press.

ORGANIZATION FOR ECONOMIC COOPERATION AND DEVELOPMENT, 2011, *Divided We Stand: Why Equality Keeps Rising*, Paris: OECD.

PHILIPPON T. and RESHEF A., 2009, "Wages and Human Capital in the Financial Services Industry: 1909-2006." *National Bureau of Economic Research,* Working Paper #14644.

---

2. A draft version of the OECD analysis found a relationship between patents per capita and inequality, although they were using this measure as a proxy for technology, rather than rents.

Will twenty-first century capitalism be as unequal and unstable as nine-teenth-century capitalism? Even as predictions proclaimed that human capital would triumph, assets held by a minority continued to increase their share of national wealth and income. The twenty-first century must invent a more peaceful and sustainable way, surpassing twentieth-century capitalism, stained as it was by two world wars.

The new prosperity of rentiers

Thomas Piketty
Paris School of Economics, Paris, France

Principally, there are two ways to get rich – by one's own labour or by inheritance. In the traditional hierarchical "three estate" societies of many European countries, and subsequently during the nineteenth and early twentieth centuries, there was no doubt that inheritance provided the best means of access to capital[1].

Classic literature, such as the works of Jane Austen, Henry James and Honoré de Balzac, provides plenty of references to the importance of inheritance during these periods. For example, Balzac's 1835 novel *Le Père Goriot* features the famous speech of the villainous manipulator Vautrin to Eugène de Rastignac, an ambitious young man keen on social advancement, in which the former provides the latter with two very different scenarios for his future life that hinge on whether he is willing to marry for money. In essence, he informs Rastignac that if he works hard and becomes a brilliant student of law or medicine, then this will lead to a certain profession which, through continued hard work, would enable him to enjoy an above average income and lifestyle. Alternatively, if he successfully managed to wed a particular heiress, then he could be assured of an entirely different future: he would inherit a great fortune and could enjoy a life of luxury, all without the effort of study and work. The distasteful conclusion of Vautrin's speech is that studies are useless and could never provide Rastignac with a standard of living consistent with his aspirations.

---

1. This article is the translation of the written transcription, validated by the author, of an oral presentation given during an interview organized by IDDRI and AFD on 20 September 2012.

Of course, although fictitious, the novel was set in a world that was far from imaginary. Balzac's words, expressed through Vautrin, are an accurate reflection of the structure of inequality at that time. It was simply impossible, through individual merit or hard work, to ever hope to achieve the same elevated standard of living as that enjoyed by those whom inherited wealth.

It might be assumed that today's societies are no longer dogged by this overriding influence of heritage and legacy on income determination and standards of living. Surely the process of development has implicitly resulted in a reduction of the benefits associated with inherited wealth, instead promoting the values of individual initiative, work and merit? Can we be certain that this has been a natural and irreversible consequence of change? Are societies of rentiers and heirs finally obsolete? The answer is "no". The historical and theoretical work of the author has revealed that in many cases inheritance plays a role in twenty-first century capitalism that is just as important as the one it played during the era of Rastignac and Vautrin. The underlying mechanism is low population and economic growth – a characteristic of nineteenth century France and also perhaps of much of the world in the twenty-first century – which automatically gives disproportionate power to inherited wealth. When capital returns exceed the rate of economic growth for a sustained period, the past tends to devour the future, and the meritocratic values on which our democratic societies are based become deeply challenged.

An imperfect measure of income inequality and inheritance

It goes almost without saying that insights from historical literature are insufficient for addressing such an important issue, and that statistical data is essential. The first step towards fulfilling this requirement is the creation of databases, these databases should then be used to provide empirical evidence of long-term changes in income. Such an approach is preferable to the simple construction of new theories or the contradiction of existing ones.

With this in mind, the author and a team of researchers constructed a historical database – the World Top Income Database – which identifies the percentile distributions of national income for France, the United States, the United Kingdom and other countries, over a long period of time. The database now covers more than 30 countries. To add a country to the database, information on its income inequalities must be collated for the longest possible period: the earliest starting point is typically the date at which income tax was established in that particular country, which is usually in the twentieth century. When I started this research around 15 years ago, historical data were only available for the United States, and only then back until 1950, which included the work of Kuznets (1955). It has taken many years to construct the current database, which enables comparisons of inequality over time and between countries.

Indeed, one of the limitations on the measurement of income through tax declarations is that it is difficult to analyse the importance of inheritance in the structure of inequalities. Firstly, there is an increasing trend for significant amounts of inheritance to escape taxation in France; secondly, even when income from assets is present in income tax documentation, it does not give specific details – in particular, it does not reveal where assets are from. If tax returns are the only basis of analysis, it is impossible to distinguish between inherited wealth and money that was earned by an individual, which is nevertheless a crucial question about the nature and justification of inequality.

Following the establishment of the World Top Income Database, the next task will be to fill the gap: to trace the sources of unearned income and to move from our world database on income inequality to a world database on inequalities in inherited wealth. These two databases should then be joined as completely as possible. The author's work on income inequality began with the building up of data for France. Then, through working in conjunction with a series of co-authors, research began on unearned income in the United Kingdom, the United States, Germany and others. The overall goal has remained constant: to study the historical dynamics of the distribution of wealth in the broadest sense over the longest period possible.

Measuring the wealth of a country, to take stock of inherited wealth, is obviously not a new idea. It was an obsession of the eighteenth and nineteenth centuries until being sidelined in the middle of the twentieth century with the development of modern national accounts. It is worth remembering that, for example, during the 1930s no government would have been able to state that: "production has decreased by 10% compared to 1932". It would have been simply impossible, as the necessary information did not exist. Clearly, this was not a very practical means of driving the economy or finding solutions to economic problems and as such provided a powerful incentive for the development of post-war national accounts. The earliest efforts in this field were based on the work of researchers – such as Kuznets in the United States, Clarke and Richard Stone in England and Dugé de Bernonville in France. Their work focused on the short-term variations in economic activity, much more than on the stock of wealth of a country. Indeed, inheritance was largely forgotten during this part of the twentieth century, firstly because of the obsession for the analysis of short-term fluctuations, recessions and crises, but also because of the strong state intervention in economic life at that time, which disrupted the structures of private property, capital and inheritance that existed at the beginning of that century. At the start of the 1950s, for example, properties were worth almost nothing. Indeed, there was a freezing of rent which led people, as Fourastié described, to spend less on their rent than they did on tobacco. In France in 1950, properties were worth nothing, so it made no sense to attempt to calculate their value. The stock exchange no longer existed, or only barely. Many activities had been nationalized. The traditional private capitalism of inheritance had been devastated by wars and then by policy responses to the economic crisis of the 1930s. For all these reasons, the measurement of inheritance was stopped. At the time, its reproduction and transmission seemed to be long forgotten issues.

Thirty years later and everything had changed. During the 1980s and 1990s, waves of financial deregulation and privatization brought a new phase of capitalism where inheritance became much more significant, and it was then realized that the statistical apparatus was lagging behind reality. A parallel can be drawn between the present situation and the 1930s: at that time, not knowing the level of economic production was a problem; similarly in more recent times, the inability to accurately measure capital stocks and their distribution in the world posed a serious problem during the global financial crisis of 2007-2008. The disadvantages of tax declarations and national accounts in terms of the determination of sources of inherited income, as briefly mentioned above, also apply at the international level. The sum of all the outputs and inputs of capital from all over the world – in other words, the sum of the balance of payments at the global level – should always be zero, unless a certain amount escapes to Mars! And yet the balance is always negative. That is to say, the dividends of outgoing interest are higher than the dividends of incoming interest. There is an obvious culprit here. The problem lies in the lack of reporting obligations for financial institutions in tax havens. Such institutions have absolutely no involvement in this statistical exercise. One of the virtues of a series of analyses such as this is that it reveals inconsistencies in the existing statistical system. In this case, the overall analysis of stocks raises major statistical inconsistencies, partly because for a long time, interest has focused on the annual flows of inheritance and less on the detail of stocks, which raises more interest today. When the instrument of observation is so imperfect, it is sometimes better to read the work of novelists rather than statisticians to find out what is happening today.

Inheritance thrives on low growth – or why growth reshuffles the cards

In the French case, by combining different sources of statistical information – especially data from the national accounts of income and wealth and data on inheritance tax[2] – I managed to reconstruct the annual value of inherited wealth in the national income from 1820 to the present day. How much does inheritance "weigh" in the national income, year after year? The first finding is that flows of inherited wealth follow a pronounced U-shaped curve over time. The annual value of inheritance flows amounted to 20-25% of national income around 1900-1910. It fell gradually to less than 10% during the inter-war period, and to less than 5% in 1950 (Figure 1). There has been a steady rise since then, with a marked acceleration in the last thirty years. We are now at a level close to 15%. In a longer perspective, the collapse of inheritance flow in the national income in the mid-twentieth century is even more spectacular. Inheritance flows during the period between 1820-1910 were stable in the region of 20-25% of national income, then from 1910 to the 1950s this figure plummeted by a factor of 5 to 6, before rising by a factor of 3 to 4 between the 1950s and the 2000s. These results are robust and confirmed by the two convergent

---

2. For more details, see Piketty T. (2011), "On The Long-Run Evolution of Inheritance: France 1820-2050", *Quarterly Journal of Economics* vol. CXXVI, Issue 3: 1071-1131.

FIGURE 1 Inheritance makes wealth again

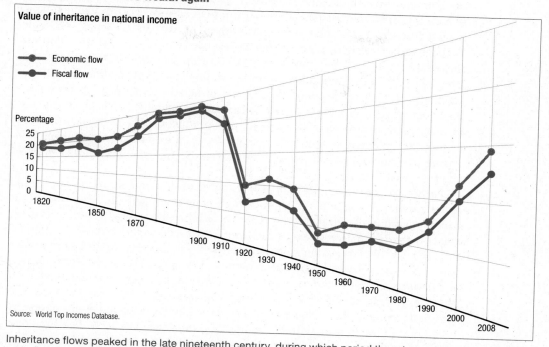

Value of inheritance in national income

- Economic flow
- Fiscal flow

Source: World Top Incomes Database.

Inheritance flows peaked in the late nineteenth century, during which period the returns on capital could be up to five times the growth rate. After a fall following the two world wars and then a low-level stabilization during the *"trente glorieuses"*, these flows have been on the rise since 1980, again due to the impact of the remuneration of capital being at a higher rate than that of growth.

estimates of the annual inheritance flow - the first on the basis of economic data (assets), the second based on tax data (successions)[3]. Note that the current level of 15% would be even higher if instead of the national income, we used the disposable income - that is to say, the national income adjusted for taxes and public transfers. Disposable income accounted for between 90% and 95% of national income in the nineteenth and early twentieth centuries, while this proportion is around 70% today - the share of taxes and transfers being simply more important. The 15% level of inheritance flow in the national income is equivalent to roughly 20% of disposable income. This is a very significant amount. It is more than the combined total of new savings made each year and roughly equal to the annual capital income of the French economy.

In which ways can these facts be interpreted? In particular, how can we account for the distinct U-shaped curve and what seems to be a return to a long-term equilibrium at the very high level of 20%? In the view of the author, there is a very simple, and also very convincing, explanation. The key lies in the comparative value of

3. Cf note 1, in particular pp. 1084-1099.

the economic growth rate and the rate of return on property. When the economic growth rate is low, lower than the rate of return on property, for example when annual growth is 1-2% and the rate of return on property is 4-5% per year, which has been the situation in France during the last two centuries - with the exception of the period of the *Les Trente Glorieuses* ("The Glorious Thirty" - the thirty years from 1945 to 1975) - then inheritance is the determining factor of wealth accumulation and the structuring of inequalities. Conversely, when the return on property is lower than the economic growth rate, then the accumulation of wealth is less influenced by inheritance compared to the year on year production of new wealth. This can be summed up in two very complementary ways. Inheritance thrives during weak growth. Or growth constantly reshuffles the cards, thus minimizing the weight of inherited wealth.

The easiest way to understand this result is to illustrate it by looking at the demographics. Imagine a society with high population growth, with five or ten children per household: this is a society where inheritance disappears. Everything must be divided by five or ten in each generation. So everyone must accumulate their own wealth. Population growth of the twentieth century, according to all available forecasts, is absolutely unique in human history. Until the eighteenth century, population growth was almost zero; it rose a little in the eighteenth and nineteenth centuries to reach 0.3% to 0.4% per year, which is already a huge change. In the twentieth century, the worldwide growth of the population stood at an average of 1.5% per year. In the twenty-first century, this rate may fall to 0.5%. This has great implications in terms of the transmission of inequality. Demographics feed growth, which as we have seen reduces the share of inherited wealth. A world of high population growth is one where the inheritance is continuously divided. Conversely, in a world that is demographically stagnant, or worse, has a shrinking population, then inheritance becomes a crucial part of the distribution of income and multiplies the inequalities related to property transmission.

The same applies to economic growth. When output growth per capita is 5% or 10% per year, then this produces a similar effect to a situation where the populace has between five or ten children each. What has been accumulated 10, 20 or 30 years ago is not important. Conversely, when economic growth is small or zero, property inherited from the past accumulates with a rate of return higher than the growth rate. This causes extreme inequality. In the contemporary situation, where the growth rate is less than 1% per annum, with a higher rate of return on property - it doesn't have to be double-digits, just 3%, 4% or 5% is sufficient - then the cumulative effects on wealth give an absolutely staggering importance to the past. When presented with these results, a common reaction is: "But this is not possible forever. It cannot always be the case. There is a logical inconsistency." But in fact, it is perfectly possible. Human history is an illustration of this relentless mechanism of accumulation by successive transmissions. Roughly speaking, with the exception of the twentieth century, the growth rate has been less than 1% per year, with a much higher rate of return on property, i.e. the rate of the rent. Even small values

FIGURE 2 **Toward a new century of rentiers in France?**

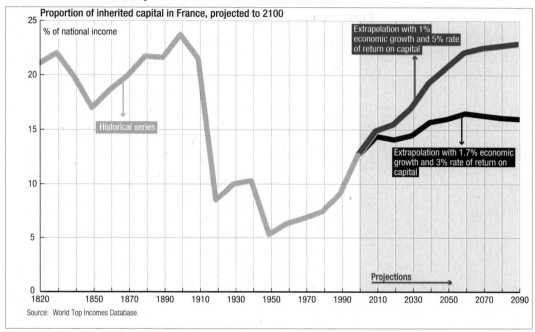

Proportion of inherited capital in France, projected to 2100

Source: World Top Incomes Database.

The study of saving habits from 1820 to 2008 allows us to construct scenarios of rent building for the twenty-first century. According to the evolution of economic growth and the return on capital after tax, the share of capital in national income should either be stabilized at around 15% to 20%, or exceed 20%.

like 3% or 4%, compared to a 1% growth, produce decade after decade of immense cumulative effects. It is here we find one of the evils of capitalism.

Admittedly, and thankfully, there are many kinds of public policies and institutions in place to reduce the accumulation of inherited wealth. Moreover, nominal growth rates (including inflation) are of the order of 5-6% per year, so that inert heritage, inherited from the past, weighs little against the new wealth generated each year. We are not yet back to the situation in the nineteenth century, which was also a world without inflation, where growth was in the region of 1% to 1.5% per year, and where the rate of return on inert capital was very much higher than growth. We are not there yet because there are reserves of population growth and economic growth. But we have seen that when population growth falters, with it falls the direct reduction of inequality by transmission, in addition to those inequalities induced by growth, which should automatically falter too. Conditions are met - from a strictly logical point of view when comparing the evolution of the rates of growth and return - so that at one point, during the twenty-first century, we should expect to return to a very low level of growth, that is much lower than the rate of return on capital, recreating a world of great inequality (Figure 2).

New rentiers

In the nineteenth century, the United Kingdom and France owned a large part of the capital of the rest of the world, and partly lived on pure rents. From 1850 to 1914, the United Kingdom and, to a lesser extent, France, were in permanent trade deficits to other countries throughout the world. However, these two countries benefited from a balance of payments surplus, that is to say that the rents paid by the rest of the world allowed these two countries not only to finance their trade deficit, but also to continue to accumulate at the expense of other countries. This is the power of capital: when you become an owner, you no longer need to work. Nineteenth century trade balances demonstrate this fact: some countries were rentiers compared to others. Although this doesn't mean that the rentiers stopped producing, in fact they continued to produce, but less than they were consuming. On the eve of 1914, English and French national incomes were 10% higher than domestic production, and the gap was financed by the rent paid by the rest of the world. Politically, such a situation is highly confrontational and violent. Is this a world that we wish to return to? The great fear in Europe today is that such a situation could indeed occur again, but with reversed roles where Europe becomes the possessed, rather than the possessor.

The resurgence of inheritance in a situation of low growth may ultimately lead to the absurd situation, which in the opinion of the author is socially and politically untenable, where millions of households pay rents to globalized, anonymous billionaires. Such a scenario reignites certain nineteenth century fears. Ricardo once said: "At the end of the nineteenth century, the rent will have absorbed all the national income" (RICARDO, 1817). While this prediction was not quite accurate, if we replace ground rent by property prices in capital cities or the price of oil, the same kind of predictions wouldn't seem outlandish today.

Something radically new has emerged in the structure of inequality that has developed particularly in the United States, which is the appearance of a kind of superstar entrepreneur, the *working rich* millionaires that claim their wealth is the result of hard work and not capital. There are no equivalent figures in history and their existence is a sign of complete institutional failure. It is simply absurd that people at the head of large US companies should be allowed to set their own salaries. What else can we expect in this situation? These people are simply helping themselves to company coffers. Since there are no limits to restrain them, they consequently build themselves a substantial heritage. The problem is not only greed, but also the inability of the market economy to properly control the remuneration of executives of very large companies. The invisible hand of the market cannot touch these people.

It is possible to calculate the marginal productivity for replicable functions, such as for staff in a McDonald's restaurant or an assembly line worker, i.e. the additional productivity an individual in such a role brings to the business. But such a calculation is not possible for non-replicable functions, such as for a chief financial officer. Nobody has conducted a test to see how much a business would lose without having a chief executive officer for ten years. Over such a period, even with all the controls

FIGURE 3 Distribution of national income between wages and profits

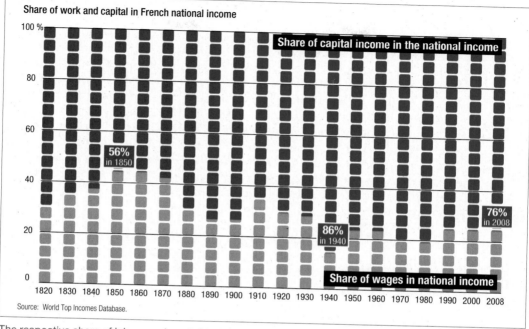

Share of work and capital in French national income

Share of capital income in the national income

56% in 1850

86% in 1940

76% in 2008

Share of wages in national income

1820 1830 1840 1850 1860 1870 1880 1890 1900 1910 1920 1930 1940 1950 1960 1970 1980 1990 2000 2008

Source: World Top Incomes Database.

The respective share of labour and capital in the French national income has been relatively stable over the past two centuries. Since 1820, capital has thus been generating 30% of the national wealth on average. During certain periods, such as the late nineteenth century, this share reached 40%. It fell below 20% in 1940 and has been fairly stable (24%) since the late 1980s, above its level of the 1970s, the end of the "Trente Glorieuses".

that can be imagined, the economic environment will have changed so much that the results would be inconclusive. This is a typical example of something that the market cannot do, which highlights the need for institutions that can.

This phenomenon of very high salaries, which transform into rent, is also symptomatic of a type of meritocratic extremism that has developed in the United States. The common justification for the exponential increase in some salaries is to say: "they allow new people, self-made people, to compete with very wealthy heirs." Essentially, we have set up a race between Forbes-listed individuals who inherit fortunes and those who earn several million dollars at Goldman Sachs. The problem here is that 90% of the population are excluded from the race - the vast majority do not enjoy any inheritance or receive very high salaries for their work, and in addition they are told that this situation is fair. In many ways this represents the worst of all worlds: here we have both the inequality of the past, but accompanied by the moralizing meritocratic discourse of the twenty-first century.

The first priority is to dispel the myths concerning *Les Trente Glorieuses* in France. The particular structure of inequality during this period was marked by low wage differentials, a very small role for inheritance as a proportion of the national income and property values that had fallen to zero in some cases, together with strong economic growth. This type of structure is now long gone.

Staying with the example of France, which is the country that has experienced the strongest break-ups during the twentieth century that can be divided into two periods between 1950 and 2010. These 30-year (i.e. one generation) periods between 1950-1980 and 1980-2010 were times of revolutionary change. The growth rates of wages, incomes and production stood at about 5% per year during the first period, compared to 1.5% in the second. Rises of 1.5% or 5% in wages, income, per capita output over a generation, were remarkable and represented a complete overhaul. The problem is precisely the length of these periods. The first period lasted so long that people eventually believed it was permanent, and having taken this experience on-board, the second period was assumed to be transitional... except that we are still in the second period, that has now lasted as long as the first one. Some even believe that we have moved into another historical phase - a perpetual *Trente Glorieuses* perhaps? However, we are likely to pay dearly for such an assumption.

We have yet to emerge from this transitional phase and some expect a return to a "golden age" if we just wait a little longer. This hope is based on the impression that such a world, although not without inequality, had inequalities that were much less pronounced. That is to say that inequalities existed between the blue-collar worker and the executive, with wage differentials from 1 to 3 or 1 to 5, but that these differences were not extreme and were mainly justifiable in light of the work that each brought to the production and the common good. Each had a common vision of the value of work. It was a period when arbitrary inequality, such as arbitrary rent, i.e. money without any possible justification that was there for some and not others, seemed to have disappeared. Many delusions exist about this period, there is the idea for example that technological and technocratic rationality had enabled the competent executive to replace the idle shareholder.

We now realize that the share of national income that goes to human capital and labour in the broad sense may be a little higher today than in Balzac's era, but not much more. That is to say, that the share that goes to pure capital - rent, interest, dividends, which are paid by the mere fact of ownership of capital without the addition of individual work - has declined little compared to the nineteenth century. Then this proportion stood at roughly 35-40%; today it is around 25-30%. This is not an indication of a revolutionary change in civilization (Figure 3). It was during the 1950-1970 period, that the share of capital in national income fell to significantly lower levels due to rent controlling mechanisms such as nationalization and the implementation of strong policies, which had the result of breaking up capital and inheritance so that it was mostly new savings that supplied the capital, meaning that the return on capital was more fairly distributed.

Many French people who have lived through *Les Trente Glorieuses* still regard themselves as self-made entrepreneurs, as people who have not inherited much wealth but have accumulated a lot through their own hard work. All this continues to weigh on the collective imagination. These people thought that after the war, the world had entered into a new era, an enchanted world where the inequalities of the past had permanently disappeared. Things seem very different to those born between 1970 and 1980. To take a specific example, people born between the years 1970 and 1980 are not able to buy property in Paris or in any big city, unless they inherit a considerable sum or their incomes are within the top 1%. Without inheriting sufficient wealth, even those with salaries in the top 10%, have little choice but to pay rent throughout their lives to the children of owners. This reality simply did not exist for people born between 1930 and 1950. There has been a complete changeover, the cause of which is associated with low growth.

Reshuffling the cards without strong growth

While low growth feeds the importance of inheritance, the obsession for strong growth is equally barren: by focusing overly on the creation of growth, other issues are forgotten - including issues that we actually know how to address. The creation of better institutions, particularly fiscal ones, can help solve the problems associated with growth. Taxes on capital must be developed in the same way that income taxes were developed in the twentieth century. Such taxes on capital must be international, or perhaps European-wide in the first instance. Europe makes a good starting point as it is the world's richest economic area, with the largest number of multinational companies in the global Top 500 list, and the largest number of billionaires. Everything is in place for a taxable base, the tax just needs to be implemented. All this could be achieved at a specific growth rate and could solve many of today's economic problems. We could improve public health and education systems, and much more besides, if we broadened the focus away from the narrow goal of obtaining a 0.1 percentage point of growth, and if we finally accepted the idea that the average growth rates observed for thirty years are already very high. Annual growth of 1-1.5% in an economy that is already highly developed is actually very fast. Perhaps the best way forward is to stop considering the rate of growth on an annual basis, but rather view it in terms of generations. So a 1% annual growth rate is actually a 30% increase over a generation (30 years); while 1.5% equates to 45%, i.e. in just 30 years almost half of the economy has been renewed. In these terms, the growth rate is huge! If we consider only the annual growth rate, then it is possible to think that nothing has happened for the last 30 years in rich countries, because during this time growth has hovered around 1.5% per capita. Whereas, in reality half of the economy has been renewed. While such growth is not sufficient to wipe away the advantage of inheritance, the development of tax tools is much more reasonable than relying solely on the automatic resorption of inheritance by virtue of a very high rate of growth.

Today, wages constitute a significant proportion of the rent. To address this issue, rigid rules on the highest salaries are necessary. Confiscatory tax rates are needed to prevent salaries reaching beyond a certain level. This is the only way to calm the market frenzy. Otherwise, without self-regulation of the market, all other efforts to address this issue are doomed to fail. As discussed above, we can work out the value of people who work at a McDonald's restaurant, but how do we value the executives at the company's headquarters? The latter may have great ideas on how to improve McDonald's menus across the world. But we have no idea how to value this contribution. Similarly, it is very difficult to gauge the value of academic or scientific researchers. Their marginal productivity is not written on their foreheads. In the absence of a suitable means to value their work, the market needs rigid rules so that certain limits cannot be exceeded. Otherwise we know what happens: a company calls in consultants to determine salaries, they check the average in the sector and add 1% so that everyone's happy. The next CEO does the same thing. And 10 years later, wages have soared.

During the time of the US President Roosevelt there were many successful experiments with near-confiscatory income taxes. In fact, there is little cause to seek for new ways to address the problem of excessive salaries. The paradox is that, although France is developing a 75% tax rate, it is not the country where it is most needed. A taxation of 75% would be much more useful in the United States, but here we encounter a political problem: it seems that once individuals in the US reach these high-income levels, they are able to influence the political process and thus can prevent any reform. In France, where such individuals are much less numerous, those with excessively high incomes have much less ability to influence government.

It is the French wealth tax that can today be considered as the closest example of an ideal tax on capital. It has many merits. Created by left-wing politicians in 1981 and then reformed in 1988-1989, it represents a much more modern tax than, for example, the property taxes that were abolished in Germany, Spain and Sweden. These other taxes actually dated from the nineteenth century and much resembled the French property tax, which also dates from that period, and is based on completely obsolete cadastral values. At least the French wealth tax is based, as it should be if we want a global tax on billionaires, on the market value of property.

Consider the Forbes ranking of the world's wealthiest people. Every year these men and women become 7% to 8% richer. So, if global GDP increases by about 5% per year, we may think that their wealth grows at a rate that is only marginally above that of GDP. However, most people who work in rich countries have a salary that rises by just 1%, or even 0% per annum. This may seem like a small difference, but over 30 years, the effect of accumulated wealth is enormous. There are very strong scale effects at work: from 100,000 euros worth of assets, the returns are modest; with one million euros, the returns are much better; while 100 million euros will yield far higher returns. The effect of this from 1990 to 2010 is quite simple: the wealth of those listed in the Forbes rich list has multiplied almost by a factor of ten. This is true for both Bill Gates and Liliane Bettencourt– i.e. those who have worked to earn their fortune, and those who have not. Gone is the idea that capital income disappears with time because the world is becoming more rational. In fact, exactly the opposite is true: an efficient market fosters the continuation of the transmission of inherited wealth from one generation to the next.

Perhaps one day soon we will realize the folly of making free trade agreements with most countries of the world, without directly including agreements on the transmission of all information on capital flows and flows of interest and dividends. For example, it is senseless to implement free trade on goods and services with Switzerland and not to have in counterpart a total transmission of information on who are the beneficiaries of the flows of interest and dividends into Swiss bank accounts. Allowing this to persist is merely giving our adversaries a stick to beat us with, and ensures that the full potential of our tax base is eaten away. ■

▌ REFERENCES

KUZNETS, S., 1955, "Economic Growth and Income Inequality." *American Economic Review* 45(1):1–28.

RICARDO D., 1817, On The Principles of Political Economy and Taxation.

The fight against poverty: the central axis of development policies?

Serge Tomasi Organisation for Economic Co-operation and Development (OECD), Paris, France

From the Washington Consensus to the New York Consensus, the fight against poverty has become the central axis of development policies in the late 1990s. In the eighties and the early nineties, the so-called "Washington Consensus" largely dominated the development agenda. Faced with the debt crisis and the structural macroeconomic imbalances of many developing countries (internal and external deficits, high inflation, low economic growth), international financial institutions, notably the World Bank and IMF, advocated the establishment of structural reforms to restore macroeconomic balances and strengthen competitiveness through Structural Adjustment Programmes (SAPs). The Washington Consensus proposed the liberalization of foreign trade and the establishment of supply policies to strengthen economic competitiveness and to reduce budget deficits and balance of payments disequilibria. While these policies, along with efforts towards the massive external debt relief of heavily indebted poor countries (HIPC), have helped to improve the situation on the macroeconomic level (lower inflation, the restoration of internal and external balances in particular), they have often had a deflationary effect and a high social cost in the short term.

The first direct criticism of the Washington Consensus came from the publication of the UNICEF report "Adjustment with a human face" in the late eighties, which warned of the human impact of these policies. In 1990, the publication of the first report on human development, and the development of the Human Development Index (HDI) by the UNDP, began the reorientation of the development agenda. Offering a composite indicator that measured both per capita income growth but also access to basic social services (education, health), the authors proposed an indicator of development that went beyond mere monetary wealth and included more qualitative elements focused on the creation of human capital. Major United Nations conferences in the nineties, including Rio (sustainable development), Cairo (population and development), Beijing (women and development) and Copenhagen (social development), have also been influential in pushing the direction of the development agenda towards human development.

From Structural Adjustment Programmes toPoverty Reduction Strategies

In addition, the World Bank, under the leadership of James Wolfensohn and with the impetus of chief economists who are specialized in inequality issues (Joseph Stiglitz and François Bourguignon), has gradually made the fight against poverty the central axis of its action. Its 2000/2001 World development report (WORLD BANK, 2001) marked a turning point, the Bank advocated a multidimensional approach to poverty, going beyond the monetary approach in terms of poverty lines, to integrate capacity and "empowerment". Such theoretical consideration was given its operational implementation through national poverty reduction strategies (PRSPs).

The late 1990s was also characterized by the emergence of the themes of pro-poor growth and human poverty. The 1997 UNDP Human Development report (HDR) introduced a human poverty index for the first time, while the 1998 UNDP Human Poverty report advocated the implemented pro-poor growth strategies. The Millennium Declaration and the attached Millennium Development Goals (MDGs) represented the culmination of a long process of theoretical reflexion and a political coming-of-age, which would put the fight against poverty at the heart of the development agenda, discussed both from the point of view of monetary income (objective 1) and of opportunities/capacity (objectives on health, education, food security and gender equity).

The French approach: the fight against poverty and inequality

The issue of inequality has never really managed to impose itself as a consensual objective of the international community. However, the French Cooperation strategy has developed proposals for an agenda that focused not only on the fight against poverty, but also on the fight against inequality. In a working document published on the eve of the Millennium Summit (DGCID, 2001), it clearly inscribed its approach within the framework of the theoretical work of economists specializing in inequality, including Roland Barro (BARRO, 2000) who highlighted the constraints to growth in poor countries that are caused by inequality, Philippe Aghion who advocated redistribution policies to correct market imperfections, and François Bourguignon who called for transfers of cash, or payments in kind, to poor families. The approach taken by the French Cooperation strategy also called on the political economy to integrate the political dimension and the analysis of power relations that influence the distribution of national income within a country. The IMPACT network, set up by the former Director General of the French International Cooperation, has for a long time been a place for the French Ministry of Foreign Affairs to conduct research and empirical studies on poverty and inequality. It has often made reference to the work of, for example: Bruno Losch on the coffee and cocoa sector; Jean-François Bayard on the State in Africa; and Alice Sindzingre on the political economy of reforms in Africa.

Inequalities are back in the headlines

The issue of inequality and its impact on growth and human development has, however, never been recognized as a central axis of development cooperation, despite efforts from France and others. Priority has been given to the fight against absolute poverty and to the support of human development. Nevertheless, inequality is now making a return to the heart of the debate, with rising income inequality attracting major media attention during the last decade. The OECD report "Divided We Stand" shows that in all OECD countries, and also in most emerging countries with the exception of Brazil and Indonesia, household income inequality measured according to the Gini coefficient has increased between the early 1990s and the end of the last decade (OECD, 2011). See figure 2, chapter 1.

The main source of these inequalities in OECD countries is the growing inequalities in labour income[1]. In emerging countries, the same report noted a sharp increase in the dispersion of income since 1990 in China (+24%), India (+16%) and to a lesser extent in South Africa (+4%), whereas it has stabilized in Indonesia and decreased in Brazil (-10%), although Brazil has by far the highest levels of disparity (the income of the richest 10% is more than 50 times the income of the poorest 10%, compared to nine times the average in OECD countries).

These developments, in the case of emerging countries, are logically leading to a reopening of the debate on the link between growth and inequality. Are we seeing here the classic Kuznets curve effect (emerging countries have not yet fully entered into the second phase of their growth process, which is characterized by a combination of growth in GDP/capita and the reduction of inequality)? Or is it due to the consequences of an external growth model that requires the long-term suppression of real wages to maintain a competitiveness differential?

Such developments also revive the debate on the measurement of poverty and the way in which inequalities are taken into account in the development agenda. The UNDP, as early as the 1990s, sought to go beyond the simple measure of absolute poverty by developing the human poverty index, which has since been replaced by

---

1.These inequalities in labour income are determined by differentials in wages and in the number of working hours (explosion in part-time working) and by the inactivity rate (rising unemployment). Reducing tax progressivity and redistributive social policies, because of funding and competitiveness problems, only very partially correct these inequalities at the level of the final disposable income of households.

the multidimensional poverty index (MPI). The MPI seeks to measure poverty not only in terms of low monetary income, but to provide a more qualitative approach in terms of capability deprivation (10 core indicators are used to measure the three dimensions of poverty: human health, education, living conditions). The 2011 HDR, in addition to monitoring the MPI of 109 countries, provides a sub-national monitoring in 66 countries to measure regional disparities.

In its 2006 report on equity and development, the World Bank emphasized the need to better take into account equity in development policies (WORLD BANK, 2006). In an imperfect market, the distribution of wealth may affect the allocation of investment opportunities and economic efficiency by creating rent-seeking situations and preventing some players from expressing their full potential. The State may then play a role to compensate for market imperfections and to enhance the efficiency of the economy, either through a redistributive policy or by a longer-term policy to strengthen economic opportunities or by supporting the distribution of assets and the capacity of the weakest to express themselves. This action also strengthens social cohesion. The report did not avoid the questions of the political dimension, inequalities in access to power or the political expression that can promote rent-seeking behaviour and the reproduction of these inequalities.

In the same vein, the latest report from the OECD Development Centre (OECD, 2012) promotes the idea that social cohesion is a prerequisite for sustainable development. The report highlights progress in developing countries over the past decade: 83 developing countries had a per capita income growth that was double that of the OECD countries, compared to only 12 in the 1990s, while 50 developing countries have a GDP/capita growth rate greater than 3.5% per year. It underlines, however, that most developing countries are now faced with rising inequality along with rising middle class expectations in terms of their standard of living and for a fairer redistribution of national income. This is reflected in the levels of public dissatisfaction over living conditions, despite the progress made in terms of per capita income (graph below). The situation in Tunisia is particularly interesting as it shows a high dissatisfaction index despite a 4% increase in GDP/capita on average over the last decade. The report therefore recommends the strengthening of social cohesion through appropriate fiscal policies, employment policies, education and social protection, and suggests that certain grants should be called into question as they are overly favourable to the wealthier classes (e.g. subsidies for the consumption of fossil fuels, which according to the International Energy Agency reached 450 billion USD in 2010).

It is hoped that this work and a growing awareness of the issue of inequality will enable the post-2015 agenda to go beyond the measurement of absolute poverty alone. Indeed, a growing number of experts are arguing for the integration of relative poverty indicators (such as, for example, the UNDP's indicator of measuring the proportion of people with an income of less than half the median income) into measurement indicators. This approach would be easier to implement if, as advocated by the OECD, targets and indicators were not limited to the overall objectives and indicators of comparability between countries, but they incorporated national objectives with indicators to monitor a country's progress in relation to its own situation. ∎

REFERENCES

BARRO R., 2000, Inequality and growth in a panel of countries. Journal of economic growth. March 2000.

DGCID, 2001, Fight against poverty, inequality and exclusion. Working Paper.

OECD, 2011, Divided we stand. Why inequality keeps rising.

OECD, 2012, Perspectives on global development 2012. Social cohesion in a shifting world. OECD's Development Centre.

WORLD BANK, 2001, World development report 2000/2001, Attacking poverty.

WORLD BANK, 2006, Development and Equity.

FIGURE 2 Judging the quality of one's own living conditions

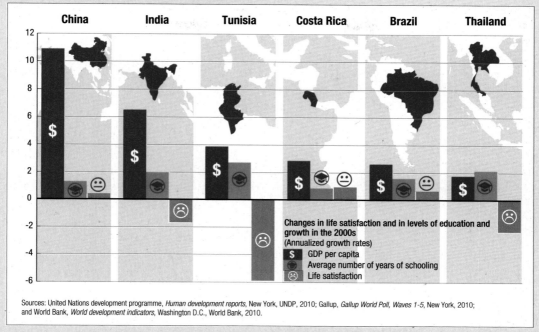

Sources: United Nations development programme, *Human development reports*, New York, UNDP, 2010; Gallup, *Gallup World Poll, Waves 1-5*, New York, 2010; and World Bank, *World development indicators*, Washington D.C., World Bank, 2010.

The expectations of the middle class are rising in many developing countries, along with rising incomes and education levels. The fastest growth of the sample (China) and the lowest one (Thailand) correspond respectively to the highest and lowest levels of a population's satisfaction with its living conditions. In Tunisia however, despite positive indicators in terms of increasing revenue and education level, the population remains largely unsatisfied.

CHAPTER 3

Controversial indicators of standards of living lie at the heart of inequality issues. A history of international comparisons of living conditions shows that these indicators definitely help change how the world is seen and whether human rights are recognized. By putting everyone into a space of equivalence that enables quantification, statistics serve as new tools for generating discussion about the reconfiguration of power relationships.

Inequality, the emergence of a political idea in the 20th century

Vincent Bonnecase
Les Afriques dans le Monde, Bordeaux, France

n historical terms, the measurement and understanding of inequalities in the world are relatively recent concerns. During the first part of the twentieth century, when most of the countries that would later become known as "developing countries" were undergoing colonization, there was no question of comparing the living standards of European populations, or those of European origin, with the situation of African or Asian populations, nor of reducing the gap between one and the other. At the time, a barrier of incomparability existed between colonized peoples and those who were not, which, depending on the various colonial empires, was expressed in a legal form, but also on the basis of differences in race and civilisation: the view was held that "whites", "blacks" and "yellows" could not have the same needs or social aspirations. Without doubt, the development of international statistical data has, since the nineteenth century, played a role in the beginnings of a hierarchal definition of living standards across the world. But this remains "geographically limited to civilised countries" (HORVATH, 1972): in other words, concerning mainly European and North American countries which, due to their assumed degree of "civilization", share the same referential space. The emergence of comparative data on living standards for societies that underwent industrialization in the nineteenth century is also closely linked to the development of social legislation intended to "govern misery" (PROCACCI, 1993), something which did not apply in the colonies.

The aim of this article is to put into perspective the conditions under which comparable standards of living in the world emerged in the mid-twentieth century, focusing particularly on the contradictory role that may have been played by the data on one side, and the paradigm of race on the other. More specifically, this article focuses on the first ever collection of data on living conditions in French colonial Africa. How has this knowledge been materially developed? To which questions, both internal and external to the empire, was it addressed? What were the different political uses of such data? Through the analysis of these questions, a number of contemporary issues will be raised regarding the measurement of inequality in the world, issues which echo controversies that appeared some sixty years ago.

The first evaluations of inequality in industrial societies

Since the mid-nineteenth century, a number of industrial societies have collected statistical information to measure and compare the living conditions of populations in terms of collective standards. Although most of this data primarily resulted from the initiatives of individual scholars, industrialists and doctors, it was correlated with new social legislation that was being established in certain countries. In England, where the adoption of the *Poor Law Amendment Act* in 1834 led to multiple controversies over the government's management of poverty, several major surveys were thus made in the second half of that century to estimate the numbers of poor people living in certain cities. The most important of these surveys were conducted successively by Charles Booth and Benjamin Rowntree who are now considered as the main precursors of the "poverty line" concept: from the perspective of their research, poverty became a category that was defined by a quantitative threshold, allowing it to be compared from one place to another (CARRÉ, RÉVAUGER, 1995). At around the same time, similar surveys on the working classes were being conducted in France, while from 1841 onwards the first social laws were passed, which were expected to reduce the hardships endured by the workers. One of the stated objectives of these surveys was to allow "a comparison between places and people" in the words of Frederic Le Play, who was the author of an important series of monographic studies conducted in the second half of the century on workers" conditions (LE PLAY, 1879).

From such research the concept of social inequality emerged, in the sense that it is currently perceived (DESROSIERES, 2008), although at the time these social inequalities mainly remained thought of at the level of a single country, where the same assistance and management mechanisms applied. Admittedly, there were some examples of cross-national comparisons in this area, particularly the work of Le Play (1879) and Rowntree (1910), but also within the framework of the first international statistical congresses that, in the second half of the nineteenth century, gathered specialists in demography, health and work (BRIAN, 1989). Unemployment figures in particular – which, from the 1880s, gradually replaced poverty as a category of public action in industrial societies (TOPALOV, 1994) – led to international comparisons of the actual situation itself, but also of the policies that were put in place to deal with the problem. But such comparative approaches to the understanding of living conditions remained rare until the early twentieth century.

Between the two world wars, the measurement and international comparisons of living conditions became more formalized due to the influence of the League of Nations (LON) and the International Labour Office (ILO). At the disposal of these institutions was quantitative data that governments were collecting on an increasingly routine basis for political purposes, although the production of statistics in this manner did not necessarily obey the same methodological framework. One of the LON's objectives was to work towards a standardization that would enable the comparison between circumstances in different nations and also the different ways in which the public authorities were managing the issues. This was particularly important in the 1930s as the economic crisis had resulted in the deterioration of living conditions throughout most industrialized countries. In 1932, the ILO thus published a "study of international comparisons of costs of living" that was based on a series of surveys involving working people from 15 cities in Europe and the United States. In 1935, the LON Health Committee launched a programme to assess levels of nutrition in the world by adopting universal standards on calorie and nutritional requirements, and guidelines to harmonize the methods of investigation. In 1938, the ILO carried out another study on "the living standards of workers" in which, for the first time by an international organization, some "generally accepted objective standards" of living were proposed (BONNECASE, 2011).

Such activities of measurement and comparison, while enabling a figure to be put on inequality in the world, remained however largely confined to *a white and civilised world*: colonized populations were generally excluded from this common reference point. Significantly, discussions at the ILO and LON during the inter-war period, when touching on Africa, did not concern living conditions and social legislation, but rather so called specifically African problems, especially slavery and forced labour (COOPER, 2004), the persistence of which was an ongoing concern in international fora. However, when the issue under consideration was health, nutritional conditions or mortality trends, the debate tended to focus mainly on industrialized countries. Indeed, colonial administrations had very little quantitative data on these issues. While the improvement of living conditions of colonized peoples was a key aspect of the colonial justification for conquest, it was not considered that this required measurement in order to be demonstrated: as evidence of such improvement, reports of clinics, agricultural development work and schools counted more than statistics. Certainly, colonial administrators produced an abundance of statistics within the framework of the routine management of their territories, but they related more to the colonial work itself, rather than to the lives of colonized peoples. What tended to be measured were things like the number of people treated or vaccinated in the clinics, the number of tonnes of grain produced in a region, the number of children enrolled in schools, i.e. the performance of the different colonial services. However, such data ultimately said very little about the way people lived in colonies: no administrator sought to specify to what extent colonized populations were likely to eat a poorer diet or to die younger than European populations. Inequality between these two population groups was not measured until the early 1940s, simply because it was considered that they did not belong to the same world.

Mobilization and internationalization of knowledge

Following the Second World War, the colonial empires were embroiled in a crisis of legitimacy led by heterogeneous actors, including new United Nations (UN) bodies and mobilized populations within colonies. French and British Africa had already witnessed great strikes in the late 1930s. In the British Empire, these strikes contributed to the adoption of the Colonial Development and Welfare Act of 1940, which represented a real break in colonial policy: the improvement of living conditions in the colonies, which until then was based primarily on local budgets, became the object of metropolitan public investment. In the French Empire, a similar break occurred in 1946 with the establishment of investment funds for economic and social development, while the colonies were shaken by a new phase of protests (COOPER, 2004).

This combination of institutional reforms and social mobilizations fundamentally altered the understanding of living conditions within imperial territories. On the one hand, new laws and policies to establish the transfer of funds from metropoles to colonies, encouraged administrations and the public to put the socio-economic disparities between the two population groups under further scrutiny; while on the other hand, colonial populations that had been mobilized in the fight to improve their living conditions eventually began to compare their own situation with those living in the metropolitan state. For example, railway workers in French West Africa, who were among the originators of the major strikes that caused alarm in the post-war colonial federation, requested that their working conditions and wages were determined according to the same rules as applied throughout the entire Empire. It was ultimately colonial differentialism, in terms of a growing awareness of living conditions, that was at the heart of the conflict.

The then newly formed UN organization became one of the main initiators of external pressure, on top of the internal social protests in imperial territories. In the post-war period, the UN quickly adopted an anti-colonial stance under the influence of the USSR and the United States, countries that officially opposed colonization, and also that of former colonies which had gained independence. While most criticism focused on the legal status of colonized peoples and their exclusion from the political sphere, the issue of living conditions was also taken on board. According to the charter adopted in January 1945 by the UN, Member States which "assume responsibility for the administration of territories whose peoples do not administrate themselves yet [...] accept the obligation to promote as much as possible their prosperity". They commit themselves "to this end to communicate regularly [...] statistical information and others of a technical nature relating to economic, social and educational conditions in the territories for which they are respectively responsible" (UNITED NATIONS CHARTER, Article 73 e). According to this clause, itself marked by an "ideology of development" that grew following the War (RIST, 1996), colonial powers were obliged to provide statistical proof of their willingness to improve the social and economic situation of colonized populations.

This political reconsideration of living conditions in the world in general, and in the colonies in particular, went together with the technical effort within international organizations to produce new evaluation standards. Each specialized institution exerted standardizing actions within its own field. FAO, for example, in 1946 launched the first major "world food survey" and three years later instituted a "Committee on

Calorie Requirements", which reviewed the validity of the pre-war minimum food requirement standards that were set by the LON, but which had most often been applied only to populations in Europe and North America. The primary objective was to collect standardized food information in territories where it was clearly lacking: in retrospect it was realized the extent to which, when undernourishment and malnutrition was considered in the 1930s, "we were almost always thinking of Eastern and South-Eastern European countries, with the Bosphorus [appearing] as the limit of the intellectual horizon" (FAO, 1955). Subsequently, the mental picture of food inequality was expanded to include non-European populations.

More generally, it was the overall measurement of living conditions across the world that became the subject of debate within international organizations. The United Nations General Assembly (UNGA) thus adopted a first resolution in 1949 requesting the Economic and Social Council to assess the social situation in the world from "quantitative indices of satisfaction of needs whose existence is universally recognized". Three years later, it adopted a second resolution in which it called for the development of "adequate statistical methods and techniques so as best to facilitate the gathering and use of pertinent data in order to enable the Secretary-General to publish regular annual reports showing changes in absolute levels of living conditions in all countries" (Bonnecase, 2011). The intention was to bring all of the world's populations into the same field of reference, where differences were both comparable and measurable, so that it became no longer only living conditions that were under discussion, but also living standards.

This led to the formation of a committee of experts from the United Nations Economic and Social Council, which in the early 1950s was charged with considering "the definition and evaluation of standards of living in an international perspective". It included economists, demographers and other experts who, like Louis-Joseph Lebret in France, had previously worked on the theme of poverty in different countries and was by then dedicated to the study of inequalities in living standards internationally. Several controversies afflicted the work of this committee. The main one concerned the relevance of a single index for the standard of living, since "the use of a uniform and universal system of values" could contribute to "penalising international technical progress in the West". Infant mortality rate and life expectancy were discussed at this time, although it was said that "longevity does not necessarily indicate a degree of sanitary quality". However, the main statistic highlighted was the national income per capita: it appeared as a "fairly comprehensive indicator of the determinants of living conditions as a whole", even though it may generate "rather false conclusions on the differences between living standards in different regions of the world", since "the non-market goods and services are partly excluded from the measurement" (ECONOMIC AND SOCIAL COUNCIL OF THE UNITED NATIONS, 1954).

These controversies are of interest as they foreshadow more recent debates, particularly on the dominance of productive indicators in the measurement of well-being, but also on the relevance of universal indices applied to different populations, regardless of how these populations may experience their own living conditions (DESTREMAU,

FIGURE 1 Measuring living standards internationally

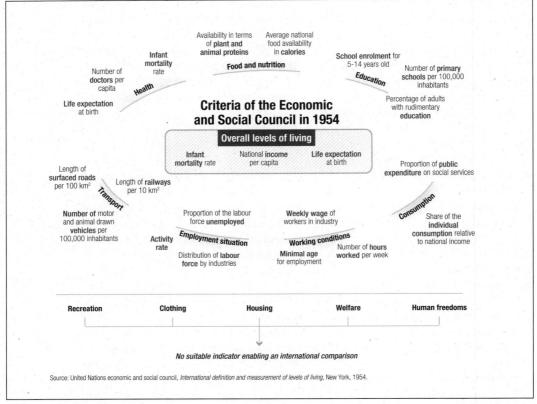

Source: United Nations economic and social council, *International definition and measurement of levels of living*, New York, 1954.

The use of living standards indicators to enable comparisons between all of the world's countries is a recent approach. The first trials of these indicators were conducted in the mid-1950s, showing that the objective to take multiple facets of life into account is not new, but the earliest attempts were hampered by the absence of measurable factors or statistical systems.

SALAMA, 2002): such controversies, far from appearing in the last twenty years, were present from the outset in the history of the international measurement of living standards.

Compiling statistics

The international demand for statistics was locally translated into a proliferation of surveys on living conditions in the colonies, which was sometimes met with resistance from colonial administrators who were initially responsible for such investigations and often reluctant to internationalize knowledge. Taking the food situation in French West Africa as an example, the first ever research conducted here into nutrition was entrusted to a new agency, known as the Anthropological Mission, largely comprising military doctors and pharmacists. In the second half of the 1940s, the

Mission carried out an extensive survey in several of the federation's colonies, which involved the observation of family meals and the weighing of food that went into the composition of these meals. For the first time the French government was seeking to quantify, according to clearly defined methodological procedures, the average calorie and nutritional intake in African towns and villages. However, underlying this innovative research was the racial assumption that Africans and Europeans did not necessarily have the same physiological needs: the fact that the people surveyed did not have a more malnourished bodily appearance, given their calculated food intake, led to the assumption that "the body of black people does not operate like [that of the whites]" (PALES, 1954). Investigators then tested this hypothesis for a number of nutrients before dismissing it, on a case by case basis, and concluded the uniqueness of the human physiology.

Despite these prejudices, research did however reveal the relative importance of nutritional problems in African populations, which was not obvious at the time. According to the results, the average calorie intake over one year was sufficient on average, while showing large variations depending on the timing and on the location studied: the strong decrease in the level of consumption during the "hunger gap", although a widely known phenomenon, appeared in retrospect to have been underestimated. The same applied to qualitative deficiencies, which appeared relatively high in terms of what was considered by FAO nutritionists to be normal requirements. The administration, however, did not readily accept these findings as evidence, particularly due to the small number of surveys on which they were based, which called into question their validity in terms of the whole of West Africa. Furthermore, the researchers knew that the people they observed strongly distrusted them, meaning that, in the eyes of the former, there was an additional parameter that significantly distorted the value of the results: for example, when the calculated intake appeared too low, the studied populations were sometimes suspected of concealing a proportion of their nutrient intake; or, conversely, when the intake was higher than expected, investigators suspected individuals of making exaggerated claims about their wealth (BONNECASE, 2009).

In the 1950s, this process of quantifying calorie intakes was continued, but under the auspices of new players: the colonial administrators, whom had previously held a quasi-monopoly on research in the colonies, began to be gradually replaced by professional nutritionists, sociologists and economists. New organizations acquired a central role in the compilation of data on living standards, especially ORSTOM (Office of Overseas Scientific and Technical Research), which was created in 1944, and the INSEE (National Institute of Statistical and Economic Studies), established in 1946. Methods of investigation were also changing, particularly through the adoption of the sampling technique. Thus, in 1957, the first food surveys based on probability samples were conducted in francophone West Africa. The same type of research was carried out in British colonies where Nutrition Committees were established after the War. By the late 1950s, Africa was still not yet considered as the main continent of hunger, in comparison to perceptions thereafter. However, compared to the situation

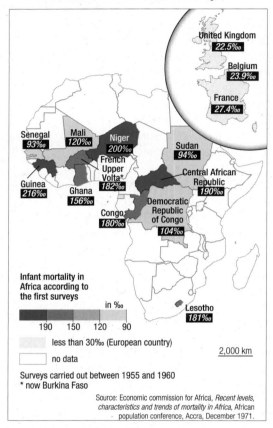

FIGURE 2 **Initial assessments of infant mortality in Africa**

United Kingdom
22.5‰

Belgium
23.9‰

France
27.4‰

Senegal
93‰

Mali
120‰

Niger
200‰

Sudan
94‰

French
Upper
Volta*
182‰

Central African
Republic
190‰

Guinea
216‰

Ghana
156‰

Congo
180‰

Democratic
Republic
of Congo
104‰

Lesotho
181‰

Infant mortality in
Africa according to
the first surveys

in ‰

190   150   120   90

less than 30‰ (European country)

no data

Surveys carried out between 1955 and 1960
* now Burkina Faso

2,000 km

Source: Economic commission for Africa, *Recent levels,
characteristics and trends of mortality in Africa*, African
population conference, Accra, December 1971.

Initial demographic sample surveys, aiming in particular to measure infant mortality, have been conducted in sub-Saharan Africa since the 1950s. The results, despite uncertainties, highlight significant differences across the world, with the infant mortality risk being three to ten times greater in Africa than in Europe.

ten years earlier, there was increasing recognition - backed up by data - of the level of undernourishment and malnutrition experienced by a number of African populations (BONNECASE, 2011).

A similar trend was emerging in the assessment of health levels, while demographics and infant mortality rates in particular were regarded by international organizations as the key indicators. In the immediate post-war period, colonial administrations had only a very small amount of synthetic data on the issue: most of the demographic knowledge available was based on administrative censuses that were regularly organized in various districts for tax purposes. Besides the fact that these figures did not paint a remotely accurate picture of reality, because many people developed strategies for concealing information from the census enumerators, they had not previously been regarded as of particular significance in terms of living conditions. If administrators were keen to take up the fight against "the depopulation of Africa" in the inter-war period, known in the French Empire as the "decline of the black race" (CONKLIN, 1997), it was mainly because it was seen as an obstacle to the development of the continent,.

During the 1950s, demographers in Africa instigated the first large population studies. In 1950, the French Imperial government ordered a review of its territories, not only to investigate whether population growth was compatible with an "industrial take-off", but also to assess "the elevation of the health status and the improvement of the way of life" (BONNE-CASE, 2011). Some demographic sample surveys were organized by INSEE agents which, for the first time, enabled the establishment of synthetic data at the level of entire colonies. Certainly, even in the eyes of their creators, these surveys produced results that appeared quite random, a fact that was due to the material difficulties encountered during the investigations, as well as the people's persistent distrust of enumeration efforts. However, these figures, especially the ones on infant mortality, enabled a hierarchy of health to be drawn up in which African territories now had their place. These data, in the absence of alternatives, continued to be regarded as

FIGURE 3 Initial comparisons of national income per capita in developing countries

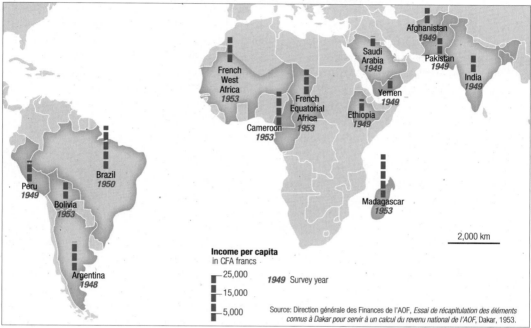

Income per capita
in CFA francs
— 25,000
— 15,000
— 5,000

1949 Survey year

Source: Direction générale des Finances de l'AOF, *Essai de récapitulation des éléments connus à Dakar pour servir à un calcul du revenu national de l'AOF*, Dakar, 1953.

Income measurement and its comparison have given a new prominence to inequalities in the world, while also reinforcing the idea that the need to catch up with developed countries should be at the heart of any development policy.

definitive by international bodies until the first general population censuses on the continent in the 1970s.

National income was a third fundamental research area that contributed to the ranking of colonial territories on a scale of living conditions in the post-war period. On this aspect, a lack of knowledge was not a colonial specificity: even in industrial countries it was not until the 1930s or 1940s that the public authorities made regular records of national income while also developing their economic policies in the wake of Keynesianism (VANOLI, 2002). In the United States, the Senate called for the establishment of "national income estimates" for the first time in 1934, in a context of new investment policies that had been set in place to deal with the crisis; in Great Britain, such calculations became systematic from 1941 for the purpose of rationalising the war effort; in France, this trend towards modern national accounts emerged slightly later with the creation in 1945 of the Commissariat du Plan and the INSEE in 1946 (DESROSIERES, 2003). The earliest calculations of national income in the colonies was closely linked to the launch of proactive investment, the formulation of which, if not the practice, required new macroeconomic data. However, the compilation of such data also reflected the will to evaluate the effects of policies "on raising living standards, [...] by generating from all existing statistical data a single figure for each country and for each year, a figure which should indicate what is commonly called, in European countries, the national income" (MINISTÈRE DE LA FRANCE D'OUTRE MER, 1955).

The first national incomes of colonial territories were obtained from 1948 onwards in British Africa, and from 1951 in French Africa: some statisticians, generally from the Central Statistical Office or the INSEE, sought to apply an accounting system in overseas territories that had already been applied in the metropoles. However, they remained extremely cautious about the value of their results, in part because the validity of the statistical production on which their calculations were based remained questionable, due to the practical conditions in which they were developed by the colonial administrations, and secondly because it was difficult to define "the boundaries of production" (JERVEN 2009), i.e. to agree on which activity sectors – especially the non-monetized sectors of the domestic economy – should be included in the calculations. The meaning accorded to the averages obtained was also a subject of controversy: while figures on national income per capita were intended to reflect the standard of living of colonial populations, the interpretation and "international comparisons that could arise" remained highly objectionable to statisticians, because of the strong heterogeneity of calculation conditions from one country to another (COURCIER, DUBOIS, FABRE, 1958). Harmonization efforts were undertaken in the 1950s under the auspices of the UN (UNITED NATIONS STATISTICAL OFFICE, 1957), which at the beginning of the next decade gave rise to the establishment of "national accounts manuals adapted to developing countries" (COURCIER, LE HEGARAT, 1963). But many differences remained between countries with regard to the classification of economic agents, the monetary transcription system of non-market activities, the manner in which they were or were not included in the calculations or, more fundamentally, empirical data upon which the evaluation of production was based (COURCIER, ADY, 1961).

The circumstances under which the statistics on national incomes developed did not however prevent them from being used in ways that their designers had not intended, and once established it wasn't long before international fora appropriated the data. Statistics on hunger or infant mortality were used to formally place colonized people into an international hierarchy of living standards, placing them on the same continuum as non-colonized populations. Viewed through the prism of "development", these scales indicated the degree to which each territory had "advanced". Although this placed them in a position of relative inferiority, it appeared that they were now being promised the same social and economic future as developed countries: the gap between colonized and non-colonized populations became measurable, which simultaneously gave rise to the belief that it would be possible for them to catch up.

Discussing inequalities in an imperial context

The significance of such statistics, beyond the technical conditions in which they were developed, therefore became eminently political. Not only did the data serve to highlight the existence of food, health and socio-economic issues in the territories concerned, but it also contributed to the emergence of a new cognitive framework from which the world's inequalities could be expressed, thereby providing a basis for new demands for equality.

These demands first manifested through international activism, and especially through the notion of "Third Worldism" which developed during the 1950s, a notion which takes its name from the works of Alfred Sauvy, a French economist and demographer who coined the term Third World in 1952, who referred to this Third World as "exploited, scorned like the Third Estate", and which "also wants to be something" (SAUVY, 1952). This ideology, in addition to the various economic theories and political struggles that structured it, was initially fuelled by data that showed the inequalities between the "third world" and "developed worlds". In the symbolic area of food, the 1950s were the years that saw the emergence of the concept of "world hunger", which implied the comparison of levels of food and nutrition throughout the world. At this juncture it is worth noting the story of Josué de Castro, a Brazilian geographer who was the first pamphleteer of books on this subject: he conducted research into the food shortages that afflicted his own country in the 1940s, before establishing in the 1950s a global "geopolitics of hunger" largely informed by statistical data (CASTRO, 1951), which served as a reference for many international campaigns over the next decade.

In the 1950s, knowledge on living standards also provided new opportunities for, sometimes antagonistic, discussion for the political actors in the colonial empires. From the point of view of metropolitan governments, they served as a means of legitimization while new policies of investment were implemented in the colonies. For example, it became possible through the calculation of data on national income to quantify the "overall progress" delivered by colonisation, whatever the technical quality of the figures. In the French Empire, the strong growth of African economies during the 1950s was thus quickly indexed by the colonial authorities, both as evidence that "thanks to French efforts, living standards had risen in colonies" and as an encouragement to "pursue development policies" that had been undertaken 10 years previously. Admittedly, the per capita income in African territories is often "characteristic of underdeveloped countries". But other nations, among the most opposed to colonialism in international fora, are "equally underdeveloped" and even "in a more serious manner" (AOF GENERAL GOVERNMENT, 1953).

Conversely, from the perspective of trade unions and the mobilized political parties of the colonies, the new data on living standards supported a denunciation of poverty, a state in which many people within the empire continued to live in, even calling into question the very idea of "colonial achievement". In the French Empire, newly elected African Parliamentarians thus became able to highlight alarming statistics to the National Assembly, such as "dietary intakes that were often less than 2000 calories" and "rates of infant mortality between 25% to 50%, compared to 4% to 7% in European countries", denouncing the insufficient efforts to improve living conditions. In the colonies, trade unions, equipped with supporting figures, became able to demonstrate the contrast between the "imperialist bourgeoisie, living in luxury," and "the poverty experienced by the vast majority of colonial populations" (BONNECASE, 2011). Within colonies, the new statistical knowledge even enabled the quantification of differences that had never previously been measured: in French West Africa for example, national income data were used to calculate that "living conditions" in the federation were on average 40 times higher "among whites" than "among blacks", finding that "modern sector revenues accrue mainly to the former" while income from "mixed and traditional sectors" were more for the latter (CAPET and FABRE, 1957). Ultimately, a new expression of justice had emerged within the imperial territories: while colonial knowledge on the social situation in colonies had long been based on the idea of a natural difference between the colonized and those who were not, it became possible with the introduction of statistics to imagine that the former could become equal to the latter, not only in terms of political rights and legal status, but also in terms of material living conditions.

Conclusion

In *The statistical argument*, Alain Desrosières explains that "applying and building a space of equivalence enabling quantification, and thus measurement, has both political and technical results. It is political in that it changes the world: comparing the aristocracy with commoners led to the night of the 4th August [abolition of feudalism during the French revolution]; comparing blacks with whites called for the abolition of slavery; comparing women with men called for a real universal suffrage that included women" (DESROSIERES, 2008). Statistical information, such as that described in this article, has undoubtedly helped change the way in which people see the world, if not actually directly changing it. We should not, however, credit such data with too much importance nor view them as causal agents in the history of political change: ultimately, these statistics only served as a new tool to engender discussion on the reconfiguration of power relations, but they have not in their own right changed the nature of inequality.

Finally, how can such a story enlighten us in terms of the modern controversies on the measurement of inequality in the world? The first lesson is that arguments over the choice of a "good indicator" – and over the place granted to productive criteria in particular – have not appeared in the 1990s with the advent of the Human Development Index, or in the 2000s with discussions on the "Measurement of Economic and Social Performance" (FITOUSSI, SEN, STIGLITZ, 2009): they were already part of the international debate on the definition and evaluation of living standards in the 1950s. The second lesson is that these first statistics on the world's living standards were used without consideration for the material conditions under which they were developed, which again foreshadows more recent realities: while contemporary statistics on poverty can sometimes resemble a "great swindle" (LORRAINE DATA, 2009) in both the North and the South, this does not prevent them from indicating realities and being used to either manage or refute them. A third lesson is that the first international standards of living statistics have contributed to the building of a common space of possibilities, and this may nuance the normative and somewhat oppressive dimension that they can also carry. The emergence of post-war "development" has often been seen as a device of power, the imposition of a social and economic trajectory onto large populations that was mainly informed by Western history (ESCOBAR, 1995). However, historically this knowledge was also considered by some of these populations, that had experienced a form of government based on race, as a means to express a fundamental claim: to be considered, if not measured, in the same way as everyone else. ∎

▌REFERENCES

BONNECASE V., 2009, "Avoir faim en AOF. Investigations et représentations coloniales (1920-1960)", *Revue d'histoire des sciences humaines*, n° 21, pp. 151-174

BONNECASE V., 2011, *La pauvreté au Sahel. Du savoir colonial à la mesure international*, Paris, Karthala.

BRIAN É., 1989, "Statistique administrative et internationalisme statistique pendant la seconde moitié du XIXe siècle", *Histoire et mesures*, IV 3/4, pp. 201-224

CAPET M. and FABRE R., 1957, *L'économie de l'AOF depuis la guerre*, Paris, Imprimerie Guillemot et de Lamothe.

CARRÉ J. and RÉVAUGER J.-P., 1995, *Écrire la pauvreté. Les enquêtes sociales britanniques aux XIXe et XXe siècles*, Paris, L'Harmattan.

CASTRO J. (de), 1951, *Geopolítica da fome*, Rio de Janeiro, Casa do Estudante do Brasil.

CONKLIN A., 1997, *A Mission to Civilize. The Republican Idea of Empire in France and West Africa, 1895-1930*, Stanford, Stanford University Press.

COOPER F., 2004, *Décolonisation et travail en Afrique*, Paris, Karthala.

COURCIER M. and ADY P., 1961, Les Systèmes de comptabilité nationale en Afrique, Commission de coopération technique en Afrique au Sud du Sahara, in collaboration with the OEEC.

COURCIER M., DUBOIS G., FABRE R. et al, 1958, *Comptes économiques 1951-1956. Compte-rendu sommaire de travaux effectués depuis 1951, concernant certains États d'Afrique et de Madagascar*, Paris, Service statistique de la France d'outre-mer.

COURCIER M. and LE HEGARAT G., 1963, Manuel de comptabilité nationale pour économies en voie de développement, Paris, ministère de la Coopération, Centre de documentation.

DESROSIÈRES A., 2003, "Naissance d'un nouveau langage statistique entre 1940 et 1960", *Courrier des statistiques*, n° 198, December 2003, pp. 41-52

DESROSIÈRES A., 2008, *L'argument statistique* (I. *Pour une sociologie historique de la quantification* et II. *Gouverner par les nombres*), Paris, Presses de l'école des mines.

DESTREMAU B. and SALAMA P., 2002, *Mesures et démesure de la pauvreté*, Paris, PUF.

ESCOBAR A., 1995, *Encountering Development. The Making and Unmaking of the Third World*, Princetown, Princetown University Press.

FAO, 1955, *So bold an aim. Ten years of international co-operation toward freedom from want. Quebec 1945-Rome 1955*, Rome, FAO

FITOUSSI J.-P., SEN A. and STIGLITZ J., 2009, *Report of the commission on the measurement of economic performance and social progress*, Paris, Ministry of Economy, Industry and Employment.

GENERAL GOVERNMENT OF AOF, 1953, *Essai de récapitulation des éléments connus à Dakar pour servir à un calcul du revenu national de l'AOF*, Dakar, Direction générale des Finances.

HORVATH R., 1972, "**Le concept de statistique internationale et son évolution historique**", Revue Internationale de Statistique, vol. 40, n°3, December 1972, pp. 281-298

JERVEN M., 2009, "**The Relativity of Poverty and Income: How Reliable are African Economic Statistics?**", *African Affairs*, 109, pp. 77–96

LE PLAY F., 1879, *La Méthode sociale*, Tours, Alfred Mame et fils.

LORRAINE DATA, 2009, *Le grand Trucage. Comment le gouvernement manipule les statistiques*, Paris, La Découverte.

MINISTÈRE DE LA FRANCE D'OUTRE mer, 1955, *Essai de détermination du revenu national des principaux territoires d'outre-mer en 1947 et en 1953*, Paris, Direction des Affaires économiques et du Plan.

PALES L., 1954, *L'alimentation en AOF. Milieux, enquêtes, techniques, rations*, Dakar, Mission anthropologique de l'AOF.

PROCACCI G., 1993, *Gouverner la misère. La question sociale en France (1789-1848)*, Paris, Le Seuil.

RIST G., 1996, *Le développement. Histoire d'une croyance occidentale*, Paris, Presses de Sciences Po.

ROWNTREE B., 1910, *Comment diminuer la misère. Études sur la Belgique*, Paris, Giard et Brière.

SAUVY A., 1952, "Trois mondes, une planète", *L'Observateur*, 14/8/1952, n° 118, p. 14.

TOPALOV C., 1994, *Naissance du chômeur. 1880-1910*, Paris, Albin Michel.

UNITED NATIONS ECONOMIC AND SOCIAL COUNCIL, 1954, *International Definition and Measurement of Levels of Living*, New York.

UNITED NATIONS STATISTIC DIVISION, 1957, *Method of National Income Measurement*, Studies in methods, Series F, No 8, New York, United nations.

VANOLI A., 2002, *Une histoire de la comptabilité nationale*, Paris, La Découverte.

International statistics on inequality: political and spatial constructions

Benoît Martin, Sciences Po/Ceri, Paris, France

This article aims to situate, in chronological terms and in terms of ideas, the emergence of international statistics on inequality. We highlight the limitations of the data that are most commonly used to quantify inequalities, such as national income per capita and the Gini coefficient, and present some alternatives that have been launched over the last 20 years. The contribution of geography to an evolving statistical corpus is demonstrated.

The limits of national accounting for understanding internal inequalities

International organizations are the main producers of economic data enabling comparisons between countries. These databases are supplied by official State bodies, such as National Statistical Institutes (NSI), ministries, commissions and governmental agencies. Economic statistics such as Gross National Income (GNI) and Gross Domestic Product (GDP), which record the total market added value for all goods and services sold in a year (on the basis of nationality for the former, and territory for the latter), are often used to compare inequalities between countries; and also to provide a picture of inequality in terms of economic power. The GNI, through a simple division, is commonly converted to a per capita figure and thus used to compare the average income per person. The "unit of account" is transformed from the nation to the individual, but this ratio completely masks the gaps within societies.

The GNI and GDP were not in fact designed for the quantification of inequalities. At the heart of what is called national accounts, these indicators were developed in the early 1940s, originally in the United States and later in Europe by researchers as tools of management and short-term forecasting of economic flows (the increase in production value and, in the context of the 1930s and 1940s, its possible contraction) as outlined by Thomas Piketty in this volume. These tools were originally part of a Keynesian approach, where the State affirms itself as the driver of the economy (VANOLI, 2002). Today, the GNI refers to a set of robust and standardized statistics, calculated with quarterly regularity in most countries. It remains valuable for longitudinal comparisons and/or retrospective estimates enabling the reconstruction of series that cover several centuries (MADDISON, 2006).

In addition to the GNI, the Gini index on income reveals information about inequality in terms of a society's internal income distribution, within a particular country. Created in the 1920s and released at the international level by the World Bank and the OECD, this index is the only one to benefit from having the noun "inequalities" mentioned in the databases of both institutions, thus highlighting the emphasis that international organizations have placed on the strictly monetary aspects of inequality. The number of countries for which there are no recent Gini indicators (and sometimes no Gini indicators at all) is also very important[1]. The financial and human effort entailed in the determination of the GDP or GNI remains much higher than that deployed for the exhaustive quantification of domestic inequalities. Without doubt, the first priority of

---

1. On the World Bank's data website (http://data.worldbank.org/indicator/SI.POV.GINI), data under 5 years exist for only 34% of countries, 46% of which concern the period 1991-2007 and no Gini index is reported for 20% of States.

the World Bank is to establish accurate assessments of the macroeconomic situations of its debtors (CLING and ROUBAUD, 2008), while understanding the evolution of their internal inequalities does not take precedence, because such data does not directly provide information on the ability of countries to repay their debts. In response to the quantifications from the national accounts, which are primarily tools for States, alternative indicators of inequality are organized in two directions: not strictly monetary development and environment.

Challenges and alternatives to the quantification of monetary inequalities

From the report of the Club of Rome (MEADOWS, MEADOWS, RANDERS and BEHRENS III, 1972) to that of the Stiglitz commission (STIGLITZ, SEN and FITOUSSI, 2009), most of the critical debates on inequality indicators focus on what GNI/GDP actually quantify and on the overemphasis they place on economic growth. The limitations of GNI/GDP, which have been well known for a long time, include: only taking market activities into account (the entire informal sector is excluded) and ignoring their many negative externalities, for example on the environment (pollution of air and soil, greenhouse gas emissions, etc.) (GADREY and JANY-CATRICE, 2005). While knowledge of these limitations originally emerged in academic research environments, NGOs and a number of international institutions, such as the UNDP, now convey these criticisms.

Although the normative power of the UNDP is definitely lower than that of international donors such as the World Bank, in 1990, through its Human Development Report Office (HDRO), it launched the Human Development Index (HDI). The HDI's originators intended it to be an alternative to GDP, moving the basis of the quantification of human well-being onto individuals, rather than on macroeconomic income growth. The HDI has evolved over time, evidenced by its abandonment of UNESCO's official statistics on Education, to use international surveys instead (BARRO and LEE, 2010), and then the use of GNI instead of GDP to take into account income transfers between residents and non-residents.

In response to continued criticism of the HDI as merely an average value that masks inequalities within societies,

---

BOX 1. Quantification of inequalities by Human Development Index (HDI)

There are three main methods used for the quantification of inequalities:

1. A version of the HDI adjusted to inequality – the IHDI – has been in use since 2010, which goes down when internal inequalities are high.

2. The Multidimensional Poverty Index (MPI), which considers the multiple deprivations faced by the poorest. This initiative, which was launched by the University of Oxford, has been adopted and supported by the HDRO.

3. Gender disparities are quantified through the gender inequality index (GII).

It is worth noting that the latter two indicators do not take the monetary criterion of income into account. The independent status of the HDRO, vis-à-vis the UNDP and its Member States, gives it a freedom to create such indicators. The HDRO functions as a de facto research centre and has the ability to make relatively unrestricted decisions about the statistical sources that it considers relevant.

---

in 2010 the HDRO introduced an adjusted version of the index, taking inequalities into account (Box 1). The popularity of the HDI has led to a global spread of its use at subnational scales, by provinces or even by counties (such as in Brazil, where the HDI is updated annually for the 5560 *municípios*).

Taking the environmental dimension into account

A significant part of the criticisms aimed at indicators of monetary inequalities derives from the fact that they neglect or only barely consider environmental aspects. In the early 1990s, before the Earth Summit (Rio, 1992), two researchers from the University of British Columbia (Vancouver, Canada), William Rees and Mathis Wackernagel, defined and produced the first quantifications of the Ecological Footprint (EF). The innovation of this indicator is that it is expressed in global hectares and obtained by subtracting the total amount of resources consumed

FIGURE 1 Comparison of indicators of inequality in South America, 2011

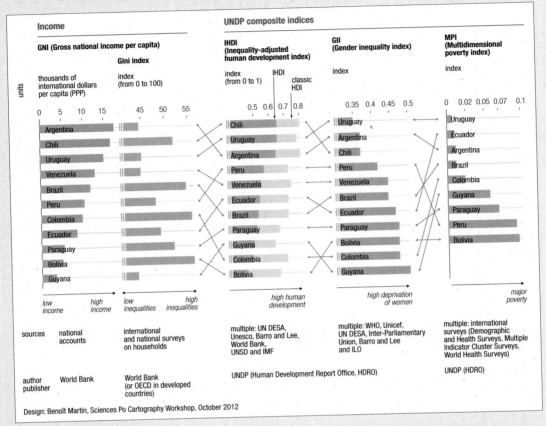

Design: Benoît Martin, Sciences Po Cartography Workshop, October 2012

by humanity from the Earth's regenerative capacity. A negative value indicates a depletion of the Earth's reserves, while a positive value indicates the sustainable use of resources. The design of the indicator allows it to be used to calculate the EF for different territorial levels (States, cities, regions, etc.) and for various actors (companies, governments, individuals, etc.). Supported by the World Wide Fund for Nature in the early 2000s and then highly publicized, the EF became the symbol of the alternative environmental indicator: experimental and "unofficial" in the beginning, and now commonplace in institutional reports and government rhetoric. Today the EF is a trade-marked concept, organized in a global network that brings NGOs and academic centres together.

Faced with these initiatives, international organizations in turn integrated environmental factors into their own indicators, even if they remained largely monetary-based. Thus, in 2002 the World Bank launched the concept of "Genuine Savings". Expressed as a share of GNI, it is calculated by subtracting the damage caused to economic and natural capital from gross savings (from the national accounts), followed by the addition of investment in education. In addition, very recently at the 2012 Rio +20 Summit the United Nations University (IHDP) and UNEP seized the opportunity to present its tests involving several countries on the measurement of an "Inclusive Wealth Index" that is intended to provide an alternative to per capita GNI and HDI.

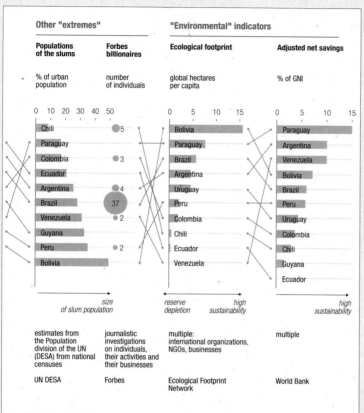

Other "extremes"

Populations of the slums | **Forbes billionaires**

% of urban population | number of individuals

"Environmental" indicators

Ecological footprint | **Adjusted net savings**

global hectares per capita | % of GNI

estimates from the Population division of the UN (DESA) from national censuses | journalistic investigations on individuals, their activities and their businesses | multiple: international organizations, NGOs, businesses | multiple

UN DESA | Forbes | Ecological Footprint Network | World Bank

◄ There are many possible indicators of inequality. All of these indicators, however, or nearly all, rank the performance of states differently – in this case for Latin America. It is difficult to see the emergence of a general dynamic: some countries tend to stay at the same level (intermediate for Brazil, the highest for Argentina), while others, such as Chile or Bolivia, show very different standings depending on whether one focuses on economic performance, human development or environmental sustainability. In addition to these indicators, slum population estimates reveal that countries that rank highly in this regard, particularly Brazil, may also have numerous billionaires (including as a proportion of the population).

Figure 1 shows a comparison between the results of a number of inequality indicators that were applied for South America. It is important to note that the levels and rankings of States change significantly according to the choice of indicator. A general dynamic is difficult to emerge: some countries tend to retain their rank (intermediate for Brazil, top ranking for Argentina), while others, such as Chile or Bolivia, show very different positions depending on whether one focuses on human development or environmental sustainability.

The contribution of geography

International statistics that use the nation as the "base unit" cover very heterogeneous situations. Demographic giants with over a billion people (such as India for example) are contrasted with islands of a few hundred thousand people (e.g. some of the Pacific Islands). In terms of densities, continent-States with low population densities, such as Russia, differ considerably from totally urbanized city-states like Singapore. The so-called "anamorphic" maps (or cartograms) where each country is swollen or shrunk according to the size of its population, partly enable these differences to be highlighted (LEVY, 2008). In addition to the quantification of inequalities within societies, it seems necessary to "zoom in" to finer spatial scales – what geographers would consider as "large scales" – such as provinces or municipalities. Figure 2 shows that national (federal in the case of India) averages can mask strong

FIGURE 2 Multidimensional Poverty in Indian States

The Multidimensional Poverty Index (MPI) is a synthetic indicator.
10 sub-indicators are gathered in three dimensions: nutrition and infant
mortality are used for health; years of schooling and number of children
enrolled are used for education; electricity, water, toilets, cooking fuels,
soil type and the possession of assets are used for the standard of living.

MPI helps with the understanding of inequalities, in the sense that it is based
on the accumulation of deprivations suffered by the population.

**Share of the population living in multidimensional poverty
(%)**

| 14.2 | 20 | 36 | 55 | 67 | 81.5 |

Federal average of India: 55%

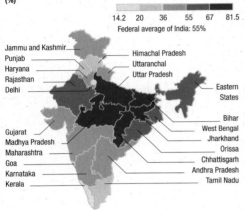

Jammu and Kashmir
Punjab
Haryana
Rajasthan
Delhi

Himachal Pradesh
Uttaranchal
Uttar Pradesh

Eastern
States

Bihar
West Bengal
Jharkhand
Orissa
Chhattisgarh
Andhra Pradesh
Tamil Nadu

Gujarat
Madhya Pradesh
Maharashtra
Goa
Karnataka
Kerala

International comparisons of shares
(proportion of the population living in poverty, in %)

| China 12.5 | Morocco 28.5 | Laos 47.3 | Haiti 57.3 | Sierra Leone 81.5 | Niger 92.7 |

| 14.2 Delhi | 32.4 Tamil Nadu | 44.7 Andhra Pradesh | 58.3 West Bengal | 81.4 Bihar |

International comparisons of numbers
(number of people living in poverty, in millions)

| Egypt 5.4 | Brazil 16.7 | Indonesia 48.3 | Nigeria 100.5 |
| Kerala 5.6 | Chhattisgarh 17.2 | Rajasthan 42.0 | Uttar Pradesh 134.6 |

Design:
Benoît Martin, Sciences Po Cartography Workshop, August 2012.

Sources: Sabina Alkire and Maria Emma Santos, *Acute Multidimensional Poverty:
A New Index for Developing Countries*, 2010, Oxford Poverty & Human
Development Initiative (OPHI), University of Oxford;
UNDP, *Human Development Reports*, http://hdr.undp.org,
accessed 30 June 2011.

internal geographical inequalities and that, according to this multidimensional poverty index, the Indian States experiencing the worst situations are comparable to some sub-Saharan African countries. The necessary fine scale microdata for this purpose do not fall within the open data movement that exist for some indicators, and are therefore often difficult to obtain or require payment.

In addition, cities and urban areas carry a greater weight in both demographic and economic terms. Today, more than half of the world's population inhabit urban areas, which are emerging as essential sites and nodes for globalization processes (SASSEN, 2007). It is a damning indictment of international organizations that they do not provide a level of analysis sufficient to take urban areas into account, given that such data is critical for understanding inequality. Cities concentrate the rich elites and also the poor, with the contrast being particularly pronounced in developing countries (Rio de Janeiro, Johannesburg, Bombay, Mexico, etc.) where gated communities coexist alongside slums. The statistical initiatives of international organizations such as UN Habitat attempt to go beyond the State as the account unit (which does not allow the consideration of urban areas spanning over several countries) by providing quantitative comparisons between cities in different countries. The GaWC university network (Globalization and World Cities Research Network), which initially focused on the connectivity between global cities, also

◄ The MPI overcomes the purely economic approach (income) to analysing living conditions. When applied at the sub-state level, it enables the comparison of Indian states with other countries in the world, both in terms of proportion of the population affected and of the number of individuals involved. Thus, in terms of ratio, the lowest levels (in Delhi) are close to those of China, while the highest (Bihar) are comparable to those of Sierra Leone. As for numbers, the poor are more numerous in Uttar Pradesh than in Nigeria.

provides many relevant indicators (infrastructure, living standards, population density, services, companies, etc.) to enable the study of inequalities between cities (Taylor, 2004).

Finally, the current "Westphalian" statistical system (which has the nation-State as its unit) appears obsolete and inadequate for the capture of the deep dynamics of inequalities that depend both on global logics (affecting the entire globe) and transnational logics (which escape, even partially, the control and actions of States) (Durand et al., 2013). Thus, the recent cases of transboundary pollution caused by oil spills (in the Gulf of Mexico for example) or from nuclear disaster (Fukushima) on the one hand, and the flows (migration or financial, legal or otherwise) on the other, show that States, confined to their national territories, cannot provide adequate statistical tools to quantify these phenomena.

We see a familiar theme emerging in the production of new data that is better able to provide valuable information on contemporary challenges, compared to the existing statistical system: as was the case for the GDP, or more recently for the Top Income Database, it is often academics who initiate the criticism of the existing systems and then launch new indicators that are better adapted to measuring changes in inequality. International organizations have fully understood the advantages of such a dynamic and develop

multiple partnerships with academic research centres. In this hybrid collaboration, the latter benefit from the visibility and institutional authority of the former, in return, they bring scientific credentials. ■

REFERENCES

Barro and Lee, 2010, *Educational Attainment Dataset*, www.barrolee.com

Cling J.-P. and Roubaud F., 2008, *La Banque mondiale*, Paris, La Découverte.

Durand M.-F. et al., 2013, *Atlas de la mondialisation*, Paris, Presses de Sciences Po.

Gadrey J. and Jany-Catrice F., 2005, *Les nouveaux indicateurs de richesses*, Paris, La Découverte.

Lévy J. (dir.), 2008, *L'invention du monde: Une géographie de la mondialisation*, Paris, Presses de Sciences Po.

Maddison A., 2001, *The World Economy: A Millennial Perspective*, Paris, OECD Development Center Studies.

Meadows D. H., Meadows D. L., Randers J. and Behrens III W. W., 1972, *The Limits to Growth. A Report for the Club of Rome's Project on the Predicament of Mankind*, New York, Universe Books.

Sassen S., 2007, *A sociology of globalization*, New York, W.W. Norton & Company.

Stiglitz J., Sen A. and Fitoussi J.-P., 2009, Report of the commission on the measurement of economic performance et social progress, http://www.stiglitz-sen-fitoussi.fr/en/index.htm

Taylor, P.J., 2004, *World City Network. A Global Urban Analysis*, London, Routledge.

Vanoli, A., 2002, *Une histoire de la comptabilité nationale*, Paris, La Découverte.

CHAPTER 4

Since the 1950s, the relationship between inequality, economic growth and poverty has fuelled intense academic debates that have shaped national policies and development organization strategies. The history of economic ideas reveals changes in the growth paradigm, with a progressively greater focus on how the most disadvantaged can accumulate productive assets. New measurement tools, social programmes and modalities for steering public policy substantiate this change in focus.

Inequalities and growth: A comprehensive ideology emerges in 1990-2010

François Bourguignon,
Paris School of Economics, Paris, France

Before the World Bank integrated the concepts of inequality and equity into its strategic thinking at the beginning of the 2000s, a lively debate about poverty reduction was taking place in the academic community. It centred on the relationship between poverty, inequality and economic growth on the one hand, and the definition of poverty and in particular its multidimensional nature on the other. We will briefly review the academic history of these ideas before examining how they have permeated operations in the field.

Since poverty reduction depends in large measure on economic growth, the debate about poverty in development economics has long been – above all – a debate about growth. The 1990s saw a double turnaround: growth returned to developed economies, and growth – and therefore development – returned as a topic in economics literature. The early 1980s had seen a major macroeconomic adjustment: inflation born in the aftermath of the oil crisis led the United States to change its monetary policy, increasing scarcity in the money supply and generating higher interest rates. This caused growth to slow worldwide. As the 1990s began, the world came out of this slow-growth period, and what appeared to be sustainable growth took hold. The topic of growth reappeared in economics literature.

First came foundational articles for the "endogenous growth" theory (ROMER, 1986; LUCAS, 1988), followed by two ground-breaking papers by Robert J. Barro (1991) and Mankiw, Romer and Weil (1992) that tried to identify determinant factors for growth through econometric analysis of cross-country data. An entire literature then developed around this identification of growth factors. The endogenous growth theory had a considerable impact. It contrasted with the 1950s vision of economic growth (e.g. Robert SoLow, 1956), which argued that growth is essentially exogenous over the very long term, determined mostly by technological progress and managerial or organizational innovations without taking into account the drivers of that progress. Robert E. Lucas and Paul Romer showed instead that long-range growth rates arise from the preferences of economic agents and from the production and organizational features of a given economy. Their contribution paved the way for subsequent research on the specific growth determinants of individual countries.

However, poverty reduction requires not only growth, but also "inclusive" growth that benefits everyone. The notion of inclusion opens an important second chapter in the poverty-reduction debate: the relationship between growth and inequality. In effect, the relationship goes in two directions, from growth to the inequality of income distribution on the one hand, and from inequality to growth on the other. On the first account, an important hypothesis by Kuznets (1955) suggests that growth can generate more or less inequality depending on the development stage of a country. The theoretical underpinning of the hypothesis had to do with what Lewis (1954) saw as the fundamental ("classical") model of development. On the second account, some theoretical models show how inequality in wealth distribution and access to credit or education can constrain growth. This runs contrary to the positive relationship previously suggested by some economists, notably the Keynesian Nicolas Kaldor[1] (1960); in fact, the recent literature has completely overturned such models. In situations of strong inequality, for instance, entrepreneurs who lack collateral (and therefore access to credit) cannot undertake privately and collectively profitable investments. By contrast, entrepreneurs with collateral or even cash to invest will pursue projects, even those that eventually provide mediocre returns. Through that mechanism, an unequal society may grow more slowly – therefore reducing poverty more slowly – since it misses profitable investment opportunities. Early papers rigorously formalizing this idea include Galor and Zeira (1993) and Banerjee and Newman (1993).

This kind of analysis provided the starting point for a voluminous literature and body of thought on the "poverty-inequality-growth" relationship. Two very frequently cited articles are those by Persson and Tabellini (1994) and Alesina and Rodrik (1994). They show what appears to be a negative correlation between economic growth rates in a sample of countries and the degree of income inequality in these countries. That was enough to convince some in the development community that maintaining inequalities counters growth and poverty reduction, and that reducing inequalities should favour development. Later, development economists and others in the field realized that the situation was far more complex, and that these first empirical constructs were, in fact, weak and little convincing. Better and more

---

1. Kaldor argued that the wealthy saved more than the poor and consequently, even if distribution was unequal, there were more savings therefore more growth (KALDOR, 1960).

complete data showed no unambiguous empirical relationship between inequality and growth[2].

The debate on inequality and growth is directly related to poverty reduction only inasmuch as poverty is defined in monetary terms, as for instance the threshold of 1.25 US dollars a day per person used by international organizations. Yet, such a view seems unduly restrictive. In effect, a multidimensional conception of inequalities has gradually taken hold, with the conviction that economic growth – even egalitarian growth – will not necessarily eradicate all dimensions of poverty. This evolution in thinking owes much to Amartya Sen (1985) and his "capability approach," which postulates that what matters is not so much an individual's level of consumption as his or her potential for generating the level to which he or she aspires. Poverty thus means the lack of education, healthcare, access to justice and other opportunities as much as it means material deprivation. Researchers quickly realized that the correlation between various aspects of poverty (thus defined) and income were far from perfect.

Together, these two currents of thought, about the relationship of inequality and growth and the multidimensional character of poverty or ability contributed to considerably expanding the development paradigm by emphasizing the fact that, in the relationship between inequality and growth, it is the inequality of opportunities – that is, unequal access to productive resources, such as education, credit, justice, and government decisions. It is the distribution of such opportunities that ultimately determines both the pace of economic growth, the distribution of income and, therefore the extent of monetary poverty. The 2006 World Bank report entitled *Equity and Development* exemplifies this evolution in thought: within the World Bank itself, it represented considerable conceptual progress in development policies and strategies.

Growth and inequality: what social insurance model to use?

Social insurance is an important instrument to promote the equality of opportunities and to fight poverty; corresponding policies give some indication about governments" attitudes in this area[3]. As a matter of fact, it can be observed that governments adopt different attitudes, often changing stances from one period to the next. In developed countries, the 1980s saw the neoliberal revolution, spearheaded by Ronald Reagan and Margaret Thatcher. It led to important reforms in both countries. In the United Kingdom, in particular, the government cut deeply into social insurance programmes, considered too generous and consequently economically inefficient.

---

2. Forbes (2000) found a positive relationship between inequality and growth, whereas Banerjee and Duflo (2003) showed none of the previous relationships were robust. In the same way that the first attempts at testing Kuznets" hypothesis on a cross-section of countries initially showed an inverted-U relationship between inequality and GDP per capita (cf. ALHUWALIA, 1996) – a finding that proved non-robust later on with better and more complete data.

3. For the explicit introduction of social protection policies in the inequality-growth framework alluded to earlier, see Benabou (2000).

In continental Europe, the share of social insurance in the gross domestic product (GDP) did not diminish, and even increased in several cases. The shift towards a more liberal view came later. Governments imitated the British model principally by trying to isolate the social insurance system from the functioning of the labour market to minimize its negative effect on economic efficiency. In Denmark, France, Germany and the Netherlands, social insurance systems were initially very much linked to the salaried employment status of people. Initially, only wage-based employment gave entitlement to health insurance, retirement benefits, and certain other social welfare expenditures. Gradually, governments undertook significant reforms to this model. For example, in France a minimum income known as the "active solidarity income" or *revenue de solidarité active* (RSA, formerly the RMI) is allocated independently of the recipient's employment status. An increasing share of health insurance is now financed through income taxes rather than through employment taxes. In several continental European countries, governments have moved away from the Bismarckian[4] model based on salaried or other work toward a Beveridgien[5] model that offers safety nets to everyone, independent of employment status. Of course, this change did not occur in every country; the perception of a common model is illusory. However, the "flexicurity" model used in Denmark has gained in popularity everywhere; it frees market mechanisms while protecting individuals from the risk of entrapment in poverty.

In developing countries, we see great diversity in social insurance systems and entitlements. Latin American countries have adopted Bismarckian European systems in a particular way, without achieving universal coverage. In postwar Europe, social insurance tied to salaried employment expanded readily, because salaried workers progressively composed nearly 80%-90% of the labour force. That left the self-employed, professionals, small merchants and a small number of farmers who soon acquired a status similar to that of salaried workers. In Latin America, the extension of the social insurance system did not occur in the absence of sufficiently rapid growth sustained for an adequate period. A dual system resulted: formal-sector labour received social insurance while, until recently, informal-sector workers had none.

Asian countries offer little social insurance, perhaps because of their very rapid growth. In an economy that constantly creates new jobs, households can handle mishaps through increased participation in the work force; this constitutes a kind of insurance. Oddly enough, it took the 1997 Asian crisis to make South Korea recognize the need for a safety net so that individuals could avoid economic hardships. China is coming to the same conclusion for other reasons. Its government is trying to encourage households to consume more to activate its internal growth engine as a future substitute for foreign markets. Chinese households' excessive savings

---

4. Translator's note: A social insurance system restricted to wage-earning workers in formal companies, and their direct dependents, named after the German chancellor von Bismarck.

5. Translator's note: A universal social insurance system named after the British economist Lord Beveridge.

stems, in part, from the fact that coverage for health problems or retirement remains uncertain or very limited.

Africa presents a special case inasmuch as a large part of its population works in the informal sector, largely escaping the formalism of social insurance; it is the extended family, above all, that covers basic risks.

From "growth at all costs" to accounting for inequalities

International financial institutions have long considered the question of inequalities and social policies of minor importance. In the 1990s, these organizations were very impressed by the Asian model, as evidenced in the publication of a World Bank report, *The Asian Miracle*: it presented the Asian experience as *the* model to follow. In countries with very rapid growth, redistribution and social insurance appear to be less acute needs than may be the case elsewhere. In its entry hall, the World Bank inscribed the slogan "Our dream is a world without poverty." However, the Bank has conceived poverty reduction exclusively as a matter of economic growth; the Asian experience seemed to validate that approach.

By the end of the 1990s, the rather disappointing growth experience of most Latin American countries gave many observers and analysts the feeling that inequality was a powerful impediment to development. This region of the world did not experience the sustained growth seen in Asia, inequality being one of the most obvious differences between the two groups of countries. Inequality was weak in South Korea, Taiwan and Vietnam, and a little less so in China; at the same time, these countries had become the champions of growth worldwide. This fuelled the hypothesis that early inequalities could hamper growth. This comparison, together with an analysis of growth failures in some African countries under predatory political elites – the height of inequality – progressively bolstered the idea that inequalities might play a key role in the growth process.

Today it is widely recognized that poverty does not necessarily and automatically diminish with economic growth, if inequality increases as the economy grows. In Africa, some countries have recently seen rapid growth with, apparently, no poverty reduction. Very high commodity prices lay behind the rapid growth, making it possible to invest in construction and infrastructure, but the growth benefited only a small part of the population. Obviously, in economies with double-digit growth, such as China, it is hard to imagine that the growth process would exclude very much of the population. Yet, it is now well known that poverty declines less quickly with growth when inequality is high, and that at slower growth rates a moderate increase in inequality might be enough to prevent a decline in poverty (BOURGUIGNON, 2003).

In the late 1990s, the World Bank and similar organizations began to consider inequalities an important subject. Joseph Stiglitz and Nicholas Stern, my predecessors as chief economist at the World Bank, were persuaded that inequality was a fundamental dimension of development. In 1996, James Wolfensohn, president of the Bank and friend of Amartya Sen, hired Stiglitz as chief economist. Both had a vision of development that went far beyond per capita GDP growth, but only a minority of the Bank's staff shared their vision. When I came to the World Bank in 2003, questions of inequality were still seldom discussed, but progress was inarguable. By 2006, the *Equity and Development* report was a sign that the World Bank, and other international financial institutions, had finally accepted that distribution and redistribution mechanisms played a key role in fostering economic growth and in curbing poverty.

Other international organizations did not need this shift in perspective. In particular, the United Nations (UN) always had inequality at the centre of their development vision; the long-dominant discourse of the World Bank and International Monetary Fund (IMF), which extolled growth at all cost, had never been as strong in the UN. It is true, however, that these two types of institution play very different roles in developing economies. In particular, the UN can have only a limited influence on national implementation policies compared with the substantially more robust means that the international financial institutions may deploy.

However, questions arise about the way these means could be, have been or are actually deployed to serve a certain vision of development. First, it must be understood that a good part of the activity of the World Bank and other development banks is similar to commercial banking and has limited impact on development. Middle-income countries borrow from the World Bank as they would do from any big, international commercial bank, were it not for the Bank's limited control over the nature of the projects being financed. The views that World Bank staff might hold on development mean little in such cases. In emerging and intermediate-income countries, the ties between loans and development "programmes" have increasingly loosened. The difference with the 1990s is stark. It arises from the expansion of international capital markets, the ease with which emerging countries can take on debt from international commercial operators and the weakening appeal of loans from international financial institutions. This lesser appeal also lessens the leverage that the latter can bring to bear on the development strategies of the countries that they finance.

That said, development programmes have not entirely disappeared, and the World Bank and other international development banks remain present in their implementation, but in a very different way. The banks act more as technical advisers or consultants than as project owners and financiers, as was the case in the past. In Brazil, the World Bank participated in the launch of the conditional transfer programmes to the poorest known as "Bolsa Escola", which later became "Bolsa Familia," but has a limited role in the programme's financing." Likewise, the Bank was present in the monitoring of "Progresa"[6] in Mexico without being involved in its financing. The Bank can share its enormous developing-world and development experience with its partners. This may be a more valuable capital than its ability to raise money on

---

6. Translator's note: PROGRESA (*Programa Nacional de Educacion, Salud y Alimentacion*) was an anti-poverty programme begun in 1997 to provide poor mothers in rural Mexico with education grants

global capital markets for lending middle-income and emerging countries.

The situation is different in low-income countries where the World Bank Group, through its International Development Association, constitutes a genuine development agency like France's *Agency Française de Développement* (AFD) or the United Kingdom's Department for International Development (DIFD); the only difference is that the World Bank can marshal much greater resources. In low-income countries, development projects and programmes still mean a lot, and the evolution of the World Bank's development vision (as discussed above) takes on its full meaning.

In those countries, a large share of the work of the World Bank and that of regional development banks now centres on individual "capabilities." This aspect of development was neglected for a long time. After the "trickle-down" or "let's grow and poverty will automatically lessen" doctrine, which was followed by "let's grow and redistribute", we have entered a new stage that aims to facilitate the most-disadvantaged groups" accumulation of productive assets – both "hard" assets, such as land, equipment or housing, and "soft" ones, such as education or access to justice. Such strategies are believed to accelerate both growth and poverty reduction and, of course, to reduce inequalities. In low-income countries, conditional transfer programmes, drawing on the example of *Bolsa Familia* or *Progresa*, support the poorest households on the condition that they send their children to school up to a certain age, and that they have their children medically examined twice a year. Such redistribution programmes reduce poverty and also help the poorest accumulate immaterial assets, reducing inequality for future generations. Other types of action with the same overall objective include market-based land reform, irrigation, microcredit, free basic health care and minimum pensions.

Furthermore, while the World Bank has less and less of a role to play with its programmes and loans in emerging countries, it maintains a major role in generating ideas. It often serves as a think tank by producing high-level, original research in fields such as measuring income inequality or the inequality of opportunities. It also very much serves by evaluating specific interventions in terms of their economic efficiency and their impact on poverty. The World Bank publishes reports that discuss alternative development strategies and that recommend specific public policies in China, India and Mexico; these studies often have a major impact because the work is done professionally and supplies innovative development ideas and concepts. From this point of view, the Bank has recently played a major role in reasserting inequality's place at the centre of governmental concerns.

Governments show greater sensitivity to inequalities

Governments have clearly shown a change in attitude. In the past, a country's growth process was evaluated through its GDP growth rate; today, growth rate analysis combines with the distribution of growth's income production through the population. This involves studying so-called "growth incidence curves," which show how individuals starting with different income levels have seen their income grow over time. These measurements have become commonplace tools as ideas have evolved

FIGURE 1 How economics has addressed inequality

	~1956	1970	1980	1990	2000
Growth	Solow (1956) formalizes a growth model that is rapidly becoming the basis for all subsequent analyses; Lewis (1954) formalizes the dualistic model of development based on an unlimited supply of labour in the traditional sector		Romer (1986) and Lucas (1988) introduce the idea of endogenous growth	Debates on growth factors and endogenous growth; Barro (1991) formalizes the first empirical growth model, taking into account human capital and economic policies; Mankiw, Romer and Weil (1992) extend the Solow model by including investment in education	Rodrik, Subramanian and Trebi (2004) and later Acemoglu, Johnson and Robinson (2005), emphasize the role of initial conditions and political and economic institutions
Poverty and inequality		Sen (1976) formalizes one of the first, non-utilitarian measures of poverty (monetary)	Sen (1985) introduces the concept of "capability"	Roemer (1998) formalizes the measurement of unequal opportunity	Bourguignon and Chakravarty (2003) attempt to formalize the measurement of multi-dimensional poverty; Another approach is proposed by Alkire and Foster (2011) and implemented by the United Nations
Discussions		1973 and 1979 oil crises	1982 overall adjustment and debt crisis; Return to growth in developed countries; Economic liberalism; Advances in microeconomic data collection in developing countries (Demographic and Health Survey, 1984; Living Standard Measurement Surveys, 1985)	The fall of planned economic systems; Soaring Asian economies	The World Development Report 2006 puts equity at the centre of development issues and strategies
Impact of growth on inequality		Lewis (1954) formalizes the dualistic model of development which implies an inverted-U relationship between inequality and income level; Kuznets (1955) notes that inequality tends to increase and then decrease in the development process; Chenery et al. (1974) introduce redistribution and inequality in development analysis; Ahluwalia (1976) provides an empirical test of the Kuznets hypothesis		Aghion and Bolton (1997) propose a model describing the circular relationship between income level, inequality and growth	Forbes (2000) finds a positive relationship between inequality and growth in cross-sectional and longitudinal data
Impact of inequality on growth		Kaldor (1960) argues that the rich save more than the poor. Unequal distribution supports saving and therefore growth.		Galor and Zeira (1993); Banerjee and Newman (1993); Persson and Tabellini (1994); As well as Alesina and Rodrick (1994) formalize a positive relationship between the degree of equality of an economy and growth rate	Dollar and Kraay (2002) show that the incomes of the poor increase on in average at the same rate as the average income; Banerjee and Duflo (2003) conclude that there is no robust relationship between inequality and growth

Source: compilation by the author.

and statistics have become available, which was not the case 10-15 years ago. In fact, in parallel with the evolution of ideas stands a revolution in statistics. In an increasing number of countries, we now have the means to produce these graphs and to follow what happened to specific groups of people in the course of development; they have become indispensible tools for decision-makers who want to orient their policies and communicate on their results.

It would be an exaggeration to say that this changing of ideas is universal. But it must be noted that sensitivity to inequality issues has increased in many countries. For example, in China – the champion of growth over the last 30 years – the rise in inequalities has already preoccupied the country's leaders for some time. The preceding Eleventh Five-Year Development Plan will come to an end this year; its title was "Toward a Harmonious Society" – harmonious in the sense of a more equal and more equitable society. The same concern hovers over several Latin American countries, beginning with the Brazil of Lula da Silva and Dilma Roussef, where great initiatives have begun. Brazil is and remains one of the world's most unequal countries, but inequality has spectacularly diminished over the last 10-12 years. In the developed world, inequalities remain a source of constant concern for governments in several European countries, including France. Paradoxically, this is less true for the United States, even though inequality is higher there and has sharply increased.

The leading elites do not simply have moral or ethical sensitivities, but also political ones. The elites know that an increase in inequality may lead to conflicts and social tensions. Furthermore, putting social insurance systems in place meets a demand produced by the economic development process. As an economy grows, populations demand more consumer goods, and also more security. Social insurance, above all, is an instantaneous redistribution. It can also bolster an economy's dynamism. Economic agents feel better about undertaking projects that may be riskier but also more profitable when they feel protected from sickness, old age, or an unexpected loss of income.

A particularly sensitive type of inequality concerns access to decent jobs. The Maghreb and the Arab Spring provide examples, but the situation is equally worrisome in several other Middle Eastern cities, where many young people who have completed their studies are not ready to accept jobs that do not match their expectations. This mismatch in the job market may have serious consequences. It may also exist in other regions of the world. The "decent work" recommended by the International Labour Organisation is certainly a need and perhaps a "right," but few have access to it in the poorest Asian or African countries. ■

REFERENCES

AHLUWALIA M., 1976, "Inequality, poverty and development." *Journal of Development Economics*, 6: 307-342.

ALESINA A. and RODRIK D., 1994, "Distributive politics and economic growth." *Quarterly Journal of Economics*. 109(2): 465-490.

BANERJEE A. and NEWMAN A., 1993, "Occupational choice and the process of development." *Journal of Political Economy*, 101(2): 274-298.

BANERJEE A. and DUFLO E., 2003, "Inequality and growth: what can the data say?" *Journal of Economic Growth*, 2003, v8(3,Sep), 267-299

BARRO R. J., 1991, "Economic Growth in a Cross Section of Countries." *The Quarterly Journal of Economics*, 106(2): 407-443

BÉNABOU R., 2000, "Unequal societies: income distribution and the social contract." *American Economic Review*, 90(3): 96-129.

BOURGUIGNON F., 2003, "The growth elasticity of poverty reduction: explaining heterogeneity across countries and time periods." In T. Eicher and S. Turnovski (eds), *Growth and Inequality*, 3-26. Cambridge, MA: MIT Press.

CHENERY H., AHLUWALIA M., BELL C., DULLOY J. and JOLLY R., 1974, *Redistribution with Growth*. Published for the World Bank and the Institute of Development Studies, Sussex. Oxford: Oxford University Press.

FORBES K. J., 2000, "A reassessment of the relationship between inequality and growth." *American Economic Review*. 90(4): 869-887.

GALOR O. and ZEIRA J., 1993, "Income Distribution and Macroeconomics", *The Review of Economic Studies*, 60(1): 35-52.

KALDOR N., 1960, *Essays on Value and Distribution*. Glencoe, Ill: Free Press.

KUZNETS S., 1955, "Economic Growth and Income Inequality", *The American Economic Review*, 45(1): 1-28.

LEWIS A., 1954, "Economic Development with Unlimited Supplies of Labor." *Manchester School of Economic and Social Studies*, 22: 139-191.

LUCAS R., 1988 "On the Mechanics of Economic Development", *Journal of Monetary Economics*, 22(1): 3–42.

MANKIW G., ROMER D. and WEIL D., 1992, "A contribution to the empirics of economic growth," *The Quarterly Journal of Economics*, 107(2): 407-437.

PERSSON T. and TABELLINI G., 1994, "Is inequality harmful for growth?" *American Economic Review*. 84(3): 600-621.

ROMER P., 1986, "Increasing Returns and Long-Run Growth", The Journal of Political Economy, 94(5): 1002-1037.

ROEMER J., 1998, *Equality of Opportunity*. Cambridge, MA: Harvard University Press.

SEN A., 1985, *Commodities and Capabilities*. New York: Oxford University Press.

SOLOW R., 1956, "Contribution to the theory of economic growth", *Quarterly Journal of Economics*, 70(1): 65-94.

WORLD BANK, 2005, *World Development Report 2006: Equity and Development*. Washington, DC: World Bank Publishing.

REFERENCES OF THE CHRONOLOGY

ACEMOGLU D., JOHNSON S. and ROBINSON J., 2005, Institutions as the fundamental cause of long-run growth, in Aghion et Durlauf (eds), Handbook of Economic Growth, Elsevier, 386-415

AGHION P. and BOLTON R., 1997, "A Theory of Trickle-Down Growth and Development", *The Review of Economic Studies*, 64(2): 151-172.

ALKIRE S. and FOSTER J., 2011, "Counting and Multidimensional Poverty Measurement", Journal of Public Economics 95(7-8): 476-87

BOURGUIGNON F. and CHAKRAVARTY S., 2003, The measurement of multidimensional poverty, *Journal of Economic inequality*, 1, pp 25-49

DOLLAR D. and KRAAY A., 2002, "Growth Is Good for the Poor", *Journal of Economic Growth*, Springer, vol. 7(3), pages 195-225

RODRIK D., SUBRAMANIAN A. and TREBBI F., 2004, "Institutions Rule: The Primacy Of Institutions Over Geography And Integration In Economic Development," *Journal of Economic Growth*, 2004, 9(2): 131-165.

SEN A., 1976, Poverty: an ordinal approach to poverty measurement, *Econometrica*, 44(2): 219-231

Inequalities and crisis recovery

Raymond Torres, Stefan Kühn and Matthieu Charpe, International Labour Organization, Geneva, Switzerland

The global crisis which erupted after the collapse of Lehman Brothers in 2008 has led to significant debate regarding the importance of adequate financial regulation. The G20 Summit which was held in 2009 in Pittsburgh, for example, highlighted the critical role that improved financial regulation should play in securing sustainable economic growth. Important as it is, however, financial reform will not be enough to tackle the crisis. Indeed, some authors have called for the emphasis to be shifted onto the "real" factors behind the crisis, particularly inadequate employment growth and excessive income inequalities (KUMHOF and RANCIÈRE, 2010; TORRES, 2010).

This paper draws on this literature and shows how addressing employment and income gaps could contribute to the rebalancing of the real economy and promote recovery. We examine the appropriate policy mix needed to tackle the crisis. In this regard, the pros and cons of fiscal austerity measures and labour market deregulation are assessed[1].

In order to achieve this, a model which takes into account the connections between macroeconomic policies and labour markets has been developed by the International Labour Organization (ILO)[2]. Importantly, the ILO model takes into account the impact that changes in income distribution may have on aggregate demand. Based on this model, the paper i) assesses the impacts of fiscal austerity and certain structural reforms on jobs; ii) examines how the labour market situation, in turn, affects macroeconomic performance; and iii) discusses what strategy would help meet both employment and fiscal goals.

Fiscal austerity is detrimental to output growth and employment...

The analysis is performed by way of three economic and social scenarios for the period 2012-15, based on the ILO model. The first encompasses further fiscal austerity through a cut in public spending starting from the first half of 2012, hereafter referred to as the "fiscal consolidation scenario". The second analyses the effect of reforms that end up reducing wages and weakening workers' bargaining power, hereafter referred to as the "lower labour standards scenario". This second scenario also discusses the ability of minimum wage to limit income losses. In the third scenario, the "ILO scenario", the effects of a policy mix combining sound fiscal policies to stimulate investment with policies that achieve balanced income developments are assessed over the selected period.

---

1. The IMF and OECD propose three scenarios based on the Global Integrated Monetary and Fiscal Model (GIMF). In a first scenario, further fiscal consolidation leads to lower output and employment due to its negative impact on aggregate demand. In a second scenario, lower taxes on labour income and profits as well as more flexible labour markets have strong supply side effects leading firms to increase labour demand and production. In a third scenario, rebalancing in Asia reduces global imbalances between high income and emerging economies.

2. For further details, see Charpe and Kühn (2012). More information on the Global Economic Linkages (GEL) model can be found at: http://www.ilo.org/public/english/bureau/inst/research/global/index.htm. See also Charpe and Kühn (2011).

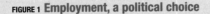

FIGURE 1 Employment, a political choice

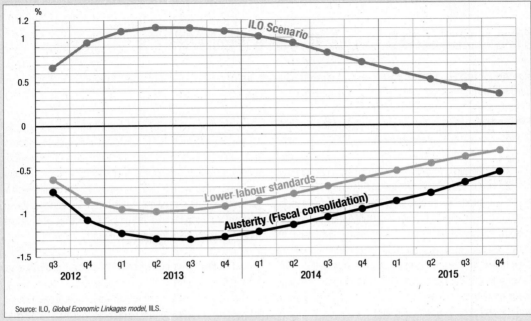

Source: ILO, *Global Economic Linkages model*, IILS.

This simulation examines the dynamic evolution of employment in the different scenarios. In a scenario of fiscal consolidation, public sector spending as a share of GDP is reduced by 1.4 percentage points. In the scenario of lowering labour standards, the share of labour income in total income is reduced by 1.8 percentage points. The ILO scenario combines infrastructure spending and labour incomes that are aligned with the increase in productivity in all countries. Policies are intended to apply in all countries and enter into force in mid-2012. Their effects are measured until the end of 2015.

Figure 1 shows the main outcomes of the three above-mentioned scenarios. Employment trends over the next two and a half years are compared with a "baseline scenario", which includes the economic and labour market projections as developed in Global Employment Trends 2012[3].

In the first scenario, further fiscal austerity would reduce employment vis-à-vis the baseline. Fiscal austerity is modelled here as a cut in public spending as a share of GDP by 1.4 percentage points in high income countries. Output declines by 1.6 percentage points at peak and by 0.6 percentage points by 2015. Similarly, employment decreases by 1.3 percentage points at peak and 0.5 percentage points by end 2015 (dash-dotted line in

Figure 1). This corresponds to 2.84 million fewer jobs in high income countries by end 2015 as compared to the baseline scenario (see Table 1). In low and medium income countries, fiscal austerity is milder with the ratio of public spending to GDP declining by 1.1 percentage points only. This is translated into 11.5 million fewer jobs by end 2015[4].

The result arises because fiscal consolidation reduces aggregate demand, in turn, affecting labour demand. Importantly, this simulation takes into account the fact that lower

---

3. ILO. Global Employment Trends (2012)

---

4. OECD Quarterly data on government accounts shows that spending to GDP ratio has declined by 1.4 percentage points between the third quarter of 2010 and 2011 in 25 advanced economies. Similarly, the World Economic Outlook forecasted a decline in spending to GDP ratio of 1 percentage point in developing economies between 2009 and 2011.

public spending creates room for higher private spending. However this positive "crowding-in" effect is outweighed by the direct negative impact associated with lower public spending. The deflationary pressures exacerbated by spending cuts tend to push up the real interest rate, which discourages private investment. Fiscal austerity does not succeed in stimulating private investment, which declines by 1.3 percentage points at peak. Additionally, budget cuts are costly to the public purse since they depress economic activity and raise unemployment, thus eroding tax revenues and adding upward pressure on social spending. The result is that short-term budget savings from fiscal austerity do not materialize. Indeed, public debt increases by 1.1 percentage points by end 2015.

...the same goes with policies that reduce the bargaining power of workers...

The second scenario illustrates the employment effects caused by a further deterioration in the bargaining power of workers. In the ILO model, the distribution of income between workers and firms depends on a parameter which captures the workers' bargaining power over wages[5]. The experiment conducted in the second scenario is to decrease this parameter such that the corresponding decline in the labour share of income is 1.8 percentage points. This drop corresponds to the decline in the labour share of income, which took place in the United States over the period 2008-2010.

In the second scenario, output declines by 1.2 percentage points at peak and 0.5 percentage points by end 2015, while employment declines by 1 percentage point at peak and by 0.36 percentage points by end 2015 (Figure 1, dashed line). This corresponds to a decline in the global number of jobs by 10.53 million, compared with the baseline scenario (Table 1).

The logic behind this result is that, even if lower wages may boost labour demand for any individual firm, a generalised fall in wages would affect household demand at the aggregate level, thereby depressing total output and employment. This means that, in the model, the negative demand effect dominates the positive impact that higher profits (associated with lower wages) may have on business investment. The positive effects of lower wages on profits are not materialized since the sharp decline in consumption pushes the economy into a liquidity trap. Private investment drops by 1.2 percentage points at peak. As with the first scenario, the second scenario is associated with a widening in budget deficits owing to lower tax revenues and larger spending related to increased unemployment benefits. Importantly, however, the model does not consider the possible effect that lower wages in the public sector would have on budget deficits.

The negative effects of lower labour standards may be attenuated by labour market regulations in the form of minimum wage. Minimum wage sets a floor on wages and therefore limits the fall in labour incomes. It follows that consumption drops less and employment losses are limited. Figure 4 shows the employment dynamic following a decline in labour standards with and without minimum wage. In the presence of minimum wage, employment "only" drops by 0.3 percentage points against 1 percentage point in its absence. Additionally, the recovery is faster and employment is restored to its pre-crisis level by end 2015.

...whereas a global job pact would help on both the employment and macroeconomic fronts.

The third scenario looks at the effects of a crisis response inspired by the Global Jobs Pact, i.e. the implementation of the decent work agenda at times of crisis. Although such an agenda encompasses a large variety of tools and policy actions, numerical simulations can only be performed on a restricted set of instruments. For simplicity, the ILO scenario is here defined as a combination of i) infrastructure investment equivalent to 1 percentage point increase in the public investment to GDP ratio[6] and ii) a

---

5. In detail, wage setting is subject to Nash bargaining over the surplus from an additional match. Wages therefore depend on a variety of elements such as the marginal productivity of labour, the replacement wage of workers, the interest rate as well as a parameter capturing the bargaining power of workers.

6. The 1 percentage point increase takes place on impact. Spending then gradually declines at a rate of 10 per cent per quarter during the simulation period until they return to their starting value.

FIGURE 2 Social safety net does not constrain job creation

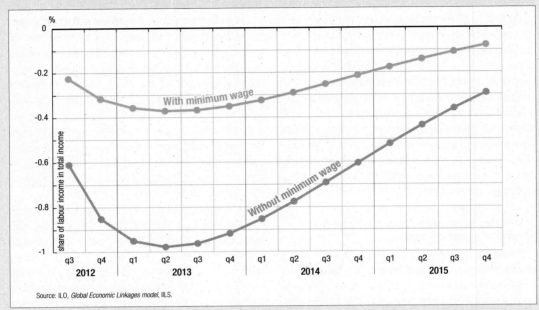

Source: ILO, *Global Economic Linkages model*, IILS.

This figure shows the dynamics of employment in the scenario of a lowering of labour standards, with or without minimum wage. This scenario is characterized by a decline in the share of labour income in total income by 1.8 percentage points. As in the previous illustration, policies are intended to apply in all countries and enter into force in mid-2012. Effects are measured until the end of 2015. It shows that the existence of a social safety net does not constrain job creation.

rebalancing of the share of labour incomes in total income, corresponding to an increase in the share of labour income in total income by 1.8 percentage points[7].

The component of infrastructure spending intends to capture the aggregate demand effect of public spending as well as the productivity-enhancing effect for the private sector of well designed public investment. Infrastructure investment plays the role of a positive externality on firms, since public capital is an input in the production function of firms. This measure captures the set of instruments advocated by the ILO to support enterprises. The stabilization of labour share in total income captures the measures promoting rights at work and social dialogue as well as

those measures aimed at achieving a more balanced income distribution.

These policies are especially relevant given the relative inefficiency of monetary policy in the current deflationary environment that prevails in most advanced economies: monetary authorities are faced with a liquidity trap as they are left with little room to further reduce interest rates to stimulate investment.

In the ILO scenario, output increases by 1.8 percentage points at peak and by 0.8 percentage points by end 2015, while employment increases by 1.1 percentage points at peak and by 0.35 percentage points over the same period (solid line in Figure 1). This translates in an additional 12.74 million jobs created worldwide (Table 1). Well-designed public investments are enterprise friendly to the extent that they generate a crowding-in of private investment, amounting to 1.1% of GDP by 2015.

7. This experiment relies on the assumption that this policy mix is undertaken jointly by all countries and that no country engages in strategic games leading to free riding behaviour.

Public debt declines in the short run due to additional tax revenues. This increase is however moderate and does not exceed 1.6 percentage points of GDP at peak value. This scenario shows that the debt level is mainly driven by revenue associated with economic activity.

Comparison with other model results

Compared to other modelling studies, the ILO model yields similar results concerning the effects of fiscal austerity. For instance, the IMF global model (GIMF) shows that in a situation of underemployment of productive resources, fiscal austerity will worsen the employment situation. Similarly, public investment has beneficial demand effects while also boosting enterprise investment and labour demand. Neither model, however, take into account the risk premium which financial markets might impose on government refinancing costs.

As to the effects of labour standards, the findings of the ILO model are more favourable than is the case with GIMF. This is because the ILO model takes into account the impact that changes in income distribution may have on aggregate demand. Indeed, in contrast to the GIMF model, the ILO model features bargaining over wages between workers and firms. Due to the low substitutability between capital and labour in the short run, a reduction in wages (due to lower labour standards) entails limited labour/capital substitution. By contrast, with many households relying exclusively on labour income, the fall in wages lowers aggregate demand, depressing employment prospects. Recent IMF research, such as for instance Kumhof and Ranciere (2010), has taken into account income distribution effects and finds results in line with the ILO model.

Importantly, the ILO model assumes that policies are coordinated across countries. In the absence of policy coordination, ILO friendly policies carried out by one country in isolation may yield much less gains than projected in the third scenario.

Finally, and crucially, none of the alternative models consider the implications of a prolonged labour market recession from the point of view of labour market participation ("hysteresis" effects). This means that employment effects of fiscal austerity and certain structural reforms are probably under-estimated. It is expected that later developments of the model will remedy this important knowledge gap. ■

REFERENCES

Arpaia A., Pérez E. and Pichelmann K., 2009, 'Understanding Labour Income Share Dynamics in Europe'. *European Economy Economic Papers* (379).

Baxter M. and King R. G., 1993, 'Fiscal Policy in General Equilibrium'. *American Economic Review* 83: 315–334.

Bom P. R. and Lighthart J. E., 2008, 'How Productive Is Public Capital? A Meta-analysis'. *CESifo Working Paper Series* (2206).

Calvo G. A., 1983, 'Staggered Prices in a Utility-maximizing Framework'. *Journal of Monetary Economics* 12 (3): 383–398.

Charpe M. and Kühn S., 2011, 'Effective Employment Policy Under Tight Fiscal Constraints: An Application Using the GEL Model'. In *World of Report 2011*. Chapter 6. http://www.ilo.org/public/english/bureau/inst/download/wow2011.pdf.

Charpe M. and Kühn S., 2012, 'Bargaining, Aggregate Demand and Employment'. *MPRA Paper No. 40189*.

Choi S. and Rios-Rull J.-V., 2009, 'Understanding the Dynamics of Labor Share: The Role of Noncompetitive Factor Prices'. *Annals of Economics and Statistics* 95/96: 251–278.

Christiano L., Eichenbaum M. and Rebelo S., 2009, 'When Is the Government Spending Multiplier Large?' *NBER Working Paper* 15394: 1–68.

Galí J., López-Salido J. D. and Vallés J., 2007, 'Understanding the Effects of Government Spending on Consumption'. *Journal of the European Economic Association* 5 (1) (March): 227–270.

Gertler M. and Trigari A., 2009, 'Unemployment Fluctuations with Staggered Nash Wage Bargaining'. *Journal of Political Economy* 117 (1): 38–86.

ILO. Global Employment Trends. 2012. 'Preventing a Deeper Job Crisis'. ILO. http://www.ilo.org/wcmsp5/groups/public/---dgreports/---dcomm/---publ/documents/publication/wcms_171571.pdf.

Hall R.E., 2009, 'By How Much Does the GDP Rise If the Government Buys More Output?' *Brookings Papers on Economic Activity* 2009 Fall: 183–249.

Kühn S., 2010, *Government Spending in Dynamic General Equilibrium Models*. Universitaire Pers Maastricht.

Kumhof M. and Ranciere R., 2010, 'Inequality, Leverage and Crises'. *IMF Working Papers* 10/268.

Mortensen D. T. and Pissarides C. A., 1994, 'Job Creation and Job Destruction in the Theory of Unemployment'. *Review of Economic Studies* 61 (3): 397–415.

Torres R., 2010, Incomplete crisis responses. International Labour Review.

Equality and Efficiency: Is there a trade-off between the two?

Andrew G. Berg, International Monetary Fund, Washington, United States of America
Jonathan D. Ostry, International Monetary Fund, Washington, United States of America

In his influential 1975 book *Equality and Efficiency: The Big Tradeoff,* Arthur Okun argued that pursuing equality can reduce efficiency (the total output produced with given resources). The late Yale University and Brookings Institution economist said that not only can more equal distribution of incomes reduce incentives to work and invest, but the efforts to redistribute—through such mechanisms as the tax code and minimum wages— can themselves be costly. Okun likened these mechanisms to a "leaky bucket." Some of the resources transferred from rich to poor "will simply disappear in transit, so the poor will not receive all the money that is taken from the rich"—the result of administrative costs and disincentives to work for both those who pay taxes and those who receive transfers.

Do societies inevitably face an invidious choice between efficient production and equitable wealth and income distribution? Are social justice and social product at war with one another? In a word, no.

In recent work (BERG, OSTRY, and ZETTELMEYER, 2011; and BERG and OSTRY, 2011), we discovered that when growth is looked at over the long term, the trade-off between efficiency and equality may not exist. In fact equality appears to be an important ingredient in promoting and sustaining growth. The difference between countries that can sustain rapid growth for many years or even decades and the many others that see growth spurts fade quickly may be the level of inequality. Countries may find that improving equality may also improve efficiency, understood as more sustainable long-run growth.

Inequality matters for growth and other macroeconomic outcomes, in all corners of the globe. One need look no further than the role inequality is thought to have played in creating the disaffection that underlies much of the recent unrest in the Middle East. And, taking a historical perspective, the increase in U.S. income inequality in recent decades is strikingly similar to the increase that occurred in the 1920s. In both cases there was a boom in the financial sector, poor people borrowed a lot, and a huge financial crisis ensued (see "Leveraging Inequality," *F&D*, December 2010 and "Inequality = Indebtedness" in this issue of *F&D*). The recent global economic crisis, with its roots in U.S. financial markets, may have resulted, in part at least, from the increase in inequality. With inequality growing in the United States and other important economies, the relationship between inequality and growth takes on more significance.

How do economies grow?

Most thinking about long-run growth assumes implicitly that development is something akin to climbing a hill, that it entails more or less steady increases in real income, punctuated by business cycle fluctuations. The pattern in Figure 1 – which shows the level of real (after-inflation) per capita income in two advanced economies, the United Kingdom and the United States – is consistent with this idea.

The experiences in developing and emerging economies, however, are far more varied (see Figure 2). In some cases, the experience is like climbing a hill. But in others, the experience is more like a roller coaster. Looking at such cases, Pritchett (2000) and other authors have

FIGURE 1 **The climbing of the hill**

FIGURE 1 **The climbing of the hill**

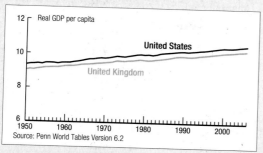

Source: Penn World Tables Version 6.2

For many advanced countries such as the United Kingdom and the United States, real per capita income has grown at a more or less steady pace over the long run.

FIGURE 2 **Growth in emerging countries: the roller coaster**

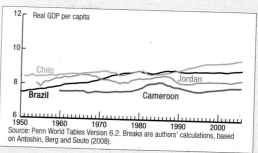

Source: Penn World Tables Version 6.2. Breaks are authors' calculations, based on Antoshin, Berg and Souto (2008).

The experience of developing and emerging market countries has been much more varied, and very few have had only steady growth. Instead, countries have experienced periods of rapid growth, decline and stagnation.

FIGURE 3 **Equality supports growth**

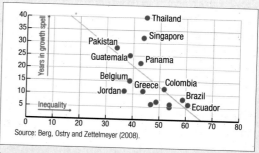

Source: Berg, Ostry and Zettelmeyer (2008).

Inequality may create richness but it does not support long-term growth which demands political stability and public support to policies to secure investments.

concluded that an understanding of growth must involve looking more closely at the turning points – ignoring the ups and downs of growth over the horizon of the business cycle, and concentrating on why some countries are able to keep growing for long periods whereas others see growth break down after just a few years, followed by stagnation or decay.

A systematic look at this experience suggests that *igniting* growth is much less difficult than *sustaining* it (HAUSMANN, PRITCHETT and RODRIK, 2005). Even the poorest of countries have managed to get growth going for several years, only to see it peter out. Where growth laggards differ from their more successful peers is in the degree to which they have been able to sustain growth for long periods of time.

Income distribution and growth sustainability

In our research we looked at the extent to which the duration of a growth episode is related to differences in country characteristics and policies. The quality of economic and political institutions, an outward orientation of an economy, macroeconomic stability, and human capital accumulation have long been recognized as important determinants of economic growth. And we found that they matter for the duration of growth episodes too.

We argue that income distribution may also – and independently – belong in this pantheon of critical determinants of growth duration. At the level of simple correlation, more inequality seems associated with less sustained growth.

Figure 3 shows the length of growth spells and the average income distribution during the spell for a sample of countries. We define a growth spell as a period of at least five years that begins with an unusual increase in the growth rate and ends with an unusual drop in growth. The measure of inequality is the Gini coefficient, which varies from zero (all households having the same income) to 100 (all income received by one household).

It may seem counterintuitive that inequality is strongly associated with less sustained growth. After all, some inequality is essential to the effective functioning of a market economy and the incentives needed for investment and growth (CHAUDHURI and RAVALLION, 2007). But too much inequality might be destructive to growth. Beyond the risk that inequality may amplify the potential for financial crisis, it may also bring political instability, which can discourage investment. Inequality may make it harder for governments to make difficult but necessary choices in the face of shocks, such as raising taxes or cutting public spending to avoid a debt crisis. Or inequality may reflect poor people's lack of access to financial services, which gives them fewer opportunities to invest in education and entrepreneurial activity.

Against this background, the question is whether a systematic look at the data supports the notion that societies with more equal income distributions have more durable growth.

We study growth spells as medical researchers might examine life expectancy. They study the effects of age, weight, gender, and smoking habits on life expectancy; we look at whether factors such as political institutions, health and education, macroeconomic instability, debt, and trade openness might influence the likelihood that a growth spell will end. The result is a statistical model of growth duration that relates the expected length of a growth episode (or, equivalently, the risk that it will end in a given year) to several of these variables. We compare the risk that the spell will end in a given year with the values of these variables in previous years – at the beginning of the spell or the previous year – to minimize the risk of reverse causality. In the face of the usual difficulties involved in disentangling cause and effect, and the risk that we have been unable to find good measures of important variables, the results we report below should nonetheless be interpreted only as empirical regularities ("stylized facts").

The analysis suggests that a number of variables found to be important in other contexts also tend to be associated with longer growth spells (see Figure 4). To show the importance of each variable, the chart (which covers 1950 to 2006) reports the increase in the expected duration of a growth spell for a given increase in the variable in question, keeping other factors constant. To compare the effects of the different variables on growth duration, we calculate expected duration when all the variables are at their median values (the value greater than that observed in 50 percent of the observations in the sample). Then we increase each variable, one variable at a time, and look at what happens to expected duration. We want the size of each of these increases to be readily comparable. To achieve this, we increase each variable by an amount such that it moves from the median value to a value greater than that observed in 60 percent of the sample (a 10 percentile increase).

Hazard to sustained growth

Somewhat surprisingly, income inequality stood out for the strength and robustness of its relationship with the duration of growth spells: a 10 percentile decrease in inequality (represented by a change in the Gini coefficient from 40 to 37) increases the expected length of a growth spell by 50 percent. The effect is large, but is the sort of improvement that a number of countries have experienced during growth spells. We estimate that closing, say, half the inequality gap between Latin America and emerging Asia would more than double the expected duration of a growth spell in Latin America.

Remarkably, inequality retains its statistical and economic significance even when we include many potential determinants at the same time, a claim that we cannot make for many of the conventional determinants of good growth performance, such as the quality of institutions and trade openness. Inequality still matters when we allow for regional differences in expected growth duration (such as between emerging Asia and Africa). This all suggests that inequality seems to matter in itself and is not just proxying for other factors. Inequality also preserves its significance more systematically across different samples and definitions of growth spells than the other variables do. Of course, inequality is not the only thing that matters but, from our analysis, it clearly belongs on the list of well-established growth factors such as the quality of political institutions or trade openness.

Do these statistical results find a voice in the political

FIGURE 4. **Inequality as a determining factor**

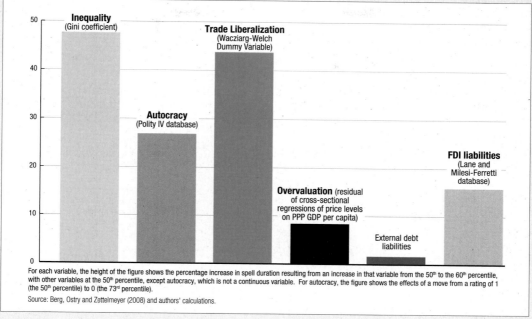

For each variable, the height of the figure shows the percentage increase in spell duration resulting from an increase in that variable from the 50th to the 60th percentile, with other variables at the 50th percentile, except autocracy, which is not a continuous variable. For autocracy, the figure shows the effects of a move from a rating of 1 (the 50th percentile) to 0 (the 73rd percentile).

Source: Berg, Ostry and Zettelmeyer (2008) and authors' calculations.

Inequality is as strong a factor as trade orientation to explain the length of growth spell in developing and emerging countries. It seems to be even stronger than the quality of political institutions.

and economic narratives of the actual country growth episodes?

It appears to be the case in, for example, Cameroon. Growth averaged 7 percent from 1978 through 1985. Then the economy fell apart and declined by 6 percent a year over the subsequent decade. Oil wealth in the 1970s initially financed large increases in the public sector, particularly in public employee wages, which proved very difficult to cut when oil prices fell. "Although these measures [to cut government spending] were necessary to rescue the country from further economic crisis, they were very unpopular because they least affected the political elite and those in the upper echelon of government, whose privileges remained intact" (MBAKU and TAKOUGANG, 2003). Our statistical model of growth duration suggests that the risk that the growth spell would end in 1985 was very high – more than 100 times higher than would be typical for a country enjoying a growth spell. The model

attributes this high risk mostly to Cameroon's unusually high inequality as well as its low inflow of foreign direct investment and high degree of autocracy.

Cameroon is typical. We have examined six historical cases, including Colombia, Guatemala and Nigeria. These cases, and our broader statistical analysis of a large number of growth episodes, suggest that inequality is an underlying feature that makes it more likely that a number of factors – external shocks, external debt, ethnic fractionalization – come together to bring a growth spell to an end.

Raising the tide

One reasonably firm conclusion is that it would be a big mistake to separate analyses of growth and income distribution. To borrow a marine analogy: a rising tide lifts all boats, and our analysis indicates that helping raise the smallest boats may help keep the tide rising for all craft, big and small.

The immediate role for policy, however, is less clear. More inequality may shorten the duration of growth, but poorly designed efforts to reduce inequality could be counterproductive. If these efforts distort incentives and undermine growth, they can do more harm than good for the poor. For example, the initial reforms that ignited growth in China involved giving stronger incentives to farmers. This increased the income of the poor and reduced overall inequality as it gave a tremendous spur to growth. However, it probably led to some increased inequality among farmers, and efforts to resist this component of inequality would likely have been counterproductive (CHAUDHURI and RAVALLION, 2007).

Still, there may be some win-win policies, such as better-targeted subsidies, better access to education for the poor that improves equality of economic opportunity, and active labour market measures that promote employment.

When there are short-run trade-offs between the effects of policies on growth and income distribution, the evidence we have does not in itself say what to do. But our analysis should tilt the balance toward the long-run benefits – including for growth – of reducing inequality. Over longer horizons, reduced inequality and sustained growth may be two sides of the same coin.

The analysis calls to mind the developing country debt crises of the 1980s and the resulting "lost decade" of slow growth and painful adjustment. That experience brought home the fact that sustainable economic reform is possible only when its benefits are widely shared. In the face of the current global economic turmoil and the need for difficult economic adjustment and reform in many countries, it would be better if these lessons were remembered rather than relearned. ■

REFERENCES

BARRO R. J., 2000, "Inequality and Growth in a Panel of Countries", Journal of Economic Growth, Vol. 5, No. 1, pp. 5–32.

BERG, A., OSTRY J. D., 2011, "Inequality and Unsustainable Growth: Two Sides of the Same Coin?", IMF Staff Discussion Note 11/08 (Washington: International Monetary Fund).

BERG, A., OSTRY J. D., ZETTELMEYER J., 2011, "What Makes Growth Sustained?", forthcoming in Journal of Development Economics.

CHAUDHURI S., RAVALLION M., 2007, "Partially Awakened Giants: Uneven Growth in China and India", in Dancing with Giants: China, India and the Global Economy, ed. by L. Alan WINTERS and Shahid YUSUF (Washington: World Bank).

HAUSMANN R., PRITCHETT L., RODRIK D., 2005, "Growth Accelerations", Journal of Economic Growth, Vol. 10, No. 4, pp. 303–29.

MBAKU J. M., TAKOUGANG J., eds., 2003, The Leadership Challenge in Africa: Cameroon, under Paul Biya (Trenton, New Jersey: Africa World Press).

OKUN A., 1975, Equality and Efficiency: The Big Tradeoff, Washington: Brookings Institution Press.

Polity IV Project, www.systemicpeace.org/polity/polity4.htm

PRITCHETT L., 2000, "Understanding Patterns of Economic Growth: Searching for Hills among Plateaus, Mountains, and Plains," World Bank Economic Review, Vol. 14, No. 2, pp. 221–50.Wacziarg,

WELCH R. and K. H., 2008, "Trade Liberalization and Growth: New Evidence," World Bank Economic Review, Vol. 22, No. 2, pp. 187–231.

CHAPTER 5

Research has shown a strong empirical link between economic inequality and biodiversity loss. Gender equality helps stabilize human population growth and mitigate the pressure on other species and on natural resources. A minimum level of equality also appears necessary to successfully manage renewable natural resources for the benefit of all.

Economic equality as a condition for biodiversity conservation

Economic equality, a worthy political goal in its own right, also greatly benefits the individual health of, and social harmony among, human beings (WILKINSON and PICKETT, 2009). Might equality also promote environmental quality? Theorists and empiricists have debated this question for several decades now (for example, OLSON, 1965; BOYCE, 1994; BALAND et al., 2007). In 2007, Mikkelson et al. reported a strong empirical link between economic inequality and biodiversity loss – in other words, a strongly positive relationship between equality and biodiversity (MIKKELSON et al., 2007). They found such a relationship at two different scales: across countries throughout the world, and states throughout the US.

This chapter builds upon Mikkelson et al. (2007) in several ways. First, we examine subsequent analyses of equality-biodiversity links among different countries. We do not know of any further published studies of such links among different states or provinces within any country. One of the subsequent between-country analyses affirms a positive connection between equality and biodiversity (HOLLAND et al., 2009), while the other denies such a connection (PANDIT and LABAND, 2009). This chapter thus first aims to explain this contrast. Second, we speculate about pathways through which equality may benefit biodiversity. These potential mechanisms partially overlap with linkages between biodiversity and poverty (ROE, 2010; ROE and WALPOLE, 2011; BILLÉ et al., 2012), on one hand, and biodiversity and wealth or over-consumption (SUKHDEV, 2010; MIKKELSON, in review), on the other. Their identification could have a marked effect on public policy.

Raphaël Billé,
Institute for Sustainable Development and International Relations, Paris, France

Gilles Kleitz,
Agence Française de développement Paris, France

Gregory M. Mikkelson,
McGill University, Montreal, Canada

Third, we make a few suggestions about how to get economic equality onto the biodiversity protection agenda. Fourth and finally, we offer some thoughts about how best to achieve equality. While progressive taxation leaps first to many people's minds, deeper political and economic changes seem needed to ensure equality in the long term. We focus here on worker cooperatives – a far more egalitarian, and surprisingly competitive, form of business organization relative to typical corporations. A crucial defining feature of cooperatives – whether worker, consumer, or community co-ops – is that they operate democratically, i.e., one person, one vote (UN, 2012). In contrast, typical corporations (which we henceforth call "corporations" for short) not only subordinate workers to both managers and shareholders (GLASBEEK, 2002), but also place ultimate control in the hands of the shareholders on a plutocratic basis – one dollar, one vote. Shifting the economy from corporations to co-ops will require changes in law and policy at all levels of government – local, regional, national and international (SCHWEICKART, 2011).

Recent controversy and future research: A case of non-monotonic improvement in data quality

As mentioned above, Mikkelson et al. (2007) found an equality-biodiversity link both among countries and among US states. But country-level data, in particular – on both economic equality and biological diversity – tend to be incomplete and inconsistent. Mikkelson et al., as well as Holland et al. (2009), and Pandit and Laband (2009), all drew upon the best data available at the time, produced by the Pitt Inequality Project (PIP) and the International Union for the Conservation of Nature (IUCN). However, they used very different versions of the PIP data.

The PIP corrected for several kinds of inconsistency between assessments of income inequality in different countries (BABONES and ALVAREZ-RIVADULLA, 2007). After performing these corrections, the PIP made three different data sets available. Mikkelson et al. used one of these, the Standardized Income Distribution Database, Version 1.0 (SIDD-1; see Reference # 17 in Mikkelson et al.). The SIDD-1 included corrected values for only those country-year combinations in which inequality had actually been measured. Holland et al. also made clear that they used only those measured country-year combinations (see p. 4), though they did not specify whether they drew from the original SIDD-1 or its revision, the SIDD-2. Pandit and Laband, in contrast, used the SIDD-3 (see p. 3222), which extrapolated and/or interpolated each country's inequality figures to yield estimates for every year from 1955 to 2005.

These extrapolations and interpolations inflated the data set by nearly six-fold, from the 1,218 country-year combinations in the SIDD-1 and SIDD-2 to 7,242 such combinations in the SIDD-3 (142 countries x 51 years). For some countries, the extrapolation was so extreme as to render the estimates for most years quite unbelievable. For example, for Barbados – one of the countries included in Pandit and Laband's analysis (see p. 3225) – the SIDD-3 lists precisely the same Gini index of inequality (0.5326) for all 51 years. The Gini index theoretically ranges from 0 – perfect equality – to 1, the case where one person takes all the income in a country.

The fact that in the SIDD-3 Barbados has the same value for all years indicates that it contains only one corrected Gini index for that country, extrapolated all the way back to 1955 and forward to 2005. This spurious invariance contrasts markedly with the variation over time shown by the measured-then-corrected Gini indices in the SIDD-1 and SIDD-2. In the extreme case, Armenia's inequality rose by more than 0.35 after the fall of the Soviet Union.

Pandit and Laband did not mention the inclusion of such indefensibly long extrapolations as Barbados'. Instead, they touted the fact that they could include 87 countries in their analysis rather than just 45 as Mikkelson et al. had done. Controlling for the same set of other variables as Mikkelson et al. had, Pandit and Laband failed to detect any statistically significant relationship between equality and biodiversity. We conjecture, however, that this failure results from the likely fact that the vast majority of data points in the SIDD-3 used by Pandit and Laband are extrapolations or interpolations, rather than measured-then-corrected Gini values.

Holland et al. provide additional support for this conjecture. Their study differed a fair bit from that of Mikkelson et al., regarding their choice of other variables to control for. Yet it supported the same general conclusion: more unequal countries have more species headed toward extinction (i.e., plant and vertebrate species that are "threatened" according to the IUCN). Mikkelson et al. and Holland et al. both controlled for the total number of plants and vertebrates (threatened plus non-threatened), human population size, and gross domestic product (GDP) per capita corrected for the differential purchasing power of a dollar in different countries (purchasing power parity, or PPP). However, unlike Holland et al., Mikkelson et al. also controlled for geography by including a dummy variable for each continent. For example, if a country is in Asia, they assigned a value of 1 to the "Asia" dummy variable; if not, they assigned a value of 0 to that variable. They also controlled for one aspect of political history, through another dummy variable denoting whether or not each country is ex-communist or not. Unlike Mikkelson et al., Holland et al. controlled for a measure of environmental governance, the proportion of vertebrate species that are endemic (i.e., limited to one country only), and each country's development category according to the United Nations. Despite employing this distinct set of control variables, Holland et al. confirmed Mikkelson et al.'s finding of a statistically significant, positive link between economic inequality and biodiversity loss.

Future country-level studies of equality-biodiversity relationships can have the best of both worlds: bigger sample sizes than Mikkelson et al.'s or Holland et al.'s, but more reliable inequality data than the SIDD-3 used by Pandit and Laband. This is because, while the PIP has removed all versions of the SIDD from the web, Solt has made a new and improved inequality data set available (the Standardized World Income Inequality Database, or SWIID). Although the SWIID includes some interpolated values, it includes no gross extrapolations such as the Barbados example discussed above (SOLT, 2009). The latest version of the SWIID includes Gini estimates for 4,549 country-year combinations. In addition to better inequality data, future equality-biodiversity studies can also draw upon the latest updates and refinements of the IUCN Red List.

FIGURE 1 Equality and Plant Conservation by Countries

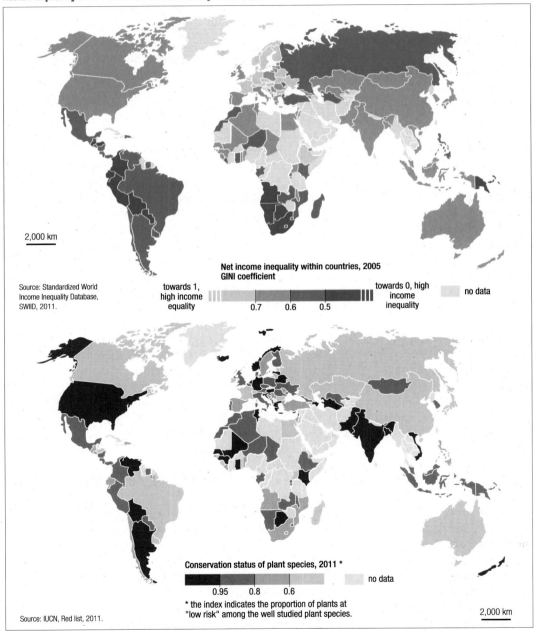

2,000 km

Source: Standardized World
Income Inequality Database,
SWIID, 2011.

Net income inequality within countries, 2005
GINI coefficient

towards 1,
high income
equality

0.7   0.6   0.5

towards 0, high
income
inequality

no data

Conservation status of plant species, 2011 *

0.95   0.8   0.6

no data

* the index indicates the proportion of plants at
"low risk" among the well studied plant species.

Source: IUCN, Red list, 2011.

2,000 km

Documenting the link between economic equality and biodiversity conservation demands the collection and
construction of comparable data sets such as the Standardized World Income Inequality Database, or SWIID.

Figure 2 offers a preview of such studies. Derived from the 2011 versions of both the SWIID and the Red List[1], Figure 2 shows a strong positive relationship between economic equality and plant conservation status among 122 countries (Kendall's = 0.31). This relationship is highly statistically significant ($p < 10^{-6}$), and preliminary analysis indicates that it holds up after controlling for potentially confounding variables. As Figure 1 shows, in all countries with an equality index (one minus the Gini index of inequality) greater than 0.70, more than 60% of well-studied plant species are considered to be at "lower risk" of extinction by the IUCN. In fact, in the great majority of these most equal countries – 21 out of 23 – more than 80% of such plant species are relatively secure. This suggests that achieving high levels of economic equality within a given country suffices to protect most of the plant species within that same country.

Possible mechanisms for the equality-biodiversity connection

Though Mikkelson et al. (2007) reported evidence for a causal connection between economic inequality and biodiversity loss, they did not detail the mechanisms by which equality may influence biodiversity. In this section we will therefore briefly discuss a few factors that may, upon further investigation, prove to be important. A first and probably important factor is population pressure. In an analysis of the 2004 Red List, the IUCN emphasized human population growth as an important socioeconomic driver of other species" population decline (IUCN, 2004). Figure 3 shows a strongly negative connection between economic equality and human population growth (Kendall's = -0.35, $p < 10^{-8}$). This inverse relationship holds up after controlling for per-capita income.

How might equality slow human population expansion? We hypothesise that gender equality will figure more prominently in the answer to this question than will other aspects of economic or political equality. Engelman (2008) identified gender equality as a key prerequisite – along with access to safe and effective contraception and abortion – to stabilising human population size. Gender equality also has at least one other advantage that benefits both human and non-human species: i.e., lower carbon emissions (ERGAS and YORK, 2012).

A second possible mechanism for the equality-biodiversity link is the role of equality in promoting good governance. For example, Stiglitz (2012) stresses the importance of equality for guaranteeing access to justice. As we discuss below, a fair and efficient justice system may be a prerequisite for the effective management of environmental problems. In addition, Solt (2008, 2010) shows that economic equality enhances citizens' levels of political interest, political discussion, and electoral participation. We conjecture that such civic engagement induces governments in more equal societies to protect biological diversity more effectively, through

---

1. See myweb.uiowa.edu/fsolt/swiid/swiid.html and www.iucnredlist.org/about/summary-statistics.

FIGURE 3 **Demographic pressure, a product of inequality**

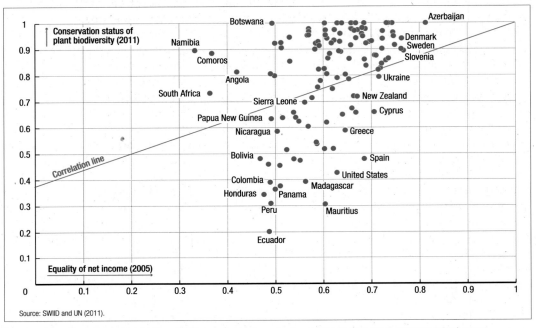

Income equality, compared to the effect caused by income level, tends to have a stronger and more sustained impact on slowing a country's population growth. It also tends to make citizens more interested in public affairs, including the protection of biodiversity.

conservation and restoration of habitat, reduction of pollution, and regulation of hunting and gathering.

A certain level of equality also seems necessary for successful community-based management of renewable natural resources (Ostrom, 1990). Natural resource management experiments in developing countries provide a particularly clear illustration of this. Whether for social forestry, the management of wildlife, protected areas, land ownership, or coastal fisheries, levels of equality affect poor rural stakeholders" access to biological resources, and the security of this access over time as the operators of globalised commodity chains exploit these resources ever further afield and more intensively.

Without sufficient levels of equality, the most disadvantaged stakeholders often lack the legal means required to secure long-term exclusive access to the biological resources vital to their welfare, because of either problems of access to land, the status of the resources themselves, the limited attention given to customary law in relation to written law, informal advantages granted to the most powerful companies or collusion between major economic actors and political leaders. For example, the development of agriculture (soybean, cattle ranching) in the Amazon, the major plantations in Indonesia, or the expansion of agricultural land into African savannah all reveal a transformation of natural rural landscapes composed of family farming areas with low externalities and considerable natural infrastructure into agricultural systems made up of large farms with high externalities and limited natural infrastructure. These situations have an adverse impact on biodiversity.

Socio-economic inequalities thus depress biodiversity through the "crushing" of small rural stakeholders due both to their relative weakness (less formalized, poorly respected rights, inferior social status, cultural stigmatisation, limited negotiating capacities) and to an effective coalition between major farmers, industries and politicians (one-sided resource exploitation contracts, large-scale land leases, assumption of risks and guarantees favouring major national and international stakeholders, weak trade unions and little representation of small farmers, etc.). For poor rural stakeholders, these inequalities result in land insecurity, unpredictability and a lack of transparency regarding access to resources. They diminish their capacity for self-organization, encourage the individualistic race to appropriate resources and limit the benefits and possibility of improving the sustainability of production systems.

Integrating economic equality into conservation practice

Conservationists tend to focus on mitigating proximal causes of biodiversity loss, chief of which is habitat destruction for agriculture and aquaculture (SALAFSKY et al., 2008). The equality-biodiversity connection discussed herein calls for greater attention to more distal socioeconomic causes – and ultimately to cultural causes. See White (1967) for an early, and now classic, cultural explanation of environmental destruction.

As discussed earlier, slowing growth in human numbers may be an important part of the mechanism by which equality mitigates species loss. It may also serve as a bridge between political economy and processes more familiar to conservation practitioners. Other pathways by which equality favours biodiversity take on special significance in the current context of the domination of concepts and instruments based on the economic value of biodiversity – especially economic assessments of environmental services and payments for environmental services – which tend to relegate approaches based on rights and statuses to the sidelines.

One of the first lessons to be drawn is that approaches based on the economic value of biodiversity must be systematically accompanied by a reduction in the political weakness of rural producers and direct users of ecosystems, by working on their rights of access to resources, their representation, and their capacities for negotiating and controlling local resources. Failing this, unequal dynamics result in greater insecurity for many local stakeholders, the rapid development of production systems with high profitability and externalities and an increase in adverse environmental and social impacts. A second lesson is linked to the fundamental inequality between the rich, who are often urban, and the rural poor: the former have the privilege of being able to shop independently of the state of local resources, with commodity chains moving around the world as ecosystems are depleted and opportunities provided by the weakest rights and regulations. Reducing this inequality of access and the associated biodiversity loss implies combining scales of action: for example, organizing sustainable local production systems for certified globalized suppliers; and reducing the relocation of urban supplies and better connecting cities to their peripheral rural areas.

A third lesson is that large-scale capitalistic production and exploitation must meet a rise in opposition and whistle blowing, as well as a consolidation of environmental rights. Actions to finance large-scale plantations (oil palm, rubber trees, etc.) must thus give way to stronger regulatory safeguards, transparency, and assistance for civil society.

How to attain equality

How then should societies go about increasing economic equality? With regard to the consequences for human well-being, it does not seem to matter. Wilkinson and Pickett (2009) used Sweden and Japan, and Vermont and New Hampshire, to illustrate this point. Sweden and Japan rank among the most equal countries in the world, in terms of net income (gross income, minus taxes, plus government transfers). Likewise, Vermont and New Hampshire rank among the most equal states in the US. Sweden, Japan, Vermont, and New Hampshire all have high life expectancies, levels of trust between citizens, etc. Yet while Sweden and Vermont attain their high levels of equality through progressive taxation and government transfers, Japan and New Hampshire achieve it through more equal gross income.

Figure 1 suggests that the route to high levels of net income equality does not matter for biodiversity conservation either. All of the most equal countries shown in Figure 1 also have relatively good plant conservation status. Nevertheless, Wilkinson and Pickett (2009) argue that one route to equality would achieve its end more securely and permanently than tax and benefits policies. Governments can quickly undo progressive tax policies, and they often have. In contrast, if an economy underwent a wholesale shift from domination by corporations – an inherently inegalitarian form of business organization – to cooperatives, it would fundamentally change the nature of work and investment (MIKKELSON, 2011). Such a shift would therefore have more staying power than policies governing individuals' taxation and benefits.

Capitalist firms – what most of us know as, and we are calling in this paper, "corporations" for short – rely on inequality for their very existence, and deepen it once they do exist. They rely on inequality because they presuppose a distinction between two kinds of people – those who already have enough money to survive, and can therefore invest an additional amount in the firm (the shareholders); and those who must instead sell their labour in order to survive (the workers). Corporations deepen this initial inequality because they put the shareholders, instead of the workers, in the "driver's seat". It is the shareholders, rather than the workers, who ultimately control the corporation. And it is the shareholders, rather than the workers, who reap the profits which, unlike wages, have no pre-established upper limit. Of course, some corporations go out of business, causing their shareholders to lose some of their money and their workers to lose their jobs. But on average, corporations make more money for shareholders than they lose. Otherwise, only extreme risk-lovers would invest, and the stock market would collapse for good (SCHWEICKART, 2011).

In contrast, worker cooperatives foster economic equality, in at least two ways. First, the profits go to the relatively poor workers, rather than to the relatively rich shareholders. Second, such co-ops operate democratically: the workers ultimately control the firm, and each has an equal vote. When workers decide on wages, they do elect to pay executives more than others, because they have an incentive to attract and keep managerial "talent" so that the firm succeeds, and its workers thus keep their jobs. But workers do not vote to pay executives hundreds of times more than others in the same firm. For example, in 2010 the highest-paid executive in the Mondragon federation of Spanish worker cooperatives earned just eight times the lowest wage in Mondragon (RAMESH, 2011). In contrast, by the early 21st Century the ratio between the highest and average wages in large capitalist firms had reached nearly 20 in Spain, not to mention over 500 in the United States (BRUCE et al., 2005).

Despite the egalitarian advantages of co-ops, most firms are corporations, and most people work at the latter. Many have assumed that some kind of competitive disadvantage must explain the relative paucity of worker-controlled firms. However, the empirical record shows decisively that co-ops actually out-compete otherwise comparable corporations (Dow, 2003). To use a biological analogy, co-ops have a lower "death rate" than corporations. However, co-ops also have a much lower "birth rate", mostly due to inadequate investment. The only solution to this long-standing problem seems to be public investment. In other words, if co-ops are to take over the economy, governments must replace stock markets as the main source of capital for new firms (SCHWEICKART, 2011).

For some, this would raise the spectre of central planning, still feared two decades after the collapse of the Soviet Union. However, it is one thing for governments to provide initial investment funds, and another for them to unduly control the firms they fund. The whole idea of a co-op is that its members (along with the market for its goods or services) control its behaviour. Another suitable guarantor of de-centralization would be to place most initial-investment decisions in the hands of local public banks, whose officials would be democratically accountable to the citizens of individual municipalities, rather than to a central government alone (SCHWEICKART, 2011).

Conclusion

In this chapter we have reviewed work to date on the link between inequalities and biodiversity loss, discussed some possible mechanisms by which economic equality may benefit biodiversity conservation, suggested ways to integrate equality concerns into the conservation agenda, and discussed worker control of firms as a promising route to equality. We conclude that equality does seem to have an important relationship to biodiversity. This relationship bears further study and action at various levels from the local to the global. In particular, social and environmental activists should heed the equality-biodiversity connection, and work together to transform economies in a way that distributes resources more equitably both within the human species, and between humanity and the myriad of other species with a rightful claim to life and to flourish on Planet Earth.

In addition, official development assistance should aim to improve equality through the conservation projects it supports, and urge recipient countries to do the same. For funders increasingly concerned about demonstrating the effectiveness of their action and setting clear objectives, enhancing equality also presents the advantage of being measurable in the long term (for example using indicators such as the Gini index). Consequently, the introduction of at least one equality target in the post-2015 development objectives and/or in future sustainable development goals is imperative. ■

REFERENCES

BABONES S. J. and ALVAREZ-RIVADULLA M. J., 2007, Standardized income inequality data for use in cross-national research. Sociological Inquiry 77:3-22.

BALAND J. M., BARDHAN P. and Bowles S. (eds), 2007, Inequality, Cooperation, and Environmental Sustainability. Princeton University. Princeton, NJ.

BILLÉ R., LAPEYRE R. and PIRARD R., 2012, Biodiversity conservation and poverty alleviation: A way out of the deadlock? S.A.P.I.E.N.S 5(1): 1-15.

BOYCE J. K., 1994, Inequality as a cause of environmental degradation. Ecological Economics 11:169-178.

BRUCE A., BUCK T. and MAIN B. G. M., 2005, Top executive remuneration: A view from Europe. Journal of Management Studies 42:1493-1506.

COBURN D., 2004, Beyond the income inequality hypothesis: Class, neo-liberalism, and health inequalities. Social Science & Medicine 58:41-56.

Dow G. K., 2003, Governing the Firm: Workers' Control in Theory and Practice. Cambridge University. New York, NY.

ENGELMAN R., 2008, More: Population, Nature, and What Women Want. Island. Washington, DC.

ERGAS C. and YORK R., 2012, Women's status and carbon dioxide emissions: A quantitative cross-national analysis. Social Science Research 41:965-976.

GLASBEEK H., 2002, Wealth by Stealth: Corporate Crime, Corporate Law, and the Perversion of Democracy. Between the Lines. Toronto, ON.

HOLLAND T. G., PETERSON G. D. and GONZALEZ A., 2009, A cross-national analysis of how economic inequality predicts biodiversity loss. Conservation Biology 23:1304-1313.

INTERNATIONAL UNION FOR THE CONSERVATION OF NATURE (IUCN), 2004, 2004 IUCN Red List of Threatened Species. A Global Species Assessment. data.iucn.org/dbtw-wpd/html/Red List 2004/completed/Executive Summary.html.

MIKKELSON G. M., 2011, Equality: Economic and ecological. Canadian Dimension 45(2): 35-38.

MIKKELSON G. M., forthcoming, Growth Is the Problem; Equality Is the Solution. Submitted.

MIKKELSON G. M., GONZALEZ A. and PETERSON G. D., 2007, Economic inequality predicts biodiversity loss. Public Library of Science (PLoS) ONE 2.e444.

OLSON M., 1965, The Logic of Collective Action: Public Goods and the Theory of Groups. Harvard University. Cambridge, MA.

PANDIT R. and LABAND D. N., 2009, Economic well-being, the distribution of income and species imperilment. Biodiversity and Conservation 18:3219-3233.

RAMESH R., 2011, Basque country's thriving big society. The Guardian, March 30th.

ROE D. (ed), 2010, Linking Biodiversity Conservation and Poverty Alleviation: A State of Knowledge Review. Secretariat of the Convention on Biological Diversity, CBD Technical Series Number 55.

ROE D. and WALPOLE M., 2011, Linking biodiversity conservation and poverty reduction: Why and where? Working Paper IIED UNEP-WCMC.

SALAFSKY N., SALZER D., STATTERSFIELD A. J., HILTON-TAYLOR C., NEUGARTEN R., BUTCHART S. H. M., COLLEN B., COX N., MASTER L. L., O'CONNOR S. and WILKIE D., 2008, A standard lexicon for biodiversity conservation: Unified classifications of threats and actions. Conservation Biology 22:897-911.

SCHWEICKART D., 2011, After Capitalism. Rowman and Littlefield. Lanham, MD.

SOLT F., 2008, Economic inequality and democratic political engagement. American Journal of Political Science 52:48-60.

SOLT, F., 2009, Standardizing the World Income Inequality Database. Social Science Quarterly 90:231-242.

SOLT F., 2010, Does economic inequality depress electoral participation? Testing the Schattschneider hypothesis. Political Behavior 32:285-301.

STIGLITZ J., 2012, The Price of Inequalities: How Today's Divided Society Endangers our Future.

SUKHDEV P. (ed), 2010, The Economics of Ecosystems and Biodiversity. www.teebweb.org.

UNITED NATIONS, 2011, World Population Prospects: The 2010 Revision. esa.un.org/unpd/wpp/unpp/panel_population.htm.

UNITED NATIONS, 2012, International Year of Cooperatives 2012. social.un.org/coopsyear/index.html.

WHITE L. Jr., 1967, The historical roots of our ecologic crisis. Science 155:1203-1207.

WILKINSON R. G. and PICKETT K. E., 2009, The Spirit Level: Why More Equal Societies Almost Always Do Better. Penguin. New York, NY.

Biodiversity conservation and the reduction of inequalities: the Namibian experience

Constance Corbier-Barthaux, Agence Française de Développement (AFD), Paris, France
Renaud Lapeyre, Institute for Sustainable Development and International Relations (Iddri), Paris, France

The ambiguous relationships between biodiversity, its conservation and poverty alleviation are the subject of much discussion (BILLÉ et al., 2012). While clear causal links have yet to be proven, evidence is starting to emerge from the field that supports the thesis of a possible synergy between biodiversity conservation policies and the fight against poverty and inequality.

The Namibian Community-Based Natural Resources Management (CBNRM) programme provides an interesting example of the ongoing promotion since the 1990s of participatory approaches to biodiversity management in southern and eastern Africa (CAMPFIRE in Zimbabwe, ADMADE in Zambia, NRM in Botswana, group ranches and conservancies in Kenya, etc.).

Namibia, with its population of about 2 million, has only been independent since 1990 and it continues to suffer today from the legacy of South African occupation. During South African rule almost all of the apartheid laws were imposed in Namibia (the black population was prohibited from property ownership, there was residential segregation and Bantustans were created, etc.). Despite a per capita income of 4,700 US dollars which places Namibia in the World Bank's group of upper middle income countries, rural poverty remains high (27% in 2010, compared to urban poverty of 9% and an overall national level of 19.5%) and inequalities in the country are among the world's highest, with a Gini coefficient of 0.6 in 2010 (the world average was 0.39 in 2007).

In this context, and based on a rich, diverse and endemic flora and fauna, the new democratic government has for 20 years tried to promote sustainable development that would simultaneously reduce poverty and inequality.

Devolution of use rights over flora and fauna

During the South African occupation, apartheid laws expropriated almost all of the black population's rights of ownership and their use of land and natural resources. In 1990, around 4,000 white farmers privately owned 44% of the land in Namibia and were entitled to harvest wildlife on it, while communal lands (which represented 41% of the territory) were populated by the majority of the black population (more than 1.5 million people) and remained the property of the South African government[1]. On communal land, management and use rights over flora and fauna remained the prerogative of the South African administrator. Faced with a total lack of rights over land and associated resources, poor rural communities were often forced to hunt and harvest plants illegally to survive, which led to rapid degradation of biodiversity (a situation that had already been aggravated by the independence war and drought). For example, in 1970 there were 300 desert elephants in the West of the country, a figure that was reduced to 70 individuals by 1982 (LONG and JONES, 2004). On the contrary, on the private land owned by white

---

1. National parks, also owned by the South African government, represent the remaining 15% of land.

FIGURE 1 Community conservancies, an important tool for nature conservation in Namibia

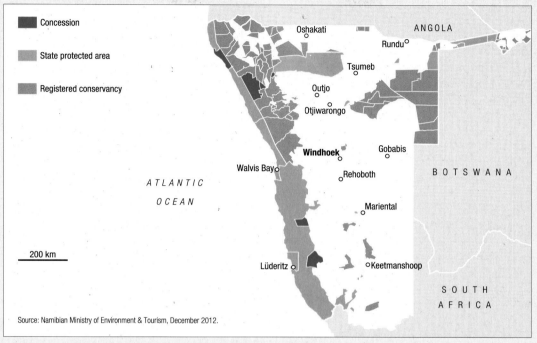

Concession

State protected area

Registered conservancy

ANGOLA
Oshakati
Rundu
Tsumeb
Outjo
Otjiwarongo
Windhoek   Gobabis
Walvis Bay
Rehoboth   BOTSWANA
ATLANTIC
OCEAN
Mariental
200 km
Lüderitz   Keetmanshoop
SOUTH
AFRICA
ATLANTIC OCEAN

Source: Namibian Ministry of Environment & Tourism, December 2012.

Between public protected areas, concessions and registered community conservancies, biodiversity is protected in more than a third of Namibian territory. 15% of the total population and most rural households live in these conservancies and thus benefit from the sustainable use of biodiversity.

farmers, wildlife abundance increased by 80% between 1972 and 1992 (Barnes and Jager, 1996).

Two laws were enacted to solve this situation. The first, known as the Nature Conservation Ordinance Amendment Act, was implemented in 1996 and allowed rural communities living on communal lands to create conservation areas (known as conservancies) where the community manages natural resources. Once a conservancy has been created and officially registered by the State, the community obtains rights of management and conditional use of the fauna and flora present on its territory. Specifically, the community receives hunting quotas that it can use at its discretion. To be recognized as a conservancy, a community must define a geographical area (with GPS-defined borders), agree on a constitution (defining the institutional rules of operation) and a list of members, elect an executive committee and draft a natural resources management

plan for the area, and vote on it, as well as a distribution plan for the generated income. The second law to be enacted was the Communal Land Reform Act of 2002, which further devolved land use rights to these conservancies that now control the allocation of land leases in their territory (rights of leasehold) for commercial purposes (mainly tourism).

Each conservancy can use these different rights that relate to the biodiversity on their territory to generate monetary and non-monetary benefits for its members. Possible activities include trophy hunting, hunting for the sale of game meat, subsistence hunting, the sale of live wild animals and also tourism. Each community is free to use these rights and to manage these activities on their own; or may delegate the management of commercial activities to a private operator, such as a professional hunter, butcher or tourism operator. In this case, the community signs a formal partnership agreement with the private company and/or the state (known as a joint venture or public-private partnership) and receives, on top of the private sector jobs created, lease fees and royalties from the private operator. All of the generated income stays in the locality (conservancy bank account) and is managed by the Executive Committee, which presents the annual accounts at the General Assembly's AGM for approval; there is no local or state tax on this income.

Increased biodiversity and the significant generation of local revenue

Since 1996 and the enactment of these laws, the number of conservancies has continued to increase in rural areas. There were four conservancies in 1998, by late 2003 this number had risen to 29, and in December 2012 there were 77. This represents 19% of the national territory and involves 15% of the total Namibian population. To this total, if we add the national parks, the private land under wildlife management status, as well as community concessions and forests, 37% of the Namibian territory is thus included within an institutional framework for the sustainable management of natural resources and biodiversity.

Such exponential growth has been made possible through the major support of local and international conservation associations (IRDNC, NNF, WWF, NACSO, etc.), as well as from international donors (USAID, GEF, FFEM, EU, etc.). This support for Namibian conservancies places the emphasis on the development of initiatives with a business economic logic: promotion within the conservancy of partnerships with the private sector as well as individual entrepreneurs, encouraging the emergence of small private economic businesses and the diversification of alternative economic activities.

In this context, financial and non-monetary benefits are significant, especially when compared to the income earned from agriculture or livestock breeding. In 1998, the annual benefit derived from conservancies, both economic and non-monetary combined, was estimated to be around 150,000 euros, while in 2010 this had escalated to 4 million euros. It is income earned from partnerships between conservancies and the tourism sector (1.9 million

BOX 1 **Work undertaken by the French Global Environment Facility (FGEF) in Namibia**

Through a project supported by the FGEF, the Namibian CBNRM programme has, among other goals, enabled the restoration of water points and the direct reintroduction of a total of 4,700 animals from rare species in 33 conservancies, one national park and one area of private land. At the local level, the Khoadi Hôas conservancy, which is located in the northWest of the country, has greatly benefited from this new community management of biodiversity: firstly, black rhino and black-faced impala were reintroduced here and are now managed locally; secondly, an EU-funded community lodge was built here, in partnership with a private operator (the Grootberg Lodge). By providing tourists with the opportunity to observe this rare wildlife, the lodge is able to employ and train 30 locals and pay royalties to the conservancy, which reinvests them in conservation and public infrastructure. Lapeyre (2011) showed that in 2007, between the 23 employees and their family dependents, the Grootberg Lodge provides livelihoods for about 115 people in the conservancy. Social mobility is also made possible: for example, a former farmer was initially appointed as a conservancy's game guard before being employed by the Lodge as a maintenance worker and then a black rhino tracker, before finally becoming a tour guide (after passing his driving licence, which was funded by the employer). This is a very good example of the possible synergy between empowerment, biodiversity conservation and income generation for local people.

euros in 2010, including lease fees, royalties and wages) that accounts for the largest part of these benefits, while hunting for sport is the second most important activity, bringing in 1.1 million euros in 2010 (i.e. 75% of the 2010 total can be attributed to these two activities).

A significant proportion of these incomes and non-economic benefits generated by the utilization of biodiversity covers the maintenance costs of a conservancy (employee wages, including community game guards and administrative staff, the purchase of all-terrain

FIGURE 2 Rising incomes in conservancies

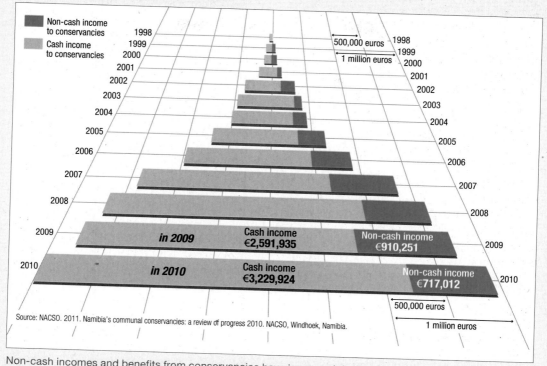

Non-cash income to conservancies

Cash income to conservancies

in 2009 — Cash income €2,591,935 — Non-cash income €910,251

in 2010 — Cash income €3,229,924 — Non-cash income €717,012

Source: NACSO. 2011. Namibia's communal conservancies: a review of progress 2010. NACSO, Windhoek, Namibia.

Non-cash incomes and benefits from conservancies have increased dramatically since 1998, as have cash incomes from partnerships with private tourism and trophy hunting operators. These incomes are mainly distributed in the form of local wages and royalties paid to rural communities.

vehicles and equipment for the monitoring of activities); while the rest is distributed as wages (for the employees of tourism lodges in conservancies, the trackers and other staff involved in trophy hunting operations, etc.); free housing for the lodge employees; free game meat distribution among local households; student scholarships; and dividends, which are paid to each family member but also fund community infrastructure (the purchase of ambulances, school or clinic construction, etc.)[2].

At the ecological level, the development of conservancy

areas has enabled a very significant improvement in the state of wildlife species. Indeed, populations of rare endemic species have increased since the mid-1990s, including mountain zebras, wild dogs, desert lions, desert elephants and black rhinos.

Do conservancies reduce poverty and inequality at the local level?

As mentioned above, the Namibian CBNRM programme generates income for the rural households in conservancies, but does this enable the reduction of socio-economic inequalities? Only a few studies have attempted to answer this question, to go beyond the simple analysis of the flow of financial income and the non-monetary benefits at the local level. Bandyopadhyay et al. (2004) conducted one such analysis, which was based on a survey of nearly

2. In 2009, 37% of income and benefits from the use of biodiversity in conservancies were used to cover the costs of conservation, while more than 40% of the profits were distributed in the form of wages by the private operators to employees of the tourism lodges. About 15% paid for the free distribution of game meat to families in the conservancies.

1,200 households in seven conservancies (in the regions of Caprivi and Kunene) and showed ambiguous results in terms of poverty and inequality reduction. It seems that, on the whole, conservancies have a positive effect on the financial wealth of households situated therein, but have a much more mixed impact on poor households specifically. On the one hand, because conservancies provide low-skilled jobs (such as game guards), less educated households (in terms of the level of education of the household's head) see their standard of living increase faster (measured through expenditure) than more educated households, although this is only marginally significant; similarly, in conservancies in the Caprivi region, the poorest households in terms of physical assets (durable goods) tend to see their living standards rise faster than richer households. On the other hand, in the Kunene region, households that are poor in physical assets have not benefited from a relative improvement in income from the establishment of conservancies, as compared with richer households; and neither have households that are poor in terms of livestock (goats and sheep) seen their standard of living rise faster than households that were richer in livestock. In general, as confirmed by Bandyopadhyay et al. (2010) through a 2006 survey of 965 households in eight conservancies, even if the Namibian programme does not favour elite capture of revenue (often cited as a potential limitation of community biodiversity management projects), neither is it demonstrably pro-poor[3].

Studies based on the sustainable livelihoods approach, such as Long (2004a, b) and Lapeyre (2010, 2011), draw similar conclusions: the benefits derived from activities in conservancies, especially through wages paid to local residents employed in partnership lodges and the income earned from tourism community projects (e.g. associations of guides), allow rural households, including poor ones, to increase their human capital (payment of school fees), their physical capital (purchase of livestock) and their social capital (contact with NGOs and donors) and thus serves as a safety net to reduce their vulnerability to economic and climatic downturns. However, it seems that these incomes, especially from tourism and from positions likely to be filled by less educated people, are still low and therefore serve more as a potential springboard towards stable employment, rather than a real way to reduce rural poverty. In this context it is also notable that better educated individuals usually monopolize the most qualified and best paid jobs in conservancies, in particular in the lodges, potentially accentuating inequalities at the local level.

Risks and limitations of the programme: its capacity to reduce inequality in rural areas

The model promoted by the CBNRM programme focuses primarily on charismatic wildlife and its habitat (elephants, rhinos, lions, etc.), and its commercial use via the upmarket private sectors of tourism and hunting, which are geographically and temporally volatile by nature. This approach seems most appropriate in conservancies that have the potential to be successfully managed in this way, which are those in the areas of Kunene and Caprivi. In these regions, the data show that a large majority of the programme's total benefits (high royalties and large numbers of employees) is derived from the small number of conservancies that have managed to enter into partnership agreements with a limited number of very reputable private tourism and hunting operators. Conversely, many conservancies have little tourism and wildlife potential and thus generate little revenue at the local level. Empirically, Lapeyre (2009) demonstrated that the four conservancies located in the Kunene region, which are very well endowed (wildlife, spectacular landscapes and UNESCO World Heritage listed monuments) and have a low population density, generate very significant income (for example, the Uibasen/Twyfelfontein conservancy in the northWest, with 230 inhabitants and a land area of 286 km², generated an income of 120 euros per capita and 98 euros per km² in 2007). In contrast, conservancies in the north of the country, which are much more populated and less well endowed (more agricultural landscapes with less charismatic fauna) have benefited little from the programme; for

---

3. Bandyopadhyay et al. (2010) even show that the probability of being a member of a conservancy, and thus to reap the associated benefits (see above) increases with the level of education of the household head.

example the Uukwaluudhi, King Nehale and Uukolonkadhi/ Ruacana conservancies generated between 0 and 2 euros per capita in 2007. This disparity is explained by the fact that tourism activities in conservancies (partnerships with private operators or community enterprises) are highly geographically concentrated: in 2007, four partnership lodges out of 25 generated half of the profits derived from this type of tourism, and nine lodges generated nearly three-quarters of this income. While seven tourism community projects out of 38 concentrated 80% of the distributed profits.

In summary, the programme requires a rethink on some of its policies if the objective is to ensure a balanced development on the entire national territory and to avoid reinforcing inequalities between conservancies or between members of the same conservancy. In this context, it seems appropriate that these activities involving biodiversity usage should be better linked and coordinated with "conventional" activities, such as agriculture and rural development, through a less sectorized ecosystem approach. ∎

REFERENCES

BANDYOPADHYAY S., HUMAVINDU M.N., SHYAMSUNDAR P., WANG L., 2004, "Do Households Gain from Community-Based Natural Resource Management? An Evaluation of Community Conservancies in Namibia", *World Bank Policy Research Working Paper*, n°3337

BANDYOPADHYAY S., GUZMAN J.C., LENDELVO, S., 2010, Communal conservancies and household welfare in Namibia, *DEA Research Discussion Paper* 82, Department of Environmental Affairs, Ministry of Environment and Tourism, Windhoek, Namibia, 29p

BARNES, J.I. and DE JAGER J.L.V., 1996, "Economic and financial incentives for wildlife use on private land in Namibia and the implications for policy", *South African Journal of Wildlife Research*, 26: pp.37-46.

BILLÉ R., LAPEYRE R., PIRARD R., 2012, "Biodiversity conservation and poverty alleviation: a way out of the deadlock?", *S.A.P.I.E.N.S.*, 5(1): pp.1-15.

LAPEYRE R., 2009, *Rural communities, the State and the Market: A New-Institutional Analysis of Tourism Governance and Impacts in Namibian Communal Lands*, PhD thesis, University of St Quentin-en-Yvelines, France.

LAPEYRE R., 2010, "Community-based tourism as a sustainable solution to maximise impacts locally? The Tsiseb Conservancy case, Namibia", *Development Southern Africa*, 27(5), pp.757-772

LAPEYRE R., 2011, "The Grootberg lodge partnership in Namibia: towards poverty alleviation and empowerment for long-term sustainability?", *Current Issues in Tourism*, 14(3), p.221-234.

LONG S.A., 2004, *Livelihoods and CBNRM in Namibia: The findings of the WILD Project*. Final technical report to the WILD project, Ministry of Environment and Tourism, Windhoek, Namibia, 289p

LONG S.A., JONES B.T.B., 2004, "Contextualising CBNRM in Namibia", in Long, S.A. (ed.), *Livelihoods and CBNRM in Namibia. The findings of the WILD Project*. Final technical report to the WILD project, Ministry of Environment and Tourism, Windhoek, Namibia, 289p, pp.25-40.

ACRONYMS

ADMADE: Administrative Management Design project

CAMPFIRE: Communal Areas Management Programme for Indigenous Resources

CBNRM: Community-Based Natural Resource Management

IRDNC: Integrated Rural Development and Nature Conservation

NNF: Namibia Nature Foundation

WWF: World Wildlife Fund

NACSO: Namibian Association of CBNRM (Community-Based Natural Resource Management) Support Organisations

NRM: Natural Resource Management project

USAID: United States Agency for International Development

GEF: Global Environment Facility

FFEM: Fonds Français pour l'Environnement Mondial

FGEF: French Global Environment Facility

EU: European Union

UNESCO: United Nations Educational, Scientific and Cultural Organization

In their book, The Sprit Level: Why More Equal Societies Almost Always Do Better, Richard Wilkinson and Kate Pickett develop a thesis – "equality is healthy" – that has been incorrectly interpreted. The authors do not argue that income and wealth inequality directly and entirely cause dysfunctional societies, nor do they call for an equalizing of incomes to achieve absolute equality. Ultimately, improvements in living conditions depend on the quality of programmes funded through taxation and redistribution policies.

Income inequalities, health inequalities and social progress

Sridhar Venkatapuram
London School of Hygiene and Tropical Medecine, London, United Kingdom

Different kinds of inequalities within low and middle-income countries as well as global or "North-South" inequalities have been recognizable for a long time. However, since the global economic crisis of 2008, inequality has resurfaced as a major public and political concern within rich countries. This crisis brought to light the unprecedented scale of the personal incomes and wealth of bankers, corporate executives and the top one per cent of the population in countries such as the United States and the United Kingdom. Greater awareness of the absolute and relative levels of wealth also produced much discussion about the causal role of the pursuit of personal wealth, on a scale of millions and billions, in the near collapse of the global financial system. The resulting social demonstrations such as the "Occupy" movement, many post-2008 election campaigns and anti-austerity protests have focused on inequalities – in wealth, job prospects for the young, education costs, social security, old age security, and so forth. It could also be argued that the political revolutions across the Middle East were motivated by inequality. After all, the Arab Spring was catalysed by a Tunisian fruit seller who set himself on fire as a form of protest expressing frustration at his relative inequality of opportunity to achieve a minimally decent life.

The global economic crisis and other world events created an unusually receptive environment for the publication of Richard Wilkinson and Kate Pickett's book, "The Sprit Level: Why More Equal Societies Almost Always Do Better" (hereafter "TSL") in 2009. The book has been fantastically popular in many countries because it purports to provide scientific evidence about how inequality is bad for societies as well as what to do about it. TSL's greatest appeal is perhaps that it is understood to argue specifically for the case that income and wealth inequality is bad for societies and, therefore, aggressive redistribution of income and wealth is, or will be, good for societies. The authors have given speeches around the world to a wide range of audiences, often managing to reach inaccessible and influential policy makers. The wide interest in their book is partly due to the context of great uncertainty and debate about what constitutes good social and economic systems. The authors seem to provide academic and scientific arguments that are more coherent, evidence-based and legitimate than the demands from the protestors in the streets or the opinions of media pundits.

A careful reading of the book, however, as well as an appreciation of the body of scientific literature that TSL draws from, shows that neither one of the two popular take-away messages is accurate. The authors do not argue that income and wealth inequalities directly and wholly cause dysfunctional societies or cause the lives of people to go badly. Nor do they advocate a simple wholesale redistribution of income and wealth, or an "equalizing down" of incomes to achieve absolute equality. So if these two take-away messages are not accurate reflections of TSL, then what exactly is their argument?

Income inequality and health

The central thesis of TSL is that in countries that are above the Gross National Income (GNI) threshold of $25,000 per person there is a positive relationship between income inequality and a wide variety of social problems. That is, above the $25,000 GNI per capita threshold, the more income inequality in a country, the greater amount of social problems including poor health, teenage births, homicides, imprisonment rates, low educational performance of children, and so forth (WILKINSON and PICKETT, 2009: p. 19). This thesis challenges a variety of dominant views about the causes of "social bads" in a variety of domains, and most prominently it argues against the view that material poverty is the main cause of such problems. Wilkinson and Pickett show that average levels of income across countries, and across regions and states within countries, do not have a statistical relationship with the levels of social ills. They interpret this finding as meaning that in rich countries (i.e. above $25,000 GNI per capita) there has been a delinking between absolute material conditions and quality of life and that, in comparison, the level of income inequality has a positive statistical relationship with levels of social problems above this threshold.

The identification of this relationship has led many to conclude that inequality in incomes directly *causes* many social problems and therefore, reducing income inequalities, most immediately through income redistribution, is the necessary remedy. Such a conclusion may be understandable because a whole variety of ideologies and intuitions about equality support the idea of income equality or at least, support the reduction of gross inequalities between the rich and the poor. However, this interpretation or policy prescription does not accurately reflect the conclusions presented in TSL. While the authors highlight that countries that do better regarding

FIGURE 1 A fairer society is less sick

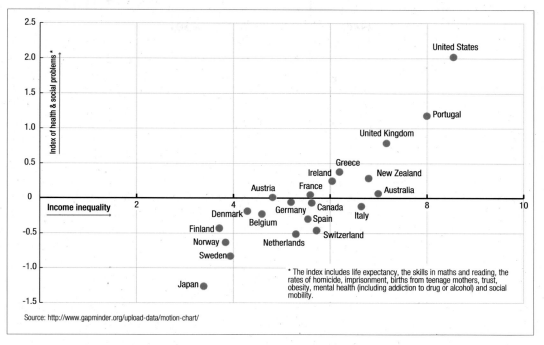

Source: http://www.gapminder.org/upload-data/motion-chart/

The work of Wilkinson and Pickett shows that the degree of inequality in a society is strongly correlated with the level of social problems experienced by that society. The most egalitarian societies (Japan, Sweden, Finland, Denmark) are also those with the lowest levels of certain problems, including obesity, incarceration rates, numbers of teenage mothers and people with low mathematical ability.

various health achievements and social bads have redistributive tax systems and large state welfare programmes, they also suggest that there are many different ways to achieve such outcomes (WILKINSON and PICKETT, 2009: Ch. 16). To understand why the equalization of incomes or the limitation of income inequalities prior to taxation is only one possible avenue to improving social progress requires a deeper look into the research. Wilkinson and Pickett argue that income inequality shows how hierarchical a society is; income inequalities show the social distances between people and the functioning of social stratification (WILKINSON and PICKETT, 2009: p. 27). Income inequalities reflect social inequalities, and they both reinforce each other.

Furthermore, evidence is also presented that seems to show that the steeper the social gradient of a particular social problem – i.e. the more skewed the distribution of a problem is towards the bottom of the socio-economic hierarchy – the stronger the relationship with income inequality. Moreover, the authors argue that a relationship between income inequality and social bads exists, or only becomes visible, when comparing groups that have meaningful social differences; income inequality would not appear as a contributing factor to problems among families within a deprived neighbourhood, but would appear when comparing neighbour-hoods of different levels of wealth. Something about the social differences between groups of people, most easily represented by income differences, seems to play an important part in the levels of social ills experienced by those at the bottom *as well as* the higher levels experienced throughout the *entire* population. But what are these social differences if not directly income inequality, and how do they shape the pathways to various social problems?

Social Epidemiology

Research on social gradients (i.e. inequalities across the socio-economic hierarchy) and influence of social factors on human deprivations, particularly health related issues, have been a central focus of the relatively new discipline of *social epidemiology*. It is often contrasted with "classic" or "biomedical" epidemiology in which the scope of research on the causes of disease is limited to individual-level factors that include individual biology, individual behaviours, and individual-level exposures to harmful organisms and physical particles. These three categories of factors are often metaphorically described as making up a multi-factoral "causal pie" or forming the links in a "web of causation" (Krieger, 2000; Rothman et al., 2008).

Despite its dominance for most of the 20th century, this individual-level biomed-ical model of disease has been increasingly challenged over the past four decades because of its persistent limitations in fully identifying the causes of many chronic and degenerative diseases, as well as its inability to explain the dynamics and distri-bution patterns of population-level health (Syme, 1996; Krieger, 1994; Krieger, 2001; Susser and Susser, 1996a; Susser and Susser, 1996b; Schwartz et al., 1999; Susser, 1999). Molecular epidemiology, which delves even deeper into the individual, has been promoted as a panacea to the classic model's explanatory limitations. In contrast, social epidemiology, which focuses on supra-individual factors, and the basic tenets of its research, has received considerably less public attention – despite its insights and productivity (Marmot and Wilkinson, 1999; Berkman and Kawachi, 2000; Marmot et al., 1997). The lack of greater public awareness of social epidemiological research may or may not be surprising, depending on one's worldview, as social epidemiology brings to light two very politically charged issues: that of the social causation of preventable illness and mortality, and the unequal social distribution of illness and mortality. Unlike classic or molecular epidemiology, social epidemiology puts social conditions, policies and choices squarely in the causal explanations of preventable illness and mortality and their social patterning.

Moving away from the classic biomedical model that was very productive and dominant in the late twentieth century, social epidemiologists are expanding the causal chain outward from the proximate individual-level factors to include the *causes of the proximate causes*, and identifying their discrete and cumulative effects throughout the life cycle, starting from the womb. Social epidemiology also expands the causal chain upwards to incorporate multiple levels of factors – such as the

FIGURE 2 Life expectancy depends on equity

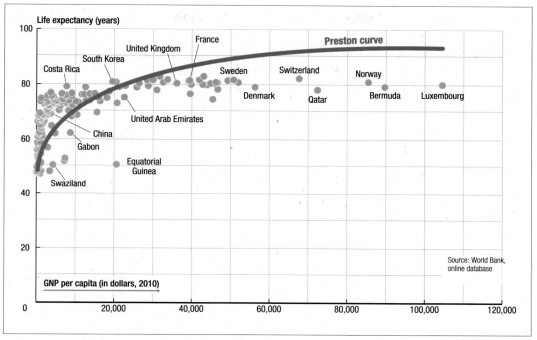

The Preston curve is a standard tool for studying the relationship between health and equity. Strong equity increases the average life expectancy of members of a society. The life expectancy of a Norwegian or Luxembourgian, people who live among the world's most egalitarian societies in terms of income, is more than 30 years higher than that of a Swaziland resident, where the degree of inequality is among the highest in the world.

macro political, economic, and social policies and processes – that affect health. These factors are being quantified and integrated into an epidemiological model of causation and distribution of illness and mortality in individuals and groups. This bridging or integrating of the social and the biological has been characterized as creating a "Chinese boxes" paradigm (SUSSER and SUSSER, 1996a; SUSSER and SUSSER, 1996b). The metaphor aims to reflect the understanding that an individual's health is determined by multiple and increasingly distal factors, which at the same time profoundly shape the immediate context or the more proximate factors. To consider this another way, just as the sun is distant from Earth, but still fundamentally determines the parameters of the biological functioning of human beings across the entire planet; similarly, there are many social factors from the global level downwards that, although remote, profoundly impact the functioning of individuals differently in different places in the world.

The focus on social factors affecting health is not fundamentally new. There is a long history of research into the identification of the role of the social environment in community and social medicine, while Louis-René Villermé and Rudolph Virchow conducted epidemiological work in this field in the 19th century. However, modern social epidemiology harnesses the most current epidemiological tools and methodologies combined with sociological analysis to explicitly identify supra-individual social phenomena that affect both the *causation and distribution* of ill-health across individuals and social groups, within and across countries (BERKMAN and KAWACHI, 2000; MARMOT and WILKINSON, 1999).

In light of the productivity and profound insights of social epidemiology, the late J. W. Lee, then Director-General of the World Health Organization, set up the WHO Commission on Social Determinants of Health ("the Commission") in 2005. Its mission was to collect and synthesize global evidence on the social determinants of health, assess their impact on health inequity, and make recommendations for action to address that inequity[1]. Members of the Commission and its secretariat were motivated by three driving forces: a belief in social justice, respect for evidence, and frustration that there was far too little action on the social determinants of ill health and health inequalities[2]. These powerfully motivating forces led to three years of detailed work compiling and analysing research, consultations with experts from around the world as well as across many disciplines and professions, meetings with governments and practitioners, and the production of a final report and recommendations. Rather than being an end in itself, the work of the Commission and the resultant report, *Closing the gap in a generation: Health equity through action on the social determinants of health* was intended to instigate discussions within institutions and the public sphere, and help promote social action and policies to advance health and health equity, both within countries and transnationally.

In the first truly global application of social epidemiology, the Commission articulated the causal nested framework in the following way:

1. The conditions of daily life in which individuals are born, grow, live, work and age determine their experience of morbidity and length of life span.

2. These daily living conditions produce proximal determinants, such as exposure to harmful substances and biological risks; availability of material needs, such as food, potable water, shelter and health care; as well as social environments that affect psychobiological pathways and health-related behaviours.

3. These daily conditions in turn have structural drivers or "'causes of causes" – the economic, social and political conditions that, together with background social

1. Information about the Commission is available at http://www.who.int/social_determinants/thecommission/en/index.html. For the complete final report, see Commission on Social Determinants of Health, Closing the gap in a generation: Health equity through action on the social determinants of health. Final Report of the Commission on Social Determinants of Health (Geneva: World Health Organization, 2008). Available at http://whqlibdoc.who.int/publications/2008/9789241563703_eng.pdf.

2. This frustration is associated with two main areas. First, that the concern for addressing preventable ill-health and mortality has to go beyond healthcare to also include the causes, particularly the social conditions. Most global and national health policies often focus only on healthcare. The second source of frustration was that despite decades of epidemiological research findings on the social causes of ill-health and mortality, health policy makers were not making use of the findings.

and cultural norms, create and distribute the proximate causes across individuals and social groups.

The starting point of social epidemiology is that individual-level factors do not provide sufficient causal explanations for the significant health differences between groups of human beings defined by such social characteristics as nationality, education, income, occupation, gender, race/ethnicity or geographical residence. The hypothesis is that factors created by the social environment have a significant influence in the causal pathways to illness in individuals and unequally distribute ill-health across social groups. Under this general hypothesis, there are a number of different pathways or explanations that are currently being researched (BAMBRA, 2011; MACKENBACH, 2012). Following this line of reasoning, the Commission started from the premise that there is no purely biological causal explanation for the marked differences in life expectancies across countries; for example, the gross inequality in life-expectancy between the Japanese (83 years) and Malawians (48 years) cannot be explained by differences in the biological endowments of the Japanese compared to Malawian populations. Rather, the Commission argued that differences in life expectancies and health profiles are determined by social environments – by economic, political, and social policies and processes driven by social and cultural values that create and distribute the daily living conditions of people in different locations around the world.

Importantly, social epidemiological research not only explodes outward the classic model of epidemiology from the individual unit of analysis, but the research also militates against the various social consequences of applying the biomedical model. Some of these social consequences include the narrow focus on health care provision and behavioural change as the primary avenues to improving health; being inattentive to social group inequalities in health; exaggerating individual volition and responsibility in health outcomes; and focusing on the material poverty of the most disadvantaged while ignoring psychosocial environments that produce preventable ill health in the entire population. Such drawbacks of a narrowly individual-level analysis are not only a concern for domestic health policies, but also for global health policies. These can include, inter alia, development assistance for health programmes, transnational health policies, or domestic health policies addressing extraterritorial health threats.

The Wilkinson Thesis

It is this context of expanding the scope of epidemiology and identifying the social determinants of ill health and premature mortality as well as their distribution that has produced the TSL. Starting in the early 1990s Richard Wilkinson began publishing research findings showing that greater income inequality in societies correlated with a lower average population health and higher social inequalities in health (WILKINSON, 1992). The "Wilkinson thesis" which was narrower in scope than that presented in TSL, asserted that in countries above a $25,000 GNP per capita threshold, larger average income differences between classes are associated with a steeper gradient in health achievements and higher, overall premature mortality in the entire population (KAWACHI et al., 1999; WILKINSON, 1997; WILKINSON, 2000). Below the threshold, income inequality shows no correlation with the gradient or distribution in health outcomes.

Across a number of industrialized countries, and within regions of countries, Wilkinson shows that the steepness of the health gradient is indeed associated with level of income inequality. In TSL Wilkinson and Pickett show that income inequality is linked with a wide range of social problems aside from disparities in health achievements (WILKINSON and PICKETT, 2009). While many have understood this research as referring to material determinants of health, Wilkinson argues that the effect of income inequality lies first in the *psychosocial* effects of being of lower social status, experiencing subordination, or being denied respect (WILKINSON, 1996). Entrenched and increasing income inequality affects social standing and in turn, leads to particular biological processes in the individual, such as chronic anxiety, permanent increases in stress hormones such as cortisol, more atherosclerosis and poorer immunity. The total result of these processes that occur through psychobiological pathways is said to be analogous to rapid ageing (KAWACHI et al., 1999, p 493). In TSL, Wilkinson & Pickett further argue that an environment of gross inequality undermines trust between people and community life, including increased violence. It also increases status competition and consumerism. And, by affecting early life, it affects people's abilities to build relationships, empathize, and their aggressiveness (WILKINSON and PICKETT, 2009: p. 231).

The Wilkinson thesis, development and health inequalities

A quick review of the literature on social epidemiology soon reveals that most research on the social determinants of health and social inequalities in health achievements has so far been done mostly in developed economies. Social epidemiology begins with an interest in the persistence of ill health and the unequal distribution of preventable ill health and mortality despite the availability of healthcare and social programmes to meet basic needs. In contrast, health research in developing countries has largely been focused on the causes of infectious diseases and controlling fertility, and less focused on the social inequalities in health achievements. The lack of research on social determinants in developing countries appears to support the economist Angus Deaton's argument that for centuries the better-off have often benefited from new health technologies first (DEATON, 2011). That is, rich people and rich countries are often the first beneficiaries of state-of-the-art technologies, including research.

However, the Commission argued that social determinants of health and health inequalities affect all countries (WORLD HEALTH ORGANIZATION and COMMISSION ON SOCIAL DETERMINANTS OF HEALTH, 2008). The final report showed how social gradients are visible in rich as well as poor countries. But efforts to apply social epidemiology and to globalize concern for the social determinants of health appear

FIGURE 3 Child well-being is an indicator of societal equity

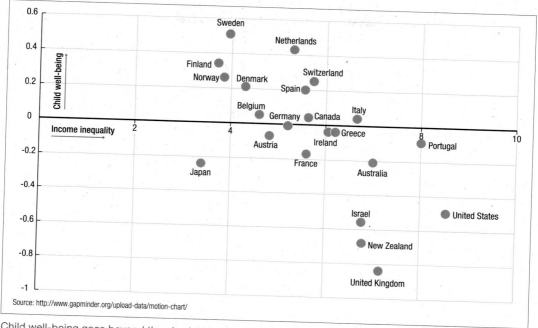

Source: http://www.gapminder.org/upload-data/motion-chart/

Child well-being goes beyond the physical health of children. Equitable societies offer a better development framework for their younger members, with interesting exceptions such as Japan, which despite having a very equal distribution of income does not rank highly for child well-being.

to be weakened by research coming from within social epidemiology. In particular, by Wilkinson's thesis that it is only above the threshold level of $25,000 GNI per capita that the levels and gradient in mortality correlate with income inequality. This threshold, he writes, "represents a transition from the primacy of material constraints to social constraints as the limiting condition on the quality of human life" (KAWACHI et al., 1999: p 27).

However, while his main finding is about what is happening above the threshold, Wilkinson may be far too quick in his conclusions about what is happening below it, and in making a peculiar distinction between material and social constraints. Under this threshold, it is far from certain that the determinants and distribution of premature mortality and impairments in societies can be adequately explained as being due largely to material constraints, including a lack of commodities such as healthcare. There may be a danger here of making the common mistake of confusing the cure with addressing the cause. For example, the poor reproductive health of girls and women, including deplorable rates of maternal mortality which are largely preventable, or the spread of HIV/AIDS are caused by social and cultural practices as much as they are by material deprivations, if not more so. To conclude that poor health and premature mortality below the threshold is caused primarily by material constraints, based on a finding about income inequality above $25,000 GNI per capita, seems to simply represent the reassertion of a theory as being applicable to poor countries, when this theory is being forcefully rejected as having any relevance to rich countries. Just as the relationship between material conditions and ill health and quality of life is not straightforward in rich countries, nor is it the case in poor countries.

It would be even an greater error to conclude from Wilkinson's thesis – given its identification of a threshold level or turning point of $25,000 GNI per capita –that economic development in the form of rising GNI per capita up to the threshold automatically brings with it improvements in life expectancy and lower prevalence of impairments. The argument that material conditions and health achievements are delinked above the GNI threshold may lead some to the conclusion that below the threshold, rising GNI automatically improves these material conditions and consequently improves health and quality of life. There is a widely held view, particularly among economists, that economic growth *inevitably* leads to dramatic improvements in life expectancy and infant mortality, while decreasing the overall burden of impairments and improving social prosperity (Bloom and Canning, 2007; Pritchett and Summers, 1996). This theory, which is often attributed to Samuel Preston (Preston, 1975; Preston, 2007), underlies a popular theory of epidemiological transition describing the movement of societies from an initial "under-developed" stage with a high burden of infectious diseases, to an "industrialised" stage with a high burden of chronic diseases (Omran, 1971). However, Simon Szreter and others argue that there is little historical evidence of an automatic link between economic growth and the improvement of health or welfare of individuals (Szreter, 1997; Biggs et al., 2010b; Sen, 1981).

In fact, Szreter, a public health historian, argues that industrialization released very disruptive forces into British society that were managed by the politics of public-health advocates and institutions. That is, social action had an influential role in the management of the process and the consequences of industrialization which do not appear to be captured by Preston's and Omran's theories. Amartya Sen also points to the modern-day importance of public discussion and agitation in the domain of health policy in such places as Thailand, India and China (Sen, 2011). In parallel discussions in economics, Sudhir Anand and Martin Ravallion show that indeed growth in GNP per capita is correlated with increasing life expectancy. But those improvements in life expectancies are largely explained by poverty alleviation programmes and spending on public health goods and services (Sen, 1999; Anand and Ravallion, 1993). In fact, after accounting for these two factors, there is not much left of the link between improvements in average incomes and life expectancy. So, a rise in GNP improves health only when resources are marshalled towards public health goods and services. Sen and Jean Drèze show a similar situation in India (Drèze and Sen, 2002). More recently, Biggs and colleagues have looked at 22 Latin American countries and shown that the relationship between GDP per capita and health is mediated by poverty levels and income inequality (BIGGS et al., 2010a).

It is worth expounding on the relationship between economic development and health because it is social factors that determine health and longevity, both above and below Wilkinson's GNI per capita threshold. Wilkinson's distinction between social versus material "constraints" on either side of the threshold seems based on the role of psychological factors related to relative social status and their influence on the onset of disease, factors that become prominent above the threshold. He contrasts these psychosocial pathways with material conditions affecting the health of individuals below the threshold. But why should psychosocial factors be considered as the only social factors affecting health? Given the wide variety of social factors that are currently the focus of social epidemiological research, it is surprising that the proximate cause model of disease and health impairment is being reasserted in poor countries. Much of the above-cited research (by Szreter, Anand, Ravillion, Biggs, Sen and others) has shown that economic growth on its own does not automatically improve health and longevity and, in particular, it does not ensure equitable achievements across populations. These improve because economic growth is usually accompanied by various social policies and provisions, such as poverty alleviation and investment in medical and public health programmes, as well as education. Economic policies are themselves important social determinants. And, of course, there are the exemplary cases of Costa Rica, Cuba, Sri Lanka and the Indian state of Kerala which achieve better health outcomes than many developed economies, despite their low GNP per capita, because of the positive impact of their social choices on the proximate causes of health (SEN, 1999, pp. 46-47).

The identification of a threshold where psychosocial factors related to relative inequality influence ill-health (and other social problems) should not be understood to mean that social factors do not affect health below the threshold. Indeed, social factors underlie both the psychological pathways in richer countries and the material pathways in poorer countries. In both rich and poor countries, going back in the chain of causation of ill health or any kind of impairment will inevitably lead to a meaningful social factor. TSL has largely been of interest to audiences in rich countries because of the public interest in income inequalities. However, for a global audience, an emphasis on the threshold as the tipping point at which material factors give way to socio-psycho-biological factors risks perpetuating the idea that rising GNP or economic growth automatically, without additional social policies, leads to health improvements. The notion that economic growth without supplementary social strategies will achieve improvements in health and quality of life has been profoundly contested in mainstream economics, but such debate does not seem to have reached social epidemiologists, perhaps because they mainly work in developed country contexts with little exposure to development related literature.

The relative influence of different factors on health varies across rich and poor societies, and across individuals. Wilkinson showed that in the United States and United Kingdom, psychological pathways have a great affect on health. In other countries, such as those researched by development economists, health may be more influenced by material pathways determined by levels of public spending on social goods and programmes. The important thing to recognize is that even the proximate material causes of ill health in developing countries have social determinants that can range from acts of commission as well as social neglect.

It is also worth noting that Wilkinson and Pickett identify a variety of interventions to increase social equality, including reducing gross income differences before tax, redistributive taxes and welfare programmes. In the study of social hierarchy phenomena, it is clear that acting on incomes is really only one possible means of reducing distances between social positions. Given that income inequality does not directly cause poor health – the fact that one person's monthly wage is less than another's does not directly induce disease in the former – the real focus is on what is happening in the lives of individuals in relation to other individuals and groups. Income intervention is only one way to help individuals to avoid disease and other social deprivations. Above and below the GNI threshold, the actual target is an individual's *ability* to achieve various physical and mental functionings, including the ability to avoid illness and premature mortality.

In light of the expansive scope of social epidemiological research to supplement the biomedical model, as well as the need to integrate debates on health and development, there is a pressing need for a "unified theory" of health causation and distribution. Social epidemiologists are aware of the need for a better paradigm for epidemiology that captures both individual and macro-level factors. But as the above discussion highlights, even the best social epidemiology research has not yet integrated state-of-the-art research on health and sustainable development, and it requires a better grounding in the realities of rich and poor societies. In addition, micro and macro analyses remain confined to developed country contexts and various assumptions about developing countries are not being sufficiently explored. There is a need for a unified theory that is applicable to the entire human species to defensibly allocate responsibility for health causation and distribution among the four categories of nature/biology, social conditions, environmental conditions and individual behaviour/agency. While a number of candidate paradigms exist, Amartya Sen's work on development as a form of increasing capabilities offers great potential as a basis for such a theory (VENKATAPURAM, 2011). Sen was a member of the WHO Commission and a significant influence on the Commission's arguments.

Conclusion

Given the renewed focus on income inequality as a result of TSL, it seems relevant to draw attention to long-standing discussions on precisely this subject in economics and especially, development economics. For decades, Sen has argued for a single or unified approach to evaluating social progress or sustainable development for all countries whether they are rich, poor or middle income. A central idea in this approach is the need to shift social and analytical concern from income inequality to economic inequality (SEN, 1997). Reflecting a long established view held by many economists, Sen argues that the importance of income is instrumental and circumstantially contingent rather than intrinsic and categorical (this conclusion is reaffirmed by Wilkinson's research which highlights income's effect on health and quality of life, rather than its intrinsic nature). Sen demonstrates the important insights that are revealed when the impact of other social and economic influences on the quality of life are examined, aside from incomes and their inequalities. While not wholly discarding concerns over income inequality, which does have important consequences, Sen argues for an approach that targets capabilities, or the freedoms that individuals have to be and do what they have reason to value.

Integrating this approach with the Wilkinson thesis would mean that our moral and practical target is not a narrow focus on income inequality but the unequal capabilities of people to achieve good health or live a good life. Indeed, Wilkinson has clearly found that there is something about the how unequal societies are which affects the inequalities in the capabilities of individuals in society to pursue flourishing lives. Inequality in this view is not only morally bad as it reflects inequalities in the abilities of people to pursue good lives. It is doubly bad because the higher the inequality, the less free the people are in the lower parts of the social hierarchy, and the less free is the entire population.

While income inequality is indicative of social inequality, and also a cause of it, there is a wide range of social factors that cause ill health and other social ills. The focus on income alone therefore constitutes an incomplete and possibly incorrect approach. Wilkinson and other social epidemiologists have brought to light the important social factors that negatively impact on the lives of individuals in rich countries, while other researchers, particularly development economists, have shown how social action and public policies, in addition to economic growth, impacts on health achievements in poor countries. The goal now is to establish an analysis framework that addresses the entire human species on a single plane, which the Commission is attempting to do with its framework on the causation and distribution of health across the world. The great insight of Wilkinson's thesis is that social inequalities in different domains, one of which is income, have a profound influence on the overall levels and distribution of constraints on the quality of life of individuals, social groups and national populations. It would be a shame if this major insight was forgotten and replaced by a more familiar focus on income inequality. ■

REFERENCES

ANAND S. and RAVALLION M., 1993, Human development in poor countries: On the role of private incomes and public services, *Journal of Economic Perspectives,* 7, 133-150.

BAMBRA C., 2011, Health inequalities and welfare state regimes: theoretical insights on a public health "puzzle". *Journal of Epidemiology and Community Health,* 65, 740-745.

BERKMAN L. F. and KAWACHI I. O. 2000. *Social epidemiology,* New York, Oxford University Press.

BIGGS B., KING L., BASU S. and STUCKLER D., 2010a, Is wealthier always healthier? The impact of national income level, inequality, and poverty on public health in Latin America. *Social Science & Medicine.*

BIGGS B., KING L., BASU S. and STUCKLER D., 2010b, Is wealthier always healthier? The impact of national income level, inequality, and poverty on public health in Latin America. *Social Science and Medicine.*

BLOOM D. E. and CANNING D., 2007, Commentary: The Preston curve 30 years on: Still sparking fires. *International Journal of Epidemiology,* 36, 498-499.

DEATON A., 2011, What does the empirical evidence tell us about the injustice of health inequalities? Princeton: Princeton Center for Health and Wellbeing.

DRÈZE J. and SEN A. K., 2002, *India : development and participation,* Oxford, Oxford University Press.

KAWACHI I., KENNEDY B. P. and WILKINSON R. G. (eds.), 1999, *The Society and Population Health Reader. Income Inequality and Health,* New York: The New Press.

KRIEGER N., 1994, Epidemiology and the web of causation: has anyone seen the spider? *Soc Sci Med,* 39, 887-903.

KRIEGER N., 2000, Epidemiology and social sciences: Towards a critical reengagement in the 21st century. *Epidemiologic Reviews,* 22, 155-163.

KRIEGER N., 2001, Theories for social epidemiology in the 21st century: an ecosocial perspective. *Int J Epidemiol,* 30, 668-77.

MACKENBACH J. P., 2012, The persistence of health inequalities in modern welfare states: The explanation of a paradox. *Social Science & Medicine,* 75, 761-769.

MARMOT M., RYFF C. D., BUMPASS L. L., SHIPLEY M. and MARKS N. F., 1997, Social inequalities in health: next questions and converging evidence. *Soc Sci Med,* 44, 901-10.

MARMOT M. G. and WILKINSON R. G., 1999, *Social determinants of health,* Oxford; New York, Oxford University Press.

OMRAN A. R., 1971, The epidemiologic transition. A theory of the epidemiology of population change. *The Milbank Quarterly,* 49, 509-38.

PRESTON S. H., 1975, Changing Relation between Mortality and Level of Economic-Development. *Population Studies-a Journal of Demography,* 29, 231-248.

PRESTON S. H., 2007, Response: On "The changing relation between mortality and level of economic development". *International Journal of Epidemiology,* 36, 502-503.

PRITCHETT L. and SUMMERS L. H., 1996, Wealthier is healthier. *Journal of Human Resources,* 31, 841-868.

ROTHMAN K. J., GREENLAND S. and LASH T. L., 2008, *Modern epidemiology,* Philadelphia, Wolters Kluwer Health/Lippincott Williams & Wilkins.

SCHWARTZ S., SUSSER E. and SUSSER M., 1999, A future for epidemiology? *Annual Review of Public Health,* 20, 15-33.

SEN A., 1981, Public Action and the Quality of Life in Developing-Countries. *Oxford Bulletin of Economics and Statistics,* 43, 287-319.

SEN A., 1997, From Income Inequality to Economic Inequality. *Southern Economic Journal,* 64, 384-401.

SEN A., 1999, *Development as Freedom,* New York, Knopf.

SEN A., 2011, Learning from others. *Lancet,* 377, 200-1.

SUSSER M., 1999, Should the epidemiologist be a social scientist or a molecular biologist? *International Journal of Epidemiology,* 28, S1019-S1022.

SUSSER M. and SUSSER E., 1996a, Choosing a future for epidemiology: I. Eras and paradigms. *Am J Public Health,* 86, 668-73.

SUSSER M. and SUSSER E., 1996b, Choosing a future for epidemiology: II. From black box to Chinese boxes and eco-epidemiology. *Am J Public Health,* 86, 674-7.

SYME S. L., 1996, Rethinking disease: where do we go from here? *Ann Epidemiol,* 6, 463-8.

SZRETER S., 1997, Economic growth, disruption, deprivation, disease, and death: On the importance of the politics of public health for development. *Population and Development Review,* 23, 693-.

VENKATAPURAM S., 2011, *Health Justice. An Argument from the Capabilities Approach,* Cambridge, Polity Press.

WILKINSON R. G., 1992, Income distribution and life expectancy. *Bmj,* 304, 165-8.

WILKINSON R. G., 1996, *Unhealthy societies : the afflictions of inequality,* London, Routledge.

WILKINSON R. G., 1997, Socioeconomic determinants of health. Health inequalities: relative or absolute material standards? *Bmj,* 314, 591-5.

WILKINSON R. G., 2000, The need for an interdisciplinary perspective on the social determinants of health. *Health Economics,* 9, 581-3.

WILKINSON R. G. and PICKETT, K., 2009, *The spirit level: why more equal societies almost always do better,* London, Allen Lane.

WORLD HEALTH ORGANIZATION and COMMISSION ON SOCIAL DETERMINANTS OF HEALTH, 2008, Closing the gap in a generation. Health equity through action on the social determinants of health. Geneva: World Health Organization.

Towards universal social health protection in Cambodia

Virginie Diaz Pedregal, Agence Française de Développement, Paris, France
David I. Levine, University of California, Berkeley, United States of America
Stéphanie Pamies-Sumner, Agence Française de Développement, Paris, France
Ian Ramage, Domrei Research and Consulting, Phnom Penh, Cambodia

Cambodia has to tackle a "double epidemiological burden". The country faces the typically characteristic pathologies of developing countries (tuberculosis, dengue, malaria...), and also diseases more specific to prosperous societies (diabetes, cardiovascular diseases, cancer...). Exacerbating the problem is the fact that Cambodia is poorly equipped to address these issues.

Self-prescription and self-treatment are common practice (Poursat, 2004). Members of the population frequently consult private doctors and traditional therapists who have had widely varying amounts of training. The public authorities do not yet have control over this lucrative private sector. Meanwhile, public facilities go underused (according to the 2010 Demographic and Health Survey (DHS) only around 25% of the population sought first treatment in the public sector (DHS, 2010)). Unofficial payments often add to the costs of official treatment prices (Meessen et al., 2008). Public staff are poorly paid, which often encourages doctors and nurses to look for work in the private sector. This lack of regulation allows the flagrant abuse of the price setting of services and of the quality of prescriptions (Duffau, Diaz Pedregal, 2009).

The Cambodian Government finances only 10% of national health expenditure, while international donors contribute more than 20%. The remaining 70% of the total cost has to be met by the users. This represents a considerable burden for the average household in Cambodia, especially in rural zones. Health costs are around 25 USD per person per year in these zones, which is more or less a month's salary for a rural inhabitant.

First steps towards universal social health protection in Cambodia

Social health protection in Cambodia combines an assistance scheme for poor people (health equity funds - HEF), a voluntary insurance scheme for the informal sector (community health-based insurance - CBHI), a mandatory scheme for the formal sector (social health insurance - SHI), as well as a private health insurance scheme (PHI) for the wealthiest of the population. Other types of health financing schemes are also found in Cambodia – although these remain minor in terms of coverage (Annear, Ahmed, 2012) – such as maternal health vouchers, global health initiatives and national programmes for patients with tuberculosis, malaria, AIDS and for child vaccination schemes. The majority of Cambodians (89% of women and 92% of men) still do not have health insurance (DHS, 2010).

HEFs provide the most important health protection scheme in Cambodia, in terms of the number of individuals covered. The Cambodian Government considers 26% to 30% of its population as poor (Royal Government of Cambodia, 2011) and that the majority of the poor are eligible for HEF or fee exemption. However, due to discrepancies between official statistics and actual coverage, this represents only around 6% to 9% of the Cambodian population (DHS,

FIGURE 1 **The construction of heath insurance**

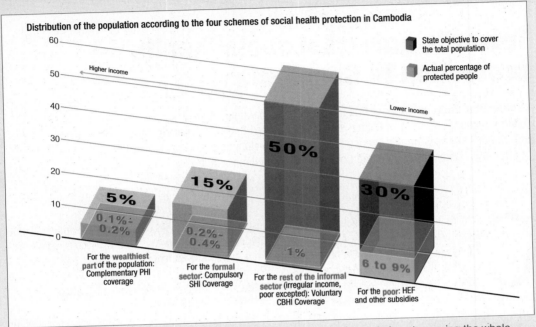

The Cambodian State has designed a complex system of health insurance aiming at covering the whole population. The discrepancy between State objectives and the actual percentage of the population covered is clearly discernable.

2010)[1]. Poor individuals who do not benefit from an equity fund have to finance their own health care expenditure ("out-of-pocket expenditure").

The second most important social health protection scheme, when considering the number of individuals insured, is CBHI. Today, however, only 1% of the population is insured by one of the nine CBHIs in Cambodia. A State objective is for the whole informal sector (with the exception of the poor) to have access to CBHI (see figure 1). In practice, there are many reasons why so few people are covered by CBHI, these include: a lack of knowledge or understanding of the concept of "insurance"; the low level of trust towards legal institutions; a lack of "willingness to pay" for a hypothetical risk of disease; and the weakness of the medical infrastructure and public care services (Duffau, Diaz Pedregal, 2009; Ramage et al, 2012; Polimeni and Levine, 2012).

At present, SHI is still under construction. This type of insurance is intended to be obligatory for people working in the formal sector (mainly civil servants) and will be wage-based. The objective is that SHI will eventually cover approximately 15% of the population.

Finally, PHI targets the wealthiest section of the Cambodian population, which represents approximately 0.1% of the population (DHS, 2010). These insurance packages are

1. According to the Royal Government of Cambodia (2011), 68% of poor people are protected under HEFs and fee exemption, which represents 18% to 20% of the total Cambodian population. The discrepancy between the figures in the 2010 DHS and the numbers given by the Royal Government of Cambodia may be explained by the fact that some poor people are "theoretically" covered and are therefore included in the official figures. However, many potential beneficiaries are either unaware of this protection or have not used it, so they declare themselves as not covered to DHS administrators.

FIGURE 2 Assessing the equity and quality of health protection mechanisms

Characteristics of the scheme	Breadth (Who is insured?)	Depth (Which benefits are covered?)	Height (What proportion of the costs is covered?)	Place where the health care is delivered	Financial cost of the access to the scheme for beneficiaries
H E F Health Equity Funds	Poor people.	Primary and hospital care. No medicine.	Moderate.	Public health centres and public hospitals; weak service.	None.
C B H I Community-based Health Insurance	Nearly poor people, "middle class", informal sector.	Primary and hospital care. Medicine usually covered.	Strong.	Public health centres and public hospitals; weak service.	Moderate.
S H I Social Health Insurance	Civil servants, employees, formal sector.	*A priori*, primary and hospital care.	Strong.	Public health centres, firm health centres and public hospitals; weak service.	Moderate.
P H I Private Health Insurance	Wealthy individuals, tourists, expatriates.	All types of care (depends on the level of the contribution).	Strong or weak (depends on the contribution level).	Private hospitals (national and foreign hospitals); medium service.	High or low.

Source: authours' compilation.

The developing health protection schemes in Cambodia give poor households access to basic health care. However they do not enable families to overcome the fragmented nature of the health care system, which remains dependant on financial resources.

expensive but quite efficient, giving a reasonable level of social health protection to affiliated individuals.

A tentative assessment of social health protection schemes

The combined coverage of these four social health protection schemes amounts to less than 10% of the Cambodian population (HEFs: 6% to 9%; CBHI: 1%; SHI and PHI: 0.5%). Social health protection schemes usually cover the costs of primary care and hospitalization, but this does not always extend to medicines. The international Global Fund finances the treatment of certain diseases, such as tuberculosis, malaria and AIDS. This means that people affected by these diseases should not have to face out-of-pocket expenses (except for the costs incurred by travelling to and from the health care centres). In theory, the Government provides the necessary funding to cover chronic diseases (such as high blood pressure, diabetes, etc.). Conversely, most of the for-profit health schemes (such as private insurance) do not cover these diseases, as such coverage is not financially profitable. The disturbing reality is that patients suffering from chronic diseases do not always know how to access public healthcare services; while many live too far away from public health centres, making regular treatment impossible.

As disease frequencies in Cambodia are often unknown, calculating the "risk factor" is a complex process that makes the design of appropriate insurance-based schemes all the more difficult. With regard to CBHI, a 2010 experimental study conducted in rural areas showed that these types of schemes have the potential to significantly decrease the health-related out-of-pocket expenditure of insured households, leading to less debt and less asset sales (LEVINE et al., 2012; also

BOX 1 Insuring health or insuring wealth? Main results from an experimental evaluation of health insurance in Cambodia

In 2007, AFD initiated[1], in conjunction with the University of California, Berkley and DOMREI, a Cambodian research institute, one of the first rigorous micro-health insurance impact evaluations, based on a randomized control trial, in Cambodia[2,3]. The study aimed to measure the impacts of a micro-health insurance programme, known as SKY (Sokhapheap krousar yeung – health for our families), and also to analyse the determinants of its take-up. The SKY insurance programme had originally been developed by an NGO called GRET in 1998.

This study highlights the difficulties faced by such a scheme in terms of reaching the large populations in rural Cambodia. Without subsidies, take-up of the micro-health insurance programme is shown to be very low (less than 5% on the "control group") and proves unstable (drop-outs are frequent after the initial six-month coverage). It is found that some households are unfamiliar with the concept of insurance, therefore indicating that educational and cognitional barriers are involved. Some evidence indicates that the less (financially) risk-averse households are the ones that purchase

1. The study was jointly funded by AFD and USAID.

2. All the results of this research program can be found on http://www.skyie.org and on the AFD website.

3. This study partially drew on the only large-scale randomized experiment examining the effects of health insurance, set in the 1980s in the United States, called the RAND Health Insurance Experiment.

SKY insurance, suggesting that SKY is perceived as a "risky product". However, demand for insurance is found to be rather elastic to the level of the premium. A decrease of 80% of the insurance price leads to a 41 percentage points increase in purchase.

Despite the slow "adoption" of micro-health insurance in rural Cambodia, the experiment confirms its strong potential economic benefits. SKY decreases total health care costs of serious health shocks by over 40%, leading to a one-third reduction in debt compared to uninsured households and to a significant reduction of asset sales. SKY is also successful in terms of its goal to shift rural Cambodians away from unregulated private providers and drug sellers and into the public system. However, the experiment does not find any reduction in the delay period prior to individuals seeking first healthcare; and nor an increase in the overall level of care received (in particular, preventive care).

Finally, the study points to the strong influence of the public healthcare supply in sustaining insurance membership. Many households think of public facilities as being of poor quality (compared to private ones). When this perception is compounded by the fact that people often have to travel very long distances to reach such facilities, then it is enough to persuade many new SKY members to continue using costly private care (in particular for minor health problems), and eventually to drop-out of SKY. Overall, the evaluation highlights the advantages but also the limits of voluntary health insurance, compared to other health protection schemes like HEF.

see box)[2]. It is also worth noting that the financial cost of utilizing the social health protection system varies considerably, ranging from zero to quite high figures, depending on the scheme considered (see figure 2).

Conclusion

Cambodian social health protection has been conceived on the basis of individual wealth and employment type (formal or informal sector). In 2012, State objectives to extend the breadth of protection are still far from being reached, thus leaving the great majority of Cambodian people without access to social health protection.

To improve social health protection coverage and reduce inequalities, other criteria in addition to individual wealth and employment formality should be taken into account. Schemes to target medically vulnerable individuals (the elderly, disabled people, patients suffering from chronic diseases…) are urgently required. There is also a need for systems that take less socially visible groups into account (women, children, ethnic minorities, homosexuals, and so on). A good start in this direction is to give healthcare vouchers to pregnant women (ANNEAR, SHAKIL, 2012).

---

2. According to the DHS (2010), only 2% of money spent on healthcare by persons seeking treatment in Cambodia came from a health equity fund and 0.5% from a CBHI. Indeed, wages, pocket change and savings remain the most common sources of money for minor illnesses. For severe illnesses, the main sources of funds are borrowed money, the sale of assets and gifts from relatives or friends.

For the continuation of the struggle against inequalities in developing countries, these new ways of targeting beneficiaries should be incorporated into Cambodian public policy, while the sustained financial support of donors is also essential.

REFERENCES

ANNEAR P. L. and AHMED S., 2012, *Institutional and operational barriers to strengthening universal coverage in Cambodia: options for policy development*, Working Paper Series, n°18, Health Policy and Health Finance Knowledge Hub, The Nossal Institute for Global Health, University of Melbourne, March.

NATIONAL INSTITUTE OF STATISTICS (MINISTRY OF PLANNING), Directorate General for Health (Ministry of Health), 2011, *Demographic and Health Survey 2010* (DHS 2010), September 2011.

DUFFAU A. and DIAZ PEDREGAL V., 2009, *Micro Health Insurance and Public Health Policy. To What Extent Does Non Profit Private Micro Health Insurance Contribute To Improving Public Health Care?*, FACTS (Field Action Science) Reports, 3 (1).

LEVINE D., POLIMENI R. and RAMAGE I., 2012, *Insuring health or insuring wealth? An experimental evaluation of health insurance in rural Cambodia*, AFD Ex-post collection, Impact analyses series, no. 08, March.

POLIMENI R. and LEVINE D., 2012, *Going beyond adverse selection: take-up of a health insurance program in rural Cambodia*, AFD Ex-post collection, Impact analyses series, no. 11, December.

POURSAT C., 2004, *Quelles articulations entre politique de santé et micro-assurance ? Réflexions à partir du projet de micro-assurance santé du Gret au Cambodge*, Gret, Coopérer aujourd'hui, n° 37, 33 p., June.

RAMAGE I., RAMAGE K. H., MAZARD E., KAVENAGH M., PICTET G. and LEVINE D., 2012, *SKY impact evaluation, Cambodia, 2010 village monographs*, AFD Ex-post collection, Impact analyses series, n° 9, August.

ROYAL GOVERNMENT OF CAMBODIA, 2011, *National Social Protection Strategy for the Poor and Vulnerable (2011 – 2015)*, 104 p.

CHAPTER 7

The greatest inequalities appear in cities in low and moderate-income nations. These urban areas concentrate more than 2.8 billion inhabitants, particularly in informal settlements where residents are subjected to intolerable discrimination. The scale and depth of urban poverty is often underestimated because of the methodology used to measure it. An analysis of numerous initiatives to improve access to basic services in cities across the world identifies the conditions needed for local governments, civil society, aid organizations and development institutions to reduce inequality.

Inequalities within the urban half of the world

Within a world where more than half the population lives in urban areas and draws their livelihoods from urban-based enterprises, some of the largest and most astonishing inequalities are within urban populations. Across the world urban settlements show a wide variation in terms of health outcomes, housing conditions, provision for services, protection of asset base, provision for voice and the quality of work environment.

David Satterthwaite and Diana Mitlin
International Institute for Environment and Development, London, United Kingdom

But detailed data on such inequalities within national urban populations or within individual cities has been relatively rare. Now, important research is emerging that is providing new insights into the field. This article discusses some of this recent data, summarized in Table 1, which highlights the contrast in the conditions between some of the worst and the best performing urban settlements.

One path breaking study on which this paper draws is the study of informal settlements in Nairobi by the African Population and Health Research Center (see APHRC 2002). This provides evidence from Nairobi for many of the inequalities listed in Table 1. Infant and child mortality rates are shown to be very high (to an extent that should be completely unacceptable) in the informal settlements that house around half of Nairobi's population (see Figure 1). In addition, a growing number of studies are showing that many informal settlements in cities have conditions similar to those listed in Table 1, which are among the worst performing urban settlements (MITLIN and SATTERTHWAITE, 2012; SVERDLIK, 2011; SUBBARAMAN et al., 2012).

FIGURE 1 **Infant mortality is indicative of urban living conditions**

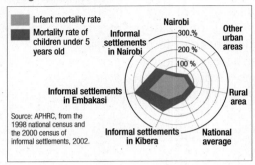

Children are among the first victims of poor environmental and health conditions. Informal settlements of Nairobi thus display an infant mortality rate that is three times higher than the city average.

At the upper end of the scale

In high-income and some middle-income nations, many of the inequalities highlighted in Table 1 have been removed or dramatically reduced – even if income-inequality has usually increased. Although low-income urban dwellers in these nations may still face poor housing conditions, they do not live in informal settlements lacking basic infrastructure – most have water of drinking quality piped to their home 24 hours a day, along with connections to sewers, drains, paved roads, electricity and street lights. In such urban settlements, regular household waste collections are provided and residents have access to health care, schools and emergency services (for fire or acute illness/injury) and there is policing in the neighbourhoods. Most inhabitants have legal addresses and are able to join voters' registers. Most populations of high-income countries are eligible for state cash transfers if they become unemployed, are rendered unable to work or they retire. Although somewhat eroded and often challenged by neo-liberal policies over the last 30 years, these countries offer a range of state or state-supervised provisions that dramatically reduce the type of non-income inequalities listed in Table 1. The inhabitants of such countries recognize that the state has responsibilities for the universal provision of many services, which should be available to all regardless of income[1]. Other such services include early warning systems for extreme weather, public response measures to extreme risks (e.g. temporary evacuation for those in sites where cyclones are due to strike), provision for needs following disasters, land-use planning and management systems to restrict development on dangerous sites, and many more. There are also public services that must be paid for, but are affordable for most, for instance public transport, piped water, sanitation, solid waste collection and electricity; and measures are often in place to make these services cheap or free to those on low incomes. Standards are enforced to protect health in the workplace and to regulate housing, manage road traffic and to protect consumers. Of course, there is a legal and institutional framework that underpins all the above that protects civil and political rights, and that seeks to reduce or remove discrimination in access to all public entitlements and rights. These societies are far from perfect and considerable levels of structural disadvantage remain, but there are also measures that seek to ensure that a minimum level of basic needs is met which serve most of the low-income population.

The inequality-reducing measures mentioned above did not materialize without a

---

1. Of course, taxpayers contribute to the costs of service provision; while some services incur additional payment from users.

FIGURE 2 Measuring inequalities in living conditions in urban areas

In the **poorest** urban areas...	In the most **favoured** urban areas...
Social services, transport, security...	
... **public services** (schools, health, safety, welfare, etc.) are of **poor quality**.	... **public services** are of **good quality**. Incomes allow access to **private services**.
... police do not enforce the law. The level of **violence** may be high.	
... there is **no public transport**.	... **public transport** is of **good quality**.
	... early warning and **response** systems to **natural hazards** exist.
... **environment is hazardous**. There is no compensation for income loss.	... **environment is safe** and the rules are respected. There are systems of compensation for loss of income.
Housing...	
... is of **poor quality**, built using flammable and recovered materials. Bare earth floors. **Poorly ventilated** and often damp.	... is of **good quality**, they comply to official rules of health and safety.
... is **very small**, often with only one room per household and less than 1 m² per person.	... is larger, offering 20 to 50 m² per person. Bedrooms are individual.
... solid waste is **not collected**.	... household waste is **regularly collected**.
... there are **no toilets in houses**. Collective or public toilets are difficult to access, rarely clean.	... **every household has a toilet**, that is easy to clean and has hand washing facilities.
... **drinking water** is **not easily accessible**. It is very expensive when bought from vendors, kiosks or tanks. Getting water is time consuming.	... drinking water is **available** in kitchens, bathrooms and toilets, **24/7**.
... there is **no power supply**. The use of dirty fuels (including waste) causes serious air pollution in homes.	... **electricity** is **available 24/7**. Cooking and heating (if necessary) use clean fuels.
... **risks** of landslides and flooding are strong, **fires** are **frequent** due to the high population density and the nature of the materials used.	... houses are built on **safe sites**.
... ownership of houses and land is uncertain. The **risk of eviction** is constant.	... **occupancy rights** protect against evictions.
... there is **no storm drain**.	... very **efficient storm drains** protect from floods.
	... near and safe **playgrounds** are available for children.
	... **Loans** are accessible to buy or improve houses.
Health	
120 infants out of one thousand	**3 infants** out of one thousand ... die at birth
250 children out of one thousand	Less than **5 children** out of one thousand... ... die before they are 5 years old.
1,500 women out of 100,000	Less than **10 women** out of 100,000 ... die in childbirth
13% of children are at risk of suffering from bloody diarrhea.	
More than **50%** of children are not of average weight or size.	
Life expectancy at birth...	
... is **20 years old**.	... is **over 85 years old**.

Source: author's compilation

It is not only the incomes of the inhabitants that determine the inequalities that exist between the richest and the most disadvantaged neighbourhoods in cities. The quality of building construction, the existence of basic services and infrastructure, of a public or private supply of specialized services, and even the physical safety of people, are all factors that fundamentally determine the experience of urban life.

long struggle by those who did not have such infrastructure, services and government accountability. They required political organization and pressure (TILLY, 2004). Such measures were also driven in large part by the death tolls of epidemics (especially cholera) and their economic impact, which persuaded businesses and higher income groups to join the call for action (ROSENBERG, 1962); these conditions may no longer prevail in urban settlements today, where elites have developed new ways to protect themselves (CHAPLIN, 1999; McFARLANE, 2008). The limited information available for the period 1850 to 1900 on inequalities in cities in what are today high-income nations show that most of the inequalities listed in Table 1 were present at that time (see for instance BAIROCH, 1988), including infant and child mortality rates comparable to those in the above mentioned informal settlements of Nairobi (ibid).

Low- to middle-income countries

Although progress has been uneven, available data on cities in Latin America show that some of the inequalities listed in Table 1 have been reduced in many cities – or within national urban populations. This region has also seen important changes in attitudes within city governments, away from regarding informal settlements as aberrations in contravention of the law (and thus bulldozing them) to the realization that such settlements house a large part of the city workforce, which plays a major role in the economy, and that these settlements can be upgraded. Thus, the upgrading of informal settlements – which considerably reduces many of the inequalities listed in Table 1 – has become simply a routine task for many city or municipal governments.

One of the largest and most effective national programmes for upgrading informal settlements is the Baan Mankong "slum" upgrading programme in Thailand (more details below) (BOONYABANCHA, 2005, 2009). It will be interesting to see the scale and nature of reductions in inequality that such a programme will deliver, and also in this instance to examine its effects on reductions not only in inequalities in housing conditions, insecure tenure, infrastructure and services, but also in citizen and community participation and interaction with local governments. However, despite these improvements in a number of countries, large sections of the urban populations in low-income and many middle-income nations face astonishing inequities – despite 60 years of development assistance. For instance, it is common for 20 to 80 per cent of households in cities or within national urban populations to lack water piped into their homes (UNICEF and WHO 2012, MITLIN and SATTERTHWAITE, 2012) and therefore to rely on public standpipes, wells, water vendors or kiosks. These people usually have to pay far more per litre of water than middle- and upper-income groups that have water piped to their homes (UN Habitat 2003). It is also common for 30 to 80 per cent of the urban population in low- and middle-income nations to have no sewers or storm drains. For example, there are many large cities in sub-Saharan Africa with no sewers or covered storm and surface drains – or where they do exist, they are only available to 5 to 10 per cent of the population (MITLIN and SATTERTHWAITE, 2012). Similarly, in many cities in low- and middle-income nations, between 20 to 70 per cent of the proportion of urban dwellers live in buildings that do not meet building standards and where occupation of the land or its development is illegal. Today, some 2.8 billion people live in urban areas in low- and middle-income nations (UNITED NATIONS, 2012). A very significant proportion of this urban population does not have the infrastructure, services, rule of law and citizen entitlements that governments are meant to provide or ensure provision for. This is despite recognition and formal commitments by almost all governments and international agencies during the 1970s to ensure universal provision of "basic needs" - for instance for water, sanitation, health care and primary and secondary education.

Inequalities in political influence and social status underlie unequal access to government transfers, goods and services, and, at least to some extent, disadvantageous positions within labour markets. Inequalities in access to infrastructure and services reflect inequalities both in income and political power. While the housing markets and particularly the gap between the costs of housing and what low-income groups can afford may be used to explain the inadequacies in infrastructure and service provision in low-income settlements, infrastructure investments are essentially political decisions (rather than market transactions). In many cities, it is the interests of political elites that are primarily responsible for the lack of access to essential infrastructure and services, such as piped water and sanitation, faced by much of the population.

In addition, those living in informal settlements so often face discrimination in labour markets and access to services. Having an inadequate income means having to live in an informal settlement which often means facing discrimination on the basis of where you live – which can then be part of the discrimination faced on the basis of race, gender and ethnicity. At the same time, informal labour is struggling as a result of unequal access to decision making. City governments may decide to beautify central city areas, expelling informal traders and/or informal settlers in the process (BHAN, 2008; CROSSA, 2009; FERNANDES, 2004). Many city governments seem to think that their city should follow the "Dubai" or "Shanghai" vision of the modern urban centre, this means that the populations in many informal settlements are likely to be threatened with eviction since the inclusion of these residents is rarely prioritised.

The inadequacy of poverty lines in accounting for urban inequalities

It is not just that incomes are unequal – very little attention is given to the unequal costs of living and the adverse prices faced by the poor across a spectrum of essential goods and services. Poverty lines are set and applied in almost all low- and middle-income nations. These do not show a detailed picture of inequality but they do distinguish between those who are considered "poor" and those who are "not poor."

Most governments now apply two poverty lines – the "extreme poverty line" (which is usually the income needed to get sufficient food) and a higher poverty line that is meant to include income for non-food needs. From this comes statistics on the proportion of the national population (or the urban or rural population) that is below whichever poverty line is defined. This is hardly a sophisticated measure of inequality – but the proportion of the national, urban or rural population below the poverty line does at least provide some measurement of those who are poor.

Although such measures of "absolute poverty" do not focus on inequality (and were never intended to do so), if accurately applied they should reveal one aspect of inequality, which is that they highlight the proportion of the population with incomes too low to meet their needs.

Unfortunately, the definition and application of poverty lines remains very crude in most nations. It is rare for poverty lines to be implemented on the basis of surveys that assess the real costs of non-food needs and for adjustments to be made according to the location, to take into account the differences in the costs of food and non-food needs in various locations. This latter omission is particularly perplexing given that the costs of many non-food needs clearly vary considerably by location – and are likely to be particularly expensive in large and prosperous cities. The cost of public services is also likely to be particularly high for urban populations that are not reached by infrastructure – as these populations have to buy water from kiosks, vendors and tankers and pay for public toilet sanitation (they do not have toilets in their homes). As government schools frequently refuse admission to the children of low-income groups in informal settlements, the families have to pay for their children to go to private schools, which are usually poor quality schools located in these settlements. They also have to pay for private health care (again because of inadequate or no public provision). Yet none of this is taken into account when setting many poverty lines – especially the dollar a day poverty line which assumes that the income needed to avoid poverty, when adjusted for purchasing power parity (PPP), is the same everywhere. This is surprising given that international experts working in development are able to make far more sophisticated allowances for the differences in living costs between different locations within nations and between nations in the rates set for their daily costs (accommodation, food and others). Why therefore is the same logic not also applied to poverty lines? According to the dollar a day poverty line, there is virtually no urban poverty in many nations – including nations in which the scale and depth of urban poverty is known to be very significant. For instance, Ravallion, Chen and Sangraula (2007), in applying the dollar a day poverty line (US$1.08 a day at 1993 PPP) in 2002, claim that less than one per cent of the urban population of China, the Middle East, North Africa, East Europe and Central Asia was poor; that less than 10 per cent of the urban population in Latin America and the Caribbean was poor; and that for all low- and middle-income nations, 87 per cent of their urban population was not poor. The documentation of the scale and depth of urban poverty in most nations in these regions shows the lack of validity for such statistics – and for the dollar a day poverty line that is used (MITLIN and SATTERTHWAITE, 2012). What is more worrying is that the dollar a day poverty line is being used in the assessment of progress for the Millennium Development Goals and in discussions on the post-2015 development framework and this means greatly underestimating the scale and depth of urban poverty in most nations.

There are also other problems with data on inequality. The lack of interest in inequality by national governments and international agencies can be seen in the data they choose to collect and the methodologies for doing so. The priority has been data collected from sample surveys – usually national ones. This can be seen in the support given by international agencies to the Demographic and Health Surveys and other national sample surveys. Such surveys have sample sizes that are too small to show much detail on inequalities in the provision of the types of infrastructure, services and entitlements noted above. Also, they do not provide data on where those with the highest levels of deprivation live – beyond very general categories – e.g. for rural and for urban populations. The questions they ask are also very inadequate in regard to being able to assess who has adequate provision for (among other issues) water, sanitation and the quality of housing. As the official UN statistics on provision for water and sanitation state, they cannot provide data on who has safe and adequate provision for water and sanitation, as there are no data sources on this for most nations.

Discussions of inequality usually focus on income inequalities. Very rarely do they consider inequalities in living conditions and access to services. For instance, the Gini coefficient is much used in assessing income-inequality and for making comparisons between nations in terms of income inequality. There are also cities for which Gini coefficients have been calculated (UN HABITAT, 2008). But no coefficients have been developed to assess inequalities in housing conditions or access to infrastructure and services, or in the political structures that underpin many aspects of inequality.

What then has informed us of the many forms of inequality faced by low-income urban dwellers? Our knowledge in this area derives from a limited number of detailed studies of informal settlements, see in particular the work of Caroline Moser, who has researched and visited the same informal settlement in Guayaquil for over 30 years (MOSER, 2009), Nancy Scheper-Hughes (SCHEPER-HUGHES, 1992) and Janice Perlman (PERLMAN, 2010). While these works cannot be considered as representative, they are supported by a much larger body of literature that shows comparable aspects of inequality – including the discrimination that the residents of these informal settlements face in their daily lives. Many governments and higher income groups still portray those living in informal settlements as dirty or illegal, or label them as rural migrants that should return to their villages. They are considered as a drain on the public purse (see for instance BHAN, 2009), when in reality the city economy (and many of the services enjoyed by middle and upper incomes) would collapse without them. In addition, a high proportion of these people are not rural migrants and very few get any public entitlements, so they hardly constitute a drain on public funds. However, these negative and inaccurate stereotypes serve as justifications for the bulldozing of settlements, especially where they "offend" nearby middle-income groups or where the land is particularly valuable.

How local governments can reduce inequalities

One important reason for widening the measurement of inequality beyond incomes is that governments and international agencies (and civil society organizations) have far more scope to reduce many other aspects of inequality – for instance in the quality of housing and the quality of provision for water, sanitation, drainage, health care, schools, emergency services and energy sources (moving away from dirty fuels and their health impacts). This is especially the case for local governments and for organizations formed by those who face among the greatest inequalities – the residents of the informal settlements. Indeed, one reason why inequalities in these aspects have remained so large is that too little attention has been given by national governments and international agencies to these two key sets of actors. This does not mean ignoring income-inequalities. But the scope for governments is limited (especially local governments) to influence labour markets to give better incomes to lower income groups. Even the scope for workers themselves to influence employers is limited. Agarwala (2004) reports on how informal workers in India focused their efforts to improve access to basic services (in a context in which informalization in labour markets has been rising and industrial disputes falling).

Local governments can only address inequalities within their jurisdiction. It is commonly found that the weakest local governments are among those with the highest proportion of their population lacking basic infrastructure and services. In contrast, as noted in the introduction, city and municipal governments in high-income and some middle-income nations have reduced or removed inequalities in many of the aspects listed in Table 1. Such examples from middle-income nations usually exhibit a combination of: strong political leadership (for instance a mayor committed to addressing inequalities); a national government with the will to drive through the necessary changes; a responsible and accountable local government (including elected mayors and city governments); and grassroots organizations that can represent the needs and priorities of those living in informal settlements.

There have been successful examples of large-scale "slum" and squatter upgrading programmes in many cities in Latin America. These programmes have achieved reductions in inequalities in access to piped water, sewers and drains (CAMPBELL, 2003; GILBERT and DAVILA, 2002; ALMANSI, 2009; SATTERTHWAITE, 2009). Such work is often supported by national governments through a strengthening of local government capacity to take action. In Thailand for example, the large-scale Baan Mankong community-driven "slum" upgrading programme, which did much to reduce inequalities in housing conditions, infrastructure and services, was supported by a national agency (the Community Organizations Development Institute). The many innovations in reducing inequality in cities in Colombia and Brazil are in part the result of local governments having more accountability, power and capacity.

Achieving universal provision for basic infrastructure and services for urban populations greatly benefits from national measures to channel support to the weaker and less well-resourced local governments. However, many city governments have demonstrated their own capacities to reduce a range of inequalities. Hundreds of city governments have instituted or supported participatory budgeting schemes as a way to make their decisions and actions more accountable to citizens and also to allow residents in each neighbourhood to influence priorities in public investments (CABANNES, 2004). In Rosario, Argentina, the current mayor and the mayor that preceded him have implemented a range of measures that have reduced inequality within the city, despite little support from higher levels of government (both mayors were from an opposition party and, until recently, the same was true for the provincial government). Measures included a decentralization of services that improved provision and accountability, a municipal health care system available to all and much increased provision for parks and other forms of public space (ALMANSI, 2009). In the city of Manizales in Colombia, over the last two decades, many mayors have supported the improvement in housing conditions for low-income groups, the reduction of the disaster risk (especially for those living in informal settlements on dangerous sites), the increasing of public space and the implementation of an "environmental traffic lights" public monitoring system, which informs residents of the environmental conditions in the city's different neighbourhoods (VELASQUEZ, 1998, 2005). An increasing number of city governments are addressing disaster risk reduction within their boundaries which so often means working with residents of informal settlements to upgrade housing and infrastructure (UNISDR 2012). All these examples highlight the importance of competent city and municipal governments that can demonstrate political leadership and are held accountable to those facing the most serious inequalities.

How civil society can reduce inequalities

Addressing most of the inequalities listed in Table 1 depends not only on change within national and local governments but also on more space and influence for those suffering these inequalities. The dramatic reduction in inequalities in housing, infrastructure and services that has occurred in high-income and some middle-income nations was driven by urban poor groups becoming organized and obtaining the necessary political changes. Over the last 15 to 20 years, organizations and federations of "slum" or shack dwellers have developed in many nations in Africa and Asia, with savings groups (mostly comprised of and led by women) at their foundation. All have undertaken initiatives, such as the upgrading of homes, improvement of water or toilet provision, while many have managed to negotiate for housing land, either for free or at a low price, which has allowed them to demonstrate their capacity to build. Many of these organizations have undertaken detailed enumerations (in effect censuses) of informal settlements and city-wide surveys of all informal

BOX 1 THE NECESSITY TO SURVIVE AND IMPROVE A DIGNIFIED LIFE

Bayat (2000) documents how individuals challenge urban governance outcomes in cities of the Middle East. He argues that the occupation of streets by informal traders, the expansion of housing in contravention of formal regulations and the non-payment and illegal tapping of basic services are all part of a quiet encroachment that reflect an inability to challenge disadvantageous outcomes. He suggests that it is helpful to see such "...activities not as a deliberate political act; rather, they are driven by the force of necessity – the necessity to survive and improve a dignified life" (ibid, 547). But in so doing he highlights the extent to which exclusion from resources and from the rules that influence control over resources, create difficulties in the struggle to secure urban livelihoods.

settlements that then allow dialogue with local governments over planning for city-wide upgrading and, where needed, resettlement (PATEL and BAPTIST, 2012; DOBSON and SAMYA, 2012; LIVENGOOD and KUNTE, 2012; CHITEKWE-BITI et al., 2012; FAROUK and OWUSU, 2012). Most have initiatives underway for upgrading or for developing new housing supported by local government – including in India (PATEL and MITLIN, 2004; BURRA, 2005), South Africa (BAUMANN, BOLNICK and MITLIN, 2001; see also the web site http://www.sdinet.org/), Thailand (BOONYABANCHA, 2005, 2009), Namibia (MITLIN and MULLER, 2004), Malawi (MANDA, 2007, 2009), Kenya (WERU, 2004), the Philippines (YU and KARAOS, 2004) and Zimbabwe (CHITEKWE-BITI, 2009). Over 200,000 families within these federations secured tenure between 1993 and 2008 and upgrading in the form of housing and infrastructure improvements has taken place in most such settlements (URBAN POOR FUND INTERNATIONAL, 2011). These federations have also formed a small umbrella organization – Slum/Shack Dwellers International – to help organize exchange visits, manage external funding and help negotiate with international agencies.

Many city governments now work with the organizations and federations of "slum"/shack dwellers to directly address a range of inequalities that include housing tenure, infrastructure, services, rule of law and participation. All these programmes directly or indirectly address one of the most profound aspects of inequality – the discrimination faced by those living in "slums" or informal settlements in all the above. For instance, the mayor of the city of Iloilo in the Philippines has a strong partnership with the Homeless People's Federation of the Philippines, helping house or rehouse those whose homes have been damaged or destroyed by floods and working on disaster prevention (CARCELLAR et al., 2011). Many city governments in Asia contribute to Community Development Funds that were set up in their city by savings groups formed by residents of informal settlements to fund improvements in infrastructure and services (BOONYABANCHA and MITLIN, 2012).

The inequality in who gets aid and who influences its use

One of the most profound inequalities is in who receives the funding from aid agencies, international NGOs and development banks. Very little aid is actually available to low-income groups and their own grassroots organizations, even if the work of such international agencies is legitimated on the basis that it addresses the needs of these groups. Even when, in rare instances, a limited amount of aid funds becomes available to low-income groups, its use is subject to the conditions and priorities established by the aid-provider. These international agencies emphasize accountability and transparency – but they have very little or no accountability or transparency to low-income groups (SATTERTHWAITE, 2001).

Official aid agencies and development banks were not set up to work directly with low-income communities. They were set up to work with and fund national governments. Aid agencies have to be accountable to the government that funds them (and beyond this to the voters who put the government into office). Multilateral development banks such as the World Bank and the Asian, African and Inter-American

Development Banks have to be accountable to the governments that sit on their boards – especially those that provide them with funding. Initially, it was assumed that international funding agencies would support national (recipient) governments to address unfulfilled needs. It was also hoped that this approach would encourage stronger economies in the expectation that it would lead to investments to address unfulfilled needs through increased incomes and larger government capacity to provide the basics – secure housing, water, sanitation, health care, schools, rule of law and provision for voice.

What would a development finance system look like if it had a commitment to reducing inequality? Certainly, this would have to include more influence for those facing the worst inequalities. Might there be a form of participatory budgeting for any funding allocated by international to national governments? But there is also the profound inequality in the support available to low-income groups to take action.

There are two working examples to draw from that have provided funding to support the initiatives of low-income groups. The first, the Urban Poor Fund International, supports the national federations of "slum"/shack dwellers or homeless people's federations to decide on how available funding is used. Since 2002, it has channelled over US$15 million to over 100 grassroots initiatives and activities in 17 nations. These include: tenure security (through land purchase and negotiation) in Cambodia, Colombia, India, Kenya, Malawi, Nepal, Philippines, South Africa and Zimbabwe; "slum"/squatter upgrading with tenure security in Cambodia, India, Kenya, Philippines and Brazil; bridge financing for shelter initiatives in India, Philippines and South Africa (where government support is promised but slow to be made available); improved provision for water and sanitation in Cambodia, Sri Lanka, Uganda and Zimbabwe; enumerations and maps of informal settlements in Brazil, Ghana, Namibia, Sri Lanka, South Africa and Zambia that provide the information needed for upgrading and negotiating land tenure; exchange visits by established federations to urban poor groups in Angola, East Timor, Mongolia, Tanzania and Zambia (in Tanzania and Zambia, these helped set up national federations); community-managed shelter reconstruction after the 2004 Indian Ocean tsunami in India and Sri Lanka; and Federation partnerships with local governments in shelter initiatives in India, Malawi, South Africa and Zimbabwe[2].

The second example is the Asian Coalition for Community Action (ACCA). Since 2009, this has provided small grants to 950 community-initiatives to upgrade "slums" or informal settlements in 165 cities in 19 nations. Each community initiative is chosen by residents. Up to US$3,000 of grant finance is available, and communities use this, for instance, for the construction or improvement of their water supply systems or toilets, drains, roads, paths or bridges, community centres, household waste management, playgrounds or parks. Up to US$40,000 has been available for larger initiatives at the city scale, as loans. While these sums seem very small in relation to the scale of the problems they seek to address, the organizers explain

---

2. For more details, see the website of the Slum/Shack Dwellers International at http://www.sdinet.org/

that there is not enough development money to fund "sufficiently" all that needs to be done in all informal settlements. The funding available to community groups may be small but it is available quickly and can be used for whatever they choose and is enough to allow them to address one of their priority needs. Insufficient funding catalyses new ways of using finance – people have to think harder about what resources they can contribute, what additional support they can negotiate and who they can work with – and so forge partnerships to address other needs. ACCA supported the setting up of 107 City Development Funds – across the ACCA countries – and also financed 110 larger housing-related initiatives (ACHR 2010, Boonyabancha and Mitlin, 2012).

These two examples show a working finance system in which those who face the largest inequalities within cities have the power to decide what is funded and implemented – and the decision-makers are accountable to these low-income groups, as well as to external funders. The initiatives funded by these two sources are planned and undertaken by the residents of informal settlements as collective processes: collective information collection (settlement mapping, city-wide surveys), collective definition of problems and search for shared solutions, collective funding systems managed by networks of savings groups (the City Development Funds), and new collective relations as linkages are built between those living in informal settlements and local governments.

Conclusions

This chapter has made clear the many aspects of urban inequality and the often severe implications for health, education, living standards, quality of life and economic opportunities. It has emphasized how an interest in addressing inequality needs to go beyond income-inequality and to include reducing differentials in access to safe, secure housing with infrastructure and services, access to schools, policing, the realization of civil rights and opportunities to have political influence that puts pressure on the government to be more accountable and transparent. As the focus on inequality is widened to include these, so the key roles of local governments and representative organizations of the urban poor become evident.

This chapter also noted the profound inequalities in access to or influence over funding from aid agencies and development banks. It suggests a need to go beyond considering how governments and international agencies can address inequalities to consider how they can support individuals, households and communities to address the inequalities they face. The examples given of the Asian Coalition for Community Action and the Urban Poor Fund International show how support given directly to community-based organizations within informal settlements and the larger federations or networks they form in many nations addresses not only the inequalities in infrastructure or service provision, but also those related to the provision of voice and the capacity to act – and critically in the capacity to engage with local government and negotiate to obtain positive responses. ■

REFERENCES

ACHR, 2010, *107 Cities in Asia; Second Yearly Report of the Asian Coalition for Community Action Program*, Asian Coalition for Housing Rights, Bangkok, 48 pages.

AGARWALA R., 2006, "From Work to Welfare", *Critical Asian Studies* 38:4, 419-44.

ALMANSI F., 2009, "Rosario's development; interview with Miguel Lifschitz, mayor of Rosario, Argentina", *Environment and Urbanization* 21:1, 19-35.

APHRC, 2002, *Population and Health Dynamics in Nairobi's Informal Settlements*, Nairobi: African Population and Health Research Center.

BAIROCH P., 1988, *Cities and Economic Development: From the Dawn of History to the Present*, London: Mansell, 574 pages.

BAUMANN T., BOLNICK J. and MITLIN D., 2001, *The age of cities and organizations of the urban poor: the work of the South African Homeless People's Federation and the People's Dialogue on Land and Shelter*, IIED Working Paper 2 on Poverty Reduction in Urban Areas, London: IIED.

BAYAT A., 2000, "From 'Dangerous Classes' to 'Quiet Rebels': Politics of the Urban Subaltern in the Global South" *International Sociology* 15:3, 533-57.

BHAN G., 2009, "This Is No Longer the City I Once Knew." Evictions, the Urban Poor and the Right to the City in Millennial Delhi, *Environment and Urbanization*, 21:1, 127-42

BOONYABANCHA S., 2005, "Baan Mankong; going to scale with "slum" and squatter upgrading in Thailand", *Environment and Urbanization*, 17:1, 21-46.

BOONYABANCHA S., 2009, "Land for housing the poor by the poor: experiences from the Baan Mankong nationwide slum upgrading programme in Thailand", *Environment and Urbanization*, 21:2, 309-330.

BOONYABANCHA S. and MITLIN D., 2012, "Urban poverty reduction: learning by doing in Asia", *Environment and Urbanization*, 24:2.

BURRA S., 2005, "Towards a pro-poor slum upgrading framework in Mumbai, India', *Environment and Urbanization*, 17: 1, 67-88.

CABANNES Y., 2004, "Participatory budgeting: a significant contribution to participatory democracy" *Environment and Urbanization* 16:1, 27-46.

CAMPBELL T., 2003, *The Quiet Revolution: Decentralization and the Rise of Political Participation in Latin American Cities*, Pittsburgh: University of Pittsburgh Press.

CARCELLAR N., JASON CHRISTOPHER RAYOS Co and HIPOLITO Z. O., 2011, "Addressing vulnerabilities through support mechanisms: HPFPI's Ground Experience in Enabling the Poor to Implement Community-rooted Interventions on Disaster Response and Risk Reduction", *Environment and Urbanization*, 23.2

CHAPLIN S. E., 1999, "Cities, sewers and poverty: India's politics of sanitation", *Environment and Urbanization*, 11:1, 145-158.

CHITEKWE-BITI B., 2009, "Struggles for urban land by the Zimbabwe Homeless People's Federation", *Environment and Urbanization*, 21:2, 347-366.

CHITEKWE-BITI B., MUDIMU P., MASIMBA NYAMA G. and JERA T., 2012, "Developing an Informal Settlement Upgrading Protocol in Zimbabwe - the Epworth Story", *Environment and Urbanization*, 24:1.

CROSSA V., 2009, "Resisting the entrepreneurial city: street vendors' struggle in Mexico City's historic center" *International Journal of Urban and Regional Research* 33:1, 43-63.

DOBSON S. and SAMYA E., 2012, "Enumerations in five cities in Uganda", *Environment and Urbanization*, 24:1.

FAROUK B. R. and OWUSU M., 2012, "If in Doubt, Count: the role of community-driven enumerations in blocking eviction in Old Fadama, Accra", *Environment and Urbanization*, 24:1.

FERNANDES L., 2004, "The politics of forgetting: class politics, state power and the restructuring of urban space in India" *Urban Studies* 41:12, 2415-30.

GILBERT A. G. and DAVILA J. D., 2002, "Bogota: progress within a hostile environment" in David J. Myers and Henry A. Dietz (Editors), *Capital City Politics in Latin America: Democratization and Empowerment* Lynne Reinner, Boulder and London, pages 29-64.

LIVENGOOD A. and KUNTE K., 2012, "Participatory settlement mapping by Mahila Milan", *Environment and Urbanization* 24:1.

MANDA M. A. Z., 2007, "Mchenga - urban poor housing fund in Malawi", *Environment and Urbanization*, 19:2, 337-359.

MANDA M. A. Z., 2009, *Water and Sanitation in Urban Malawi: Can the Millennium Development Goals be met? A Study of Informal Settlements in Three Cities*, Water Series Working Paper 7, IIED, London, 78 pages

MCFARLANE C., 2008, "Governing the contaminated city: Infrastructure and sanitation in colonial and post-colonial Bombay" *International Journal of Urban and Regional Research* 32:2, 415-35

MITLIN D. and SATTERTHWAITE D., 2012, *Urban Poverty in the Global South: Scale and Nature*, Abington: Routledge

MITLIN D. and MULLER A., 2004, "Windhoek, Namibia – towards progressive urban land policies in Southern Africa" *International Development Policy Review* 26:2, 167-86

MOSER C. O. N., 2009, *Ordinary Families, Extraordinary Lives: Assets and Poverty Reduction in Guayaquil 1978-2004*. Washington: Brookings Institution Press.

PATEL S. and MITLIN D., 2004, "Grassroots-driven development: The Alliance of SPARC, the National Slum Dwellers Federation and Mahila Milan", in Diana Mitlin and David Satterthwaite (editors), *Empowering Squatter Citizen; Local Government, Civil Society and Urban Poverty Reduction*, Earthscan Publications, London, pages 216-241

PATEL S. and BAPTIST C., 2012, "Documenting by the undocumented", *Environment and Urbanization*, Vol. 24, No. 1.

PERLMAN J., 2010, *Favela: Four decades of living on the edge in Rio de Janeiro* New York: Oxford University Press.

RAVALLION M., CHEN S. and SANGRAULA P., 2007, New Evidence on the Urbanization of Global Poverty, WPS4199, Washington DC: World Bank.

ROSENBERG C. E., 1962, *The Cholera Years*, Chicago: University of Chicago Press.

SATTERTHWAITE D., 2001, "Reducing urban poverty: constraints on the effectiveness of aid agencies and development banks and some suggestions for change", *Environment and Urbanization* 13:1 137-157.

SATTERTHWAITE D., 2009, "Editorial: What role for mayors in good city governance?", *Environment and Urbanization*, 21:1, 3-17.

SCHEPER-HUGHES N., 1992, *Death Without Weeping: the Violence of Everyday Life in Brazil* Berkeley: University of California Press.

SUBBARAMAN R. , O'BRIEN J., SHITOLE T., SHITOLE S., SAWANT K., BLOOM D. E., APPADURAI A. and PATIL-DESHMUKH A., 2012, "Off the map: the health and social implications of being an unrecognized slum", *Environment and Urbanization*, 24:2, 643-664.

SVERDLIK A., 2011, "Ill-health and poverty: a literature review on health in informal settlements", *Environment and Urbanization*, 23:1, 123-156.

TILLY C., 2004, *Social Movements, 1768-2004*, Paradigm, 262 pages.

UN-HABITAT, 2003, *Water and Sanitation in the World's Cities: Local Action for Global Goals*, London: Earthscan Publications.

UN-HABITAT, 2008, *State of the World's Cities 2008/9: Harmonious Cities*, London: Earthscan Publications, London, 280 pages

UNICEF and WHO, 2012, Progress on Drinking Water and Sanitation; 2012 Update, Joint Monitoring Programme for Water Supply and Sanitation, New York and Geneva: UNICEF and WHO, 60 pages.

UNISDR, 2012, *My City is Ready; a Global Snapshot of how Local Governments reduce risk*, Making Cities Resilient Report 2012, UNISDR, Geneva

UNITED NATIONS, Department of Economic and Social Affairs, Population Division, 2012, *World Urbanization Prospects: The 2011 Revision*, http://esa.un.org/unpd/wup/index.htm.

URBAN POOR FUND INTERNATIONAL, 2011, Annual Report 2011, Cape Town: SDI

VELÁSQUEZ L. S., 1998, "Agenda 21; a form of joint environmental management in Manizales, Colombia', *Environment and Urbanization* 10:2 9-36.

VELÁSQUEZ L. S., 2005, "The Bioplan: Decreasing poverty in Manizales, Colombia, through shared environmental management", in Steve Bass, Hannah Reid, David Satterthwaite and Paul Steele (editors), *Reducing Poverty and Sustaining the Environment*, London: Earthscan Publications, pages 44-72.

WERU J. 2004, "Community federations and city upgrading: the work of Pamoja Trust and Muungano in Kenya", *Environment and Urbanization*, 16:1, 47-62.

YU S. and KARAOS A. M., 2004, Establishing the role of communities in governance: the experience of the Homeless People's Federation Philippines, *Environment and Urbanization*, 16:1, 107–120

Favelas - segregation in the heart of the city

Luiz Antonio Machado da Silva, Instituto de Estudos Sociais e Politicos, Universidade do Estado do Rio de Janeiro, Rio de Janeiro, Brazil

Rio de Janeiro is geographically compressed into a narrow strip between sea and mountains, which strongly determines its physical expansion and population growth. The extensive modernization of the country, which began in the twentieth century and intensified in the 1930s, means that the city has grown through two competitive processes of territorial occupation. The boundaries of the city were stretched by the construction of mass housing settlements in previously suburban areas (Santos and Bronstein, 1979). These speculative and largely illegal projects have left the new owners in a precarious situation both legally and socially (Fisher, 2008; Gonçalves, 2010; Magalhães, 2010). The fragile nature of ownership rights in these areas was accompanied by a limited or non-existent supply of public services, the new owners finding themselves obliged to pressurize public agencies to acquire these services (see many references, among which: Ribeiro, 1982; 1997; Ferreira dos Santos, 1979). It was in this way that the peripheries of Rio were established, and they today remain characterized by countless forms of illegality and a limited number of public services. Their management has been entrusted to a new dedicated administrative body (the "município", one of the three levels of the Brazilian federation). Despite their demographic weight and the many conflicts that have beset them, these mass settlements have never figured prominently on Brazil's public agenda.

In parallel, spaces within the conventional inner urban area that had been neglected because of high construction costs, started to attract the interest of the population and then of small developers. Gradually, the property market began to incorporate these spaces, which had previously been regarded as unsuitable for construction. Despite the lack of an organized collective movement, buildings that were erected by the people with the support of small informal entrepreneurs and some branches of formal activity began to be established on these areas within the heart of the urban space. These buildings became the subject of growing interest from conventional developers, due to the emergence of new construction technologies and new ways of valorization.

While the two processes have coexisted since the 1940s, the issue of favelas has eclipsed that of the suburbs in public debates. This is partly explained by historical reasons, but also by the evocative use of language, and in particular, the powerful imagery conveyed by the word "favela".

A historical representation

Three main stages can be distinguished in the evolution of the concept of favelas and therefore, in the way that the authorities have approached the issue of government intervention in disadvantaged neighbourhoods.

When favelas appeared in the early 1920s, despite the beginning of industrialization, the city was still essentially a colonial warehouse. At that stage, favela inhabitants were not yet sufficiently organized to have any influence on policies that might affect them. Their physical presence in the city was subject to access restrictions. Considered simply as insalubrious squatter settlements, as slums that should be eliminated and as a health and aesthetical problem, favelas were only of marginal interest to councillors. In the early 1930s, with the election of Getúlio Vargas as President, a new era of industrialization began, based on the idea of import substitution. While modernization

FIGURE 1 Favelas, the inner boundary

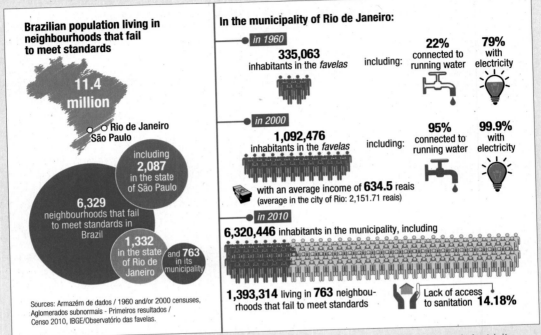

Brazilian population living in neighbourhoods that fail to meet standards

11.4 million

Rio de Janeiro
São Paulo

including 2,087 in the state of São Paulo

6,329 neighbourhoods that fail to meet standards in Brazil

1,332 in the state of Rio de Janeiro

and 763 in its municipality

In the municipality of Rio de Janeiro:

in 1960
335,063 inhabitants in the *favelas* including: 22% connected to running water — 79% with electricity

in 2000
1,092,476 inhabitants in the *favelas* including: 95% connected to running water — 99.9% with electricity
with an average income of 634.5 reais (average in the city of Rio: 2,151.71 reais)

in 2010
6,320,446 inhabitants in the municipality, including
1,393,314 living in 763 neighbourhoods that fail to meet standards
Lack of access to sanitation 14.18%

Sources: Armazém de dados / 1960 and/or 2000 censuses, Aglomerados subnormais - Primeiros resultados / Censo 2010, IBGE/Observatório das favelas.

The favelas have experienced significant urban transformations, such as access to water and electricity networks, etc., which have been obtained through the campaigning efforts of their inhabitants. However, these areas remain pockets of poverty in the heart of the city. The average household income in Rio's favelas is almost four times lower than average incomes elsewhere in the city.

programmes began to be launched in Rio de Janeiro, the situation and the fate of the favelas moved into the public arena, with profoundly different ideas emerging on the policy responses that should be designed.

Following the end of the Second World War and the re-democratization of the country in 1945, two forces favourable to the favelas appeared. "Developmentalism" was the new dominant ideology of that period, which caused high economic growth accompanied by an increase in the demand for labour, which thereby strengthened the political power of workers. The two most important political forces of that time – the church and the communist party – were diametrically opposed. The debates and conflicts between the two were particularly apparent in the favelas, where they fostered a vast public grassroots

movement. In this way, these physical locations became a symbol and the favelas entered into the public sphere, first through inhabitant associations, and then through the federation of these groups. With local variations (clientelism, revolutionary radicalism, reformism), the political emergence of the favelas was enhanced by the strong economic and demographic growth of the city. This trend towards inclusion and political normalization extended into the 1970s; eventually being brought to an end by the crisis that followed the first oil shock.

Public debate on the favelas centred on the productivity of migrants (which was criticized for being low or zero) and how they fitted into the city, i.e. mainly through the so-called informal economy. After a short period during which the State claimed it was making changes to urban governance, the military took power in 1964

FIGURE 2 A political focus on violence

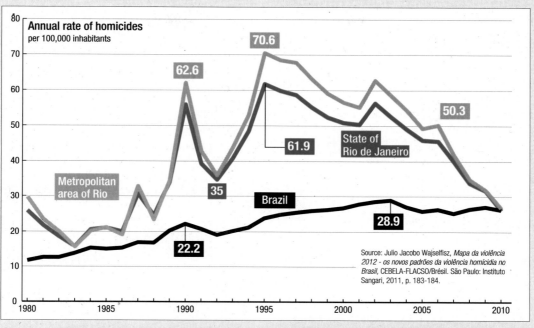

Source: Julio Jacobo Wajselfisz, *Mapa da violência 2012 - os novos padrões da violência homícidia no Brasil*, CEBELA-FLACSO/Brésil. São Paulo: Instituto Sangari, 2011, p. 183-184.

Over the past 15 years, Rio's annual homicide rate has significantly declined, even though the national rate has continued to increase and the absolute number of homicides per year remains very high: in 2010 there were 1,535 homicides in Rio de Janeiro and 49,932 in Brazil.

and the debate on favelas changed. Political organizations suffered severe repression. The only question still debated was housing. Two opposing interventions were proposed: "remoção" – the displacement of people to the outskirts of the city; and "urbanization" – the improvement of urban facilities and buildings in areas occupied by favelas (MACHADO da SILVA, 1967, 2002; LIMA, 1989; FISHER, 2008). All conflicts around issues of social cohesion, including those relating to the favelas, were only able to grow within the narrow repertoire of the claiming of rights.

With the economic crisis of the 1970s, the issue of favelas changed in the way it was perceived. It became part of the fight against the military government and the refusal to submit to violations of civil and political rights – a fight that was partly sustained by the middle class victims of repression. Then, in the 1980s, the government used the preservation of public order as an excuse to renege on the acquired rights. A "discourse on urban

violence" then emerged (MACHADO DA SILVA, 1995, 1999, 2010a, 2011) that emphasized the risks that city inhabitants had to face in daily life. Crime and violence were no longer considered as interstitial but as everyday realities that were increasingly making invasions into all areas of life. This discourse endowed the notion of the favela with an evocative and powerful symbolism. Violent crime and its daily repression by the police became the central, and relatively autonomous, subject of public attention.

The violence began to be decentralized with the emergence of various forms of private police and armed criminal groups. The government received criticism for its inability to control areas that fell under the influence of drug traffickers. Militarization was increasingly regarded as the only way to preserve public order on a daily basis (LEITE, 2001), profoundly transforming the perception of the favela as a collective problem (MACHADO DA SILVA, 2008).

In 2008, a policy to maintain urban order, which received

full public support, began to be implemented in Rio. This approach, which is still militarized, involves Pacifying Police Units (UPP) which are designed specifically for intervention in the favelas. This approach seems to have reduced the number of deaths caused by armed clashes between rival drug traffickers, and between traffickers and the police, although the homicide rate had already been in decline well before the implementation of this policy. It is worth noting, however, that these results have had little impact on the perception of violence by the city's inhabitants. In 2010, the UPPs were strengthened by the "Social UPP" state scheme (which was a way to acknowledge the brutal nature of the conventional UPP). The aim of the Social UPP is to promote access to full citizenship for the people living in favelas.

From the word to the socially invented representation

Historically, the word "favelas", which describes interstitial inner periphery settlements and examples of uncontrolled development in Rio de Janeiro's urban area, has been associated with specific social groups, a certain type of architecture, along with a number of physical and ecological characteristics. It also refers to a type of economy, or socio-economic and politico-cultural processes. This characterization, in the choice words of Valladares (2005), is a socially *invented* representation that is continually renewed. However, this depiction has not developed as a *myth*, as suggested by Valladares, but rather as a key reference in the evolution of urban forms. The term has territorialized the debate on the city's social integration problems. The strength of the favela does not lie in its ability to embody a reality that is both nearby and concealed. Instead, it comes from its ambiguous semantics and its polysemy, which give it the virtues of a political arena and the weapons of an object of struggle. ∎

REFERENCES

FERREIRA DOS SANTOS, Carlos Nelson e Bronstein, Olga. *"Metaurbanização: Rio de Janeiro"*. Revista de Administração Municipal, Ano XXV, nº 149, outubro-dezembro de 1979, pp. 06-35.

FISCHER, BROADWYN. A poverty of rights – citizenship and inequality in twentieth-century Rio de Janeiro. Stanford, Ca.: Stanford University Press, 2008.

GONÇALVEZ, RAFAEL SOARES. Les *favelas* de Rio de Janeiro – histoire et droit, XIXe ET XXe siècles. Paris: L'Harmattan, 2010.

LEITE, MÁRCIA DA SILVA PEREIRA. Para além da metáfora da guerra. Percepções sobre cidadania, violência e paz no Grajaú, um bairro carioca. Tese de doutorado (Sociologia). Rio de Janeiro: PPGSA/IFCS/UFRJ, 2001.

LIMA, NÍSIA VERÔNICA TRINDADE. *"O Movimento de Favelados do Rio de Janeiro: Políticas do Estado e Lutas Sociais (1954-1973)"*. Dissertação (Mestrado em Sociologia). Rio de Janeiro: IUPERJ/UCAM, 1989.

MACHADO DA SILVA, LUIZ ANTONIO. *"A política na favela"*. Cadernos Brasileiros, Ano IX, nº 41, maio/junho de 1967, pp. 35-47

MACHADO DA SILVA, LUIZ ANTONIO. *"Violencia y sociabilidad: tendencias en la actual conyuntura urbana en el Brasil"*. Ecuador Debate, Quito (Equador), nº 34, pp. 116-129, 1995.

MACHADO DA SILVA, LUIZ ANTONIO. *"Criminalité, Violence et Ordre Publique au Brésil"*. Les Annales de la Recherche Urbaine, Paris, nº 83/84, pp. 65-71, 1999.

MACHADO DA SILVA, LUIZ ANTONIO. *"A continuidade do 'problema da favela"*. In Oliveira, Lúcia Lippi (org.): Cidade: história e desafios, Rio de Janeiro: Editora FGV/CNPq, 2002, pp.220-237.

MACHADO DA SILVA, LUIZ ANTONIO (org.). Vida sob cerco – violência e rotina nas favelas do Rio de Janeiro. Rio de Janeiro: Nova Fronteira/Faperj, 2008.

MAGALHÃES, ALEX FERREIRA. *"O direito da favela no contexto pósprograma favela-bairro: uma recolocação do debate a respeito do 'direito de pasárgada"*. Tese de Doutorado. Rio de Janeiro: IPPUR/UFRJ, 2010.

RIBEIRO, LUIZ CESAR DE QUEIROZ. *"Espaço urbano, mercado de terras e produção da habitação"*. In Machado da Silva, Luiz Antonio (org.): Solo urbano – tópicos sobre o uso da terra. Rio de Janeiro: Zahar, 1982, pp. 29-47.

SANTOS, CARLOS N. F & BRONSTEIN, OLGA, 1979. *"Metaurbanização: Rio de Janeiro"*. Revista de Administração Municipal, Ano XXV, nº 149, octobre-décembre, pp. 06-35.

VALLADARES, LÍCIA DO PRADO. A invenção da favela. Rio de Janeiro: FGV, 2005.

CHAPTER 8

Citizens' awareness of their "well-understood self interest" can be erased by manipulating their concern for equity. Agitators and lobbyists regularly block important reforms that would benefit the disadvantaged, strengthening low-growth trends that generate inequalities, not jobs. The author calls for space for public debate to counter the diabolical game, which drags attention away from society's challenges.

Killing carbon tax with the equity argument - Lessons from the Sarkozy tax

This paper will attempt to show the mechanisms by which arguments based on equity have played a central role in the failure of the carbon tax project under the presidency of Nicolas Sarkozy. One can argue that these mechanisms are partly specific to the French institutional framework, to a precise politico-media cycle and a somewhat unusual presidency style that put the emphasis on media announcements rather than on social consultation, which was suspected of being a strategy to slow the pace of reforms. Without, I hope, falling into the trap of thinking that what happens in France automatically has universal value, I will show that the effectiveness of arguments mobilized to counter the project is indicative of broader fundamental problems that go beyond the "carbon tax" project. These problems are those of the blocking of reforms, at national or international scales, through the manipulation of the concern for equity in a media-crazed world where the primacy given to the consumer obscures the "best interests" of the citizen.

Jean-Charles Hourcade

Centre International de Recherche sur l'Environnement et le Développement, Paris, France

From general consensus to a blitzkrieg that was rapidly lost

The story of "Sarkozy's climate contribution" begins on 31st January 2007 when five of the presidential candidates[1], including the three that received the most votes in the first round (N. Sarkozy, S. Royal and F. Bayrou), signed an "ecological pact" that included a carbon tax proposal, that was drawn up by Nicolas Hulot, the host and producer of a renowned television programme, *Ushuaia*. Once elected, N. Sarkozy

---

1. These candidates gathered a total of 78.51% of the votes in the first round.

confirmed his commitment during the closing of the *Grenelle* Environment Forum on 25th October 2007, and once again during his presidential vows in January 2009. The political context seemed favourable: the election of Barack Obama to the U.S. presidency gave hope during the late-2009 Copenhagen conference that it might be possible to unblock the climate negotiations that had been becalmed by G. W. Bush; while the 15.8% of votes gained by Europe Ecology in the European elections in May 2009 at last reflected a rise in environmental concern among the public.

Finally, the choice of Michel Rocard, former Socialist Prime Minister, as Chairman of the preparation of the climate-energy contribution (CEC) indicated a willingness for a transpartisan compromise, while the appointment of Yves Martin to assist him – a senior official who has supported this idea since 1990 – was a guarantee of technical seriousness and sincerity. Conferences of experts met in early July and the Rocard report was submitted on 28th July; he advocated an immediate rate of €32 per tonne of carbon emitted that should reach €100 in 2030. M. Rocard said: *"There is something extraordinary, totally unexpected for a society as confrontational as ours, in the consensus expressed by almost all experts from all sides involved in these discussions"* (p. 67). The problem is therefore to understand how, within a period of just six months, we moved from this apparent consensus to the invalidation by the Constitutional Council on 29th December of a bill that the Chamber of Deputies and the Senate had definitively voted in favour of on 18th December, and to the permanent abandonment of the project by Prime Minister Francois Fillon on 23rd March 2010, about a year after its launch.

To fully comprehend these events, we must return to two important recommendations of the Rocard report, namely the absence of exemptions and the enactment of a social negotiation process to clarify the use of the revenue, accompanied by "the implementation of an appropriate governance on a multiannual perspective, comparable to the "Green Tax Commissions" that exist in other countries, in order to institutionalize this need for governance, assess its impact and determine how this revenue is used. Admittedly, in January, N. Sarkozy had announced that the carbon tax would be used to finance the reduction of the professional tax, a local tax paid by businesses that was unanimously considered as particularly distortionary. This announcement led to the presentation of the carbon tax as an indirect means to give a "gift to the employers" and was therefore denounced by labour unions. But the Rocard report put things back into perspective by giving prominence to usages of the tax that included a reduction of social charges, and using among others a study of the CIRED to back it (COMBET et al., 2009). Everything therefore remained open for negotiation: at this stage the second largest French union, the CFDT, had officially given its support, while the largest union, the CGT, had not vetoed the proposals.

The defeat of the bill stems back to the beginning of July when, from the angle of protecting consumers from rising energy prices and the mobilization of an anti-tax reflex, the Consumer Association, *UFC Que Choisir*, through the voice of François Carlier became very prominent in the media, calling for the handover of the tax revenue to households. The *Fondation Nicolas Hulot*, which had the ear of the president, was convinced that this option, which combined social justice and budget neutrality, would be the only one likely to be accepted by the public and would enable a rapid adoption of the CEC. On 5th July the Minister of Ecology Jean-Louis Borloo, to avoid being accused of inventing a new tax grab, then argued in *Le Point* magazine for the idea of a "green cheque" to be given to households with equal retrocession of payments. Then, on 6th July, the Budget Minister Eric Woerth declared his opposition to this idea in *La Tribune*. This clash rendered obsolete, prior to its emergence, the recommendation of a negotiation on the use of such a tax: the recommendation fell on deaf ears when it was released on 28th July and was definitively buried.

The mechanism that would lead to failure had been triggered. Public opinion did not understand the logic of a reform where money taken from them could be given back; on 3rd September, a survey by *TNS Sofres* showed that two out of three French people declared themselves opposed to the CEC. While employers highlighted the competitiveness argument and the additional costs of the carbon tax when companies do not benefit from other lower taxes. Technical points were debated in the heat of the moment before the Head of State made a decision on 10th September to implement zero taxation on electricity, provision of a green cheque to households, and exemption for industries covered by the European Emissions Trading scheme (EU-ETS). Failure was now inevitable, due to the inclusion of exemptions that the Rocard report had strongly urged against.

However, companies that are subject to the EU-ETS (i.e. the highest emitters), are only required to pay the European market-determined carbon price in the event that they exceed their allocated free quota. This leads to tax inequality, as highlighted by the Constitutional Council: "the significance [of the exemptions in relation to major emitters] was such that it was contrary to the objective of fighting against global warming and has created a characterized fracture of equality in terms of the public burden". While the butcher or the carpenter would have to pay tax on their first tonne of emissions, the steel and chemical industries would only be liable for their excess emissions. This gives weight to the argument of tax inequality that the Constitutional Council had already used in 1998 against a carbon tax proposal by the Jospin government. F. Fillon abandoned the project on 23rd March and on the 24th March, N. Sarkozy "subordinated the creation of a domestic carbon tax to a tax at the borders".

Certainly, one can accuse Sarkozy's method for this defeat, but in doing so, we would not draw any useful lessons. One may indeed wonder why the Greens or the Socialist Party (whose candidates had signed the N. Hulot pact) did not mobilize to demand a negotiation around the carbon tax, and simply welcomed the withdrawal of a tax that was considered as antisocial, without offering an alternative project for a tax that would fit better into the overall project, and did not campaign on the carbon tax during the last presidential election. In fact, the failure of the Sarkozy carbon tax is indicative of two more general problems: the first relates directly to the profession of economists and their ability to respond effectively to issues of fairness, the second concerns the way in which the media process "informs" citizens.

FIGURE 1 Can we combine efficiency and equity?

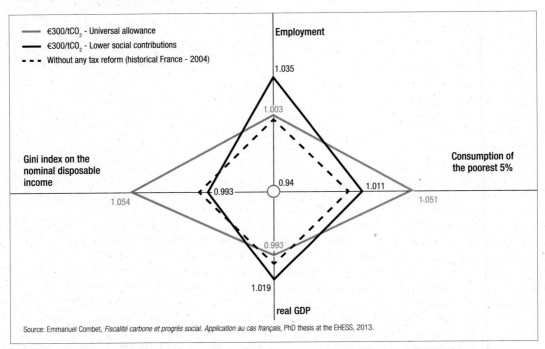

— €300/tCO$_2$ - Universal allowance
— €300/tCO$_2$ - Lower social contributions
- - - Without any tax reform (historical France - 2004)

Employment
1.035
1.003
Consumption of
the poorest 5%
Gini index on the
nominal disposable
income
1.054
0.993   0.94   1.011
1.051
0.993
1.019
real GDP

Source: Emmanuel Combet, *Fiscalité carbone et progrès social. Application au cas français*, PhD thesis at the EHESS, 2013.

The Rocard mission has used this model to compare the effects of a carbon tax of €300/tCO$_2$ in France according to the way in which it is applied: green cheque paid to the consumer (purple line), reduction of social charges (black line). The modelling shows that it is possible to combine economic efficiency (job and wealth creation) and equity. A reduction in social charges is good for the economy but does not compensate for the weight of higher energy prices on poor households. Conversely, the green cheque is inversely proportional to income and more socially fair, but it does not create additional jobs or wealth.

Did the economists lack pedagogy on the equity-efficiency links?

The mechanics of the failure of the Sarkozy carbon tax can be likened to a double-bladed razor: the first blade, that of the fairness argument, can be said to "raise the hair"; while the second one, that of the arguments of competitiveness, is the blade that "cuts it". This can only raise questions for economists who, for more than 20 years, have been involved in the development of some models of reasoning in "general equilibrium". The results of these models are certainly not consensual, but they are more than sufficient to show how the idea of a green cheque given to households is counter-productive and ignores the fact that, because of economic interdependencies, the one who pays a tax is not necessarily the one who bears the ultimate cost. This means, in practical terms, that a redistribution measure that is apparently equitable may eventually have consequences contrary to its stated objective.

This was the case of the "green cheque" as it was presented in the heat of the moment. A fee of €20 for each tonne of CO_2 that a consumer is directly responsible for would also affect companies, which will charge this extra cost to customers; this cost would be spread from sector to sector with an amplification effect on the price of final products, and a green cheque of €20 per tonne delivered to a consumer to offset rising energy costs would not compensate for the increase in prices that the extra cost of energy will have caused for the rest of the consumer's purchases. The use of the carbon tax to decrease the social charges is necessary to block this mechanism, thus offsetting the extra cost of energy by reducing the labour costs. Without this compensation, the €100 per tonne (planned for 2030 in the CEC project) that is necessary to truly "decarbonise" our economies would cause an unbearable additional cost.

Economists may bear some of the responsibility for the way in which the public and the policy makers understand the simple reality of these propagation mechanisms. If one takes stock of two decades of work on the carbon tax, the importance of the "double dividend" is striking, i.e. the fact that by using the revenue of a carbon tax to reduce the most distortionary taxes, we could have, in addition to improving the environment, an economic dividend in the form of an increase in employment activity. Opposing this theory were the many reflexes from within a profession that is always wary, with good reason, of anything resembling a "free lunch". In this case, it was important to avoid the creation of the illusion of a miracle tax, one that would solve economic problems, especially those in terms of employment. L. Goulder had introduced in 1995 a very useful distinction between "strong form" and "weak form" of the double dividend by showing that the first was not automatic and depended on specific conditions, but it should not make us forget the second, namely that an environmental tax was necessary to reduce the economic and social costs of environmental policies.

But this was not enough, and tension amongst theoretical economists continued, they pointed out that a double dividend was not possible in a so-called first best economy i.e. using optimally its resources (HOURCADE and ROBINSON, 1996) and criticized the empirical models for working on second-best economies for which economic science does not provide generalizable theoretical solutions. A second complaint, collateral to the first, is that these models only point to a double dividend assuming that the introduction of a carbon tax is carried out in parallel with reforms that have not been undertaken so far; they therefore attribute to the carbon tax the dividend of reforms that should have been adopted independently of climate policies. This argument is encapsulated in the provocatively titled paper "The double dividend is dead" by Bovenberg (2000)[2].

We can wonder whether this "tension" in the debates between "theorists" and "empiricists" is particularly relevant when one sees that the empirical models generally find modest increases in GDP, rarely above 2% over the long term, the

2. In the French debate, this position was echoed by K.Schubert (2010), and in a very nuanced way by Guesnerie (2010).

employment figures being more significant. The issue of double-dividend is numerically secondary with respect to the propagation effects of a carbon tax and the need, in order to control these effects, to use the product of this tax to reduce levies that ultimately weigh on production costs. What has been lacking in the public debate is a good understanding of this point, which induces the "weak form" of the double-dividend as an undisputed theoretical result. CIRED's IMACLIM model shows that alight *strong form* is possible in France, due to the proportion of the tax that implicitly hits annuity incomes and oil imports. But this is not the essential element; the important issue was to clearly explain the need to control the spread of rising energy costs and the fact that, without this control, the green cheque was an illusory gift.

This lack of pedagogy is perhaps due to an intellectual posture that makes sense as a step in the analysis of general equilibrium effects of a carbon tax, but not to calculate the real cost of a measure. This posture, which requires consideration on the basis of a leading universe (that is to say, assuming all the reforms are carried out to lead to optimal taxation and full use of factors of production), leads to an argument that is somewhat scholastic. In a given historical period, the only relevant question is whether a carbon tax, because it brings revenue that has to be used, facilitates or otherwise the implementation of reforms that have not been undertaken so far. Such as, for example, the reduction of social security contributions[3].

This structuring of the debate may be at the origin of the difficulties in giving equity issues the appropriate consideration. Indeed, in a leading universe, the solution is to make compensatory transfers towards households adversely affected by a reform; there is "separability between equity and efficiency". However, in the real world, this separability is far from being realized. Figure 1 shows its issues. Taken from a simulation by the IMACLIM-S model, that was used for the Rocard study, it provides a comparative analysis of the situation in France in 2004 if a carbon tax had been enacted 20 years earlier to reach the level of €300/tCO$_2$, depending on whether this tax would have been given back to the consumer in the form of a green cheque or used to reduce the social security contributions. It provides the comparison of four criteria (GDP, employment, consumption of the poorest 5% of the French population, and the Gini coefficient), the baseline situation before tax being described by the dotted square.

It is immediately clear that the use of revenue to decrease social security contributions (black diamond) allows very significant improvement in employment, significant growth of GDP and incomes of poor households, but leads to more inequality.

3. At the time of writing, the French government is initiating a downward trend in social security contributions, through increased value-added tax (VAT), which affects consumption, and through the increase in the Generalized Social Contribution (CSG), which is a form of income tax. The limits of these increases will appear very quickly, i.e. pressure on the purchasing power for the first increase, resistance of the middle and upper classes for the second. Compared to these solutions, we have shown in our work that a carbon tax has a similar effect to that of an increase in VAT and has the advantage of decreasing energy imports; the only valid question is then whether the carbon tax will be politically accepted as a means to diversify funding sources to lower social security contributions.

This result can be explained by a virtuous circle: the transfer of the tax burden on income from rents, higher salaries, lower labour costs, increased exports, lower imports (on top of the decrease in oil imports). This allows an increase in employment which is of sufficient benefit to disadvantaged segments of the population to compensate for the decline in purchasing power caused by the higher energy costs. But this device aggravates inequality (Gini coefficient degradation) because the wealthier strata dedicate a significantly less amount to energy than that which is spent by the disadvantaged. The egalitarian "green cheque" device improves the Gini coefficient, since wealthier households receive a cheque lower than the amount they have paid out, while the opposite is true for poor households. But there are negative points: it comes at the expense of growth and no gain in employment due to the degradation of production costs; rising domestic consumption triggered by the higher incomes of the disadvantaged cannot compensate for the loss in competitiveness; and, in addition, a fact that does not appear in this graph, there is a decline in investment and a higher level of national debt.

The terms of arbitration on the use of the money from the tax thus clearly appear and the goal of the social negotiation, that was recommended by the Rocard study, was precisely to see the emergence of solutions to allow compromise, with some of the tax revenue targeted towards the most vulnerable households and another part focused on the lowering of charges. However, such a substitution between carbon tax and the social security contributions could not be dissociated from the negotiations on wages and on the financing of social protection. This is a politically sensitive issue because it affects the "equal representation" between employers and trade unions in the management of social security. An important point for the starting of a virtuous economic circle is the proportion of the decrease in contributions which employees can benefit from in the form of net wage increases without preventing the decrease in production costs.

It is in this search for a compromise that two sensitive issues could have been addressed. The first is the specific arrangements for certain activities, not only those covered by the European system of tradable emission permits, but also very vulnerable activities such as fishing or mountain agriculture. The second is the importance of location in the vulnerability to energy prices. Figure 2, which is drawn from a survey of 35,000 households, shows that the share of energy expenditure in the household budget is based on income, but that its variability within the same income class is high. This is because the energy requirements are very specific to the place of residence, not only for climate issues, but also and especially for issues of dependency on economic mobility, which is highly variable depending on whether you live in the centre of Paris, where the combination of metro plus walking is very effective, or far out in the suburbs or in the mountains.

In fact, the heterogeneity of situations is a concern to economists because the scheme of compensation through money transfers to take this into account quickly leads to very complex administrative solutions, which pave the way for endless lobbying. We can only find a solution by expanding the scope of the negotiations so that what one social category loses through its energy bill, is regained on access to employment, rental costs, lower (or at least not increased) other charges, and for economically vulnerable occupations (agriculture, mountain pastoralism, fishing) an institutional framework that gives them the prospect of true economic viability. In other words, the basic reductions of carbon tax or monetary transfers are not the only tools by which the "losers" of the reform can be compensated. The major political advantage of the Rocard proposal for a specific governance on the use of the CEC revenue was the forced reconnection of issues, fears and expertise, including by encouraging specialists of retirement funding, public debt, health or social housing to examine the potential offered by environmental taxation and the complementary measures to adopt (the insulation of buildings, for example) to make it a "win-win" device, what economists call "Pareto-improving".

The dictatorship of the immediate, its reasons and modalities

The above shows why forcing the adoption of a carbon tax outside of any social negotiation could only lead to failure. The episode of the Sarkozy carbon tax is a perfect counter-example of the success of the Swedish tax, which is described in this publication by Thomas Sterner. However, this does not explain the collapse of the idea of such a tax, or the fact that it was not used by the opposition parties, and neither does it explain why the equity argument was so effective, even though it could be easily disproved.

We must firstly underline here an element of psychological context. When decisions were to be made on the carbon tax, the media hype over the climate issue suddenly stopped after the failure of Copenhagen. This can be explained by the discouragement felt by those whose expectations had been overly high. There was also a suspicion that the climate issue was not particularly serious, or was even a sham, as suggested in the title of Claude Allègre's bestseller, which was published in February 2010[4]. It is irrelevant that Allègre relied on distorted documents or that the Academy of Sciences had refuted his arguments. The important element is the mistrust vis-à-vis the predicted disasters and the anti-environmentalist reflex that was revealed by the success of this book. This reflex can be easily understood if we remind ourselves of the historical examples of prophets of doom that were proved wrong, and of course, the figure of Cassandra that the Trojans refused to believe. Such a reflex is all the more to be expected given that the population feels threatened by a financial crisis for which it feels no responsibility for, and which fears unemployment. If climate warnings are presented as catastrophes, they do not allow "enlightened catastrophism" (DUPUY, 2002). If people feel they have their backs to

---

4. Claude Allègre: The Climate fraud or false ecology, Plon, February 2010. Former Minister of Lionel Jospin's government, a member of the Academy of Sciences, Claude Allègre is a French example of a "merchant of doubt"; as a columnist in some influential newspapers, he was frequently invited during this period to voice his opinions on radio and television. Having approached Nicolas Sarkozy, he asked that the French Academy of Sciences should rule on the issue, which it did by certifying the scientific character of the work on climate change.

the wall, there is no room for choice and they become very receptive to rhetoric that presents environmental taxes as punitive and guilt-apportioning.

The effectiveness of Ségolène Royal's position, the runner up in the second-last presidential election as the leader of the Socialist Party, against the carbon tax is very symptomatic: she argued during a television debate ("*À vous de juger*" on France 2, 25th March 2010): "*If you put a tax on people before they have a choice – to buy an electric car or take public transport – it is very unfair.*" In essence, an easy response to this view is that it is precisely the low oil prices since 1983 that have discouraged the investment in such vehicles and that the failure of the CEC has undermined, for example, the strategic gamble made by Renault in 1989 to allocate more than 5,000 engineers to this field. But this is not the important element. The essential point is the sense of a "trap" that captures part of the population, illustrated as the "peaks" in Figure 1, including those among the middle and higher income bracket, because it has no flexibility in its consumer choices.

A typical example here is the dependence on cars for commuting between home and work. The power to purchase vehicular mobility has increased over the last thirty years together with the intolerance towards increases in petrol prices. The paradox is that the growth of real estate prices, combined with low fuel prices, has made the population migrate to less dense suburban areas, less served by public infrastructure, where it found itself dependent on the car, including to go to work. In the 1990s, when interviews and vox pops recorded the suffering of the motorist at each price increase (without similar coverage whenever falls in prices occurred!), it constituted a disservice to households, maintaining the illusion that the rising cost of fuel was avoidable.

It is this feeling of being trapped which explains the effectiveness of anti-environmentalism, the presentation of the carbon tax as punitive and guilt-apportioning and ultimately of the rise in the media of consumer protection. But this efficiency would have been less effective if we had used, in addition to the appeal for caution vis-à-vis climate change, other arguments to support higher prices of fossil fuels. There are at least three of them:

- The most obvious concerns energy security; indeed, during this period, there has been little emphasis on reminding the French people that the tax was a bulwark against excessive dependence on the Organization of Petroleum Exporting Countries (OPEC), and that it would be better to fund French schools and pensions rather than to contribute to an oil revenue that funds an 828 metre tower in Dubai and feeds the financial strength of the Gulf countries.

- The second is, as we have seen, the possibility of using carbon tax revenues to lower levies that are particularly disadvantageous for the economy. To this is added the fact that, by taxing energy, the level of charge that falls on the company follows the fluctuations of production and declines when business is not good; it would enable the reduction of the significant disincentive to employ people in the current system where, when the turnover is lower than expected, social security contributions increase per unit produced and represent a tax on excess employees because

FIGURE 2 **Energy consumption does not only depend on income**

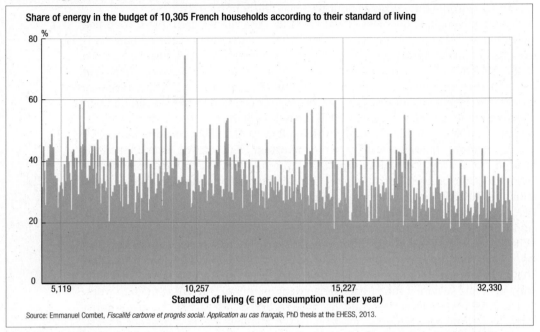

Share of energy in the budget of 10,305 French households according to their standard of living

Standard of living (€ per consumption unit per year)

Source: Emmanuel Combet, *Fiscalité carbone et progrès social. Application au cas français*, PhD thesis at the EHESS, 2013.

The more incomes rise, the less energy expenditure represents an important part of the household budget. But this trend includes high variability within the same income class. Energy needs depend on the place of residence, lifestyle as well as income.

of labour laws. In addition, there is the fact that companies have an incentive to retain skilled and committed employees to be able to respond when orders increase again. The carbon tax could have been included in a general fiscal reform to help the competitiveness of SMEs and manufacturing industries, once having responded to the concerns of heavy industry, by giving them the choice to stay in the EU-ETS system or to be taxed but to benefit from a decrease in charges.

- Finally, one could have explained how, in the long term, a carbon tax can support policies aiming at reorienting agriculture, construction and transportation systems (without carbon tax, road freight will continue to increase its competitiveness in relation to rail or waterways), and at centralized innovation or a more balanced territorial planning. This affects our agricultural model (better use of local potential, ecological engineering in substitution for more expensive energy and chemical inputs, higher transportation costs moderating competition among territories by major distribution channels) as well as our urban model (commuting distances).

By ignoring these arguments, it was easy to stir up anti-green reflexes in certain parts of the population. A polemicist from the radio station RTL even said that the carbon tax was a stupid idea equivalent to taxing babies because of the CO_2 they emit through respiration, and that N. Sarkozy had only wanted to please N. Hulot. We cannot blame the latter for the brilliance with which he imposed his pact, but his action has affected public opinion that was so little informed of the carbon tax that it was easy to label as a "bobo" fad, an idea that had been promoted since the 1990s by many economists and by the European Commission on behalf of the conciliation between environment, employment and competitiveness. It remains to be seen why these "oversights" were possible. This is where the case of the carbon tax has a value of generality, revealing the implicit anthropology of public space today, which fragments the person and the citizen.

First, there is the compartmentalization of issues and militancy that show the neglect of non-climatic arguments and the reluctance to advocate social negotiation. It is as if we had wanted this tax to remain purely an ecological issue, either by fear of diluting the environmental objective or, prosaically, to avoid having discussions with activists from other causes. A cultural gap remains between environmental NGOs and trade unions. It is exacerbated by the ease of access to the media of spokespersons for causes that are not subject to the discipline of trade unionists who are accountable to their constituents. These advocates hope for an easy victory through their impact on public opinion and policy. But public opinion turned when there was a move from abstract wishes to the determination of who should pay the bill.

Finally, there was the obstacle highlighted by the effectiveness of interventions "in the name of consumers", that started in early July 2010: the mobilization of the equity argument in a public discourse marked by the primacy of the interests of consumers and this interest being reduced to the search for the lowest price above all else. It is in the name of this consumer interest that we reject rising gas and electricity prices, or we allege to protect the population against rising fuel prices. But what the consumer does not pay today is what the taxpayer or the company will pay tomorrow, and after that so will the dismissed worker and the future consumer whose bills will be duly weighted by the spillover effects between sectors.

In fact, the way in which the concern for fairness and protection of vulnerable populations was translated through the media on the basis of a consumer figure has blocked any projection into the future; this consumer looks at price without questioning the reasons for that price and what it involves in terms of sacrifice in the present (underpayment, poor working conditions) and future (under-investment, environmental costs). The future disappears in such a game, because there is no room for the discussion of the real interests of all, as here and now consumers, but also as a consumer of tomorrow, the worker, the parent or the grandparent who is concerned about the fulfilment of their children and grandchildren.

Conclusion

In the end, Sarkozy's carbon tax was killed by the temptation for a "political coup" that, by refusing to allow time for negotiations on the use of the tax revenue, did not allow sufficient intellectual preparation to develop arguments that would speak to citizens and not to fragmented individuals, who were reduced to the state of consumer, taxpayer, bobo-green or poor…

A major issue appears here beyond the cases we have analysed: the construction of a public space for debate which blocks the diabolical game of the fragmentation of individuals and societal issues, equity questions being of course a major dimension of these issues. Perhaps this cannot be done without what Pierre-Noël Giraud calls "a vast movement of awareness in favour of equality". Here lies the heart of the issue, which is ethical in principle, that we should not only think of the "poor" (or any minority) when to do so is merely useful for blocking a measure that we do not want. A movement is necessary to counter these manipulations and to discuss the necessary solidarity, in an integrated collective project, so that the benefit of coming generations is not preserved at the sacrifice of the most vulnerable generations today. ■

▌ REFERENCES

BOVENBERG L., 2000, Preface, in R. A. de Mooij (ed.) *Environmental Taxation and the Double Dividend (Contributions to Economic Analysis, Volume 246)*, Emerald Group Publishing Limited, pp.vii-ixDOI:10.1108/S0573-8555(2000)0000246002 (Permanent URL).

COMBET E., GHERSI F., HOURCADE J.C. and THUBIN C., 2009, Economie d'une fiscalité carbone en France, 3 November 2009, http://www.cfdt.fr/rewrite/article/23599/qui-sommes-nous/nos-publications/les-etudes/economie-d-une-fiscalite-carbone-en-france.htm?idRubrique=8174

DUPUY J.-P., 2002, Pour un catastrophisme éclairé, Paris : Seuil, 216 p.

GIRAUD P.-N., 2012, La mondialisation: Emergences et fragmentations, Sciences Humaines Editions 2012.GOULDER L. H., 1995, Environmental taxation and the double dividend: A reader's guide International Tax and Public Finance, August 1995, Volume 2, Issue 2, pp 157-183.

GUESNERIE R., 2010, "Pour une Politique Climatique Globale", Editions Rue d'Ulm/Presses de l'Ecole normale supérieure, 96 p.

HOURCADE J.C., ROBINSON J., 1996, "Mitigating factors: assessing the costs of reducing GHG emissions", *ENERGY POLICY*, 24 (10/11), PP. 863-873.

SCHUBERT K., 2010, *Pour la taxe carbone. La politique économique face à la menace climatique*, CEPREMAP, ENS rue d'Ulm, 90 p.

Sweden's CO_2 tax and taxation reform experiences

Henrik Hammar, Ministry of Finance, Stockholm, Sweden
Thomas Sterner, Environmental Defense Fund and Professor at the University of Gothenburg, Stockholm, Sweden
Susanne Åkerfeldt, Ministry of Finance, Stockholm, Sweden

An important tool to achieve reduced greenhouse gas emission targets is the use of economic instruments, such as carbon dioxide (CO_2) taxes and emissions trading[1]. Pricing of CO_2 emissions is essential to make those who pollute pay for their impact on the environment. A central goal and characteristic of CO_2 taxation is to set a price for fossil CO_2 emissions irrespective of the kind of fossil fuel that is being used, thereby acknowledging the Polluter Pays Principle. The use of this principle can, however, imply distributional consequences that need to be addressed.

This chapter outlines the basics of the CO_2 tax, which was introduced in Sweden in 1991 as an important part of a major reform of the national taxation system[2*].

The Great Tax Reform in 1990/91

Sweden has applied taxation to energy carriers for a long time. Up until the 1970s, the primary reason for taxation was to raise public revenues and taxation consisted of one single tax, an energy tax.

In 1991 Sweden complemented the energy tax with specific CO_2 and sulphur taxes, as environment policy was becoming increasingly important on the political agenda. The CO_2 tax was introduced on all major fossil fuels at rates equivalent to 27 per tonne of CO_2. At the same time the energy tax rates were reduced by 50%. These two taxes combined, however, still meant a taxation increase for all fuels (although the increase varied in magnitude between fuels). All in all this still implied a pioneering – and very high – level of taxation on fuels compared to other countries.

The introduction of CO_2 taxation was part of a major tax reform that implied dramatically lower marginal income taxes on capital and labour, the elimination of various tax shelters, base broadening of the value added tax, etc. It is worth emphasizing that the political opportunity to introduce this rather unique tax consisted of the confluence of two separate political processes. On the one hand, there was a demand for a drastic reduction in marginal income tax rates which had reached very high levels (in some cases around 90%). At the same time there was an increasing interest in environmental issues politically and throughout society. The CO_2 tax was thus introduced at a moment when there was a need to fill a gap created by reduced taxes on other factors of production. According to pre-reform estimates, the rate cuts entailed

1. In this paper we refer to carbon dioxide (CO_2) taxation. The molecular weight of one C is 12 and the corresponding weight of O_2 is 32 (2×16). Hence the ratio between CO_2 and C is $44/12=3.67$. In the comparison of carbon pricing levels, it should, hence, be remembered that one tonne of carbon (C) is equivalent to 3.67 tonnes of carbon dioxide CO_2. This implies, for instance, that, a tax of €10 per tonne of CO_2 is equivalent to 36.70 per tonne of C.

2. Parts of this paper have been previously published, see Hammar and Åkerfeldt (2011). The views expressed in the paper do not necessarily reflect those of the Swedish Ministry of Finance. The usual disclaimer applies. Research funding from the Mistra program Indigo is gratefully acknowledged.

a reallocation of revenue of approximately 6% of gross domestic product (GDP). The reform can be seen as an early green tax shift reform. The tax yield from changes in energy related taxation amounted to roughly 1% of GDP in 1991, of which the introduction of value added tax on energy consumption accounted for the major part (SWEDISH GREEN TAX COMMISSION, 1997)[3].

CO_2 taxation from 1991 to 2015

The CO_2 tax rates have over the years been significantly increased, with the purpose of achieving cost effective emission reductions. The use of tax instruments is considered to be the most cost effective way to achieve emission reductions. The tax changes have, however, been implemented stepwise so that households and companies have had time to adapt. Typically, tax increases in Sweden for companies and households in the energy and environmental areas have been combined with general tax relief in other areas to avoid increases in the overall level of taxation, address undesirable distributional consequences and stimulate job growth. Such a combination of measures has been the result of a desire to design the tax scheme in a way that ensures a sufficient balance between different policy considerations. It is worth mentioning that there has over the years been a general consensus among the different political parties in Sweden to focus on the CO_2 tax as the primary instrument to achieve greenhouse gas emission reductions. Sweden has had left-wing and right-wing governments, but this has not meant any major deviations from the chosen road forward in this regard. Also, all major Government proposals are based on in-depth analysis by independent committees which include experts from different parts of society. Further, the proposals are sent out for public consultation prior to being finalized in a bill to Parliament. This general law-making procedure in Sweden enables stakeholders and other interested parties to be able to give their views on the future tax policy design.

For instance, in the area of labour taxation, increasing tax allowances for travelling to work (including fuel costs) can be seen as a measure that to some extent counteracts the potentially disruptive consequences of higher fuel taxes. Also other, more significant measures, have been carried out in the area of labour taxation over the years. These include the introduction of higher basic tax allowances targeted at low and medium income households and, during recent years, major in-work tax credits. However, the main reason for the in-work tax credit reforms has been to boost labour supply and employment during the recent recession, even if it can also be seen as a way to compensate households for raised costs caused by increased environmental taxes. This can be illustrated by the fact that during the 2007 – 2012 period environmental tax increases for households and firms amount to + 0.5 billion, while reduced taxes on labour amount to − 8.6 billion. Thus, from a Swedish point of view it is essential to regard the CO_2 tax in itself as a powerful and necessary tool to curb CO_2 emissions.

The advantage of a CO_2 tax is that it is a market-based instrument, which enables households and firms to choose measures to reduce fossil fuel consumption – and thus greenhouse gas emissions – that are best suited for their specific situation. However, the effect of the CO_2 tax can be enhanced by aid schemes for limited time periods, to ensure that real options are available for households and firms. In Sweden such schemes have for example included investment state aid during the 1990s for fossil free electricity production, mainly for biofuelled combined heat and power plants. Also, a general focus in infrastructure projects has been on ensuring well-functioning public transport systems.

The development of CO_2 taxation and the use of revenues are determined in accordance with general Swedish national budgetary rules. A central element is *not* to earmark tax revenues, but instead the spending of the tax revenues is decided in the normal, annual, national budget process. However, throughout the existence of the CO_2 tax the policymakers have aimed at ensuring a balanced tax design by, inter

---

3. For readers interested in the tax reform in general, see Agell et al. (1996).

FIGURE 1 **Taxing carbon without taxing the economy?**

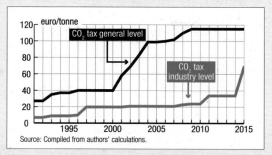

Source: Compiled from authors' calculations.

The progression of the Swedish carbon tax since 2000 has mainly concerned households and not industry. Industrial emissions have been taxed more since 2010, while the general level of taxation has remained fairly constant. This indicates a gradual transfer of the mitigation effort towards industry, to the benefit of households.*

*Nominal CO_2 tax levels, for 2010-2015 the 2010 level is used. From 2008, the level for industry outside the EU Emissions Trading Scheme (EU ETS) is shown. Fuel used for stationary motors and for heating purposes in the manufacturing process in industry. Diesel as motor fuel in tractors and other agricultural and forestry machinery is not included.

alia, a step-by-step introduction of CO_2 tax hikes and addressing for example undesired distributional consequences on low-income households by adjustment of the income tax rules.

A two-level CO_2 tax system

An essential aspect when designing the energy taxation system has been to strike a balance between fulfilling environmental objectives and accounting for the risks of carbon leakage (which in turn is related to securing the competitiveness of certain sectors that are subject to international competition)[4]. Ever since the introduction of the CO_2 tax, industry has faced a lower tax level than households on fuels used for heating purposes and for stationary motors. Figure 1 shows

how these two tax levels have developed[5]. Since it is necessary to avoid disruptive effects on competitiveness, such a lower tax level can be seen as a prerequisite for a high tax level for other sectors and has been instrumental in achieving major emission reductions in the household and service sectors[6]. This two-level system has been by far the most important element in the design of a well functioning system to curb CO_2 emissions in Sweden.

Motor fuels used in vehicles are basically taxed according to the general CO_2 tax level. The sharp increase of CO_2 taxation between 2000 and 2004 was to some extent offset by a reduction of the energy tax as far as motor fuels were concerned. The CO_2 tax proportion of the total tax on fuels (energy tax and CO_2 tax) was heavily increased. On the other hand, the sharp CO_2 tax increase was not combined with energy tax cuts on heating fuels used by households and services[7].

In 2009, the Swedish Parliament adopted a number of tax changes in the climate and energy area that would enter into force over several steps: 2010, 2011, 2013 and 2015. The purpose was to increase transparency and efficiency of the taxes in the area of climate and energy policy. In 2011 the CO_2 tax for industrial installations within the EU ETS was abolished, since national policies for emissions regulated at the EU level only cause emissions to move within the EU ETS without affecting total emissions. It is worth noting that this implied a reduction in the effective price paid by industry. This illustrates the difficulty of combining a tax policy with a cap and trade programme.

4. When high CO_2 and energy taxes imply that industries will move their production and consequently their emissions outside the "Kyoto bubble", an ambitious climate policy can give rise to undesirable effects in the form of higher global CO_2 emissions.

5. For a more detailed description of the CO_2 tax provisions for industry, see Hammar and Åkerfeldt (2011).

6. District heating has not only heavily increased its share of total residential and commercial space heating, but it is now also to an overwhelmning extent fuelled by biofuels (e.g. wood residues and pellets) and household waste.

7. The energy tax and CO_2 tax should be seen in combination, as two tax components rather than as two separate taxes. Sweden has been using these taxes as instruments to support various policy objectives. Apart from raising revenues, the energy tax takes account of other external effects than CO_2 emissions (such as noise, congestion and road wear from traffic) and also acts as a way of generally stimulating energy efficiency.

FIGURE 2 Can the carbon tax be social?

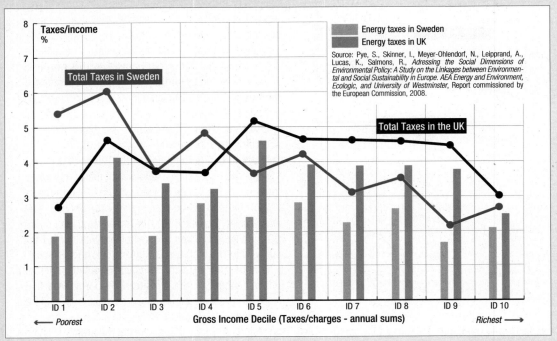

Source: Pye, S., Skinner, I., Meyer-Ohlendorf, N., Leipprand, A., Lucas, K., Salmons, R., *Adressing the Social Dimensions of Environmental Policy: A Study on the Linkages between Environmental and Social Sustainability in Europe. AEA Energy and Environment, Ecologic, and University of Westminster*, Report commissioned by the European Commission, 2008.

Swedish environmental taxation applied to energy is only slightly progressive. The middle and higher income groups are, on average, only a little more heavily taxed than the poorest 10% of the population. In other countries – such as the UK – the highest tax levels do not apply to the richest households (ID10) and nor to the poorest households (ID1). Between these two income levels, low-income households remain heavily taxed (ID2)

In 2013, the general CO_2 tax corresponds to €118 per tonne CO_2 (1.08 SEK per kg CO_2). It is interesting to compare this figure with the current permit prices within the EU ETS that are below €10 per tonne, or the minimum CO_2 tax levels in the EU proposal for a revised Energy Taxation Directive of €20 per tonne [8].

Concluding remarks

We believe the Swedish CO_2 tax experience is of interest for several reasons:

– it includes an early example of the introduction of a CO_2 tax.

– it was part of a major tax reform and the total tax share of GDP has actually fallen, so CO_2 taxation did not lead to "a bigger state".

– we have seen gradually increased tax levels that are now considerably higher than those typically considered in other countries and considerably higher than the prices in current carbon trading schemes.

– the risk of carbon leakage has been addressed through the use of somewhat lower tax levels (that are still high in an international context) for certain sectors that are more open to international competition and thus the risk of carbon leakage.

– a demonstrated and widely held political acceptance

and an evolution over time with, most recently, steps taken towards a more uniform and even higher national price on fossil CO_2.

– the Swedish experience shows that emission reductions can be combined with economic growth. During the 1990 – 2011 period, the CO_2 equivalent emissions were reduced by 16% while at the same time economic activity increased by 58%. A further important advantage of a tax (as compared with a cap and trade programme) is that the tax works well together with other instruments of climate and energy policy, such as green certificates and subsidies to renewables, regulations that have been introduced after (or in some cases before) the tax. ■

REFERENCES

AGELL J., ENGLUND P. and SÖDERSTEN J., 1996, "Tax Reform of the Century – The Swedish Experiment", *National Tax Journal*, 49(4): 643-64.

BRUVOLL A. and LARSEN B. M., 2006, "Greenhouse gas emissions in Norway: Do carbon taxes work?", in T. Sterner and A. Muller: Environmental taxation in practice, Ashgate Publishing Limited.

HAMMAR H. and ÅKERFELDT S., 2011, "La imposición del CO_2 en Suecia: 20 años de experiencia, mirando hacia el futuro" (in Spanish. English title: CO_2 Taxation in Sweden - 20 Years of Experience and Looking Ahead), *Fiscalidad Verde en Europa - Objetivo 20/20/20*, Centro de Innovación del Sector Público de la Fundación de PwC e IE Business School.

STERNER T., 2007, "Fuel Taxes: An Important Instrument for Climate Policy." Energy Policy 35 (6): 3194–3202.

SUMNER J., BIRD L. and DOBOS H., 2011, "Carbon taxes: a review of experience and policy design considerations", Climate Policy, 11(2).

SWEDISH GREEN TAX COMMISSION, 1997, *Taxation, environment, and employment*, Fritzes, Stockholm.

---

8. The CO_2 tax rate expressed in SEK per kg is used to calculate the tax rates for respective fossil fuel by volume or weight units (e.g. SEK per litre) in the Swedish tax legislation. An exchange rate of 9.1582 SEK per €, official rate per 1 October 2011, is used throughout this chapter. In USD, the current tax rate is thus over $150/ton CO_2 (or more than $550/ton C).

CHAPTER 9

Crisis contexts inevitably open the door to "rethinking development".
The current crisis involves each pillar of sustainable development, suggesting at least three types of responses – differentiating market relationships from those of society, and emphasizing their potential implications for sustainable development.

Pathways to sustainability in a crisis-ridden world

Peter Utting,
United Nations
Research Institute for
Social Development
Geneva, Switzerland

Recent global crises related to food, energy and finance, as well as
climate change and the scale of precarious employment, suggest
that we are in the midst of a broader crisis of sustainability[1]. This
is apparent in both senses of the term: the (dis)integration or
(im)balance of economic, social and environmental dimensions
of development, and chronic instability in terms of the long-
term reproduction of economic, social and ecological systems.
The Rio+20 summit positioned sustainable development as the
key challenge for contemporary development strategy. This was
symbolized in the call for a set of Sustainable Development
Goals (SDGs) to succeed the Millennium Development Goals (MDGs).

Contexts of crisis inevitably open the doors for "rethinking development". In the
wake of the food and financial crises certain features of neoliberalism, notably financialization, came under the spotlight, some new regulations and governance institutions emerged, and old and new social movements mobilized to demand policy
change that implied very different configurations of state-market-society relations
and development priorities. Similarly, as recognition of climate change has increased,
solutions associated with "green economy", environmental regulation and myriad
eco-social grassroots alternatives have gained traction.

In practice, different actors and institutions at multiple levels have called for

---

1. Peter Utting is deputy director of the United Nations Research Institute for Social Development (UNRISD),
writing in his personal capacity. This paper draws partly on Utting, Razavi and Varghese Buchholz (2012). Research
and editorial assistance from Nadine Ruprecht is gratefully acknowledged, as are comments from Shahra Razavi.

very different responses to both crisis and the sustainability challenge. This paper examines these responses through the lens of three ideal-type representations of different pathways associated with "market liberalism", "embedded liberalism" and "alter-globalization". It identifies key features of each of these approaches and reflects on their implications for sustainable development, understood here in the holistic sense of a development process that is economically developmental, socially inclusive, environmentally sound and rights-based.

A final section reflects on some of the limitations and challenges confronting each of these pathways and the prospects for change in the real world of institutional dynamics, contestation and interest group agency. While the dominant policy and institutional reforms that are currently being proposed and implemented tend to draw on elements associated with both market and embedded liberalism, it is argued that the challenge of sustainability requires far more consideration of the alter-globalization perspective within mainstream knowledge and policy circles. This, in turn, requires that social forces promoting such an agenda cohere, organize, mobilize and build coalitions for change.

Diverse pathways

Global crises not only deeply impact economic growth and people's livelihoods, they also unsettle basic ideas and assumptions about the meaning and drivers of development. In the wake of the global financial crisis a vibrant debate unfolded about "where do we go from here". This debate has been further energized by international efforts to craft a development agenda beyond the (2015) MDGs.

At the time of the financial collapse there was an instant revival of Keynesian ideas, which, in contrast to neoliberalism, elevated the role of the state and countercyclical public expenditure in development strategies. Speculative activities and financialization came under the spotlight as did the ethics of a development model that resulted in growing inequality and perverse levels of wealth for the 1%. Just as "third world" developmental states and northern welfare states eventually emerged as part of the solution to the crisis of the 1930s and geopolitical rearrangements associated with decolonization, the question arose as to whether a different approach to development and global governance might gather momentum. Or less ambitiously, would the type of policy reforms (e.g. greater fiscal "policy space" and more comprehensive social policy), which were introduced in some countries in the wake of the 1997 Asian financial crisis (KWON, 2005), be replicated?

As Bob Jessop has pointed out, a key question was whether global crises constituted a crisis "in" the system or "of" the system. If interpretations of crisis lean towards a crisis in the system then the solution centres on crisis management via adjustments in mainstream policies and institutions. But if it is a crisis of the system, then a more fundamental restructuring – involving transformations in power relations and in patterns of commodification, growth and consumption – is required (JESSOP, 2012).

A schematic representation of different responses is presented in the sections that follow[2]. The first involves stabilizing, legitimizing and sustaining *market liberalism*. It relies on market forces and technology, tweaks existing regulatory and governance institutions, and enhances some aspects of social and environmental protection. The second, *embedded liberalism*, seeks to craft a 21st century social contract via social protection, redistribution and rights, and a Green New Deal, whilst respecting the basic institutions of modernity and capitalism. The third, *alter-globalization*, calls for a more fundamental reconfiguration of state-market-society relations seen as conducive to both the social control of markets and emancipation.

Focusing on these pathways is not meant to suggest that others do not exist; these three, however, have gained considerable currency in the discursive arena concerned with issues of contemporary crisis, development and sustainability. Selected features of each of these pathways are discussed below and summed up in Figure 1.

Market liberalism

A remarkable feature of capitalism over several centuries has been its staying power and capacity to re-stabilize following episodes of crisis. From the perspective of sustainability, the contemporary challenge for the market liberal paradigm in contexts of crisis is not only how to re-energize and sustain growth and employment, but how to do so in ways that also address climate change and other environmental limits to growth, as well as threats to social reproduction and legitimacy associated with precarious employment and food insecurity.

To assuage international financial markets and investors, policies involving some combination of cuts in social spending and public sector employment, tax reform and labour market flexibilization were adopted in much of the global North after the financial collapse of 2008. The market liberalism approach leans towards enhanced public sector efficiency and safety nets as the means to limit negative social impacts of both crisis and austerity policies, as well to keep the lid on social discontent.

At a systemic level, a major challenge for elite economic interests relates to finding outlets for surplus capital by creating or expanding markets in developing countries, new industries, commodification and privatization[3] (HARVEY, 2010; GHOSH, 2010). Discourse, policies and practice associated with "green growth" (WORLD BANK, 2012b) are crucial in this regard, as are priorities of governments and corporations to secure new sources of energy, food and other raw materials. The market liberalism pathway favours approaches to green economy that are led by private investors and corporations interested in new profit opportunities associated with cleaner energy, payments for environmental services (PES) and the commodification of nature and the global commons. It positions such actors to take advantage of a market for environmental goods and services that is expected to double from

---

2. This approach was inspired by the analysis of Jennifer Clapp and Peter Dauvergne in Paths to a Green World (2011).

3. Speculation and militarization are other means that can be used.

around USD 1.3 billion around the time of the financial crisis to USD 2.7 billion by 2020 (UNEP, 2009).

In relation to the food crisis, the market liberal pathway includes the following features. Governments of a number of food insecure countries promote investment in large tracts of land in developing countries (so-called land grabs). Low productivity agriculture is identified as a key cause of food insecurity. It is also a key site for new investment in potentially profitable sectors, given the scope for productivity increases through a "New Green Revolution", which like its predecessor in the 1970s, modernizes agriculture through technology and intensification. The attraction of private investment in agriculture is further reinforced by the projected need for a 70% increase in food production to meet demand in 2050 (WORLD BANK, 2012).

High input agriculture with improved environmental management, greener technology and GMOs are seen as the way forward (PAARLBERG, 2010). Large agri-food and other corporations come to see low income populations as a largely untapped "bottom of the pyramid" market (PRAHALAD, 2005). Small farmers can be integrated in global value chains as both consumers of intermediate products and suppliers of cheap agricultural produce. Having relinquished direct control of land and production of raw materials several decades earlier, agri-food corporations need to (re-)secure raw material supplies through contractual relations that also serve to raise productivity and lock-in producers via measures associated with export orientation, training, input dependency and corporate social responsibility (CSR) (LUCAS, 2012). Discourses and practices about CSR, centred on voluntary environmental, social and governance standards, serve both to legitimize corporate expansion and mitigate certain negative externalities associated with business behaviour and global value chains (UTTING, 2012).

Concerning energy and climate, the market-liberal pathway favours market- and corporate-led green economy or lower carbon growth within a "lite" regulatory framework. Key features are carbon trading, investments in new energy sources such as bio-fuels, and gradual shifts in the energy mix from conventional fossil fuels and production methods to "cleaner" coal, gas and nuclear. This approach also involves tapping into new sources of "dirty" fuel (deep sea oil, tar sands) but adopting certain CSR practices and accepting a degree of environmental regulation. Managerial and technological solutions associated with eco-efficiency and cleaner technology are key for "relative decoupling" of economy and environment, i.e. to ensure that energy and material inputs decline relative to economic output (JACKSON, 2009).

Stabilizing market liberalism also requires discursive shifts that serve a legitimating function. This may include the rhetoric of protectionism, e.g. "buy American". Translating words into policy, however, is generally more difficult given the way "free trade" has been locked-in legally and ideologically. The discourse related to the greening of business and CSR is also key in the legitimization process. CSR emphasizes the capacity of (big) business to put its house in order through voluntary standards and initiatives. These involve codes of conduct, "sustainability reporting" by companies, and various forms of monitoring and certification. While such an approach is often dismissed as "greenwash", from a systemic perspective this "new ethicalism" (Sum, 2010) can be viewed as a necessary complement to institutional and regulatory reforms that attempted to lock-in economic liberalization and neoliberal orthodoxy through free trade agreements and WTO rules, or through what has been called "new constitutionalism" (Gill, 2003).

Embedded liberalism

A solution to the economic and social crises of the Great Depression and the two World Wars was "embedded liberalism" (Ruggie, 1982), an ideology and project which recognized that markets and economic liberalization need to be shaped by values and institutions that can mitigate market failure, social injustice and inequality. Key features of 20th century embedded liberalism were Keynesianism, state capacity to plan and regulate, neo-corporatist governance arrangements favouring organized business and labour, and the strengthening of the welfare state. In practice, these aspects were more apparent in some of the advanced industrialized countries and benefitted particular social groups, notably formal sector workers.

In today's world, embedded liberalism means addressing three challenges that were not central to mid 20th century embedded liberalism, namely: i) the structural reality of mass "informal" employment and the limited scope for universalizing social policy through the (formal) workplace and labour relations, ii) women's economic and social rights, and iii) the need for an industrial or growth model that does not destroy the environment.

Calls in recent years for a global social contract and a global Green New Deal suggest what contemporary embedded liberalism might look like (Birdsall, 2005; Brown, 2010; UNEP, 2009). In contrast to the rolling back of the state and certain types of regulation under neoliberalism, this approach leans towards enhanced state regulation, new or strengthened institutions of democratic governance and accountability; and comprehensive social (including labour market) and environmental policy. Regulations, policies and institutions of social dialogue attempt to promote "decent work" and counter labour conditions associated with precarious employment outsourcing. Key elements of the embedded liberal pathway are typically found in UN-system publications such as the report of the World Commission on the Social Dimension of Globalization, "A Fair Globalization", or more recently the statement by a group of well-known development economists, "Be Outraged: There are Alternatives" (Jolly et al., 2012), or the report of the Stiglitz Commission set up by the UN General Assembly in the wake of the 2008 financial collapse. The report of the high level panel on global sustainability, "Resilient People, Resilient Planet" brings together perspectives supportive of green economy or green growth with human rights. It was also laid out clearly by former UK prime minister, Gordon Brown, in "Beyond the Crash" (Brown, 2010).

Two recent developments point to the crafting of a 21st century social contract. First, several of the BRICS countries and some other developing economies, have broadened the scope of social policy and introduced new large-scale social programmes. Second, internationally, there is growing momentum behind the idea of a global social floor whereby all countries would provide a set of basic social benefits including access to essential healthcare and income security for children, the unemployed, elderly and disabled (DEACON, 2012; ILO, 2011b).

Of particular interest from the perspective of coupling inclusiveness or social protection and environmental sustainability, is the new policy arena of "eco-social" policy (UNRISD, 2012; GOUGH, 2012). Examples include workfare programmes in India that rehabilitate rural and environmental infrastructure, compensation in EU countries for low-income households affected by increases in energy prices, and the new IMF strategy to promote reductions in fuel subsidies in developing countries whilst simultaneously expanding social safety-net schemes, as has occurred, for example, in Indonesia (INTERNATIONAL MONETARY FUND, 2012).

Embedded liberal responses to the food crisis highlight the need to reverse the neglect of agriculture and rural development, which has occurred in national and international policy circles in recent decades, via aid and public investment in infrastructure and skills development. A key goal is to promote food security via increases in agricultural productivity, smallholder economic empowerment and multi-functional agriculture (IFAD, 2010). Regulations and standards associated with land governance or land rights, as well as ethical trade also feature prominently.

Discourse and policy associated with green economy focuses on dematerialization, subsidy reform, and the need for significant investment, training and employment generation in "cleaner" and green sectors and industries. Social dimensions of green economy are also addressed including decent work, social policy to compensate losers in the transition to lower carbon economies, and stakeholder participation in consultative processes

Alter-globalization

Major gatherings of civil society in recent years, in events like the World Social Forum and the People's Summit at Rio+20 in 2012, bring into sharp relief a third scenario of change, which we can call "alter-globalization". This suggests that dealing with current and recurring economic, food and climate crises requires not only rolling back neoliberal policies, strengthening state regulatory capacity and democratizing global governance, but also a more fundamental restructuring of market and power relations which are seen as central to social and environmental injustice.

Within the field of critical scholarship and advocacy considerable attention is focusing on the need to transform capitalist relations and institutions (BELLO, 2005; CAVANAGH and MANDER, 2004); how to reassert social control over finance, production and distribution and consumption (HARVEY, 2010); deep transformation of growth and consumption patterns (JACKSON, 2009); and emancipation from forms of domination associated with gender and ethnicity (FRASER, 2012). But the alter-globalization pathway goes beyond changing material and political aspects by calling for fundamental shifts in values. The structure of the outcome report of the Thematic Social Forum, "Another Future is Possible", prepared for the 2012 People's Summit in

Rio de Janeiro, is telling in this regard. Before addressing the question of economic transformation (Part 2) and political transformation (Part 3), it begins with the discussion of how sustainability demands new "ethical, philosophical and cultural foundations". These relate, for example, to the imperative of equity, care, stewardship, diversity, solidarity, non-violence, and recognizing the symbiosis of human life and nature (THEMATIC SOCIAL FORUM, 2012).

Sharing some commonalities with the embedded liberal approach, the alterglobalization route to sustainability lies in the creation of a people-centred economy. Here employment is generated through a fundamental retrofitting of economies, finance serves production and communities, international taxation (such as the Tobin Tax) serves to control speculative activity and mobilizes new sources of finance for sustainable development, international financial institutions are democratized, and corporations are held accountable or, indeed, "dismantled"[4].

But the concern broadens from the question of how to re-embed liberalism through social protection and regulatory reforms to the need to transform capitalism through deeper structural, cultural and political change. The challenge lies not simply with institutional adjustments but in deep changes in production and consumption patterns. A new growth model centred on low carbon economic activities and dematerialized services, community-based social enterprises, and the provision of public goods is key (JACKSON, 2009).

Deep changes in power relations are required both to curb the power of elites (not least corporations) to influence politics (REICH, 2010; MARQUES and UTTING, 2010), and to provide far greater scope for the effective participation of citizens and disadvantaged social groups. While both the market and embedded liberal pathways acknowledge, to varying degrees, the importance of "participation", this is often reduced to notions of stakeholder consultation, or in the case of embedded liberalism, to social dialogue involving organized business and labour, as well as NGOs. Under the alter-globalization approach, participation conforms more to the definition coined by UNRISD in the late 1970s, namely, the organized efforts of the disadvantaged to gain control over resources and regulatory institutions that affect their lives (UNRISD, 2003). Social agency centred on grassroots collective organization and social movements is key for meaningful participation.

The term "food sovereignty", which has been popularized by Via Campesina, can be used to sum up the alter-globalization approach to dealing with the food crisis and food strategy. Here attention focuses on securing the land rights of the disadvantaged; enhancing the scope for redistributive agrarian reform; and the importance of local knowledge, production and trade. It also upholds principles of fair trade and agro-ecology, and the need not only for smallholder economic empowerment but also political empowerment through collective organization

4. The term refers to the campaign, "Dismantling Corporate Power", launched at the People's Summit in Rio de Janeiro in June 2012.

and mobilization. The alter-globalization perspective seeks alternatives to food systems that are controlled by agri-food corporations and structured by "free trade" agreements that prioritize corporate/investor/intellectual property rights and facilitate cheap food imports from Northern countries where agriculture is heavily subsidized.

Much of the food sovereignty agenda, notably specific features such as agroecology, low-input agriculture and local trade, also relates directly to the challenge of dealing with climate change and the energy crisis. The Quechuan concept known as *Buen Vivir* or Living Well (FATHEUER, 2011), which emphasizes the rights of Mother Earth and living in harmony with nature and diverse cultures, is one descriptor for the alter-globalization approach to the climate challenge.

Elements of the alter-globalization pathway include not only relative but also absolute decoupling, voluntary simplicity which connotes the need to challenge consumerism and profoundly transform consumption patterns, and public environmental regulation and law, both national and international. This includes, for example, non- or "neo-extractivism" (Eduardo Gudynas, cited in Fatheuer (2011)) where governments are compensated for leaving oil in the ground (as proposed by the Ecuadorean government), and nationalize extractive activities, using revenues, inter alia, for social programmes, as in Bolivia.

Some proponents of the alter-globalization pathway pin their hopes on the long-term possibility that a cohesive coalition capable of challenging a capitalist class will emerge. This would involve social movements, non-governmental organizations (NGOs), trade unions, grassroots organizations and left-leaning political parties (BELLO, 2005; HARVEY, 2010). In the shorter term, some also look to populist alternatives of the type being pursued within the Bolivarian Alliance for the Americas (ALBA), as well as the scaling-up and ongoing proliferation of myriad social and solidarity economy initiatives centred co-operation and collective organization of workers, producers and communities.

Wither sustainable development?

In the midst of economic turmoil and the severe social consequences of recent crises lies the optimism that contexts of crisis will lead to progressive change associated with sustainable development. Often compared to the 1929 economic crisis (UNITED NATIONS, 2009), which led to a more pro-active management of the economy by the state and the extension of various social policies embodied in the New Deal, many commentators argued that the financial crisis could create the political space for a structural transformation needed for the challenges in the social, economic and environmental sphere (NEF, 2008). Indeed, one argument is that crises are conducive to policy change when they enable societies to enact measures that would be impossible to enact in less distortionary circumstances (Hirschman, cited in Drazen and Grilli (1993)). New social movements like Occupy Wall Street and the *indigados* of Spain and Greece, as well as global rural movements like Via Campesina or Ekta Parishad in India suggest that social pressures for change are mounting.

Tensions and blind spots

Each of the different pathways outlined above raises questions vis-à-vis the challenge of sustainability. This is apparent both in terms of the relationship between economic, social, environmental and emancipatory dimensions of development, and normative aspects associated with well-being and rights (of people and the planet) and intra- and inter-generational equity. Each pathway is characterized by certain biases, blind spots or the so-called elephant in the room syndrome.

While many social groups today are seriously affected by vulnerability and insecurity, a fundamental challenge of sustainability relates to living conditions of future generations. Unless issues of debt, inequality and decoupling are addressed head on, it is our children's children and subsequent generations that will suffer most.

The market liberalism pathway to sustainability tends to adopt a narrow, if not contradictory, approach to such issues. Attention to the debt issue centres to a large extent on austerity policies involving cuts in certain social spending. Concerns for inequality relate to equality of opportunity (not equality of outcomes), which are addressed primarily through education and active labour market policies. Decoupling involves only relative (not absolute) decoupling, largely through technological and managerial innovations associated with eco-efficiency.

The policy response to the financial crash, particularly in the United States, was designed essentially by persons closely associated with financial institutions and whose world views corresponded closely with the market liberal paradigm. Government policy may have prevented a general financial meltdown, but mainstream policy discourse narrowed the effective scope of public debate to a limited set of policy options and diverted attention from questions of institutional design, as well as from deeper causes that reproduce crisis-tendencies (Jessop, 2012).

The market liberal approach is economically and technologically deterministic. By de-emphasizing the key role of institutions and politics in shaping development processes and outcomes it leaves open key questions about state and societal capacity to engineer transition, the distributional consequences of change processes for different income or social groups, and ongoing contradictions that will arise in contexts financialization, market de-regulation and public sector retrenchment. In the context of financial crisis, capital must seek to take advantage of surplus labour through policies and practices associated with the flexibilization of labour markets. This may facilitate hiring but also firing and more precarious forms of employment (Standing, 2011). Furthermore, it can transfer risks and costs downstream towards suppliers and producers in global value chains.

Policy responses to the financial crisis included massive liquidity injections into the financial system and direct support to major financial institutions (United Nations, 2009). Much of the criticism of the bailout of the banks has been that it restored "Wall Street" and executive pay but not enterprise and employment on "Main Street". While there were signs of global economic recovery in 2009 and 2010, the world has experienced a "jobless recovery" (ILO, 2011). In 2011 the number of workers in vulnerable employment[5] was estimated at 1.52 billion. Nearly 30% of all workers (more than 900 million) were living with their families below the $2 a day poverty line, up 55 million in relation to pre-crisis trends (ILO, 2012).

Within the market liberal frame, macro-economic and structural fundamentals that underpin unsustainable development are not seriously interrogated. The key to social development fundamentally lies in reactivating employment through growth, voluntary corporate social responsibility, social protection (safety-nets for the most needy), education and training. Often sidelined are redistributive policy and public policy associated with care and social reproduction that provides women with greater freedom of choice and is important for social cohesion (FRASER, 2012). Also marginalized are various forms of mandatory regulation that can minimize tensions between market-led development and social well-being. The environmental pillar is addressed through greener technology, eco-efficiency, environmental management and better pricing signals, whilst largely ignoring the structural, institutional and political underpinnings of environmental decline and climate change. The market liberalism pathway may address the economic power of monopolies through competition policy and anti-trust regulation (THE ECONOMIST, 2012) but downplays the scale of the climate change challenge (and the need for decoupling), as well as the issue of skewed power relations and political influence of organized business interests.

Embedded liberalism emphasizes the need for stronger institutions to reshape development processes. The debt issue is addressed through such means as progressive taxation, public sector efficiencies and regulations on the reserve requirements of banks. It is more proactive in relation to inequality through certain redistributive policies and also emphasizes the need for relative decoupling of environmental impacts and growth. In contrast to market-liberalism, it extends the focus of social policy beyond social protection to redistributive policies and eco-social policy, food security and green jobs. But like market liberalism, it places great store on the growth-employment-consumer demand nexus. The notion of a 21st century social contract is directly concerned with issues of social protection and redistributive justice but within the frame of fairly conventional patterns of growth and consumption (BIRDSALL, 2005).

Embedded liberal environmentalism couples technological solutions and "getting the prices right" with stricter environmental protection and regulation. It leaves open, however, questions about the scope for absolute decoupling, i.e. the need for emissions or resource impacts of economic activity to decline in absolute terms. Whilst emphasizing the role of accountability, stakeholder or social dialogue, and global governance, it tends to downplay the need to significantly transform power relations both among social groups and North and South. Whilst strong on the need to correct certain social and environmental injustices associated with market liberalization, embedded liberalism can play down or ignore various forms of domination

---

5. The ILO defines vulnerable employment as the sum of own-account workers and unpaid family workers.

FIGURE 1 Pathways to Sustainability?

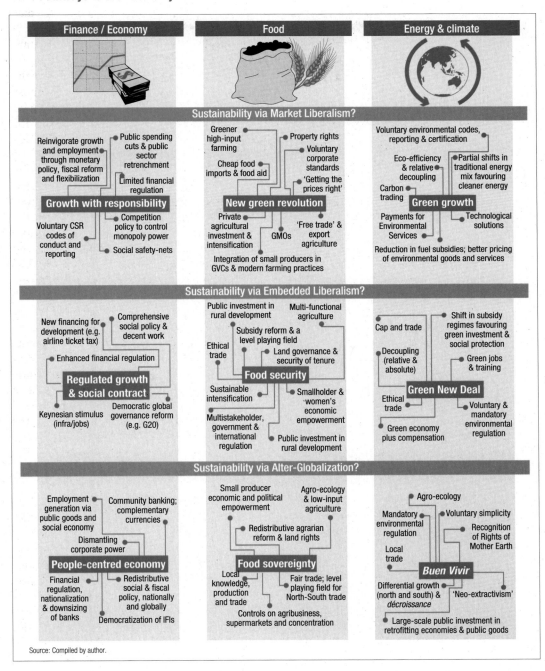

Source: Compiled by author.

associated with gender (patriarchy) and ethnicity, and the corresponding need for "emancipation" (FRASER, 2012).

Within the alter-globalization camp one finds more emphasis on issues of decoupling, inequality and emancipation. In relation to the debt problem, considerable attention is focused on such aspects as reduced government spending on defence and corporate subsidies, controls on money creation and lending by banks, as well as debt forgiveness for low income countries. As argued below, however, other aspects have been neglected. Alter-globalization sees conventional growth patterns and consumerism as central to the problem of unsustainable development, requiring either *décroissance* (degrowth) or highly differentiated growth patterns for developed and developing countries, as well as voluntary simplicity in relation to consumption patterns. The social and environmental pillars of sustainable development are addressed not only through comprehensive social policy (related to social assistance, services, care, training and redistribution) but also proactive community and local development, social and solidarity economy organizations and enterprises, and food sovereignty.

While proponents of the alter-globalization pathway tackle crucial structural issues they often ignore others that have bedevilled radical transitions (populist or socialist). These include, lack of understanding of, or capacity to anticipate, the economic, social and political consequences of disarticulating complex market systems, not only in terms of the reaction of market forces, investors, savers and consumers, but also the multiple functions of market actors and institutions that are crowded out. The fiscal issue is often downplayed. This relates to the ways and means of financing change, whether the mechanisms in place are sustainable over the long-term, and impacts in terms of debt and inflation. So too is the political question relating to the fact that leaders and parties associated with sub-altern groups need to become "hegemonic" in the Gramscian sense. This refers to the capacity to govern on the basis of consensus, rather than coercion, building broad-based coalitions and accommodating diverse interests and demands, including those of the middle class and business sectors. The political question also concerns the co-optation of social movements and civil society leaders, and the ongoing neglect of certain rights of women and indigenous peoples or injustices within communitarian society. Issues related to state capacity and legitimacy, which is crucial for transition, may receive short shrift, including problems of middle class brain drain, the competency of the civil service, and the transparency and accountability of public institutions.

The interplay of ideas, actors and institutions

Ideal-type representations correspond more to the discourse or rationalizations that different actors espouse as their preferred approach to crisis and "sustainability" than to real world policy and practice. As various literatures and writers have emphasized, reality consists of hybrids and diverse, heterodox, institutional arrangements. Complex institutional dynamics and ongoing changes in political economy mean that standardized prescriptions tend to exist more on paper than in practice.

Real world policy and institutional change associated with sustainable development will be shaped by the interplay of such factors as institutional path dependence; contestation and other societal responses to market pressures and failures; changes in political opportunity structures and state capacity; and the scope for institutional learning or "learning by doing". Indeed, as Ben Fine points out (2012), each area of policy (for example, health, education, trade, etc.) is likely to be shaped by different social, political and institutional dynamics, and each may follow a different trajectory in terms of social or distributive outcomes.

Beyond the dynamics of specific policy areas is the constant and evolving tension between, on the one hand, "capitalist logic" centred on profit maximization, commodification, "creative destruction", coercive competition, concentration, growth and consumerism, and, on the other hand, societal responses that aim to mitigate negative social and environmental effects associated with these relations through some form of social regulation (POLANYI, 2001; STREECK, 2008; HARVEY 2010). And beyond the tensions and struggles associated with commodification and decommodification are other struggles for emancipation (FRASER, 2012).

Eclecticism and hybrids, rather than anything approaching ideal-type futures or "utopias designed by committees" (WOLFE, 1996), are more likely outcomes. Spaces for progressive change may open in one area, only to close in another. For example, small farmers participating in fair trade producer groups, which promote agro-ecology, producer empowerment, and community development, simultaneously integrate global value chains dominated by transnational corporations. Such relations involve terms, standards and priorities that can deviate substantially from those associated with fair trade.

As Elinor Ostrom and others have observed, it is often a complex mix of "polycentric" institutional arrangements (state, private, community) operating at different scales (local, national, regional, global) that provide the complementarities and synergies that facilitate regulation, efficiency and governance (OSTROM, 2009; BRETT, 2009).

Diverse and often contradictory approaches may also exist at the macro level. Some welfare state regimes that typified the 20th century European embedded liberalism now conform more to a "flexicurity" model, which retains basic social services but flexibilizes labour markets and rolls back, to some extent, progressive taxation. Some governments that form part of ALBA, which promotes an alternative development model through south-south co-operation and solidarity, are simultaneously locked into free trade agreements with their ideological adversaries such as the USA.

But ideas and discourse do matter. They frame and influence public and policy debate and can influence priorities. And they shape common sense understandings about the meaning of development, ways forward, what are legitimate issues for concern and what should remain off-limits (OCAMPO, 2006).

The recent Rio+20 process and Summits (both the official and the People's Summit) intended to re-energize the political momentum for action to craft a more sustainable future. All three world views and perspectives outlined above were well represented (UTTING, 2012). The official Summit outcome document, *The Future We Want* (like that of the Durban climate conference), is a hybrid of principles, proposals and initiatives associated primarily with the market liberal and embedded liberal approaches. This outcome was perhaps to be expected in the context of ongoing economic crisis, the proliferation of geopolitical power, the influence of corporations and market forces on agenda setting and policy making, and the fragmentation of civil society voices in the build-up to Rio.

The scale and scope of contemporary economic, social and environmental crises suggests that we are at a crossroads. Policy responses and solutions must go beyond the assumption that this is a crisis "in" the system that can be resolved through "lite" institutional reform. As in the past, we can continue to draw on policy and institutional arrangements associated with the market and embedded liberal pathways. Such an approach, however, is unlikely to produce the type of institutional and structural changes that a crisis "of" the system requires. Policy makers need to think outside their comfort zone. The alter-globalization pathway provides a fertile ground for new ideas and innovations. It also identifies certain ways of living and institutions conducive to sustainability that have been tried and tested but are often in urgent need of support.

Key to the receptivity of policy makers is not only better understanding of complex problems but social and political pressures. It remains an open question whether anything resembling, for example, the power of the labour movement that contributed significantly to the post-crisis social contract in the mid 20th century can be reproduced within civil society today. The People's Summit clearly honed the capacity of disparate social movements to connect, forge alliances, launch advocacy campaigns and craft a strategy for action. If that momentum can be sustained nationally and globally, and local and global struggles can connect both in terms of their analysis of development problems and strategically, then features of the alter-globalization pathway are likely to raise their profile both in mainstream discourse and policy. ■

REFERENCES

AGARWAL B., 2010, *Gender and Green Governance: the political economy of women's presence within and beyond community forestry*, Oxford: Oxford University Press.

Bello W., 2005, *Deglobalization: Ideas for a New World Economy*, London: Zed Books

Birdsall N., 2005, "*The World is not Flat*: Inequality and Injustice in our Global Economy", *WIDER* Annual *Lecture* 9, Helsinki: UNU World Institute for Development Economics Research.

BISSIO R., 2010, *Social Watch Report 2010: Time for a New Deal after the Fall Montevideo.*

BRETT E. A., 2009, *Reconstructing Development Theory: Responding to the Crisis of Global Equality*, London: Palgrave Macmillan.

BROWN G., 2010, *Beyond the cash: Overcoming the First Crisis of Globalization*, New York: Free Press.

CAVANAGH J., MANDER J., 2004, "Alternatives to Economic Globalization: A Better World is Possible", *Report of the International Forum on Globalization*

CLAPP J. and DAUVERGNE P., 2011, *Paths to a Green World: the political economy of the global environment*, Cambridge MA: MIT Press.

CROTTY J., 2003, "Structural contradictions of current capitalism: A Keynes-Marx-Schumpeter analysis", in Gosh, J., and Chandrasesekhar, C.P., eds., *Work and Well-being in the Age of Finance*. New York: Tulika Books.

DEACON B., 2012, "Shifting Global Social Policy Discourse and Governance in Times of Crisis", in Utting, Razavi and Varghese Buchholz (eds.), *The Global Crisis and Transformative Social Change*, London: Palgrave Macmillan/UNRISD.

DRAZEN A. and GRILLI V., 1993, "The benefit of crises for economic reforms", *The American Economic Review*, Vol. 83, No. 3 598–607.

DUNCAN G., 2008, *From Poverty to Power: how active citizens and effective states can change the world*, Oxford: Oxfam International.

FATHEUER T., 2011, *Buen Vivir: A Brief Introduction to Latin America's new concept of the good life and the rights of nature*, Berlin: Heinrich Böll Stiftung.

FOOD AND AGRICULTURAL ORGANIZATION (FAO), 2009, *How to Feed the World in 2050*, Rome: FAO.

FINE B., 2012, "Financialization and Social Policy", in Utting, Peter et al., 2012, *The Global Crisis and Transformative Social Change* (New York: Palgrave Macmillan and Geneva: UNRISD) pp. 103- 123.

FRASER N., 2012, *Can society be commodities all the way down?: Polanyian reflections on capitalist crisis*. Working paper series, No. 18. Paris: Fondation Maison des sciences de l'homme.

GIBBON P., LAZARO E. and PONTE S., 2010, *Global Agro-Food Trade and Standards: Challenges for Africa*, Basingstoke: Palgrave Macmillan.

GILL S., 2003, *Power and Resistance in the New World Order*, Basingstoke: Palgrave Macmillan.

GHOSH J., 2010, "The unnatural coupling: food and global finance", *Journal of Agrarian Change*, Volume 10, pp. 172-86

GOUGH I., 2011, *Climate Change, double injustice, and social policy- A case study of the United Kingdom*, Geneva: UNRISD.

GREEN D. et al., 2010, *The Global Economic Crisis and Developing Countries*, Oxford: Oxfam International.

INTERNATIONAL FUND FOR AGRICULTURAL DEVELOPMENT (IFAD), 2010, *Rural Poverty Report 2011*, Rome: IFAD

HARVEY D., 2010, *The Enigma of Capital: And the Crisis of Capitalism*, London: Profile Books.

INTERNATIONAL LABOUR OFFICE, 2004, *World Commission on the Social Dimension of Globalization:* A Fair Globalization- *Creating Opportunities for All*, Geneva: ILO

INTERNATIONAL LABOUR ORGANIZATION, 2011b, *Social Protection Floor for a Fair and Inclusive Globalization.* Geneva: ILO

INTERNATIONAL LABOUR ORGANIZATION, 2011, *Global Employment Trends 2011: The Challenge of a Jobs Recovery*, Geneva: ILO.

INTERNATIONAL LABOUR ORGANIZATION, 2012, *Global Employment Trends 2012: Preventing a deeper jobs crisis*, Geneva: ILO.

INTERNATIONAL MONETORY FUND, 2012, "IMF Sets Path for Sustainable Development", *IMF Survey Magazine*, June 25, 2012.

JACKSON T., 2009, *Prosperity without Growth: Economics for a Finite Planet*, London: Earthscan.

JESSOP B., 2012, "Economic and Ecological Crisis: green new deals and no-growth economies", in *Greening the Economy*, Development Journal, volume 55/1, March 2012. pp. 17-25.

JESSOP B. and SUM N.-L., 2006, *Beyond the Regulation Approach: Putting Capitalist Economies In Their Place*, Cheltenham: Edward Elgar.

KWON H.-J., 2005, "An overview of the study: The developmental welfare state and policy reforms in East Asia", in Huck-Ju Kwon, ed., *Transforming the Developmental Welfare State in East Asia*, Basingstoke, Palgrave Macmillan, Geneva: UNRISD.

LUCAS L., 2012, "Food Producers: A Shift from Subsistence", *Financial Times*, August 18/19, p. 8.

JOLLY R. et al., 2012, *Be Outraged: There are Alternatives*, Brentford: Waterstone.

KUMHOF M. and RANCIERE R., 2010, "Leveraging Inequality", *Finance and Development*, Volume 47/4, pp. 28-31.

MARTENS J., 2010, *Steps out of the Global Development Crisis: Towards an Agenda for Change*, Berlin: Friedrich Ebert Stiftung.

NEF (New Economics Foundation), 2008, *A New Green Deal*, New Economics Foundation).

OCAMPO J.A., 2006, "Foreword: Some Reflections on the Links Between Social Knowledge and Policy", in Utting P. (ed.), *Reclaiming Development Agendas: Knowledge, Power and International Policy Making*, London: Palgrave Macmillan/UNRISD.

OSTROM E., 2009, "Beyond markets and states: polycentric governance of complex economic systems", *Nobel Lecture delivered in Stockholm, Sweden*, on December 8, 2009.

PAARLBERG R., 2010, *Food Politics: What Everyone Needs to Know*, Oxford: Oxford University Press.

POLANYI K., 2001 (1944), *The Great Transformation: The Political And Economic Origins Of Our Time*, Boston MA: Beacon Press.

PRAHALAD C. K., 2005, *The Fortune at the Bottom of the Pyramid: Eradicating Poverty through Profits*, New Delhi: Pearson Education/Wharton School Publishing

REICH R., 2010, "Reading America's tea leaves", *The American Interest*, Vol.VI, No.2, pp. 6-17.

RUGGIE J. G., 1982, *International Regimes, Transactions, and Change: Embedded Liberalism in the Postwar Economic Order*, Cambridge: University Press.

RUGGIE J. G., 2003, "Taking Embedded Liberalism Global: The Corporate Connection", in *Taming globalization: frontiers of governance*, Held, D., Koenig-Archibugi, M., eds., Cambridge, UK: Polity Press.

SCHUMPETER J., 1976, *Capitalism, Socialism and Democracy*, London: George Allan & Unwin.

SOCIAL FORUM, 2012, *Another Future is Possible*, Porto Alegre: Thematic Social Forum

STANDING G., 2011, *The Precariat: The New Dangerous Class*. London: Bloomsbury.

STREECK W., 2008, *Re-Forming Capitalism: Institutional Change in the German Political Economy*, Oxford: Oxford University Press.

SUM N. L., 2010, "Wal-Martization and CSR-ization in Developing Countries", in Utting, Peter and Marques, J. C., Eds., *Corporate Social Responsibility and Regulatory Governance: Towards Inclusive Development?* London: Palgrave and Geneva: UN-RISD. Pp 50-76.

THE ECONOMIST, 2012, *Special Report: The World Economy*, October 11.

UNITED NATIONS, 2009, *Report of the Commission of Experts of the President of the United Nations General Assembly on Reforms of the International Monetary and Financial System*, 21 September 2009, New York: United Nations.

UNITED NATIONS ENVIRONMENT PROGRAMME (UNEP), 2008, *Green Jobs: Toward Decent Work in a Sustainable, Low-Carbon World*, Nairobi: UNEP.

UNITED NATIONS ENVIRONMENT PROGRAMME (UNEP), 2009, "Global Green New Deal", *Policy Brief, March*, Nairobi: UNEP.

UNITED NATIONS GENERAL ASSEMBLY STIGLITZ COMMISSION, 2010, *Comprehensive Study on the Impact of the Converging World Crisis on Social Development*, 65th session, New York: United Nations.

UNITED NATIONS, 2012, *Secretary-General's High-level Panel on Global Sustainability, Resilient People, Resilient Planet: A Future worth Choosing*, New York: United Nations.

UNRISD, 2012, *From Green Economy to Green Society*, Geneva: UNRISD.

UTTING P., 2012, "Introduction: Multistakeholder Regulation in a Development Perspective", in *Business Regulation and Non-State Actors: Whose Standards? Whose Development?*, Reed, Ananya Mukherjee, Reed, Darryl, and Utting, Peter, eds., (New York: Routledge and Geneva: UNRISD), pp. 1-14.

UTTING P., RAZAVI S. and VARGHESE BUCHHOLZ R., 2012, "Overview: Social and Political Dimensions of Global Crisis: Possible Futures", in Utting, Razavi and Varghese Buchholz (eds.), *The Global Crisis and Transformative Social Change*, London: Palgrave Macmillan/UNRISD.

WADE R., 2008, "Financial Regime Change?" in *New Left Review*, September-October, Volume 53, pp. 5-12.

WOLFE M., 1996, *Elusive Development*, London: Zed Books

WORLD BANK, 2012, *Food and Nutrition Security: A framework for action for sustainable development*, Washington DC: World Bank.

WORLD BANK, 2012b, *Inclusive Green Growth: The Pathway to Sustainable Development*. World Bank, Washington, DC.

The emergence of the middle classes in sub-Saharan Africa

Pierre Jacquemot Associate researcher, Institut de Relations Internationales et Stratégique, Paris, France

Sub-Saharan Africa has experienced dramatic changes in recent times, including sustained economic growth throughout the 2000s (5% to 6% of GDP on average), major demographic transformation, the pursuit of rapid urbanization and improvements in the management of economies, along with the emergence of the "middle classes". According to the African Development Bank, this social group already comprises tens or even hundreds of millions of people. Will these middle classes induce the inclusive and democratic development that some predict? To answer this question, there are three major points to consider: the phenomenon is usually accompanied by a deepening of social inequality; social ties tend towards less solidarity; and while certain demands for democracy may be made, they are often set in a context of relative "political apathy".

A widening of social inequalities

Despite national differences, all Africa's middle classes have managed to find a place within the existing income structures, between the very poor and the very rich, this income structure being very unequal, with gaps that have widened further during periods of rapid growth. In Mozambique, Kenya and Zambia, the Gini index (a high value represents greater inequality) varies between 45 and 55, while in Botswana, Lesotho and South Africa, it exceeds 60 (African Progress Report, 2012).

South African society is incommensurately the most unequal in Africa, while it was also the country that experienced the most spectacular rise of an intermediate middle class. Post-apartheid measures of the Black Economic Empowerment, initiated after 1994, led to rapid social change. Within a decade, 12% of the black population had access to the markets of intermediate consumption. The result was paradoxical: there was both a decrease in inter-racial inequality, along with an increase in intra-racial inequality, with the entrenchment in poverty of a larger proportion of the population. It can even be argued on the basis of the South African example that the promotion of the middle class has simultaneously led to the creation of a new poor class, largely composed of foreigners, in this case from Zimbabwe, Mozambique and DR Congo, to provide services at low cost to the middle class.

An impact on the growth and diversification of domestic markets

It would be wrong to assume that the intermediate classes that have emerged in Africa demonstrate homogeneous behaviours and shared objectives. It would also be erroneous to assume that economic and social forces cannot lead to the making of "middle classes" as discrete entities. They get their impetus from this transformation itself. The identification must therefore be made in motion.

More than a decade ago, W. Easterly (2001) anticipated that a virtuous circle would be triggered by the dual phenomenon of the boom of the middle classes and of urbanization. He predicted that consumers would become more numerous and that markets would gain in size; housing construction would experience a boom; and that the banking economy would expand. To what degree have these expectations materialized in the current situation?

The changes introduced by social evolution and the emergence of new groups can be easily detected in terms of consumption. McKinsey (2010) estimates that, as a result of a major growth in GDP per capita, an additional one hundred million Africans will have access to the market for basic consumer goods in 2015. PROPARCO (a member of the Agence Française de Développement group) predicts that the number of "creditworthy consumers" will be 132 million in 2020, then 243 million in 2040, which equates to $584 billion in terms of spending in 2020 and a market of $1,750 billion in 2040, which is more than the amount spent today by the 300 million urban Chinese Internet-users. Signs of an increase in domestic demand due to the appearance of emerging groups are already visible in the growth of two key sectors: the automotive sector and telecommunications. The dramatic spread of mobile telephony and the Internet correlates perfectly with the trend of social change.

To fully understand the future impact of this phenomenon on African societies, we must go beyond the figures and extend the analysis to dimensions other than income and consumption potential.

Monographic surveys (such as those of the Bordeaux-based Laboratoire des Afriques dans le Monde, which were conducted in South Africa, Ethiopia, Kenya and Mozambique, and those collected in Afrique contemporaine, 2012) indicate that the middle classes of these countries are comprised of teachers, nurses, shopkeepers, private sector employees and mid-level officials. These surveys also show members of this class work mainly in the private sector, sometimes in sectors that have been devastated by the structural adjustment programmes of the 1980s. These people seek a "good job" that is stable, well paid and which allows them to "gain status". The wives of these workers also participate in the family economy in increasingly independent ways. Priority is given to a low-level capitalization of resources, to health and especially to the education of children. The middle classes have statistically fewer children and spend relatively more on education. Aside from their regular job, most of the people in these classes have informal second jobs. The surveys also show that the values held by the urban middle social classes are geared towards a competitive market economy, greater

BOX 1 **The three categories**

The so-called African "middle" classes are difficult to identify. The African Development Bank, which has pioneered attempts of statistical identification (for the whole of Africa), now provides the reference (AfDB, 2011). It proposes a division into three categories, showing that these emerging groups do not strictly form a single "class", but rather fit onto a scale between "neither very poor, nor very rich", in other words somewhere "in-between".

The first of these groups, known as the "floating class", is only barely above the poverty line, the intermediate group or "lower-middle class" has attained a "low level of prosperity", while the "upper-middle class", which represents 5% of the total, has an average income of more than $10 per day. There is a clear distinction between these three groups and the "possessing class", also known as the "new rich", a group that live on more than $100 per day and have a lifestyle that attracts jealousy, as well as an equal measure of sarcasm, from the intermediate categories.

The histories behind the origins of the three groups in the "middle of the pyramid" are unique from one country to another. In Nigeria, which is by far the most populous country in Africa and has benefited from the redistribution of oil revenues, the middle classes have grown in numbers with the expansion of the private sector in areas such as banking, telecommunications and the service sector, mainly in Lagos. However, it is difficult to generalize about this trend, as estimations are that two-thirds of Nigerians continue to live below the poverty line. The extreme disparity in incomes is partly explained by the low-level income diffusion effect experienced in the country. In Ghana, the rise of the intermediate classes was associated with the sums of money that were sent by those that were part of a large diaspora. In Liberia, the intermediate class is comprised of educated entrepreneurs that were involved in the restoration of peace.

BOX 2 Disparities between the middle classes

The first group, known as the "floating class", is only slightly above the very insecure category. It includes people that have between $2 and $4 per day (in purchasing power parity). It is this group, located just above the poverty line, that has grown the fastest in recent years, from just over 10% of the population in 1980 to over 20% in 2010. Members of this class have attained a level above that of the very poor, but remain in an unstable and vulnerable position, at risk of returning to poverty in the event of a critical situation (unemployment, recession).

The second group, the lower-middle, has a daily income of between $4 and $10 per day. Its members have reached a "small amount of prosperity" and obtained an improvement in social status. Representing 9% of the population, this group has escaped from a number of daily risks and enjoys an income that allows relatively easy access to certain goods on top of basic food consumption requirements.

The class above, the upper-middle, lives on more than $10 per day. Representing 5% of the population, its members typically having invested a proportion of their savings in a suburban property near a big city. This class has everything to lose from political instability, insecurity, poor public management and inflation.

The "possessing class", which live on more than $100 a day, constitute the "new rich" (including the "Black Diamonds" of South Africa, the Nigerian "Oil Blokes", the Congolese "en haut d'en haut"), i.e. a group which includes a few million people across Africa, who are at the highest level of the income hierarchy and whose lifestyle is embodied by cars, property, travel and bank transfers.

FIGURE 1 A relative reduction of extreme poverty in sub-Saharan Africa

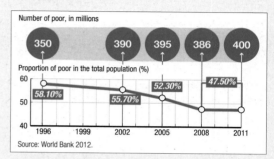

Source: World Bank 2012.

Sub-Saharan Africa has experienced a steady decline in extreme poverty since the 1990s due to unprecedented economic growth. This reduction of poverty is accompanied by the emergence of a middle class with new expectations in terms of consumption and living conditions.

political and administrative governance, greater gender equalities and more investment in science and technology.

Rearrangement of social ties

Africa's "middle classes" participate in the "urban dream". The top group, which has been in existence for many years, search for accommodation in clearly identified areas, seeking permanent houses equipped with running water and electricity. This group aims to buy rather than rent property, investing time and effort in considering ways to improve home comforts, including the purchase of electronic consumer goods. This behaviour can lead to the phenomenon of spatial segregation, particularly in terms of development and housing. The provision of housing for the middle classes and civil servants is often confused with the notion of "social housing", and it is these classes that have benefited the most from social housing and urban renewal projects. In Johannesburg, Nairobi, Libreville, Dakar and now increasingly in Bamako and Ouagadougou, there are privileged and protected archipelagos of high standard buildings, residential areas, administrative and commercial centres. These islands are surrounded by housing belts that accommodate those with a "low level of prosperity", while the outlying working-class neighbourhoods are surrounded by slums, which in turn

FIGURE 2 Social inequalities persist in sub-Saharan Africa

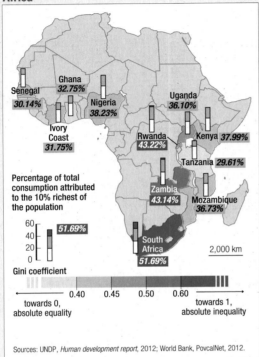

Percentage of total consumption attributed to the 10% richest of the population

Gini coefficient

0.40   0.45   0.50   0.60

← towards 0, absolute equality

towards 1, absolute inequality →

2,000 km

Sources: UNDP, *Human development report*, 2012; World Bank, PovcalNet, 2012.

The emergence of a middle class in Africa does not indicate an automatic reduction of inequalities. South Africa, which has experienced the most dramatic emergence of a middle class, is also the country with the highest rate of inequality, where the richest 10% account for almost 52% of total consumption.

are bordered by a ring of squatter settlements that provide a degree of shelter to the multitudes that are "excluded" from the modern city.

Divisions are also noticeable in terms of social ties, through a clear willingness for emancipation from the traditional model of the extended family, with references borrowed from external models conveyed by the media – television and the Internet – that these populations have access to, and of which they are great consumers. They are obliged to counterbalance two opposing aspects inherent to their status: they must take on board pressure, which remains intense, from their communities of origin with regards to the hierarchical obligations to support others; while on the other side they aspire to urban and individualistic modernity, driven by the notion of every man for himself. Since it is not possible to completely escape these ties, the social status can be seen as conferring a double bind onto the individual, making it necessary to make existential compromises that are difficult to live with.

Gradually, however, these populations change their habitus and develop new avoidance strategies, for example: ceasing to send money to their former village; no longer welcoming those that migrate from their village of origin; or no longer employing family labour. They shelter their nuclear family, their trade and business from solicitations.

A force for democracy or relative political apathy?

Some experts have raised concerns about these developments, fearing that the rise of the middle classes will bring acculturation and a loss of solidarity. The emergence of a depoliticized class, along with increasing inequalities, unchecked consumerism, lower levels of interaction, and a loss of the sense of community, could all open the door to new profiteers that take advantage of the social insecurity affecting both agents and victims of the new market forces.

At the same time there is increasing expectation that the "middle classes" may provide a driving force for democratic change. Their potential weight could, depending on local conditions, either make usurpation difficult, or mitigate the anti-democratic actions of regimes that are already in place that may have autocratic tendencies. It is also believed that the intermediate social group develops as a "middle class with aspirations", and therefore that it soon demands the construction of a state that guarantees compensation for losses of security resulting from the erosion of traditional protective institutions.

What do the field surveys tell us? They show that the African middle classes often have a certain political "apathy". These surveys reach opposite conclusions to the international and regional banks that target financial support towards the "new" middle classes, which they consider as in possession of the positive values of progress and democratization (World Bank, 2012). In fact, the creation of a new group does not always lead to collective action that would open the social system. Here we find the Olson paradox: since all members stand to gain from collective action, whether they participate in this action or not, it is therefore better to do nothing and rely on the action of others. Ultimately, if each member follows this line of reasoning, there is no collective action. Moreover, we are talking here about states where economics and power are often closely linked. It is therefore perhaps understandable that individuals may prefer not to openly challenge the elite coalitions in power, when their own position is not fully consolidated. ∎

REFERENCES

AFRICAN DEVELOPMENT BANK, 2011a, *The Middle of the Pyramid. Dynamic of the Middle Class in Africa,* Tunis.

AFRICAN DEVELOPMENT BANK, 2011b, Africa in 50 Years' Time – The Road towards Inclusive Growth, team led by Mthuli Ncube.

AFRICAN PROGRESS PANEL, 2012, *Africa Progress Report 2012 – Jobs, Justice and Equity.*

BARDELETTI J., 2011, *Petite prospérité, les classes moyennes en Afrique,* Paris, Images en manoeuvres éditions.

DARBON D. and TOULABOR C., 2011, *Quelle(s) classe(s) moyenne(s) en Afrique, une revue de la littérature,* Working document, Agence française de développement.

EASTERLY W., 2001, "The middle class consensus and economic development", *Journal of Economic Growth,* 6(4), 317-335.

JACQUEMOT P. et al., 2012, Revue *Afrique contemporaine,* n°244 (dossier classes moyennes).

McKINSEY, 2010, *Lions on the move: The progress and potential of African economies,* McKinsey Global Institute.

WORLD BANK, 2012, *Global Economic Prospects: Uncertainties and Vulnerability,* Washington.

CHAPTER 10

Deploying an effective social policy is no simple matter. Brazil, long known as one of the world's most unequal countries, is making considerable progress in reducing inequality and improving living conditions, in particular for its informal workers. To understand Brazil's success, we must look at the country's experience from 1930 to its recent Fome Zero and Bolsa Família programmes. Brazil is a major proving ground for an innovative social insurance system that may adapt itself to disparate local realities.

Brazil's social policy in the 21st century

Brazil's social achievements in the first decade of the 21st century are remarkable and have captured the world's attention. Indeed, the country became and continues to be an important kind of laboratory for the experimentation of social policies and for testing them on a massive scale. The eradication of extreme poverty and hunger is under way and, in order to keep momentum, the country now has to overcome challenges to boost the supply side of the low and middle-income strata of the economy to favour urban, rural and forest populations. These transformations are necessary for a sustainable development pattern, both socially and environmentally.

Thiago Varanda Barbosa,
Ministry of Social Development and Fight against Hunger, Brasilia, Brasil

Mayra Juruá Oliveira,
Centro de Gestão e Estudos Estratégicos, Brasilia, Brasil

The reader must be aware that this laboratory does not provide ready-to-use solutions, but rather shows that knowledge about the social problems to be tackled is a starting point. This is the basis for pragmatic governmental action; solutions must emerge from the specific institutional frameworks and social structures of individual countries. The upcoming pages describe the pathway to social inclusion undertaken by Brazil in the last decade, taking into account its specific institutional, political and social background.

Brazil's social policy in historical perspective

Poverty and hunger are social phenomena. While they are very real to anyone living under such social conditions, they may sound like a faraway tale to those who have never experienced such suffering. Be as it may, the fact is that no country, seen as a social organism, can fully develop its potential with such social atrophy remaining among its population (see chapter 4). To overcome the problem of poverty and hunger a society must have the political will to implement all embracing in-depth policies, confronting various difficulties that are caused by the lingering effects of long-standing existing policies and practices, which must be dealt with for once and for all. The very understanding of hunger and poverty phenomena may at first sight appear simple, but in reality the issue is highly complex.

Brazil became a republic in 1889. Slavery had formally been abolished just one year before. Agriculture was the main economic activity, which since it was oriented to commodity export, was based close to the ocean. Only a small part of the population benefited from this activity, specifically big farmers and traders. Throughout the hinterland, the Brazilian population formed a huge mass of deprived people.

By the 1930s the country was undergoing a transition from a commodity export-oriented economy to a more inward-oriented industrial one. By this time, there was already a rising urban middle class in the works. Social policies were being built that were structured and focused on labour rights, health and education of the formal urban worker. The great majority of rural inhabitants remained outside of this dynamic.

Throughout the next 50 years the country was to undergo a long-term industrialization process. But again, in order to support this rising reality, attention was primarily given, in terms of social improvements, to that same formal social stratum. From health networks to the gathering of social data, the focus was unequivocal: the formal urban worker. The core idea was that this social-economic pattern would one day be universalized. However, this did not turn out to be the case, not in Brazil, nor in the World-System as a whole (WALLERSTEIN, 1995).

Social policies in the re-emerging democracy

During this long-term development trend, the country was able to include into the formal segment around half of its population, until the model stagnated during the 1980s, precisely when Brazil was overcoming a three-decade long dictatorial regime. By the middle of the decade the country had re-established the right to have a civilian president, although one that was elected indirectly, and just three years later in 1988 a new Constitution was proclaimed.

However, by this time Brazil had ceased to grow at such a rapid rate and the federal budget was significantly compromised by the massive foreign debt burden that had been acquired during the previous decade. The aspirations for in-depth social reform advocated by the rising fresh new democracy were therefore obstructed. As a result, the government's social budget stagnated, caught between economic and financial contingencies and social pressure for expansive reforms.

The new Constitution established an ample spectrum of social rights and inaccurate attributions to the three executive dimensions of the nation: municipal, state and federal. The new constitutional frame was not yet backed by a legal apparatus, able to set specific responsibilities to each of the three levels of the executive branch. With unsettled legal obligations, government heads could politically and legally avoid some social responsibilities.

By the end of the first government of the post-democratization Brazil (1986-1990), one third of Brazilians under five years old remained undernourished (INAM/IBGE/IPEA, 1990). Unemployment was at around 7% of the working population (IPEADATA, 2012). Hunger and poverty acquired political relevance to Brazilian society. An increasing number of personalities from various walks of intellectual and cultural life started a movement[1] that led to a more proactive social awareness: hunger was no longer acceptable in a food-exporting country ranked among the top ten economies in the world.

The next President, Fernando Collor, did not improve on this scenario (1990-1992). On the contrary, by the time of his second year in power, food and nutrition policies underwent a budget reduction of around 80%. The subsequent government of Itamar Franco (1993-1994) inherited a political atmosphere of social mobilization. A new format of political articulation was set in motion by different government areas, while the participation of civil society in government decisions was facilitated by the creation of the National Council for Food and Nutrition Security. Its suggestion to decentralize policies to improve cooperation with municipalities began to be taken seriously by the federal government.

At the same time, Map of Hunger (PELIANNO, 1993) was published by an important public think tank[2], which highlighted the fact that 32 million people were living in hunger in Brazil. These people were dispersed throughout the country, in rural and urban areas. This publication also provided an analysis of the food production situation, concluding that Brazil produced an amount of calories and proteins that could feed a population 50% bigger than its own. A huge and alarming difference was identified between producer price and food cost to the final consumer.

Civil mobilization over the problem of poverty and hunger kept rising, in confrontation with the limits of Brazil's development process. The aim to universalize the income pattern of the formal industrial worker spread worldwide in the 20th century, pushing political forces forward in many nations to structure social security systems (WALLERSTEIN, 1995). This idea of the universalization of welfare was embedded into the 1988 Brazilian Constitution.

Health and education were established as civil rights in Brazil, but historically they had been geared towards the formal urban worker and thus for the main part only provided good quality services to this sector of society. Now, the forces pushing for democratization were pressing governments to extend these services to the entire population. However, since the budget was in decline, broadening the reach of these systems meant lowering their quality. As a result, and due to the encouragement of income tax reductions, the upper middle class moved to private education and health care.

---

1. *Ação da Cidadania Contra a Fome, a Miséria e pela Vida* (Citizenship Action Against Hunger, Misery and for life), created in 1993.

2. Instituto de Pesquisa Econômica Aplicada (IPEA), Institute of Applied Economic Research (http://www.ipea.gov.br).

This delineates the reality of welfare policies in Brazil during the 1990s: more people were able to access schools and hospitals, but they received lower quality services. Furthermore, despite the cost-cutting reduction in quality, these services were still not able to cover the entire population. Social assistance was scattered and left open to hijack by local political powers for electoral purposes, leading to problems of continuity as well as of focus away from those who were really in need. Thus, no clear-cut pathways to de facto continuous social inclusion were offered to poor families.

The great policy contribution for poverty reduction during that decade occurred in 1994 and was a side effect of the end of high inflation. The poor no longer had to deal with the month-by-month erosion of their income due to inflation. This increased the monetary value of their income, allowing them to spend more on consumption, thus taking 10 million people out of poverty (PELIANO, 2010).

From 1995 to 2002, the government of Fernando Henrique Cardoso advanced a neoliberal agenda with strong fiscal efforts. The National Council for Food and Nutrition Security was replaced by a Council with a broader focus on poverty, presided over by the first lady. An Executive Secretariat was created with no budget, its mission being that of linking and stimulating anti-poverty actions among the different ministries and with civil society.

However, contractionist macroeconomic policies were leading to increased unemployment, which reached 10.4% in 1999 (IPEADATA, 2012), along with a rise in social tension. Social policies were especially affected and, in accordance with the government's neoliberal agenda and its minimalistic idea of State, focalization on the poorest was chosen as a response to overcome budget limitations, at the expense of classical universal policies, such as education, health, pensions and other worker's rights.

The new generation of Brazil's social policies

In reaction to this neoliberal pathway that had not managed to reduce the social pressures that had emerged during the re-democratization process, Luiz Inácio Lula da Silva (popularly known as Lula) won the first presidential election of the current century on the strength of his electoral campaign which focused on a structured social agenda. The fight against hunger and poverty thus became the top priority of the new federal government.

When Lula's Workers'Party came to power at the federal executive it introduced the *Fome Zero* Programme (Zero Hunger), which was based on four lines of approach: (i) access to food; (ii) the strengthening of family agriculture; (iii) income generation; and (iv) institutional linkages, mobilization and social control (ARANHA, 2010). Furthermore, the new government had a broad development strategy based on the strengthening of the Brazilian internal market, employment creation and increasing the capacity for State action (BRASIL, 2003). Social policies became part of the arsenal not only to fight hunger, but also to stimulate the internal market and income generation in regions where they had stagnated.

A great number of policy proposals were now on the table, drawn from ideas that had emerged in debates since the 1980s and from many experiences that had been locally tested. There was also a need to continue the social policies that had been implemented by the previous government. The importance of this was realized once discontinuity, a characteristic of a fragile institutional and legal framework, was identified as a major problem associated with policies that focused on the poor. These efforts had a dispersive nature among different ministries and produced little intersectorial[3] dialogue.

The Extraordinary Ministry for Food Security and the Fight Against Hunger (MESA) was thus created to unite actions in the fight against poverty and hunger. Although it had greater institutional strength than the preceding Council that was presided over by the first lady, it still had no budget to implement policies of its own and its ability to link up different areas was redundant towards other government areas with similar functions, such as Casa Civil – which was later to become the main source of support to the President in his efforts to bring about more synergy between different areas, from infrastructure investment to action against hunger. In its first year, Fome Zero embraced 36 different actions. But the optimism for these proposals that were based on sound values was, as is usually the case, not enough: social policies must have efficacy and efficiency and, in Brazil, they must function on a massive scale.

There had been no previous experience of massive anti-poverty policies with a permanent structure and transparent rules. Some policies implemented during the beginning of the government showed good results and others were to have a complex execution or weak impact. Therefore a draft process occurred where some policies could expand, becoming structural to Fome Zero's strategy; some remained very limited in range, as if in pilot mode; and a few were simply discontinued. Federal per capita annual expenditure in social policies rose from US$950 to US$3,325 between 2003 and 2010 (IPEA, 2012); and federal social expenditure rose as a percentage of the total federal budget (see figure 2). As this budget increased in real terms, reaching US$320 billion, it is evidence that there was indeed a political effort to strengthen social protection in Brazil.

Identification and targeting

Identification of the target population and of their living conditions was the first key challenge for anti-poverty policies. Previously, identification systems were based on those who were already included in welfare policies or framed by formal employment. Such systems were designed to provide information about individuals, dissociated from their family structure. As policies were fragmented, so were their registry systems, throughout various ministries and federation levels. The creation in 2002 of

---

3. Brazil's multi party political system, its logic of coalition during elections and how each party of the winning coalition is granted with the power to appoint a Ministry or Secretary of its own, makes intersectorial work very difficult.

the Unique Database for Federal Government Social Programmes (*Cadastro Único*) and a unique social identification number was an important step to overcome this dispersion of social data sources. By the beginning of Lula's mandate, Unique Registry data still had a lot of flaws as far as quality and focus were concerned, and no federative pact had yet been built to allow for the necessary accountability.

In 2004, the Ministry of Social Development and Fight Against Hunger (MDS) was created by the linkage of the Ministry of Social Assistance, the MESA and the Secretariat for Food and Nutrition Security. The new Ministry was now able to incorporate social assistance, the *Bolsa Familia Programme* (BFP - a conditioned cash transfer programme to poor families), the Unique Registry as well as food security. At the launch of the BFP in October 2003, the President led a federal negotiation process that resulted in joint management agreements which set municipal and federal responsibilities. Registry data gathering became a municipal task and the federal government established an index for decentralized management, used both as a monitoring tool and as a formal measurement to the financial counterpart by the Union to the administrative costs of data gathering.

Income and family size are declared by families to the Unique Registry and this information is used to determine whether a household is eligible to receive a BFP grant and if so for what amount. In 2012, the BFP had 13.7 million beneficiary families with a targeting error of around 5%, which the World Bank considered to be a "very impressive targeting accuracy" (LINDERT et al., 2007:2). Federal government uses estimation criteria based on previously existing survey systems[4]. For each of Brazil's 5,565 municipalities, MDS estimates the number of poor families, setting quantitative goals for families registered by municipal staff. As informality is a characteristic feature of the poorest, although a declaration of family income is necessary to prove eligibility, there is no requirement for documental proof[5]. Accuracy comes from the knowledge of local officials regarding the poverty areas in their territories, and is calibrated using MDS's statistical estimates.

Of all policies advanced in Fome Zero's scope, the BFP has become a main pillar in terms of budget, extension, impact and public opinion. It is based on simple and clear rules, endowed with a family approach and it promotes universal policies of health and education through conditionality enforcement. For families to qualify for benefit, their children must have an 85% school attendance rate and be up-to-date with the vaccination schedule defined by the Ministry of Health, while pregnant women are required to adhere to a prenatal schedule.

Poverty and extreme poverty are defined by per capita family income. Of course poverty has many faces beyond just income insufficiency (STIGLITZ, SEN, FITOUSSI,

---

4. Brazil has well-established statistical institutions, for example the Brazilian Institute for Geography and Statistics (IBGE) that was created in 1936. The IBGE has conducted a National Household survey on a regular basis since 1967 and a National Census every 10 years.

5. MDS audits BFP's payroll using other administrative databases, such as those with data on formal workers, car owners and pensions. An additional factor that helps keep the targeting error low is social control, both among community members and by Municipal Councils composed by civil society to control local government.

FIGURE 1 **Who benefits from the *Bolsa Familia* Programme?**

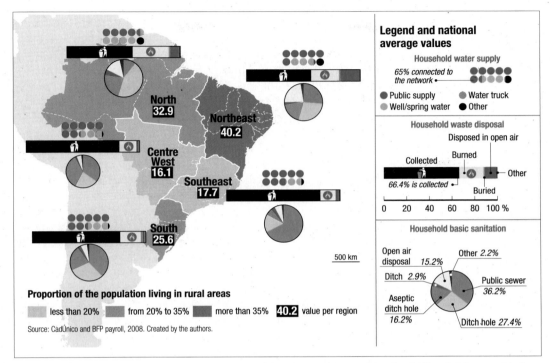

The Bolsa Familia programme has not only renewed the approach to social policy in Brazil, it has enabled the implementation of very precise statistical tools for targeting poor families on a territorial basis.

2008) but this factor has been chosen by the BFP as its sole eligibility criteria due to the fact that it is very easy to manage, it also favours the practice of social accountability. By operating in conjunction with the Unique Registry and universal policies, BFP helped government put aside the dichotomy between focused versus universal action. As both the Unique Registry and the BFP now function on a massive scale – they include 72 million registered individuals, one third of the Brazilian population, and 50 million beneficiaries – they are in a strong position to provide valuable information to other projects, such as rural electrification, basic sanitation and water supply (Table 1). Indeed, during the first stages of the implementation of massive anti poverty policies, it was easier to find poor families waiting for social inclusion. In 2011, 16 million are still excluded from Brazil's social, political and economical rights. While major efforts have not yet been enough to reach all of these people, it looks like the answer lies in targeting action towards specific populations, in terms of territories or cultural belonging, such as *quilombolas*, Indians, river side inhabitants, forest extractivists, etc. The Single Registry Department has built different strategies to reach these specific populations, and action was taken according to social movement demands. This approach has effectively reached many poverty spots that local authorities have not yet targeted.

Social assistance, a constitutional right, has now become institutionally structured through a federative treaty and specific legislation. Now, many Social Assistance Reference Centres (CRAS) have been established in areas of poverty through the work of the MDS, which aids infrastructure construction, together with municipalities, which provide human resources. They provide territoriality to a variety of social policies. Information technology is fundamental for the management of these decentralized actions. In 2010, MDS was monitoring more than 6,700 CRAS (BRASIL, 2010).

Supporting Family agriculture

On the supply side of food security policy, family agriculture has been growing in importance. Although 70% of the food consumed by Brazilians comes from family agriculture, the agribusiness had received preferential attention due to its importance in terms of the country's exports. However, since the 1990s a number of policies have started to be directed to small-scale agriculture. For example, a rural credit programme was created[6], setting in motion the registration of small farmers.

In 2006, specific legislation that defined family agriculture[7] was adopted, which created a better environment for the targeting of policies for this type of family business. An agriculture census in the same year identified 4.3 million family farms, which although occupied less than 25% of the total area of rural properties, they were responsible for 74.4% of agricultural employment (FRANÇA, DEL GROSSI, MARQUES, 2009).

Family agriculture became central to rural development strategies with policies of access to land, credit, insurance, technical assistance and commercialization. In 2009, 1.4 million small farmers accessed PRONAF credit (see footnote 6), which amounted to a total of US$7 billion in credit operations (BRASIL, 2010). Technical assistance for small crops was also improved and expanded. As usual, actions were dispersed among different ministries, so a programme was created in 2008 to link such efforts, which gave a territorial approach to government intervention on poor rural areas by defining 120 territories (made up of municipalities) where policies of all kinds should be present.

Commercialization, a long-standing problem for small farmers, especially in poor regions, was addressed by these measures. Agricultural businesses could now become financially viable through policies of public purchase from family farms, and through

---

6. The National Programme for the Strengthening of Family Agriculture (PRONAF), and the Declaration of Eligibility to PRONAF (DAP) a registry system that reaches 3.2 million agricultural families. Registration is done at the local level by rural unions or technical assistance institutions. Following registration, a family can access PRONAF credit at any bank or credit cooperative, once credit rules are approved by the National Monetary Council, a top financial authority.

7. Family Agriculture is defined by a maximum property size, where no more than two employees are hired, with the main income source deriving from agricultural activity and the farm is managed by family members.

an increase of the food expenditures of poor families. At least 30% of the school meal budget now had to be spent on produce from family farms. Another important programme in this respect is the 2003 Food Acquisition Programme, which purchases as much as R$8,000 a year from each family. In 2011, it bought 476 million tons of food, worth US$300 million, from 162,242 farms and donated to 29,800 social institutions (PAA DATA, 2012) such as schools, popular restaurants, social assistance centres, restaurants for people on low-incomes or simply directly to families. Products are also used to form public food stocks that function as price regulators and as emergency stocks in the case of climate disasters, the most common being drought and flood. At present the programme is being adapted in order to expand its figures to reach an annual budget of around US$1 billion.

FIGURE 2 Addressing poverty and the informal sector

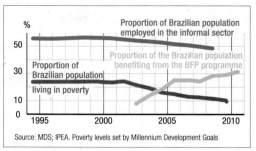

Source: MDS; IPEA. Poverty levels set by Millennium Development Goals

The Bolsa Familia programme aims to fight against extreme poverty in Brazil and to assist people that work in the informal sector. The increasing number of beneficiary families corresponds to a reduction in the number of people living on less than $2 a day or working in the informal sector.

Monitoring results and upcoming challenges

The MDS was created alongside the Secretariat for Evaluation and Information Management, which is responsible for the evaluation and monitoring of this new generation of well-institutionalized and decentralized social policies. It works in two ways: diagnosis and policy monitoring, carried out through networks with public statistical and research institutions; and policy evaluation by external institutions.

As statistical and administrative social databases have traditionally been based on the formal sector, and poverty and hunger are predominant among families living in informal situations, the management of policies that focus on the poor demanded a better understanding of the phenomena. By networking with public statistical and research institutions, MDS was able to open a methodological debate and advocated the inclusion of supplementary fields into traditional household surveys and in the all-embracing Brazilian Census. Through this effort the country is making advances in "the establishment of a broad statistical system that captures as many of the relevant dimensions as possible" (STIGLITZ, SEN, FITOUSSI, 2008).

As mentioned above, the Fome Zero strategy is linked with a broader development strategy based on internal market stimulus and employment generation. Prior to the subprime financial crisis, in 2008 unemployment had dropped to 7.8% (IPEADATA, 2012). This is important for a better appreciation of Brazil's recent social achievements. The total number of formal workers increased by 15 million between 2003 and 2010 (BARBOSA et al., 2010), during the same period minimum wage had a real value increase of 66%. Indeed, job market dynamic was responsible for 75% of the rise in household income during the first decade of the millennium (IPEA, 2012), which is a key element of poverty reduction. Inequality was also impacted, the Gini

FIGURE 3 **Structural fragility of Brazilian workers**

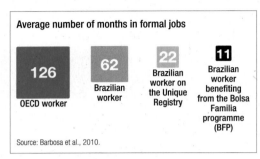

Average number of months in formal jobs

126 — OECD worker

62 — Brazilian worker

22 — Brazilian worker on the Unique Registry

11 — Brazilian worker benefiting from the Bolsa Familia programme (BFP)

Source: Barbosa et al., 2010.

The Brazilian labour market offers few stable jobs, which maintains poverty and makes the Bolsa Familia programme particularly crucial for many families.

index dropping from 0.594 in 2001 to 0.527 in 2011. Income source decomposition methods indicate the relative impact of each source on Gini reduction: employment and real wage raises, 58%; pensions, 19%; and BFP, 13% (IPEA, 2012).

Nevertheless, Brazil's job market remains a very unstable source of income for families in poverty. While OECD workers are hired for an average of 126 months, compared to an average for Brazilian formal workers of 62 months, those workers included in the Unified Registry stay hired for only 22 months – almost one third of the national average – and BFP beneficiary families on average keep their formal jobs for less than a year (Figure 3).

This reality points to the necessity of a new dynamic of social inclusion through productive means. As seen, a linked set of productive inclusion policies targeted to rural areas based on family agriculture is already in existence. But as yet no policy has emerged as a consistent solution for the stimulation of low-income businesses in urban and forest areas that is applicable on a massive scale. From the experiences gained so far, new policies should be targeted towards: (i) solidarity economy cooperatives; (ii) small business formalization; and (iii) the creation of new credit lines. Furthermore, technical assistance is still poorly adapted for small businesses. Taking these factors into consideration, in 2011 the new government of Dilma Roussef established the Brazil without Misery Plan (*Plano Brasil sem Miséria*). It was identified that Brazil still had 16 million people living in extreme poverty and that further efforts were necessary to change their situation. The Brazil without Misery Plan is based on existing policies and works on the improvement of policies through three lines of approach: income guarantee, access to public services and productive inclusion.

As seen, poor families in urban and rural areas face different deprivations that demand specific strategies from public policies. In the following section it is shown that Brazil faces not only urban and rural social challenges, but in the northern region of the country, the rainforest also poses a great challenge to social policies.

Poverty and environment

Policies that address poverty and promote social development in Brazil have always faced an additional challenge which is quite particular in relation to the majority of other countries: besides the usual dichotomy of rural versus urban, Brazil's forests represent a third dimension which demands specific consideration in national strategies. The debate on the economic use of natural resources, particularly from forests, is frequently associated with the debate on the policies and pathways to national development. The so-called Amazônia Legal, in Brazil's northern region, represents nearly 60% of Brazilian territory, provides home to 13% of the country's population, and contains the planet's largest reservoir of biodiversity and water. During the 1970s, the prevailing trend here was that of slash-and-burn clearance to create traditional rural and urban settlements. As result, two thirds of the population in the Amazon region live in urban areas, and about six million live in forest or rural areas.

At present, the rainforest is the ultimate frontier to social information and policy management. Social data on forest resident families remains absent, even though the Household Survey carried out by the Brazilian Institute of Geography and Statistics (IBGE) has been in existence for some time. While these people may be few compared to the entire Brazilian population, together with the rainforest itself they are the starting point for many solutions that the country must create to meet the necessary social and environmental sustainable development objectives of this century. In addition, forest populations are a major source of focalization error faced both by policies that fight poverty and universal ones. There is no doubt that the scattered nature of traditional settlements, inland and along the river margins, is a barrier to the implementation of social policies.

The main trajectory of rainforest resource production has been centred on mining and deforestation, which is largely illegal, upon which land agriculture and cattle ranching follow. President Lula's Minister of Environment encapsulated the nature of the problem, saying that while it is easy to dismantle an illegal sawmill in a day, it is not possible to create quality jobs for all sawmill workers at the same pace. Another important aspect should be brought to light here: that of the high amount of greenhouse gas (GHG) emissions that result from forest burning[8]. Although the Brazilian government's efforts to reduce emissions have produced impressive results, this fact alone has not been able to break the prevailing economic logic of that region.

As highlighted earlier, the dominant sociotechnical regime in the Amazon is neither environmentally nor socially sustainable. As was the case for poverty and hunger two decades ago, sustainable development has been emerging as a consensual political goal in Brazil's democracy over the last ten years. Rainforest preservation is essential for both the survival of the population and also to ensure that the rich spectrum of natural products offered by the region is not lost but sustainably used. It is now clear to all that the promotion of the sustainable use of biodiversity is key for long-term sustainable development. When the aggregate value generated by the forest "standing up" becomes higher than that of the deforestation ("forest down") activities, people will be more ready to engage in sustainable activities.

Federal government social grants (such as those from the BFP and, more recently, Forest Grant[9]) have been an important social policy for ensuring a minimum income for local populations within the Amazon region. Nevertheless, much more is needed to truly encourage sustainable development: it is of pivotal importance to promote natural resource-based productive chains that combine traditional knowledge of the uses of biodiversity along with science, technology and innovation. Certain

---

8. Deforestation is the major source of Brazilian GHG emissions.

9. Forest Grant (*Bolsa Floresta* in Portuguese), is a cash transfer programme aimed at seasonal sustainable activities.

products, such as natural cosmetics, foods, beverages and phytotherapeutics (herbal medicines) are already putting this into practice. Some large and medium-size enterprises, such as Natura and Beraca Sabará[10], have heavily invested in the sustainable development area, while at the same time they have worked with the local extractivist communities.

However, the prevailing economic activity in relation to forest resources remains based on the slash-and-burn model for providing valuable wood and useful land for agriculture and cattle ranching. Such extractivism, although recognized as an important social movement for the region, is faced with its own limitations in terms of absorbing a large proportion of the local working population without transforming its traditional techniques. This issue has become a major challenge to the development of the Amazon region and to the aim to improve extractivism through science and technology.

Conclusion

Social policies have developed in Brazil since the 1930s. At the beginning they focused on the formal urban worker, but following re-democratization in the 1980s, the problems of poverty and hunger gained political relevance for public policies. To plan and calibrate the targeting and formatting of policies, the Brazilian authorities used consolidated statistical tools. However, because the existing social databases and surveys had not been designed to capture specific information on poverty, new tools had to be created for this purpose.

These tools were not only of an informational nature. Brasilia has a well-established set of institutions at its command: three big public banks and a public investment bank; a federal universities network; statistical institutions; consolidated worker legislation; and effective external control. Politically, constitutional rights provide key parameters to social results, while more specific legislation is important to structure policies so that they can be maintained when there is a change in the ruling political party. Clear rules are fundamental for the popular acceptance of programmes and for social accountability. Social movements also play a political role by pressing for specific groups to be given access to social policies.

A new social security system has arisen in Brazil through the conjunction of policies based on universal social rights and those focused on the problems of poverty and hunger. This social security system is linked to a broader development strategy based on Brazil's huge internal market.

Brazil's social policies have many successful strategic features: the merging and strengthening of social databases to enhance the understanding of poverty in its different social environments; the decentralizing of operations to cut costs and improve targeting quality; assigning well-defined roles and responsibilities which

---

10. Natura is the largest cosmetic company in Brazil. Baraca Saba is the major organic supplier for cosmetics enterprises in the country and is a pioneer in organizing local communities to extract biodiversity products by traditional processes.

favour accountability; implementing clear and simple rules that favour social control; the targeting of cash transfer and other policies towards the poor to complement universal policies; the use of food acquisition and institutional markets to improve rural income and local circuits of wealth; the use of employment and minimum wage increase in the fight against poverty; applying a territorial focus, which favours policy intersectoriality; the specific targeting of populations to address targeting errors; the monitoring and evaluation of policies as a guide; and finally the acceptance that trial and error is inevitable and political will is obligatory.

In spite of the many successes, Brazil's social policies still face a great challenge if extreme poverty and hunger is to be eradicated. During the last decade, social policies became synergic with the country's broad development strategy by stimulating economically stagnated areas with an influx of income – through cash transfers or family agriculture incentives – and an expansion of social services and infrastructure. This dynamic of income generation led the country to acquire economic and social momentum through the expansion of low and medium-income household consumption. To maintain this momentum, the challenge now turns to the supply side of the economy, and must be met through low and middle-income entrepreneurship. Options are already evident for rural areas, such as the expansion of productive inclusion policies, while effective alternatives are required for urban and forest area production. ■

REFERENCES

Aranha A., 2010, Fome Zero: a construção de uma estratégia de combate à fome no Brasil. In Brasil. *Fome Zero: Uma história brasileira*. Brasília: MDS.

Barbosa T. et al., 2010, O Direito ao Trabalho e a Necessidade de uma Política Nacional de Inclusão Produtiva. In BRASIL. *Fome Zero: Uma história brasileira*. Brasília: MDS.

Brasil, 2003, *Plano plurianual 2004-2007*. Brasília: MP.

Brasil, 2010, *Fome Zero: Uma história brasileira*. Brasília: MDS.

Centro de Gestão e Estudos Estratégicos, 2009, *Um Projeto para a Amazônia no século 21: desafios e contribuições*. Brasília: CGEE.

Centro de Gestão e Estudos Estratégicos, 2011, *Brazilian Sectoral Report – The Amazon Region and the use of its biodiversity*. in: *Opening up Natural Resource-based industries for innovation*: exploring new pathways for development in *Latin-America*. Brasília: CGEE.

Centro de Gestão e Estudos Estratégicos, 2011, Brazilian *Fieldwork Report (cosmetics and forest management)*. in: *Opening up Natural Resource-based industries for innovation*: exploring new pathways for development in *Latin-America*. Brasília: CGEE.

Centro de Gestão e Estudos Estratégicos, 2011, Amazon Environmental Research Institute; Secretariat of Strategic Affairs of the Presidency of Brazil. REDD in Brazil: A Focus on the Amazon Brasília: CGEE.

França C., Del Grossi M and Marques V.P., 2009, *O Censo Agropecuário 2006 e a agricultura familiar no Brasil*. Brasília, MDA, 2009.

INAM/IBGE/IPEA, 1990, *Pesquisa Nacional de Saúde e Nutrição*. Brasília, março de 1990.

IPEA, 2012, Nota técnica. *Gasto Social Federal: prioridade macroeconômica no período 1995-2010*. Brasília: IPEA.

IPEA, 2012, Comunicado nº 155. Brasília: IPEA.

Ipeadata, 2012, http://www.ipeadata.gov.br/. Accessed in November 2012

Lindert K., Linder A., Hobbs J. and Brière B., 2007, "The Nuts and Bolts of Brazil's Bolsa Família Program: Implementing Conditional Cash Transfers in a Decentralized Context. In World Bank. Discussion paper nº 0709.

Oliveira M. J. G., 2006, *A importância da ciência e tecnologia no desenvolvimento da Amazônia e o caso do Acre*. Dissertação de mestrado. Brasília.

Peliano A., 1993, *O Mapa da Fome: subsídios à formulação de uma política de segurança alimentar*. Brasília: IPEA, 1993.

Peliano A., 2010, Lições da História – Avanços e Retrocessos na Trajetória das Políticas Públicas de Combate à Fome e à Pobreza no Brasil. In Brasil. *Fome Zero: Uma história brasileira*. Brasília: MDS.

Stiglitz J., Sen A., Fitoussi J.-P., 2008, *Report by the Commission on the Measurement of Economic Performance and Social Progress*. Paris, CMEPSP.

Wallerstein I., 1995, After Liberalism. New York: The New Press.

South Africa: when devolved governance fails

Thierry Giordano Centre de Coopération International en Recherche Agronomique pour le Développement, Montpellier, France

1994: Nelson Mandela is elected as the first president of the post-Apartheid era. There is much work to be done to correct the gender, racial and spatial imbalances inherited from the past regime. The Reconstruction and Development Program (RDP) is then launched by the new government, which aims to address the inequalities that exist in terms of access to education, water, energy, housing, employment and land. Meanwhile, the Commission for a Democratic South Africa (CODESA) starts working on the drafting of the new Constitution. In 1996 this Constitution is promulgated and constitutional experts deem it as one of the best in the world. A Bill of Rights is entrenched in the Constitution which stipulates that every citizen has the right of access to adequate housing, health care services, sufficient food and water, social security, basic and further education, and a safe and healthy environment. There could be no better demonstration of a serious attempt to reduce inequality than that provided by this Constitution and the first policy framework developed by the ruling party.

Over the past 18 years, much progress has been made, for instance between 1996 and 2007 the percentage of households with access to water has increased from 80% to 89%, while rising from 54% to 74% in the Eastern Cape, a former homeland. Access to electricity has also improved, increasing from 57% of households to 83%. Similar developments have been achieved in every sector (education, sanitation, refuse removal, telecommunications, housing and transport). However, access does not equate to quality, and the regular demonstrations in most townships serve as a reminder of the low living standards faced by most of the population. The reality lies beyond the national averages: income inequality remains among the world's highest; access to essential services is far from universal, especially in suburban townships and poor rural areas; and former homelands are still the country's poorest regions, while the big metropolises are thriving. What then has gone wrong? This article does not attempt to unravel the multiple causes that might explain the persistence of inequality, but rather sets out to highlight an oft-overlooked aspect of the South African governance system, in terms of inequality reduction efforts, i.e. the role of local government.

Local governance in disarray

Enshrined in the Constitution is the principle of cooperative government, i.e. the then appealing principle of decentralization, where service provision and economic development are devolved to the spheres of government that are deemed most relevant. Thus, water, sanitation, energy and housing are examples of municipal responsibilities; while education, health and transport are illustrations of devolved provincial competencies. However, in practice, decentralization appears highly dysfunctional and a cause of truly appalling consequences.

Firstly, due to their level of financial distress, every year the poorest municipalities find themselves incapable of meeting their short-term liabilities, which has serious

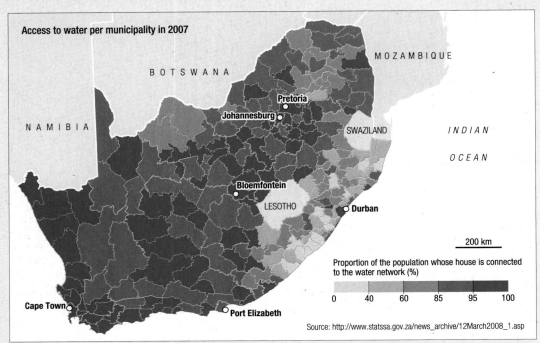

FIGURE 1 **Water, an objective almost reached in South Africa**

Access to water per municipality in 2007

Proportion of the population whose house is connected to the water network (%)

0   40   60   85   95   100

200 km

Source: http://www.statssa.gov.za/news_archive/12March2008_1.asp

Satisfaction of basic needs is enshrined in the South African Constitution and is a prevalent theme in the country's policies. Universal access to water is today an objective that has been achieved in almost all South African municipalities.

consequences on the maintenance of infrastructure and hence results in a deterioration of service quality and reliability. Secondly, many municipalities fall short, often by 30% or even 40%, of spending their entire annual capital budget allocated by the National Treasury, which again has severe consequences, in this instance on the roll-out of services and the reduction of backlogs. In February 2012, the Finance Minister reported to Parliament that the departments and municipalities had only spent 68% of the 2010-2011 R260 billion capital budget, which was intended for infrastructure development. While in 2011-2012, 54 municipalities under-spent their budget by R3.7 billion according to the auditor general report of July 2012.

These municipalities are being eaten away by a combination of corruption, conflicts of interest, cronyism, a lack of capacity and expertise (from chief financial officers

to planners and engineers, many of these positions remaining unfilled) and incompetent cadre deployment; all this against a complex social and cultural backdrop where municipal mayors and councillors are in conflict with traditional organizations and the powers of local kings and tribal chiefs. The lack of capacity is worth illustrating. The latest Local Government Budget and Expenditure Review released by the National Treasury in September 2011 reveals the grim truth about the employment situation in municipalities: on average, 36% of approved positions were vacant in 2006, with the rate reaching 51% in the metropolitan municipality of Tshwane. No one can say whether these vacancies are being compensated for through skills development, as there is no data on the training budget for official posts.

The centre of the problem appears to be poor public procurement and supply chain management processes.

FIGURE 2. South African Municipalities that remain fragile

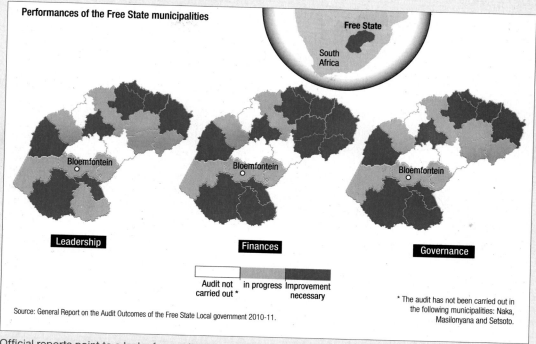

Performances of the Free State municipalities

Free State

South Africa

Bloemfontein

Bloemfontein

Bloemfontein

Leadership

Finances

Governance

Audit not carried out * in progress Improvement necessary

* The audit has not been carried out in the following municipalities: Naka, Masilonyana and Setsoto.

Source: General Report on the Audit Outcomes of the Free State Local government 2010-11.

Official reports point to a lack of capacity that prevents municipal authorities from fulfilling their mandates. This figure illustrates the performance of the Free State, which has no former homelands in its territory. It shows that most municipalities remain below national recommendations in terms of policy and financial management, as well as governance (transparency, participation, compliance). The situation is even more difficult in the former homelands of Limpopo and Eastern Cape.

Tender processes are heavily flawed. Of course, checks and balances exist, but rules and regulations are so complex and capacities so weak, that it has become easier to tweak the system rather than to enforce it. Projects are poorly prepared; technical requirements are inadequately specified; and capital expenditures are badly planned. As a result, tender bids are usually over-priced and awarded on the basis of cronyism to under-capacitated suppliers, representing a win-win situation for councillors and bidders, while the poor communities are always the losers. The same auditor general's report revealed that local governments had misspent R11 billion over the fiscal year previous to the report's publication. However, despite these findings, it would be wrong to conclude that money is not an issue. Even if the municipal budget was spent

more wisely, it would still probably take several years to reduce the current backlogs in service delivery and infra-structure maintenance. Therefore, for the time being at least, increasing the municipal budget allocation is not the answer as only 13 of the 283 municipalities have received a clean audit this year, i.e. they have produced a clear and transparent report on the use of public funds. One must keep in mind however that a clean audit does not necessarily mean that money is being spent more wisely, or that a better delivery is being achieved. Municipalities need assistance.

Taking over municipality responsibilities

The Constitution makes provision for provinces to assume control of the responsibilities of municipalities when poor management capacity is recognized. However, most provinces are fraught with the very same problems, resulting in unauthorized expenditures, unlawful conduct and violation of supply chain provision and public procurement procedures. Services that are devolved to provinces are equally poorly delivered. Given this state of affairs, how can such provinces be expected to assist and oversee dysfunctional municipalities? Furthermore, because the Constitution also makes provision for the National Department to take over provincial departments, the situation has escalated. Since December 2011, to address mismanagement and avert the collapse of essential services, the cabinet has put under national administration several provincial departments in Eastern Cape (education), Limpopo (treasury, education, health, public works, roads and transport), Free State (treasury, police, roads and transport) and Gauteng (treasury and health). The consequences of this action go beyond service provision. Recently, an engineering and construction company was liquidated following the nonpayment of contracts by provincial departments in Limpopo, KwaZulu-Natal and Free State, which resulted in the loss of 2,500 jobs in a country where the official unemployment rate exceeds 24% and job creation is the utmost governmental priority. In addition, this situation is also controversial at the national level: since the last presidential election in May 2009, several ministers (public works, local government), deputy ministers (economic development), as well as the police commissioner, have been accused of misconduct before being suspended or dismissed. The Fiscal and Financial Commission has pointed out the shortcomings of the Public Finance Management Act, stressing the lack of criteria to trigger national intervention. While this is true, could a simple revision of the Act, even one that was as comprehensive and well structured as possible, solve such systemic failures? It seems highly unlikely.

Consequently, the cabinet is stepping up to address these issues. National departments have deployed staff to the different provincial departments under public administration. In addition, the National Treasury has established a technical support unit in each province to assist municipalities with the planning and spending of capital budget. The Department of Cooperative Government and Traditional Affairs has created the Municipal Infrastructure Support Agency to support rural municipalities that lack planning and project development capacities. The Presidential Infrastructure Coordination Committee has identified 17 strategic infrastructure projects, one of which aims to assist the 23 district municipalities with the least resources (17 million people) to provide an adequate level and quality of essential services to their constituencies. Some functional provinces, such as the Western Cape, are also committed to assisting municipalities in better planning and spending for infrastructure and service delivery. What can actually be expected of these plans? Previous trials of methods of capacity building and technical support have been conducted but have had only limited success because the capacitation of local government does not eliminate the political games that are being played, which are eating away at the system. Action plans remain too vague and flimsy on this dimension. Consequently, results take too long to achieve and inequalities persist.

Solving the implementation problem

This is not to say that progress has not been made, as the reality is far from that. But the progress that has been obtained has benefited only a minority, while almost half the population continues to live below the poverty line. While it has been 18 years since the first democratic election, the Apartheid legacy remains to varying extents across the country. Many inequalities have actually increased rather than diminished: the former homelands are still lagging behind; poor black (and increasingly white) townships are still in disarray. Nevertheless, despite what certain high profile politicians would like people to believe, Apartheid can no longer be singled out as the culprit. Firstly, political parties need to seriously tackle the dysfunctional nature of local governments, to question their internal functioning, stop irrelevant cadre deployment and promote good governance. This implies, amongst other things, that councillors, mayors and municipal managers, just like provincial leaders and members of executive councils, should be appointed according to their proven ability to deliver, and not according to their position or their connections. Today, these leaders are more accountable to their political parties than to their constituencies - a situation that must be reversed. Secondly, administrative and legal shortcomings must be overcome so that unlawful practices can be effectively punished, including the implementation of effective protection for whistle-blowers. Powers and means of the public protector should be extended to promote good governance in state affairs. Anti-corruption laws should be enforced. These are only a few examples of what needs to be done. Proposals to effectively remedy the present shortcomings exist; the issue at stake more concerns the implementation of these solutions. Only once these issues have been addressed can there be a real chance to properly deal with inequality. The National Planning Commission has released its Vision 2030 report for the country: it is an ambitious plan that is generally regarded as achievable, provided that the state becomes "capable, developmental, professional and responsive". Here lies the challenge. ■

"Bottom of the pyramid" strategies combine the profit motive with development objectives. However, the idea that a multinational corporation might simultaneously drive profit and alleviate poverty has not become a reality; it requires a revised, more modest definition of promised outcomes so they may better integrate with corporate interests.

Bringing Bottom of the Pyramid into business focus

Erik Simanis,
Center for Sustainable Global Enterprise, Cornell University, Ithaca, United States of America

Like the popular Tex-Mex cuisine found across the United States, Bottom of the Pyramid (BOP) has been an effort to fuse two very different cultures. In place of culinary traditions, BOP has attempted to blend the core capabilities and resources of big business with the heart of global development institutions – a visionary fusion of profits with poverty alleviation (PRAHALAD and HAMMOND, 2002; PRAHALAD and HART, 2002).

But the theory that global corporations could simultaneously drive profits and alleviate poverty by selling products and services to the world's four billion poorest consumers has proven less than palatable in practice. Over the more than dozen years since the concept was put forward, numerous business experiments to reach BOP consumers have failed to support the profit opportunity half of the hypothesis (KARAMCHANDANI, KUBZANSKY and LALWANI, 2011; KARNANI, 2007).

Visibility into the challenge is further obscured by well-publicized corporate ventures deemed successes in the popular press by virtue of simply being operational and having expanded a pilot – actual profitability and return on investment remain far from certain. Two often referenced successes are the Hindustan Lever's Shakti initiative, an effort to build a door-to-door, rural sales channel in remote villages of India for the company's personal care and home care products by recruiting and training women micro-entrepreneurs from self-help groups; and ITC's e-choupal, which provides rural Indian farmers with market and agricultural data via village-based internet kiosks.

The disappointment hasn't been confined to the business-side of the equation. The broader development community's assessment of initial corporate ventures was less

FIGURE 1 **Estimating the size of the BOP market**

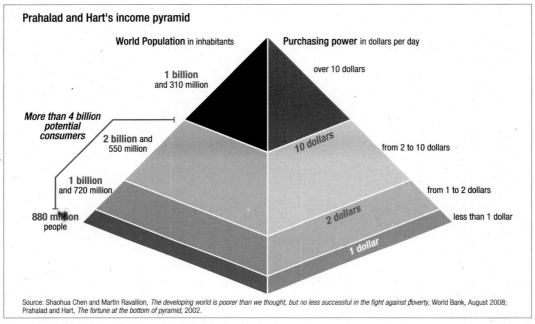

Prahalad and Hart's income pyramid

World Population in inhabitants

Purchasing power in dollars per day

1 billion
and 310 million

over 10 dollars

**More than 4 billion
potential
consumers**

2 billion and
550 million

10 dollars

from 2 to 10 dollars

1 billion
and 720 million

880 million
people

from 1 to 2 dollars

less than 1 dollar

2 dollars

1 dollar

Source: Shaohua Chen and Martin Ravallion, *The developing world is poorer than we thought, but no less successful in the fight against poverty*, World Bank, August 2008; Prahalad and Hart, *The fortune at the bottom of pyramid*, 2002.

The work of Prahalad and Stuart (2002) revealed the existence of nearly 4 billion poor consumers whose needs were not being sufficiently taken into account by the market. The idea of developing specific products for this segment of the population is the logical next step.

than rosy. Seeing efforts that – to their eyes – were little more than attempts to sell products to the poor, the term "poverty wash" entered into the BOP lexicon (KARNANI, 2007). In response to this critique, academics (including the author) and development practitioners urged corporations pursuing BOP markets to also expand the incomes of the poor by sourcing from them and incorporating them into their value chains (DRAYTON and BUDINICH, 2010); to empower and build local capacity by co-creating new businesses and products in close partnership with low-income communities (SIMANIS et al., 2008a; SIMANIS, HART and DUKE, 2008b); and to conduct rigorous assessments on the poverty-alleviation impacts of their ventures (LONDON, 2009). In short, corporations were being asked to do what non-profits do.

It's not surprising, then, that the locus of corporate interest in BOP has steadily shifted away from the profit-and-loss side of the business to the philanthropic and social responsibility departments. Danone's partnership with Grameen Bank to bring wholesome yogurt to the poor in Bangladesh through a network of rural women entrepreneurs is one such high-profile effort. Rather than a fusion of competitive returns on investment with development impact – the vision that spurred initial enthusiasm among corporations – many of today's BOP ventures are corporate-funded development projects justified on the basis of their reputational value to the company. While such corporate-social responsibility efforts do indeed bring tremendous value to the communities where they operate and should continue to be encouraged and expanded, they are a shadow of the initial vision.

The goal of this chapter is to help revive corporate interest in the BOP as a profit opportunity by bringing a business-focus back to the field. To do so, I summarize what I believe are key misconceptions concerning the roots of business success/failure in low-income markets, and the poverty alleviation potential of corporations more broadly. The issues reach from the field-level all the way up to the boardroom. I hasten to add that not only have I contributed to some of these misconceptions, but I have also guided and closely advised a number of failed corporate BOP business ventures that drew from this blueprint. This article is therefore based on hands-on experience and personal learning and reflects a fundamental re-thinking of some of my earlier positions.

Misconception 1: Build it right and they will come

First, it's common to hear and read today that the true challenge of BOP markets is, first-and-foremost, one of understanding poor consumers' needs and translating those needs into high-quality products. Companies, so the argument goes, simply don't understand how these consumers live, what they value and what their aspirations are. Should a product fail to attract sufficient consumer demand to be profitable – as so often is the case – the company is faulted for not having truly heard the voice of the customer.

In fact, this was the theory at the very start of the BOP movement in the late 1990s – that companies, by working closely together with BOP consumers to "co-create" an offering, would crack the code. This view was also appealing from a development perspective, as it was consistent with the core tenets of what is called "participatory development" – a development approach popularized in the 1980s which calls for the close and active participation of the poor in the design and implementation of all solutions. Such deep participation empowers the poor, builds capabilities and ensures that solutions are appropriate for the local context (CHAMBERS, 1983, 1997).

So what happened? Companies got on the ground, did in-depth research (in all of the projects I've led and advised in Africa and India, the teams and I did homestays in the slums and villages we aimed to serve), engaged the community in "co-creation" using various participatory techniques, launched products that seemed to address pressing needs, and then... failed. In many cases, there was no demand after all that co-creation and engagement – even for products that seemed so important to a healthy, normal life; such as clean water solutions, nutrient fortified food products, smoke-free stoves, etc.

What became clear to me is that needs aren't the same thing as a market (SIMANIS, 2009; SIMANIS, 2010). A market is a lifestyle built around a product. When a market exists, consumers have embedded a product and its value proposition into the fabric of their lives – buying and using it is second nature. In that case, market researchers and product designers can get really good consumer data, and it makes sense to work

FIGURE 2 What is the BOP market made of?

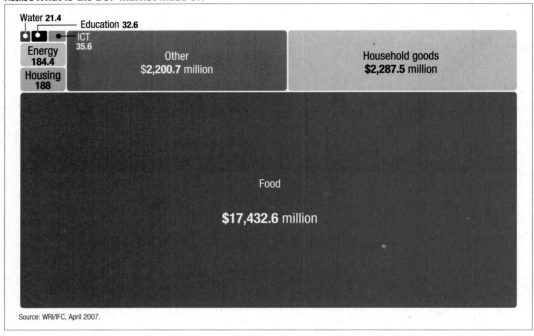

Water 21.4 — Education 32.6

Energy 184.4

Housing 188

ICT 35.6

Other $2,200.7 million

Household goods $2,287.5 million

Food

$17,432.6 million

Source: WRI/IFC, April 2007.

According to the WRI (2007), well-adapted products could meet a variety of basic needs of the poor. The two largest markets are the improvement of food and household equipment.

closely with consumers to improve a product's functionality.

But for most products launched in the BOP, there is no market – instead, a market has to be created. With market creation, traditional consumer research and data are fuzzy signals at best, as consumers have no reference point for understanding the value of the new functionality, nor the various changes to their existing routines, budgets and lifestyles that product adoption will entail. So it's possible to collect lots of data and get extensive consumer feedback – but when push comes to shove and consumers are asked to hand over money for the product they endorsed in the abstract, they balk.

Successful market creation requires a very different approach to product positioning and go-to-market strategies more broadly. The primary objectives are to help kick-start an initial consumer "sensemaking" process – a trial-and-error based form of experimentation – that invites consumers to figure out on their own terms how a product fits into their lives and the value it holds, and to then catalyse a bandwagon effect that, in sociological terms, normalizes the offering and makes it seem a necessary and vital part of any person's life. Specific marketing techniques that I've used with success in the field include pricing for repeat usage (rather than one-time sampling) and including "props" or familiar items from the consumers' context as part of the offering (as part of a rewards programme, for example). I've also tested and refined a "seed group" strategy that creates an initial group of committed users through workshops geared towards encouraging participants to model key behaviours associated with the offering and begin feeling part of a high-visibility brand community.

Misconception 2: Target high volumes at low margins and price points

A second misconception that dates back to the very first BOP articles is that profitability is a matter of setting low margins and price points, and generating high volumes. The mathematics seemed intuitively correct: BOP consumers spend a scant dollar a day, but make up two-thirds of the world's population. Mathematics aside, I believe this proposed revenue model was quickly and uncritically accepted because it helped assuage the potential reservations of managers and executives in terms of making money off the proverbial backs of the poor: getting by on razor-thin margins seemed the morally correct way of doing business at the BOP.

However, basing a revenue model on intuition and emotional resonance has proven to be a recipe for failure. The low price/low margin/high volume strategy simply doesn't work in the majority of BOP markets, as it inevitably requires an impractical penetration rate of the target market (SIMANIS, 2012). Two factors account for this:

One, costs in BOP markets are much higher than in traditional markets. Compensating for poor infrastructure (e.g., outage-prone power grids, pot-holed roads) and absent or inefficient social institutions (e.g., corrupt law enforcement agencies, poor school systems) with back-up diesel generators and in-house employee literacy training programmes drives up operational costs beyond the levels found in traditional markets. The poverty penalty to which low-income consumers are subjected, which results in their paying more than their middle-class counterparts for essentially the same goods and services (PRAHALAD and HAMMOND, 2002), exists also on the supply side of the equation.

And because of the market creation issue discussed above, acquiring and retaining customers demands a very high-touch sales and marketing strategy. Getting people to value new-to-the-world functionality and changing long-held routines and behaviours –even when it can save their lives – is extremely difficult. Think about the massive campaigns and the measures taken just to get people to wear seatbelts and bicycle helmets or to use condoms. All this drives up costs and pushes out break-even timelines, as corporations have to pay for awareness building and behaviour modification through future profits (even if it forms partnerships with local NGOs, self-help groups and governments, as they too don't work for free).

The second factor is that business units in low-income markets come pre-set with an "efficient scale" that is extremely small. In economics, "efficient scale" refers to the size of business facilities, equipment, and operations that generate the highest level of efficiency and, thereby, maximize profits. Consider the previously mentioned e-Choupal venture by ITC that provides poor farmers with agricultural information: each one of their internet kiosks serves farmers living within just a five kilometres range. The main culprit behind this phenomenon is poor transportation infrastructure. Dismal road quality across rural areas drives up costs rapidly when companies try to access consumers living further away from their base of operations. On the flip side, consumers are constrained to doing most all of their shopping within their own villages (or very nearby) because of the disproportionately high cost of local transportation. Consider that in rural Ghana the cost of a five-mile return trip using the public mini-bus is approximately $1.40. That's more than 20% of the average daily spend of a four-person farming family.

The upshot is that the business unit is forced to meet its sales volume target from the consumer base living in a narrow geographical range – one holding little more than a cluster of villages in rural areas, or several neighbourhoods in the case of larger slums. The only way to cover these disproportionately high operational costs and generate a return within a reasonable time frame without essentially converting an entire target market into repeat customers is by generating what accounting calls a high contribution per transaction (the sale price minus a product's variable costs). To raise contribution levels, a company has to raise its gross margin (by decreasing variable costs) and/or raise its sale price.

To generate very high contributions within a BOP context, companies inevitably have to restructure the entire business model: beginning with the value proposition, the pricing structure and down through the supply chain. Several generic strategies that I've outlined in prior published work that are effective in boosting contribution levels include offering a bundle comprised of bulk-format products; integrating an "enabling service" that engages customers in an activity linked to the bundle so that they self-teach themselves to maximize product functionality; and aggregating customers into peer groups (SIMANIS, 2012).

Misconception 3: High profits are unethical

A related misconception, or perhaps misunderstanding to be more accurate, concerns what constitutes an appropriate or reasonable profit level for corporations at the BOP. It's a topic for which I too have received criticism based on my argument above that very high gross margins are necessary for profitability in low-income market contexts.

While there are certainly ethical and moral dimensions to this debate, I believe that a significant portion of the confusion – particularly between the non-profit sectors and business – stems from something far less philosophical: definitional inconsistency. In other words, people are talking past one another, as they are using the word "profit" to mean very different things.

The term in common business usage refers (mainly) to three very different things – gross profitability, operational profitability, and investment profitability. When I wrote that companies needed very high profit levels, I was referring to the first two. As explained above, high gross profitability (sales minus variable costs) is necessary because of the higher-than average operational costs in these markets. If you don't start off with very high gross profitability, a business unit will find itself in the red when those operational costs are subtracted.

What is often misunderstood by those outside the business sector is that a venture can generate seemingly high year-on-year operational profitability – more or less the equivalent of net profits – but still have negative investment profitability. Investment profitability is a measure of a project's overall return on investment and represents the payoff to the people (e.g., shareholders) who risked their money to make the project possible. It's a situation that the pharmaceutical industry – which is characterized by enormous upfront research and development costs and years of clinical trials before sales can begin – periodically struggles to explain to the public. Take, for example, a business that generates $1,000,000 of operating profits every year. If $2,000,000 was invested to launch the business and it is up and running in two years, the business has strong investment profitability by almost any measure; but if $20,000,000 was invested and it took five years to start seeing those profits, those risking their money are faring very poorly when they take into consideration inflation and the guaranteed returns they could have received by simply putting their money into a savings account.

Low-income market opportunities, much like the pharmaceutical industry, invariably require very high operational profitability to generate a positive return on investment. The reasons are two-fold. The first is that many of these opportunities won't see profits for many years, given the extensive market research, development of new products, and pilot tests that are necessary before sales start in earnest.

The problem is quite literally compounded in emerging markets, as the discount rate used to assess the present value of future profits is very high – 30% or more in many corporations. To put that in perspective, the present value of $1,000,000 of net profits earned ten years from a project's starting point is only $72,000 when a 30% discount rate is used.

The second reason is that the upfront investment costs needing to be recouped are often quite high, as many BOP opportunities demand extended, multi-country project teams, draw on a wide range of corporate capabilities, and entail extensive investment in assets and new business infrastructure (particularly on the distribution side).

As this suggests, very high gross and operational profitability do not automatically lead to "unfair" levels of investment returns. By that same token, an "investment-worthy opportunity" is also not inherently extortionist – it is simply one that covers within a given period of time those upfront expenditures, the income forgone or what economists call the opportunity cost (i.e., a guaranteed return on the money, usually equal to the interest rates paid by government-backed securities), and the risk that an investor assumes. As one might imagine, the opportunity costs in developing and emerging markets are higher (because inflation levels are generally much higher in emerging markets, thereby pushing up interest rates), and there is a lot more business risk because of the market creation issue. So it's not a case of trying to make more money off the backs of the poor; rather, it is the challenging nature of the investment climate that sets a high bar for corporate BOP ventures.

That said, once some of these markets are established, the necessary level of investment profitability will probably start to decline, as business risk decreases and competition increases. It is a dynamic that financial analysts call a "reversion to the mean". It's already taking place in some markets in the micro-finance industry (PORTEUS, 2006), thus forcing companies to maintain their investment profitability by reducing their costs (as competition often doesn't allow them to increase their prices – in fact, companies usually face pressure to decrease prices). That's the so-called magic of markets and why they generally result in increasing consumer value over time.

Misconception 4: Corporations should use a blended value approach to BOP

The final misconception reaches the very heart of what makes a corporation a corporation. Increasingly, the rhetoric in the BOP space urges corporations to take a much broader approach to assessing the value of their investments – to base resource allocation decisions not simply on the expected returns to shareholders, but also on the value generated in poor communities. By this view, corporations should invest in expanding BOP ventures even if they fail to reach an internal hurdle rate of return, as the societal value of tackling poverty and providing for the unmet needs of the poor should essentially be viewed as offsetting that loss.

This discussion has been confounded by the advent of the impact investing field, which invests in social entrepreneurs first and foremost to generate a social or environmental impact and secondly to generate some financial return, and by the concept of the "social business" proposed by Nobel Prize winner and Grameen Bank Founder Mohammed Yunus. Yunus' social business is a business established to solve a social problem that covers its operational costs but pays no dividends to investors; all profits are reinvested in the business (YUNUS, 2007).

The argument is absolutely understandable and certainly appealing. But it's a platitude, and fails to give due recognition to how institutions function, in particular how the need to appeal to key resource providers dictates behaviour. This view, known as resource dependence theory, essentially states that all organizations are dependent on outside resources; to maintain a flow of those resources and ensure the organization's survival, organizations have to perform first and foremost along dimensions important to the primary providers of those resources (PFEFFER and SALANCIK, 1978). So it's not just publicly-traded corporations that are beholden to these outside forces, but so too social enterprises, non-profits, churches, teachers associations and town hall assemblies. As Bob Dylan penned in song, "it may be the Devil or it may be the Lord, but you're gonna have to serve somebody."

So organizations that operate under various "non-profit" legal designations – like social enterprises/entrepreneurs, impact investment funds, multilaterals, and foundations to name a few – aren't acting benevolently in using a blended value approach: *they have an obligation to their resource providers to do so and to prioritize social impact over profits*. Why? Because people give resources to these organizations so that they impact on external social and environmental issues – not for the sake of growing the organization for the sake of itself. Self-obsolescence is, in fact, a sign of a mission accomplished.

That's not the case for corporations – the overwhelming majority of company investors (e.g., shareholders) give funds specifically so that the company grows itself in order to repay the original investment with a dividend, much like banks are expected to pay interest on customers' savings deposits. So the changes in people's lives that a company's products and operations bring about are simply a means to the company's growth and longevity.

The point is that different institutions present different constraints and different boundaries to those working within them because of their differing obligations to resource providers. A corporation cannot do "BOP business" the same way as a social enterprise. For corporations to make BOP business part of their core operations, as Prahalad, Hart, Hammond and others initially envisioned, BOP resources will have to be allocated and the investments managed according to what capital markets and the shareholders that supply them with money set as the key benchmark of success: namely, rates of return better than or comparable to alternative investment opportunities. Corporations can, and hopefully increasingly do, bring progressive values to bear on how they achieve that target, but those values are not by themselves going to pay the bills, let the company continue growing, and attract additional investment capital.

The situation may change and a blended value approach may in fact eventually become a shareholder demand – but that day is a long way away, as institutional contexts evolve very slowly. So if you want a seat at that table today and to get corporations directing their core capabilities and core resources to social and environmental issues, the goal has to be re-framed in a way that it synchronizes with the norms, pressures and daily reality of the managers – not the other way around. As renowned 1970s community organizer Saul Alinksy argued in his seminal book, *Rules for Radicals*, if you aren't communicating within the experience of your audience, you simply aren't in the game (ALINSKY, 1971).

And that is exactly what has happened to the BOP field over the last decade. We (I include myself here) got too caught up with our own beautiful theories and abstract concepts (like mutual value creation, inclusive business) and lost sight of the pressure on managers to meet next quarter's sales and earnings forecast. We theorized ourselves out of being relevant. As I noted in the introduction, the consequence is that companies are turning away from the space or only approaching it as a corporate social responsibility project. And that's a real loss, as companies can bring unique value to the poor.

But it's a loss caused as much by the perverse pressures that drive corporate decisions, as it is by the field's lack of creativity in re-framing these concepts and goals in a way that can speak to managers – from those sitting in the "C-Suite" (the top senior executives), right down to those in the field (SIMANIS and MILSTEIN, 2012). We as a field need to start putting into practice our own recommendation about avoiding top-down or so-called "push solutions." Instead we need to get on the proverbial shop floor and come up with solutions that work for the very managers whose annual performance reviews depend on successfully implementing them.

Consider the total quality management (TQM) and just in time (JIT) management revolutions as case studies. I would wager that these management practices – ones today considered baseline skills for any respectable company – have had an order-of-magnitude greater impact on reducing firm's and industries' environmental impacts than all "environmental management initiatives" combined. But TQM and JIT have

FIGURE 3 Misconceptions of the BOP approach

	Conventional wisdom	**Emerging reality**
Product	**Co-designing products** enables the unique needs of BOP consumers to be met and to open **new markets**.	Getting BOP consumers to adopt new functionalities and product routines requires **market creation strategies**.
Business model	**Low margin**, low price and high volume models are key to success in BOP markets.	The majority of BOP markets require a **very high contribution** per transaction (high volumes plus high price points).
Investment model	Aiming for high **profitability** in BOP markets is **unethical**.	The challenging investment climate in the BOP demands **high gross profitability** and **high operational profitability**.
BOP paradigm	Corporations should consider aggregate **social, environmental and economic value** when making and evaluating BOP investments.	Make BOP **part of core business operations** by re-framing poverty alleviation goals in traditional business economic outputs.

Source: Erik Simanis.

The BOP approach, as it has been conducted, has raised hopes, achieved mobilization and led to disappointments. In the experience of the author, it is often the principles adopted by stakeholders for product definition, along with market research that have resulted in unsatisfactory outcomes. Other approaches are possible.

had such a profound environmental impact precisely because they were not undertaken for that purpose.

The goals, practices, language and metrics of TQM and JIT are focused on enabling a company to drive profitability and top-line growth – the environmental benefits were derivative of achieving the core institutional objective. It's going to take the same kind of framing and approach if corporations are to make BOP and the creation of social value a part of their core operations.

Conclusion

Audacity and bold visions are powerful and necessary tools for change. By freeing oneself from the limitations of current reality, they open minds, instil hope, catalyse motivation and spur action. The BOP concept has unquestionably had such an effect.

But visions alone – no matter how often they are repeated or how boldly they are proclaimed – will not result in lasting institutional change. Sustained change requires bringing a vision back down to earth and re-embedding it into the day-to-day realities and practices that give institutions their shape and form. That process, however, is one of mutual adaptation and negotiation – not only will the organization change, but so too the vision. And that's an unsettling process, as it requires letting go of the purity of one's vision and frequently contenting oneself with half-wins and incremental advancements.

Today, the BOP concept is faced with such a decision: either we adapt the vision to meet the realities of the corporation, or we risk the concept fading entirely from corporate business agendas. To be clear, it's not a question of going back to "business as usual" and giving up on the vision of a better world. Rather, bringing a business focus back to the BOP concept is an exciting next phase in an on-going process of change – one that will demand creativity and open up new waves of research and new opportunities for interaction and learning among academia, the development sector and global business. It is my hope that this article helps to shine a light on some of the potential new pathways that can make BOP a lasting part of corporate business agendas. ∎

REFERENCES

ALINSKY S. D., 1971, *Rules for Radicals: A Pragmatic Primer for Realistic Radicals*. New York: Vintage Books.

CHAMBERS R., 1983, *Rural Development: Putting the Last First*. Essex: Pearson Educational Longman Limited.

CHAMBERS R., 1997, *Whose Reality Counts? Putting the First Last*. London: ITDG Publishing.

DRAYTON B. and BUDINICH V., 2010, A New Alliance for Global Change. *Harvard Business Review,* September.

KARAMCHANDANI S., KUBZANSKY M. and LALWANI N., 2011, Is the Bottom of the Pyramid Really for You? *Harvard Business Review*, March: 107-111.

KARNANI A., 2007, Misfortune at the bottom of the pyramid. *Greener Management International*, 51: 99-110.

LONDON T., 2009, Making Better Investments at the Base of the Pyramid. *Harvard Business Review,* May.

PFEFFER J. and SALANCIK G., 1978, *The External Control of Organizations*. New York: Harper & Rowe.

PORTEUS D., 2006, Competition and Microcredit Interest Rates: CGAP Focus Note 33.

PRAHALAD C. K. and HAMMOND A., 2002, Serving the World's Poor, Profitably. *Harvard Business Review*, 80(9): 48-57.

PRAHALAD C. K. and HART S. L., 2002, The Fortune at the Bottom of the Pyramid, *Strategy + Business*, Vol. January: 1-14.

SIMANIS E. N., 2009, At the Base of the Pyramid, *Wall Street Journal*, Vol. October 26. New York City: Dow Jones and Co.

SIMANIS E. N., 2010, Needs, Needs Everywhere but Not a BOP Market to Tap. In T. London, & S. L. Hart (Eds.), *Next Generation Strategies for the Base of the Pyramid*: FT Press.

SIMANIS E. N., 2012, Reality Check at the Bottom of the Pyramid, *Harvard Business Review*, Vol. 90: 120-125.

SIMANIS E. N., HART S. L., DEKOSZMOVSZKY J., DONOHUE P., DUKE D., ENK G., GORDON M. and THIEME T., 2008a, The Base of the Pyramid Protocol, 2nd Edition: Towards Next Generation BOP Strategy. Ithaca, New York: Center for Sustainable Global Enterprise, Johnson School of Management, Cornell University.

SIMANIS E. N., HART S. L. and DUKE D., 2008b, The Base of the Pyramid Protocol: Beyond Basic Needs Business Strategies. *Innovations*, 3(1): 57-84.

SIMANIS E. N. and MILSTEIN M. B., 2012, Back to Business Fundamentals: Making Bottom of the Pyramid Relevant to Core Business. *FACTS Reports*, April: 79-85.

YUNUS M., 2007, *Creating a World Without Poverty: Social Business and the Future of Capitalism*. New York: Public Affairs.

Women's paid work and unpaid care responsibilities in China

Sarah Cook and Xiao-yuan Dong, United Nations Research Institute for Social Development, Geneva, Switzerland

China's economic reforms over the past three decades have dramatically changed the mechanisms for allocating goods and labour in both market and non-market spheres[1]. The role of the state and the work unit (*danwei*) as providers of social goods and services has been eroded, and responsibility for social reproduction and "care" – a domain principally of the state in the urban sector under the planned economy – has returned to the household. These processes have considerable – but largely under-researched – implications for the work and status of women in both the home and the marketplace.

This paper examines the social and economic trends that intensify the pressure on the care economy and on women in particular in playing their dual roles as caregivers and income-earners in post-reform China. What are the implications of the reform process for non-market activities, such as care for children and elders, activities which traditionally are the domain of women? How does caregiving responsibility affect women's labour market outcomes? And what are the implications of work-family conflicts for the well-being of women and their families?

The care economy under strain

The overriding concern of the Chinese government in the post-reform period has been to find the most efficient way of restructuring the productive economy, assuming that social reproduction will adjust itself accordingly. As a result, social protection for women's reproductive role have been severely eroded; the support of the government and the employer for care provision has been substantially cut back; and the contribution of women's unpaid care work has been completely ignored in the design of the emerging social security system. These policy changes have exacerbated the labour market penalty on women for their caregiving role, contributing to the deterioration of women's position in the labour market (Berik, Dong and Summerfield, 2007). Various institutional, economic and demographic changes affect childcare and elder care and intensify the pressure on women in trying to fulfill these roles in China's transitional economy.

With respect to institutional changes, nowhere have women with young children been more adversely affected than in the area of childcare provision. During the Maoist era, China established a public childcare system which provided care from the earliest months until primary school age (Liu, Zhang, Li, 2008), although publicly subsidized childcare was more accessible to families in the urban sector than in the rural sector. The economic reform has brought about two major changes in China's childcare policy. First, the post-reform policy discourse stressed the role of formal childcare for promoting early childhood education while downplaying its role for supporting working women (Zhu, Wang, 2005). Second, there has been a substantial cutback in the childcare support provided by the government and employers. According to the 2006 Chinese enterprise social responsibility survey, enterprise-run kindergartens existed in less than 20 percent of state-owned enterprises (SOEs) and only 5.7 percent of the total surveyed enterprises (Du, Dong, 2010).

Recognizing the changing patterns of childcare

---

1. This paper summarizes part of the discussion in Cook and Dong (2011).

provision, in its 2001 Guidelines for Kindergarten Education the Chinese government formally endorsed a pluralistic approach to childcare, with "state-run kindergartens as the backbone and exemplar" and "social forces (an ideologically convenient term for market forces) as the primary providers". Between 1997 and 2006, the number of publicly funded kindergartens in China fell from 157,842 to 55,069; in contrast, private kindergartens grew rapidly with their share rising from 13.5 percent to 57.8 percent. For China as a whole, the number of kindergartens decreased by 28.5 percent between 1997 and 2006 (Ministry of Education, Educational Statistics Yearbook of China, various issues). The childcare reforms have raised concerns about the availability, affordability and quality of childcare programmes in China (Corter et al., 2006; He and Jiang, 2008; and Liu, Zhang, Li, 2008).

Similarly, elder care institutions have faced new challenges during the economic transition. Like many countries in the world, in China the provision of care for the elderly is primarily the responsibility of families. Consistent with the approach to childcare, the post-reform childcare policy discourse emphasizes family responsibility and the role of markets for care provision. The Elderly Rights and Security Law which was enacted in 1996 reiterates that care for frail elderly parents is a non-evadable responsibility of adult children, despite the growing reluctance of employers to accommodate the care-giving needs of their employees.

China's ongoing demographic transition to an increasingly aged society further increases the care burden on families. According to official statistics, the proportion of the Chinese population aged 65 and above rose from 4.9 percent in 1982 to 8.3 percent in 2008 (National Bureau of Statistics, 2009, p. 90). Analysts project that China's old-age dependency ratio will surpass that of industrialized countries in 2020 and become the highest of any population in the world by the mid-twenty-first century (Poston and Duan, 2000). Due to the effect of the one-child policy on family demographics, growing numbers of married couples will have sole responsibility for four parents and one child, with the main burden of care again likely to fall on women (Chen and Standing, 2007).

The structural change of the Chinese economy from an agrarian to an industrial one has also created new tensions for the care economy. The rapid growth of industrial production and high rates of urbanization separate the workplace from the home, increasing women's needs for non-parental childcare services. However, without access to publicly subsidized childcare programmes, the vast majority of women in rural areas and migrant women in cities have to rely on informal care substitutes or fee-for-service daycare programs to enable their participation in the labour market.

Rural-to-urban migration also creates dislocation for migrant families. Due to institutional arrangements related to the residential registration system (hukou) and land use rights, as well as various other economic and cultural factors, migration remains temporary, resulting in a large left-behind population consisting of children, non-elderly married women, and the elderly (Fan, 2009). Almost 59 million children under the age of 18 years – 28 per cent of rural children – are left behind, living with only one parent (mostly mothers), grandparents or other relatives (All China Women's Federation, 2008). A growing number of rural elderly people live in "empty nests" in which elderly females take care of their spouses while having no one to take care of them after the spouse passes away (Liu, Zhang Li, 2008).

Economic growth, together with privatization and commercialization of care services and an aging population, has led to a rapid expansion of markets for domestic and care services. Analysts estimate that about 15 to 20 million Chinese workers earn a living by cleaning, cooking, and taking care of children, the elderly, and the sick for middle- and high-income families (Hu, 2010). Laid-off urban female workers and female migrants account for the majority of paid domestic workers. In China, as in many other countries, the domestic service market is poorly regulated; paid domestic work is low status, low paid and not covered by the existing social security system; domestic workers also face societal discrimination (Hu, 2010; Wang, Si and Chen, 2010). The development of domestic and care service markets has transferred the domestic and care burdens of middle- and upper-middle-class women to women struggling at the margin of the labour market, thereby perpetuating socio-economic inequality.

FIGURE 1 **How men and women in China allocate their time**

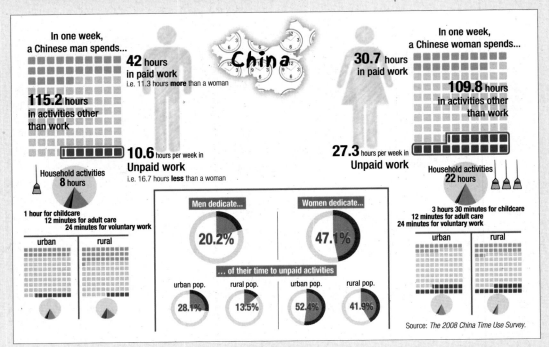

In one week,
a Chinese man spends...

42 hours
in paid work
i.e. 11.3 hours **more** than a woman

China

115.2 hours
in activities other
than work

10.6 hours per week in
Unpaid work
i.e. 16.7 hours **less** than a woman

Household activities
8 hours

1 hour for childcare
12 minutes for adult care
24 minutes for voluntary work

urban   rural

Men dedicate...

20.2%

... of their time to unpaid activities

urban pop.   rural pop.

28.1%   **13.5%**

In one week,
a Chinese woman spends...

30.7 hours
in paid work

109.8 hours
in activities other
than work

27.3 hours per week in
Unpaid work

Household activities
22 hours

3 hours 30 minutes for childcare
12 minutes for adult care
24 minutes for voluntary work

urban   rural

Women dedicate...

47.1%

urban pop.   rural pop.

52.4%   **41.9%**

Source: *The 2008 China Time Use Survey.*

Chinese women, both urban and rural dwellers, undertake the majority of family support work, which mainly comprises childcare and household activities. They spend three times longer than their partners on these activities.

The tensions between women's dual roles as caregivers and income-earners

The changes in the care economy associated with policy reforms and demographic transition have heightened the tensions between women's dual roles as caregivers and income-earners. Recent empirical analyses shed light on the implications for the well-being of women and their families caused by the growing work-family conflicts that women have to face.

Access to childcare services profoundly shapes women's labour force participation. Du and Dong (2010) examine the impact of childcare reform on women's childcare choices and labour force participation in urban China, using data from the China Health and Nutrition Survey (CHNS) for the period 1991 to 2004. The authors point out that China's pluralistic approach to childcare provision in conjunction with the legacy of employer-based

welfare entitlements has created a two-tier system. In this system, subsidized high quality childcare services mainly reach already well-off parents - employees of non-profit public organizations and large SOEs which are still able to provide childcare services, while other parents have to rely on the fee-based services of private or commercialized public kindergartens to meet their needs.

These authors also find striking disparities in women's labour force participation and access to formal childcare among different socio-economic groups. Women with less education or those that have lower levels of family income are more likely to withdraw from the labour market and are less likely to use centre-based childcare. For working women, those married to husbands with higher levels of educational attainment are more likely to enrol their children in centre-based childcare. These findings suggest that gender-blind, market-oriented childcare reforms are

FIGURE 2 High activity rates of Chinese women

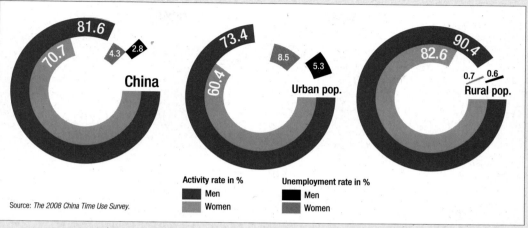

Source: *The 2008 China Time Use Survey.*

Chinese women, whether rural or urban, have high activity rates (over 70%). The reduction of formal childcare opportunities creates tensions that are difficult for families to cope with.

reinforcing socio-economic inequalities, including gender inequality as well as inequality in the quality of childcare and early education.

Rural migrant families are among the most vulnerable socio-economic groups in post-reform urban China. Yuan (2010) explores how married migrant women cope with the tension between paid work and childcare using data from the 2007 Beijing Migrant Family Survey. The analysis shows that in response to the growing demand of migrant families, private childcare services have grown rapidly in the migrant communities in Beijing. In line with the fact that migrant workers are concentrated in low-paying jobs, the childcare accessible to migrant families is typically characterized by low fees and the provision of low quality services. Most of such childcare facilities are non-registered because they do not satisfy the regulations on safety, sanitation, teacher qualification, students-teacher ratios, and so on. The presence of low-fee childcare appears to be important for migrant women's labour force participation. But, in the absence of affordable, quality childcare programmes, these women are forced to make harsh choices between earning income and the well-being of their children.

The tensions between work and child care provision are felt not just by migrant women in the cities but also by women in low-income rural villages, where services that can substitute for family provision are generally unavailable and the economic pressure to work is enormous. Wang and Dong (2010) find that grandmothers and older children are the only care substitutes available to women and the lack of access to affordable, decent childcare is a main obstacle to women's participation in off-farm employment. These findings provide strong evidence that care for young children constitutes a barrier to women's access to more lucrative off-farm employment and wage work.

Concluding remarks

The retreat of the Chinese state from the sphere of reproduction during economic transition has exacerbated the weight of domestic responsibilities which women have to balance alongside their labour force participation, limiting their occupational choices and time autonomy. Women from disadvantaged socio-economic groups have been the hardest hit. Privatization and commercialization of childcare services not only restrict the choices of women from disadvantaged socio-economic groups in the labour market but also deny their children access to quality child care. Population aging, in conjunction with the growing emphasis on Confucian values and family responsibility in policy circles, has exacerbated the dilemma for middle-aged, married women who attempt to fulfil multiple responsibilities as income-earners as well as caregivers for family members at different stages of the life cycle. Social dislocation associated with labour migration has increased work burdens of the left-behind middle-aged, married women, school-age children and elderly people. The emergence of off-farm wage employment, and the lack of affordable, decent out-of-home child care substitutes, force rural women with pre-school children into having to make difficult choices, intensifying the conflict between the employment of mothers and the well-being of their children.

These choices may compromise the care and education of children as well as the elderly. They also constrain women's labour force participation and options, and thus ultimately their own incomes and well-being. It is increasingly clear that women have been disproportionately pushed out of formal employment opportunities, are more likely to drop out of the labour market than men, and are concentrated in low paid, irregular forms of informal employment. While analysis on the labour demand side suggests explanations arising both from human capital and discrimination, the studies reported here point to the need for analysis of the supply side constraints – particularly the need to balance care responsibilities – that undermine women's capacity to undertake paid employment. The longer-term outcome is that these women have limited access to social protection or pensions, thus perpetuating the care responsibilities of the next generation. Ultimately, a gendered approach to both social and labour market policies, with investment in support for social reproduction services, will be needed to break this cycle.

REFERENCES

ALL CHINA WOMEN'S FEDERATION, 2008, "Zhongguo Nongcun Liushou Ertong Qingkuang Yanjiu Baogao"["A Study Report of the Situation of the Left-behind Children in Rural China"]. Beijing: All-China Women's Federation.

BERIK G., DONG X.-Y. and SUMMERFIELD G. 2007, "China's Transformations and Feminist Economics." *Feminist Economics* 13(3-4): 1-32.

CHEN L. and STANDING H., 2007, "Gender Equality in Transitional China's Health Policy Reforms." *Feminist Economics* 13(3/4): 189-212.

COOK S. and DONG X.-Y., 2011, "Harsh Choices: Chinese Women's Paid Work and Unpaid Care Responsibilities under Economic Reform". *Development and Change,* 42(4): 947–965.

CORTER C., JANMOHAMMED Z., ZHANG J. and BERTRAND J., 2006, "Strong foundations: early childhood care and education." Paper commissioned for the EFA Global Monitoring Report 2007.

DU F. and DONG X.-Y., 2010, "Women's Labor Force Participation and Child care Choices in Urban China during the Economic Transition." In Xiao-yuan Dong and Sarah Cook eds. *Gender Equality and China's Economic Transformation: Informal Employment and Care Provision,* pp. 173-191. Beijing: Economic Science Press.

FAN C. C., 2009, "Flexible Work, Flexible Household: Labor Migration and Rural Families in China", *Research in the Sociology of Work* 19: 377-408.

HE J. and JIANG Y., 2008, An analysis of China's child care policy and current situation from the perspective of supporting women and balancing family and work. Studies in Preschool Education (*xueqianjiaoyuyanjiu*), No. 08: 3-7.

HU X., 2010, *Paid Domestic Labor as Precarious Work in China.* Ph. D. Dissertation. Women's Studies, Simon Fraser University.

LIU B., ZHANG Y. and LI Y., 2008, *Reconciling Work and Family: Issues and Policies in China.* ILO, Asia.

NATIONAL BUREAU OF STATISTICS, 2009, China Population and Employment Statistics Yearbook 2006–2008. Beijing: China Statistics Press.

POSTON D. L. Jr. and DUAN C. C., 2000, "The Current and Projected Distribution of the Elderly and Child care in the People's Republic of China." *Journal of Family Issues* 21(6): 714–32.

WANG H. and DONG X.-Y., 2010, "Child care Provision and Women's Participation in Off-Farm Employment: Evidence from China's Low-Income Rural Areas" in Xiao-yuan Dong and Sarah Cook eds. *Gender Equality and China's Economic Transformation: Informal Employment and Care Provision,* pp.228-241. Beijing: Economic Science Press.

WANG J., MIN S. and YUEXIN C., 2010, "Domestic Workers' Access to Social Security in Shanghai: a Case Study" in Xiao-yuan Dong and Sarah Cook eds. *Gender Equality and China's Economic Transformation: Informal Employment and Care Provision,* pp.113-128. Beijing: Economic Science Press.

YUAN H., 2010, "Migrant Family's Choices of Mother's Employment and Child care: Empirical Evidence from Beijing" in Xiao-yuan Dong and Sarah Cook eds. *Gender Equality and China's Economic Transformation: Informal Employment and Care Provision,* pp.192-205. Beijing: Economic Science Press.

ZHU J. and WANG C., 2005, Comtemporary early childhood education and research in China. In B. Spodek and O. Saracho (Eds), International Perspective on Research in Early Childhood Education. Greenwich, CT, U.S.: Information Age Publishing.

CHAPTER 12

The alternative and solidarity economy leads to social emancipation. However, despite its success in bypassing the rules of a free-market economy and critiquing managerial ideology, it remains marginal in terms of trade and society. It urgently needs its own political agenda and identity

The solidarity economy: emancipatory action to challenge politics

n his analysis, the sociologist Robert Castel, shows that today, although social security has continued to expand since the post-war era and still covers a large part of the French population, and despite the fact that the labour law and the welfare state remain strong even in the face of longstanding social criticism, the category that Castel calls the "disaffiliated of the wage society" continues to grow. This category applies to those people that the last twenty years of sociological literature has described as excluded (i.e. the long-term unemployed) and those that are experiencing a series of transient and precarious work situations (which has also been discussed for a long time but is now increasingly common) (CASTEL and HAROCHE, 2001).

Bruno Frere,
senior fellow of the FNRS, University of Liège, Sciences Po Paris, France

Falling outside of the spectrum of occupations included within the wage society, which constitute the primary labour market (where people still benefit from collective agreements, trade union support, insurance, etc.), the disaffiliated make up a secondary market of unemployed people and permanent temporary workers whose services are only of intermittent interest to companies (CASTEL, 1995). This market is composed of "supernumerary", "unnecessary" people, who no longer even have the opportunity to be "exploited" by a company and to be alienated by repetitive and monotonous work, since they are deprived of long-term employment and forced to accept positions that offer a "half-wage", a "split salary status" or, in particular, a "low-paid wage". These types of jobs, which are considered as "atypical" (short-term contract, temporary, part-time, insertion, odd jobs, holiday cover, trainee positions...) have become widespread[1]; and while the salaried status remains the dominant form

---

1. 74% of new contracts in 2006 (CASTEL, 2007).

of work organization, we are probably witnessing a rapid deterioration in the status of wage-earners towards a level that is "below" that of traditional employment (scheduled to last for an indefinite period) and no longer enjoying all the prerogatives of labour laws and social protection (CASTEL, 2007, p. 416-418).

For ten years, many authors have confirmed the analysis that identifies the return, among a large number of pervasively present inequalities (gender, race, etc.), of a fundamental inequality that is creating a hierarchy between two social classes (CHAUVEL, 2001, 2004, 2006). In the twenty-first century, this inequality is no longer that which existed between the bourgeoisie and the working class. It has in fact become an inequality that separates a large disaffiliated class, the members of which do not currently realize they are grouped within it, which consists of unemployed people and those that have become the holders of downgraded jobs, from the middle class[2] (CASTEL, 1995, 2007, p. 415) which is disappearing from the bottom, since their social prerogatives are said to strain flexibility and competitiveness[3].

This new bi-polarity of social inequality is not only an inequality of "affiliation" in the traditional sense of the wage earning society. It also combines geographical inequality which, despite what we may like to believe, is not only present between North and South. Unemployment and precarious work are concentrated in certain segments of the population, in certain regions and in certain neighbourhoods. Throughout the world there are ghettos, either actual or quasi-ghettos, whose inhabitants do not have the slightest chance of being saved by a miraculous integration into the global economy. Instead, the logic of the capitalist flow continues to marginalize these "black holes", as the sociologist Manuel Castells points out, because the locations of wealth generation are connected via telecommunications (CASTELLS, 2000). The selective connections of capitalism circumvent these undesirable neighbourhoods or regions where the inhabitants cannot even expect a decent education (this is the situation in certain Parisian suburbs, U.S. cities with declining populations such as Detroit, the Chinese countryside, in Indian and South American slums, throughout almost the entirety of Africa...).

Nonetheless, within these "black holes", which are home to the majority of disaffiliated people engaged in precarious work, life organizes itself. New associations and cooperatives are formed on a regular basis, the purpose of which is to allow members to re-establish social relationships and engage in the solidarity economy that is necessary for their survival. The main hypothesis of this paper is that the strength at which this associative movement is currently developing not only enables a partial easing of the rate at which the wage society is eroding (what the public authorities expect from

---

2. The middle classes are those that fall, said Castel, along a continuum of differentiated professional positions ranging from minimum wage workers to those in higher (senior) posts, but all have the same rights in terms of labour laws and its regulations, as well as in terms of the State and its social benefits.

3. Germany is a case in point. It addressed the current financial crisis through the multiplication of "small" poorly paid jobs, that are under-protected. This was made possible by a massive reform of the labour market that was voted for in 2004 (Hartz IV reform).

it everywhere in the world), but that it also contains the seeds of another economic model, which is radically alternative, self-managing and non-capitalist. We will see that many members of the middle class are intuitively sensing the threats to the traditional wage society to which they are still integrated, and are engaging with the disaffiliated. Their efforts are not only based on charity: they live in the knowledge that at any time they may be downgraded to the less stable type of employment offered by the second deregulated labour market. A strong local solidarity economy could someday be important to these people, not just as mere volunteers or consumers of the goods and services that such a market offers.

The first part of this article focuses mainly on understanding the solidarity economy, with the help of quantitative data and examples of initiatives from Europe, the Anglo-sphere and Asia. The second part deepens the analysis with regard to the observation that the solidarity economy is an alternative in which, in the words of Karl Polanyi (1985), the economy is re-embedded into politics and democracy. We note that the solidarity economy combines two fundamental dimensions: first, although the middle classes participate in the solidarity economy, it is largely initiated *by* and *for* this new disaffiliated class regardless of the country or continent; secondly its utopian outlook is that of the overthrow of capitalism (as distinct from the market) since its organizational model draws much from associationist socialism and the libertarian principles of the nineteenth century that have been described elsewhere (FRERE, 2009).

However, it is precisely the failure of the associationist socialism movement, which is caught between Marxism and liberalism, that has taught us that such a model must be politically focused and organized to be effective. Finally, the last part of the article is devoted to the question of whether the solidarity economy today has the strength to assert itself as what it means to be, namely, an alternative potential model, rather than what the market and the State wants it to be: a management and accounting tool for tackling unemployment and disaffiliation.

An international economic revolution from below?

As Jean-Louis Laville (2011) emphasized in his latest book, a revival of associationist socialism, assimilated to the solidarity economy, is underway on all continents. We can see this in the people's economy of Latin America, in Africa's informal economy and in the social economies in Asian and English-speaking countries (the notion of "social economy" is only now beginning to be distinguished from that of the "third sector" or "charities"). All of these different forms share common practices. Today, the commonly held view is that four elements comprise the alternative solidarity movement: social currency, solidarity-based finance, North-North or North-South fair trade, and local services. All these initiatives, which occur in different variations in the North and the South, have such a vast scope that for the last fifteen years a number of specialists, such as Ortiz and Munoz, have been sufficiently confident to talk of a "counter-hegemonic globalization" (ORTIZ and MUNOZ, 1998).

The element of finance and solidarity-based savings includes a diverse range of structures, for example in France there are savings associations such as CIGALES

FIGURE 1 The social economy in France

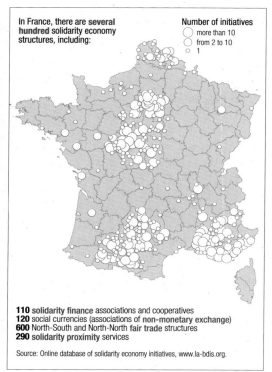

In France, there are **several hundred** solidarity economy structures, including:

Number of initiatives
- ○ more than 10
- ○ from 2 to 10
- ○ 1

110 solidarity finance associations and cooperatives
120 social currencies (associations of **non-monetary exchange**)
600 North-South and North-North **fair trade** structures
290 solidarity proximity services

Source: Online database of solidarity economy initiatives, www.la-bdis.org.

The Movement for Solidarity Economy (MES), which was founded in 2002 as a replacement for another more informal structure, now provides various French organizations with a common political platform, offering, beyond a simple representation, free participation in terms of various projects. Mapping of existing initiatives is one of the common actions undertaken. Both from the point of view of the political imaginary and from an organizational perspective, we can assume that the logic of the movement is federal and libertarian.

(*Clubs d'Investisseurs pour une Gestion Alternative et Locale de l'Epargne Solidaire* – investment clubs for alternative management and local solidarity savings) and credit unions such as *Garrigue* or the larger *La Nef* (*Nouvelle économie solidaire* – New fraternal economy), which invest in cooperative micro-initiatives that have been set up *by* and *for* collectives, precarious workers, unemployed people or people who no longer wish to hold the status of temporary workers or employees, positions that they found alienating. Most of the structures of so-called "North-North" solidarity finance have precise specifications that require, in order to qualify for funding, a structure to incorporate some solidarity dimensions relating to, for example, the social or cultural sector. Of course, the issue here, which is sometimes problematic, is to avoid reproducing micro-capitalism on a small-scale (or "barefoot" capitalism as Serge Latouche (2003) would say, targeting in particular Muhammad Yunus's micro-credit in Bangladesh), which only results in an application of the conventional market rules. Through this method of financing, various fair trade and "local" organic shops have been created, in France and elsewhere. The figures speak for themselves. While the first citizen club of CIGALES savers was established barely 30 years ago, the French territory is today covered by 136 associations that currently support some 350 companies and 1,800 potential (self-) employment positions. *La Nef*, which was formed just 24 years ago, now has 31,000 members – mostly drawn from, just like CIGALES, the middle classes that populate what Castel calls the primary labour market (engaged employees, militant civil servants, retired small-business people...). In 2010, *La Nef* invested 20 million euros in more than 350 projects.

The rise of solidarity-based finance has also taken place internationally: in 2006, Jean-Michel Servet noted that from 1997 to 2004, the increase in the number of clients and projects supported by organizations of solidarity finance members of the International Network INAISE[4] was 36%. In Japan, for example, the first community bank (Bank Mirai) was set up in 1994. Citizens who placed their savings in this bank are able to choose the micro-projects in which they want to invest, provided these projects relate to environmental, social or cultural sectors, and the project

---

4. International Association of Investors in the Social Economy.

implementers are also members of the credit union. Today, throughout Japan there are 12 such banks (known as NPO banks). The smallest are composed of around 20 members and have capital amounting to several thousand dollars, while the largest have up to 500 members and their investments in 2010 amounted to 2 million dollars (MAKINO, 2011).

Social currencies constitute a second group. They have a long history that we will not reproduce here[5], suffice to say that, while rare and isolated throughout the twentieth century, they underwent a major worldwide development from the 1980s, mainly in Europe, North America, South America and Japan. Jean-Louis Laville estimates that there are now some 2,500 such associations, which have a total of 1.5 million subscribers (LAVILLE, 2011, p.148). Their main representatives in France are the local exchange services (*Services d'échanges locaux* – SEL). These groups of people practice the multilateral exchange of goods and services using a voucher system, that is to say, their own unit of account[6], enabling the measurement of the value of internal transactions. Services are also exchanged, such as repair work, babysitting, language courses, etc. Some of the poorest associates are able to live off the fruits of this exchange. It should be noted that the French example (there are currently about 300 SEL in France), as well as Italy's time bank and Germany's *Tauschringe*, are based on units of account that are not generally exchangeable into euros. The challenge is to avoid the commoditization of goods and services that would lead to their valorization and devaloraization according to their traditional market price. The Local Exchange Trading Systems (LETS) is the Anglosphere's version of this structure, which is present in Australia, Canada, New Zealand, United Kingdom and the United States. LETS enable the matching of their alternative currencies to the dollar, so as to give their poorest members the opportunity to convert their earnings, allowing them to obtain the non-accessible elements that are necessary to their daily lives in the LETS.

Today, we cannot discuss social currencies without mentioning the Argentinian example. Here, in the mid-1990s, the first "barter clubs" were established in Buenos Aires. They were spectacularly successful and the idea was rapidly replicated by the disaffiliated and middle classes from the quasi "black holes" that were in effect most of the cities in Argentina. They boomed to such an extent that it quickly became necessary to create a global barter network (GBN) to ensure a certain amount of mutualisation. However, the network became so large that the exchanges between members of different clubs – who took the name *nodo* ("node" in the network) – became difficult because there was nothing to structure the equivalences between all currencies. The GBN therefore decided to create a single currency: the *crédito*. The phenomenon continued to grow until several problems appeared in the early 2000s:

---

5. In France, the first experiment of this type was the People's Bank created by libertarian anarchist Proudhon in 1848 (on this topic, see: Frere B., 2009, *op. cit.*). Reference is made to other European and American experiences in chapter 10 of the book Blanc J., 2000, *Les monnaies parallèles. Unité et diversité du fait monétaire*, Paris, L'Harmattan.

6. *Le grain de SEL, le Pigalle, le Piaf, le caillou,* etc.

inflation due to the over-issuance of *créditos*, the relocation of several clubs which then (re-) created their own currencies, regionalization (and division) of the GBN, the creation of a social franchise... Despite the success of the bi-monthly *mega férias* (mega markets), which were supported by the Secretariat of Industry, Trade and Labour, as well as the municipality of Buenos Aires[7], the system eventually imploded, after reaching a membership of more than 5 million people across Argentina. While there are only about twenty *nodos* left in Buenos Aires, with around 4,000 members and each operating with their own currencies, the fact remains that the Argentinian experience has shown that it is possible to set up a large scale economic system that not only incorporates the poorest, but also redraws the rules of economic exchange, since in this case, hoarding is unnecessary and a strict social equality exists between members: all goods and services have a value that is measured in time (the time taken to make the good or provide the service) and is not based on supply and demand. One hour of a CEO's or university professor's time is worth no more than that of an artisan or manual worker.

The Japanese example may be referred to in response to those who argue that any parallel economy, which is neither public nor capitalist, is systematically doomed to suffer the same decline as the Argentinian case. In Japan, the *yichikris* network brings together 270,000 associations that are autonomous and independent from the state (each consisting of 180 to 400 households). They offer all kinds of proximity goods and services to their members. As François Plassart wrote, "what *yichikris* show is that autonomous spaces of self-managed solidarity can exist in the in-between space that separates the family from the market economy, which separates the family and public services" (PLASSART, 1997).

The third element comprises the North-North or North-South examples of fair trade, which in France is embodied by networks such as the *Biocoop* shops, and the AMAP[8] (for North-North exchanges), and *Artisans du Monde* and *Andines* (for North-South). While it only represents 0.02% of the current global trade, the figures concerning fair trade are steadily increasing – in 2007 the estimated total sales in France stood at 241 million euros, which represented an increase of 157% since 2004. Worldshops, such as *Artisans du Monde*, could be counted on the fingers of one hand in the early 1970s, in the country where they originated: the Netherlands. Today, there are more than 3,500 (involving over 60,000 volunteers and 4,000 employees) across 18 European countries. Naturally, this sector is not immune from tensions, such as those that are increasing between the worldshops movement and the so-called "certification" one, the main representative of the latter being Max Havelaar. The certification group considers that it is important to get their labelled products into supermarkets in order to reach a larger public. Conversely, the worldshops group criticizes the attitude of

---

7. Following the model of "*la Fabrica*" on the property of the former textile factory La Bernalesa in Quilmes, where in 1997, 600 people exchange goods and services (electricians, hairdressers, accountants, artisans, cooks, teachers...). See in this regard the website of There Are Other Alternatives: www.taoaproject.org

8. Associations for the maintenance of small-holder agriculture.

supermarkets for the "depersonalization" of the relationship between the consumer of the North and the producer of the South, whereas fair trade was originally intended to bring the two together (by organizing meetings, providing clear information in stores on production conditions and the identity of producers, etc.). Besides which, it has become evident that supermarkets have only been using fair trade as a showcase. Over the years they have not increased the shelf space devoted to such products or changed their draconian attitude towards their suppliers and staff[9].

The most interesting aspect of fair trade is no longer only the charitable impulse that, for the last forty years, has led Northern civil society actors (mainly from the middle class) to associate themselves to Southern producers in order to overcome the inherent injustices of international markets that the latter suffer from. Now, for the last 10 years, we have seen examples emerge of North-North and South-South fair trade, representing new kinds of production and consumption cooperatives. In this respect, the French AMAPs are particularly interesting. Without providing a detailed historical account that goes back to the nineteenth century – which would, for example, include a reference to the *Commerce véridique et social*, the first true consumer cooperative initiated by Michel-Marie Derion in Lyon in 1835 (BAYON, 2002) – it is estimated that the first AMAP-type contemporary cooperatives appeared in Japan in the 1970s. The first *Teikei* (which means "cooperative") originated as a citizen reaction against intensive agriculture, which was then thriving, and enabled 11 families from Tokyo to sign a contract with a number of local farmers that did not use chemical inputs (ZIMMER, 2011). The concept was so successful to the point where today, one Japanese family in four participates in a *Teikei*. In the United States in the mid-1980s, the first CSA (Community Supported Agriculture) groups were organized in Massachusetts and New Hampshire. As was the case in Japan, the reasons behind this movement were both ideological and health-related. CSAs were also a great success in Canada, where more than 100 farms work with around 8,500 homes in Quebec alone. While in the United States, the last census reported almost 13,000 CSAs (CHARLEBOIS, 2011; FLORES, 2006).

The French AMAPs were developed later, the first one being established in 2001, but they operate in identical ways. They aim to provide their members with quality food produced close to their town or village, in exchange for involvement with the farmer regarding its distribution and/or production. The sharing of these tasks gives members access to organic products at a lower cost by the avoidance of a series of intermediaries. These initiatives represent an alternative to the industrial "organic" products sold by the supermarkets and, in particular, have the effect of relocating the commodity exchange, this is a point on which fair trade remains environmentally problematic, since the products sold may travel around the world by plane before arriving on our plates. But it should be noted that, in both cases, for "fair" or "proximity" trade, it is again the middle classes, who commit through voluntary

---

9. See in this regard the beautiful study conducted by Ferreras I. on supermarkets in 2007, *Critique politique du travail*, Paris, Presses de Sciences Po.

work, which have enabled the economies of scale to function to allow the proper compensation of producers (often precarious workers) who want to focus on quality products. AMAP's success is growing. As Fabrice Ripoll stated: "in late 2011, AMAP promoters announced that there was around 1,600 collectives, bringing together over 66,000 families and nearly 270,000 consumers, for an annual turnover estimated at 48 million euros" (RIPOLL, 2013).

"Relocated fair" trade is also developing in the South. This is evidenced, for example, by the creation in Lima, in 2001, of the Latin American Network of Community trading (RELACC) which involves 12 countries. "Its aim is to promote the increase in national trade while reducing the intermediaries, so that the mostly indigenous producers receive a better price for their work. As for consumers, they have access to basic necessities at a controlled price; in Peru, more than 3,000 popular restaurants are supplied in this way. The label *Comercio Justo México* is another example of the South-South dynamic, in terms of trade on the domestic market." (LAVILLE, 2011, p. 143)

Finally, the last element includes what experts have been referring to since the 1980s as "proximity services", which are often developed in an associative or cooperative form. Four major areas are covered: services for daily life and health (elderly assistance, etc.); services for the improvement of the quality of life (building maintenance, etc.); cultural services and recreation; and environmental services (maintenance of green spaces, recycling, etc.). The most common examples in France are the neighbourhood boards or parental crèches that have thrived in most cities since the early 1980s, which combine their resources together: public funds, the market and voluntary work. Structures exist to support the development of such services (for example, solidarity economy clusters). They bring together volunteers and professionals who are trying to support their promoters. All sometimes work with solidarity finance agencies (with the same kind of specifications) or with organic or fair trade networks.

Like all other "solidarity" groups, there are many local variations of the concept of proximity services, such as in the heart of the popular economy in Latin America, and the social economy in North America. Since the 1980s, Community Development Corporations are increasing in the United States. These structures are aimed at the revitalization of neighbourhoods and rural areas through mobilization, of people who are disaffiliated or otherwise. New cooperatives are also on the increase, including work cooperatives where the workers hold the majority of shares and where the share distribution is relatively equal between them. They represent 1,200 small entities that employ some 15,000 people. In the UK, community approaches are expressed through the development of the Community Transport Association, nationally recognized as the representative body for groups that have come together to overcome the lack of transport. These include Community Enterprises, which are numerous in Scotland, some Community Foundations and Community Development Trusts. All these initiatives are taking place in rural and urban areas where conventional market activity is in decline, leaving in its place an economic black hole. Since the 1990s, this dynamic has originated from the population itself, with the objective of counteracting the marginalization of disadvantaged areas.

With regard to environmental protection, the Groundwork Trust has helped with the take off of more than 3,000 projects, all of which have the common point of involving the participation of the inhabitants in their design and implementation, in partnership with environmental organizations, local communities and businesses. In terms of childcare, Playgrounds are places that host young children on a part-time basis: they are managed by parents in reaction to the lack of supply, there were 18,000 of them in the early 2000s, which provided 19% of the spaces available for children under 5 years old, while their Swedish counterparts provide 15%. In Germany, at the beginning of the twenty-first century, some 70,000 similar self-help structures have been identified, providing work for some 2.65 million people in the fields of health and social action (LAVILLE, 2011, p. 130-131). While in France, the ACEPP (*Association des collectifs enfants-parents-professionnels* – collective association of children, parents and professionals) which brings together parental crèches, works mainly for the establishment of its scheme in poor neighbourhoods where the self-management by parents of such structures can help to re-establish social links and enable substantial financial savings.

In the health sector, we can mention the 90 medical homes in Belgium that have been established to deliver free medical outreach in urban areas to the most vulnerable. Brazil for its part has more than 100 similar cooperative medical services, involving nearly 15,000 associated doctors. These services come under the so-called "formal" economy, unlike the vast majority of the Brazilian proximity services which are still considered as informal economic activities, at the same level as crime or underpaid activities linked to the outsourcing strategies of large capitalist corporations. However, part of this "informal" sector, which is difficult to quantify, is only based on mutual aid[10]. Many proximity services in Brazil, and other Latin American countries, are organizations of unemployed people from various sectors including collective kitchens, vegetable gardens, self-construction pre-cooperatives, organizations devoted to housing problems, etc. Common ownership of the means of production is the rule. It is estimated that at the end of the twentieth century, this popular economy represented 25% of employment in a city like Santiago. "In this country, as in others, one of the most illustrative examples is that of waste recycling. There are nearly 300,000 people, or 1% of the population, who make a living from waste recovery, including 50,000 people in Bogota" (LAVILLE, 2011, p. 120). Bogota's recycling association was created in response to the ostracism experienced by the city's recyclers, who are victims of both the formal and informal intermediaries to whom they sell, often suffering stigmatization and social contempt.

---

10. Without a doubt, many actors in the informal economy participate in both proximity services and certain illegal activities. It is important here to avoid naivety. It is thus not at all absurd to imagine that the same person could, in order to survive, be involved in drug trafficking while also investing in community solidarity activities, such as a cooperative restaurant for example.

FIGURE 2 **The social economy in Brazil**

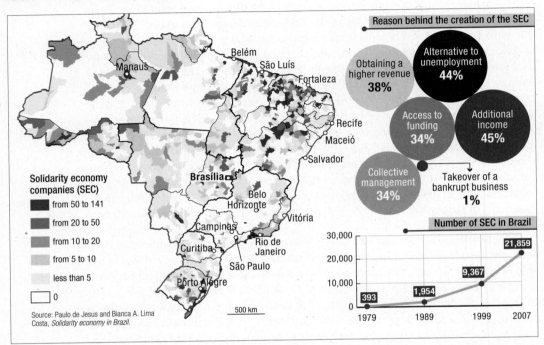

Source: Paulo de Jesus and Bianca A. Lima Costa, *Solidarity economy in Brazil.*

In less than thirty years, solidarity initiatives have developed at a surprising rate in Brazil. If we believe their progression curves, their numbers will continue to grow strongly in the coming years. The main reasons given by the actors who engage in this alternative economic pathway are practical (incomes, alternatives to unemployment) as much as ideological (collective management).

Characteristics of alternative solidarity: organization, empowerment and politicization

From the Japanese LETS, to the Brazilian proximity services cooperatives, through the British or American community enterprises, economists specializing in this sector agree that the characteristics of these initiatives are similar (DEFOURNY et al, 2009):

– their purpose is to serve members and the community, rather than profit;

– management autonomy (or self-management);

– democratic decision-making (1 person = 1 vote)

– collective ownership (cooperative or associative) of capital and means of production;

– primacy of people and work over capital in the distribution of income (fair distribution of the value-added between work and investment in the activity on the one hand, and between the workers themselves on the other);

- market activity (for proximity services, fair trade or solidarity finance) is specified by adding a final criterion: more than 50% of current resources should come from the sale of goods and services.

The uniqueness of the solidarity economy is therefore the people that comprise it: on the one hand, are the precarious and temporary workers, the tired trainees and the unemployed (the disaffiliated); while on the other are the middle class volunteers who live in the knowledge that they may one day join the ranks of the disaffiliated. This uniqueness is also its modus operandi. While, naturally all of these criteria are met to varying degrees depending on the situation, there is no doubt that they enable the very clear differentiation of the solidarity economy and that they attest to its potential desire to offer an alternative. The mere mention of criteria "1" and "4" (the rejection of the sole purpose of profit and private property) is enough to convince us that we are dealing with an economy that, ideally, does not dream of being "alongside" capitalism but rather to replace it. As for the notion of "market", it is not de-legitimized so long as it is organized collectively through cooperative and collective actions.

In addition to its public and internal modus operandi, the rejection of the "insertion sector" is another dimension of the solidarity economy which demonstrates its aim to provide an alternative. The political supporters of this sector would like to confine the solidarity economy to addressing social issues and managing the disaffiliated classes, on the margins of a public sector and a capitalist private sector, which would deal with the things that matter: politics and economics. Whereas those involved in the social economy have known for years that, for some, it is absurd to try to "rehabilitate" the "excluded" into the "primary" employment market, which only exists precisely because it has a vast secondary market at its disposal, a sub-class of disaffiliated workers who are flexible and cheap (because they are often funded by the state on the basis of "insertion contracts" (CASTEL, 2007, p. 20) and who serve as extra workforce as and when needed. These actors all agree that the exclusion/inclusion connection must be terminated, as it is this connection which makes individuals carry the responsibility for their own marginality, of their so-called difference, because they are not sufficiently "their own managers" or "leaders of their own lives" or "connected to opportunities" to find a full-time job with a permanent contract. Once these assumptions have been assimilated by the concept of exclusion, it becomes easy to say, as some authors have been doing for a long time, such as Pierre Rosanvallon, that there is no "precarious social class" and to pretend that the social issue can be addressed by imposing, hidden under the cover of the solidarity economy, "insertion" mechanisms that are singular and particularized. If no "class" exists, but only "individuals", then the answers should be "individualized" (ROSANVALLON, 1995). And here lies the problem, in at least two respects.

First, it is not unreasonable to wonder, "insertion into what?" The middle classes know that they are far more likely to become precarious workers, rather than the reverse. As touched upon above, the middle classes are gradually disintegrating. The walls that separate them from precariousness and disaffiliation are crumbling, little by little, with the lengthening of working hours (the reduction of which has been shown to increase life expectancy), the lowering of wages and of the minimum wage threshold, a forced multi-job style of employment, a scarcity of permanent contracts to be replaced by a range of increasingly sophisticated short-term contracts, a questioning of labour law[11] (which slow downs productivity), etc. (CASTEL, 2007, p. 421).

Second, the application of individual schemes to attempt to make the disaffiliated more connected, more mobile, more flexible, more adapted to the labour market and the global economy, is in a way to compel them to the labour of Sisyphus, bringing the excluded person back to the gates of the traditional wage society, to then be forever rejected. Ultimately, the utopia of insertion is to believe that it is possible to extract the disaffiliated from the black holes in the globalized information economy, and to use them to feed the secondary labour market, which the economy fundamentally needs as an adjustment mechanism.

Having gained experience of existing as an alternative, the solidarity economy refutes the logic of insertion into the conventional labour market, instead seeking to create its own. In the words of Castel, mentioned above, the solidarity economy would enrich a second labour market without trying to bridge it with the primary market, the market of the drifting middle classes.

A final element (after its public, its own modus operandi and empowerment towards the traditional labour market), which places the solidarity economy away from the capitalist economy, is its inherently political dimension. Often, these multifaceted associations are considered as a re-politicization of the economy, in the best and Polanyi sense of the term, as described above (the "re-embedding" of the economic into the social). These "solidarity" initiatives never refer to the "political" world (institutionalized) even though they reflect "a modest, ordinary citizenship." It is something other than a simple and fragile survival strategy: the management of public space where we relate to others (CHANIAL, 1998). What becomes possible, it is said, is "a public commitment of dominated groups that would at least partially become autonomous from dominant representation structures" (parties or trade unions), "becoming free from the appearance and the compulsory channels of expression, the potential inclusion of politics within the actions in the field, the potentiality of a renewed exercise of democracy" (ION, 1999).

Ultimately, as a utopian alternative to capitalism and as a vector of practical democracy, the solidarity economy would carry a true project of political economy. At the head of this project is probably the Latin variation of the movement. Beyond the proximity services and LETS which, as we have seen, are developing in various forms in both the North and South, it should be noted that an additional political dimension characterizes mainly the solidarity economy in South America. Every year, in countries such as Argentina and Brazil, many companies are being taken over as cooperatives by their workers in an attempt to create democratic management (all workers participating in the general assembly: one man, one vote). However, all is

---

11. We can think for example, in France, of the *contrats nouvelle embauche* or the *contrats première embauche*, which are clear exceptions to the labour law and give employers the opportunity to dismiss workers as and when they want, without compensation.

not rosy and the famous principle "we produce, we sell, we pay ourselves" is often very difficult to achieve. But the successes are more numerous in cases where traditional bosses, although they were highly skilled managers, were forced to give up: for example, the Impa metallurgical plant, the Bauen hotel, the Chilavert printing factory, the Fasinpat tile factory, the Catense cooperative and its 12,000 workers in the Brazilian northeast, and many more.

In light of these experiences, one may wonder why the self-management vision struggles to develop in France at a time when both unions and political parties only offer as an alternative to the delocalization and closure of industrial sites, the idea of searching for "credible buyers" and "new foreign investors". Even though of course, despite what we may pretend to believe, these new investors may well delocalize at the first opportunity. Indeed, everything transpires as if the traditional pillars of the political dialogue of our Western social democracies were so steeped in the image of the wage society (in its contemporary, most contorted, configuration)[12] that they fail to consider that a different economy could go beyond the traditional triptych of investor shareholders, bosses (CEOs and managers) and salaried employees. One paradox of this observation is that it underlines the fact that the social structure of capitalism seems to be as necessary to those intending to fight it, as it is to those who benefit from it.

But is the solidarity economy the perfect solution to everything when the unions, for example, are left behind? The answer is no, far from it, because it is very likely that the unions have a political experience and lucidity towards political power, which they have had for a long time, whereas proponents of the solidarity economy currently have a kind of moral irenicism that is somewhat naïve and on which subject we will explore further below.

Indeed, while all of these associative or cooperative initiatives attest to an undeniable citizen momentum, thereby renewing an action trend derived from associationist socialism or nineteenth century libertarianism, which was to challenge the established economic and political domination, it remains that this citizen momentum raises an unsolved question regarding its own militant universe.

This unresolved issue is that of their political organization. It is probably rather idealistic to simply magnify the democratic strength of the solidarity economy and the "political essence" that it would carry. As written by Alain Caillé, these associations are "political", certainly. But where is the large-scale organizational form that allows them to make their voices heard at European and national institutions in charge of

---

12. Our political classes and unions have directly inherited this imaginary vision from the twentieth century: they fail to think about the work "outside" the domination relationship between employers and employees, that is inherent to the traditional forms of hiring in the private sector (staff, executives, manual workers...) or the public sector (civil servants). Things would be less serious if the salaried status, to which this vision refers, was not today translated as, on top of the domination relationship, something that is "below" the traditional salaried status, some sort of new existence of this status. Individuals of precarious status are ready to sell their labour, at any price that an employer may impose without any discussion (2007, p. 422 and 426). However, collective initiatives and property, self-management and democracy make the solidarity economy difficult to understand for those whose representation of economic activity fits into this imaginary vision.

economic and social policies? Sooner or later, we will have to raise the question of power, that is to say, the question of a "meta-association between existing associations. There will have to be an emergence of associations, specialized in general problems in the issue of bindings and transversality" (Caille, 2003). Because, by carrying on pretending that the *practiced* citizenship is sufficient, we will not see the emergence of a common discourse that is likely to produce a collective scheme, such as unionism in a previous era, in which the various hopes could engage. Without an incarnation in a single place (where all could engage democratically, one after the other), power is almost squandered between diverse churches that sometimes oppose each other. This is proved by the multiplicity of international networks[13], whose number is only equal to their weakness and impotence beyond their strict impact on local development.

The idea of structuration is frightening. It evokes abandonment, verticality, the confiscation of speech and the compelled allegiance to a fixed ideological line. It is also at the crossroads of these elements that we understand the disinterest of most of the solidarity economy activists in engaging with the traditional political structures: which are very restrictive. One must give one's voice to a representative, even though, since the 1980s, a growing number of activists feel a real distrust of the political delegations and the rhetoric of their leaders, which rarely lead to real social change. In new forms of commitment, such as the alternative and solidarity economy, the autonomy is much greater. One can engage and disengage easily from an association: when we consider that the message (or products) no longer corresponds to our expectations, it is easy to withdraw and to engage elsewhere.

As Jacques Ion expertly shows, these forms of activism are better suited to a more individualized society: a lighter commitment, less time-consuming, a more personalized and less general protest (Ion et al, 2005). We chose from the menu, without feeling "forced" by a specific organization and the perception that it carries, as was the case in previous times when one became involved in trade unions or political parties with Maoist or Marxist ideologies. Ultimately, this form of commitment is the photographic negative of the engagement in contemporary capitalism for its executives: it is flexible. This is what makes both its strength and its fragility.

Certainly, by engaging into an AMAP or CSA, for example, members are being political in a practical sense. They do not just verbally denounce productivist agriculture

---

13. The suggested list below is by no means exhaustive but indicates the diversity of unions, networks and federations of the social and solidarity economy. In Europe only, there are already a large number of structures that do not have any specific links between them: ESENSEE (Eco Social Economy Network South and East Europe), REVES (European Network of Cities and Regions for the Social Economy), EESC (European Economic and Social Committee), FEBEA (European Federation of Ethical and Alternative Banks), Social Planet, RIPESS Europe (Intercontinental Network for the Promotion of the Social Solidarity Economy), IRIS (European Inter-network of Ethical and Responsible Initiatives), Cooperatives Europe, CECOP (European Confederation of Workers" Cooperatives, Social Cooperatives and Social and Participative Enterprises), etc. This diversity also exists worldwide: RIPESS, FIESS (International Forum on the Social Economy), INAISE (International Association of Investors in the Social Economy), Alliance for a responsible and united world, ICA (International Cooperative Alliance), WFTO (World Fair Trade Organization), IFAT (International Fair Trade Organization), Point Pal (international network of proximity services), RIFES (International Network of Women and Solidarity Economy), IFHE (International Federation of Home Economics), the International Federation of cooperative and mutual insurance, etc.

and the wide network of capitalist supermarkets (Carrefour, etc.). They also take practical action, reinventing a cooperative and mutualist local economy, the growing success of which may perhaps one day constitute a major concern to industrial producers and supermarket chains that hitherto had become accustomed to dictating the reality of consumption. Namely: a mass of products and customers in gigantic and impersonal spaces, away from the producers and any reflection on our ostentatious consumption modes. Instead of a verbal political criticism, without substance, these cooperative and purchasing groups put practical criticism into action through emancipation, which is direct and sometimes even thoughtless.

Beyond political inaction, what are the modes of expression, the political intermediaries? Major social advances have never happened through moral good will (that, for example, of a Max Havelaar label coffee drinker) but through the overlap of well-understood interests of social groups in a declared political struggle. But today, it is clear that if there is such a gap between political representatives and civil society, it is also because critical demonstrations by the latter, such as the solidarity economy, struggle to go from social diversity and moral *pathos* which partly characterize them ("I invest myself with and for the poor, through a community development corporation, fair trade, etc.") to the formalization of a common struggle and a political *logos*.

Daring to face the question of the organization of power, while retaining its popular essence, is perhaps the challenge that lies ahead for the solidarity economy to become a real force of political proposal. A proposal that does not forget to think about democracy, something that the radical left often do when aiming for a proletarian revolution that does not concern itself with the voice of the proletariat.

Facing the ideology of the management of precariousness

Today, the solidarity economy, in all countries, is facing a crucial problem: because it lacks an identity and a political agenda, which are necessary vectors of a economical alternative, it can only assume the identity that some parties grant it, in the best case at the margin of their programmes or public policies. This "imposed" identity is that of the "resocialization" through re-insertion with a few rare exceptions of self-management, such as those envisaged in Latin America. This would indeed be its vocation and its only raison d'être according to the left wing green and socialist parties, who might support it as such (conservative parties simply ignore it most of the time). Both in the North and South, the solidarity economy flirts constantly with public authority instrumentalization. Indeed, when it has the opportunity to "pay salaries" due to potential public subsidies, it is not uncommon that it uses the status that it decries: supported employment, short and part-time contracts. Everywhere, it is asked to "manage" the social issue in order to reformat the "excluded" according to the standards of the wage society that is today disguised with a new managerial ideology, which weighs heavily for both individuals and institutions, and is very well described by Vincent de Gaulejac. This ideology is based on a set of abstract principles that are overvalued but have powerful effects on the reality of the organization of work:

connectivity, flexibility, mobility, scalability, efficiency, performance, streamlining (DE GAULEJAC, 2005). All continuously assessed by expensive consultancy devices.

We believe this managerial ideology seems to be nothing less than the cosmetic tool used to try to disguise the metamorphosis of the wage society.

We will join de Gaulejac to conclude that, to a certain extent, the solidarity economy, the main achievements of which in the world are often born of the resourcefulness of the most disaffiliated themselves, is indeed a direct process of emancipation, especially driven by aforementioned organizational characteristics (self management, democracy, etc.) (DE GAULEJAC, 2005). This process is likely to arrest the managerial ideology, and the border of the wage society that it also intends to redefine, by ensuring the refinement of tools that allow it to link at best the secondary and primary labour market: insertion, requalification, professionalism and competitiveness.

However, it is questionable whether by putting our noses to the grindstone, without pausing for thought, either pro or anti towards the initiatives of those who suffer the violence of a globalized and financialized economy (often women, foreigners, unemployed...), some of these initiatives are not likely to strengthen the identity of a marginal spare wheel for THE real economy, the authentic one, the big one – that of the market – instead just serving as a stick that breaks the spokes. To the extent that they do not even see that the atypical wage status that are specific to the precarious disaffiliated are often present in their own associations, due to a lack of political perspective.

Indeed, events sometimes unfold as if we agreed to leave the real political power to define the solidarity economy in the hands of institutions, and as if we settled for the aforementioned *policy of local* (modest and ordinary) which is more effective. The power of the labour movement which, since the nineteenth century, has enabled so much to be achieved in the social field, was precisely to have been fuelled by people who had no other choice but to unite to carry a collective voice, beyond the commitment to the local. Today, recognizing common reasons to fight is no longer so easy in a wage society that is split between civil servants who are decreasing in number, and private sector employees who are still relatively protected but increasingly threatened in European countries, and a growing number of precarious people who are working part-time or short-term contracts and who are already ultra-flexibilized. And this lack of unity arising from the invisibility of common motivations even appears in the associative or cooperative commitment of the solidarity economy. Until now, whether it was investors in solidarity finance, fair trade coffee drinkers or work cooperatives set up by the poorest, the resourcefulness, the altruism or the pleasure of social links was prevalent among the reasons to commit... But the world has until now only been truly transformed when well-defined and collectivized interests have managed to violently enter into the established balance of power. ∎

REFERENCES

BAYON D., 2002, *Le commerce véridique et social*, Paris, Atelier de création libertaire.

BLANC L., 2000, *Les monnaies parallèles. Unité et diversité du fait monétaire*, Paris, L'Harmattan.

CAILLÉ A., 2003, "Sur le concept d'économie en général et d'économie solidaire en particulier", *L'alter-économie, quelle autre mondialisation ?, Revue du MAUSS*, n° 21, p. 215-236.

CASTEL R., 1995, *Les métamorphoses de la question sociale*, Paris, Gallimard, p. 658-659.

CASTEL R., 2007, "Au-delà du salariat ou en deçà de l'emploi ? L'institutionnalisation du précariat", in PAUGAM S., *Repenser la solidarité*, Paris, PUF, p. 418.

CASTEL R. and HAROCHE Cl., 2001, *Propriété privée, propriété sociale, propriété de soi. Entretiens sur la construction de l'individu moderne*, Paris, Fayard, p. 112-113.

CASTELLS E., 2000, *L'ère de l'information*, Paris, Fayard.

CHANIAL P., 1998, "La délicate essence de la démocratie : solidarité, don et association", *Une seule solution, l'association ? Socio-économie du fait associatif, Revue du MAUSS semestrielle*, n° 11, p. 28-43.

CHARLEBOIS J.-M., 2011, "Le projet Otesha (Canada) : la consommation alternative par la communauté intentionnelle", in PLEYERS G., *La consommation critique*, Paris, Desclée De Brouwer.

CHAUVEL L., 2001, "Le retour des classes sociales ?", *Revue de l'OFCE*, n° 79.

CHAUVEL L., 2004, in BOUFFARTIGUE P., *Le retour des classes sociales : inégalités, dominations, conflits*, La Dispute, Paris.

CHAUVEL L., 2006, *Les classes moyennes à la dérive*, Le Seuil, Paris.

DEFOURNY J., DEVELTERE P., FONTENEAU B. et NYSSENS M., 2009, *The Worldwide Making of the Social Economy. Innovations and Changes*, Leuven & The Hague, Acco: 15-40.

DE GAULEJAC V., 2005, *La société malade de la gestion. Idéologie gestionnaire, pouvoir managérial et harcèlement social*, Paris, Le Seuil, p. 317-323.

FERRERAS I., 2007, *Critique politique du travail*, Paris, Presses de Sciences Po.

FLORES H.-C., 2006, *Food Not Lawns. How to turn your Yard into Garden and your Neighbourhood into a Community*, Vermont, Chelsea Green Publishing Company.

FRÈRE B., 2009, *Le nouvel esprit solidaire*, Paris, Desclée de Brouwer.

ION J., 1999, "Engagements associatifs et espace public", *Mouvements*, n° 3, p. 67-73.

ION J. et alii, 2005, *Militer aujourd'hui*, Paris, Autrement.

LATOUCHE S., 2003, "L'oxymore de l'économie solidaire", *L'alter-économie. Quelle autre mondialisation ?, Revue du MAUSS*, n° 21, p. 145-150.

LAVILLE J.-L., 2011, *Politique de l'association*, Paris, Le Seuil.

MAKINO M., 2011, "Emerging models of social and community finance in Japan: opportunities and challenges". (available on: www.researchgate.net/publication/229050217_Emerging_Models_of_Social_and_Community_Finance_in_Japan_Opportunities_and_Challenges).

ORTIZ H. et MUNOZ L., 1998, *Globalizacion de la solidarad. Unreto para todos*, Lima, SES-CEP.

PLASSART F., 1997, *Le temps choisi, un nouvel art de vivre pour partager le travail autrement*, Paris, Charles Léopold Mayer, p. 73.

POLANYI K., 1985, *La grande transformation*, Paris, Gallimard.

RIPOLL F., 2013, "Les AMAP et dispositifs apparentés : forces et faiblesses axiologiques et stratégiques d'un succès pratique", in FRÈRE B. et JACQUEMAIN M., *Résister au quotidien ? Les formes contemporaines de l'action militante*, Paris, Presses de Sciences Po (à paraître).

ROSANVALLON P., 1995, *La nouvelle question sociale. Repenser l'État-providence*, Paris, Le Seuil.

ZIMMER M., 2011, "Les AMAP en France, entre consommation de produit fermiers locaux et nouvel ordre de vie", in PLEYERS G., *La consommation critique*, Paris, Desclée De Brouwer, p. 47-67.

Ekta Parishad, the landless people's movement in India

Émeline de Bouver, Université catholique de Louvain (UCL), Louvain-la-Neuve, Belgium

Unequal access to natural resources, especially to land, is a major issue that lies at the heart of social movements throughout the world[1]. Population growth, development models and intensive agriculture are transforming many regions into battlegrounds where conflicts are waged over natural resource use, damaging the lives of the farmers who depend on such resources (SHIVA, 2004). In India, the *Ekta Parishad* movement was created during the 1990s to support and defend the landless in a country marked by significant land pressure and where 70% of the population lives in rural areas. Dam construction, ore and cement mining, the creation of nature reserves and other wildlife parks, biofuel production… all play a role in intensifying the ever increasing pressure on land, forests and water. In the one-sided contests where businesses, landowners or the State take on indigenous peoples (*Adivasis*) or small farmers (mostly *Dalits* or untouchables), it is usually the latter group that end up the losers. "The pattern of land ownership is so unequal that 40% of the rural population are landless farm workers who labour under the control of local landowners and earn meagre daily wages" (CHINNAPPAN, 2010).

Ekta Parishad means Unity Forum. The movement[2] brings together thousands of Dalits and Adivasis from ten Indian states and unites thousands of local organizations. "Led by P. V. Rajagopal (an activist in the mould of Ghandi…)" (SINGLETON, 2004), the movement evokes the Gandhian challenge: the reduction of inequalities through non-violent social action. Ekta Parishad's activities primarily involve major demonstrations such as the *Jan Satyagraha* 2012 march, which is the most recent example. This protest, which was attended by 50,000 landless people, proved to be the greatest non-violent march in history[3], successfully enabling the voices of the excluded to be heard by government. In 2007, *Janadesh*, a similar march that gathered 25,000 people for one month, managed to help some landless people obtain land titles but mainly led to improvements in the rights of the poorest: in particular, a promise was obtained on the establishment of a National Commission for Agrarian Reform, along with amendments to the Land Acquisition Act and the Forest Rights Act. Two years later, Ekta Parishad activists began preparations for *Jan Satyagraha* 2012, a march that aimed

1. There are many active social movements that focus on access to land, both in the South and the North, the most well known being the Landless Movement of Brazil (MST). Other examples include: the *Via Campesina* international movement (based in Indonesia) which is present in all regions of the globe; the association *Terre de Liens* in France; *and Terres en vue* in Belgium.

2. Ekta Parishad activists consider that they are part of a people's movement, or a people's organization, rather than a social movement. In doing so, they put the emphasis on the fact that their movement lies in the hands of the population, the poorest, those who are involved.

3. After only ten days of walking, the action was halted following the signing of an agreement between P. V. Rajagopal and the Prime Minister, the latter undertaking to initiate the early stages of land reform within six months.

to put pressure on the government to keep its promises, most of which had not been fulfilled.

The Ekta Parishad experience has shown that far-reaching demonstrations are only the tip of the iceberg. This article mainly discusses the submerged part: the analysis of the movement suggests that large mobilizations are only one step in the process of social change.

Ekta Parishad, a multifaceted social movement

An analysis of Ekta Parishad reveals that the movement is engaged in a strikingly diverse range of actions: self-help groups, marches and sit-ins involving thousands of people, ashrams, political lobbying groups, land occupation, beekeeping training, youth camps... To the outside observer it is difficult to ascertain who is part of this movement and how it works[4]. This multiplicity of actions (often considered in mainstream analyses of social movements as spreading your resources too thinly[5]) and the different forms of the movement's objectives are achievements in line with P.V. Rajagopal's concept of activism and social change. For him, the transformation of society towards greater equality requires action on several levels. "Being an activist is not being a beggar", he often cites. For him, demanding rights for the poorest is only legitimate and relevant if, in parallel, efforts are also focused on the responsibilities of the people themselves. The advocacy of Ekta Parishad is rooted in the work of the sustainable transformation of the daily lives of Dalits and Adivasis through the implementation of local initiatives ranging from job creation in road construction to the support of organic agriculture, among others. Ekta Parishad is based in thousands of villages where its activists initiate and support many projects that are part of the alternative and solidarity economy (see article by B. Frère).

Focusing on the story of Lalita, a village coordinator who has worked with women and children in ten villages in southern India for a decade, gives us a good understanding of the invaluable work of Ekta Parishad, which is carried out locally by hundreds of activists. Lalita was employed to develop the work of Ekta Parishad in the region where she lived with her husband. Her first step, when she knew hardly anyone, was to create a village homework school that brought together children of all ages. She then replicated her school in neighbouring villages. Through her interaction with the children, she began to meet many mothers and developed an interest in their lives and the difficulties they encountered. Realizing that their need for an income was very high, she decided to address the need for jobs before anything else. With the help of other Ekta Parishad activists, Lalita ran training courses in beekeeping and sewing, giving the families an opportunity to get involved in small businesses, which provide significant material support. Through her work, a strong bond of trust has been established between Lalita and many people of the village, allowing her to advance her projects in a step-by-step manner. Before long, a children's council was established alongside the homework school, where the children are able to express their views on the strengths and weaknesses of their village. Elections are held in these councils to select leaders to discuss village problems (and solutions) in an inter-village council and then at an inter-district council. The sewing workshops do not only function as a support for job acquisition, they also serve as places where women can learn to express the difficulties they face in everyday life and to find solutions. Among these people, Lalita identifies and trains leaders: those with the potential to represent their village in public meetings and those who, like her, are suitable candidates for Ekta Parishad.

The movement has a *think local* philosophy, which primarily involves listening to people to understand their most pressing needs and working with them to find ways to respond to those needs, based on local capacities and resources. The multiplicity of initiatives is therefore the consequence of an extreme adaptability to local contexts. For the activists, *think local* also implies taking a step back from their objectives and focusing on learning non-violence, and coming to terms with realistic timescales for the

4. This multiplicity is also reflected in the various titles that are assigned to members of the movement. There are workers (those employed by *Ekta Parishad*), activists (including all other denominations), local leaders, national leaders (leaders are responsible for the coordination of the movement's action in a village, a region or a state).

5. For a critical view of the assimilation of multiplicity and dispersion, see Benasayag M. and Aubenas F. (2002).

achievement of their goals. Unlike many movements that put the acceleration of change as a priority, the distance of Ekta Parishad activists vis-à-vis the results of their efforts allows them to appreciate the slow pace of transitions. Their first objective is to deal with whatever reality they are faced with, at the risk of appearing inconsistent. An outside observer must remember to view the work of Ekta Parishad in a diachronic context. For example, it is possible to regard Lalita's seamstresses simply as poor women working for a pittance. To jump to this conclusion, however, means missing the most important element: these women have been inserted into a process that will enable them to develop much greater resilience. For Lalita, supporting these women to help them find a job to lift themselves and their families out of extreme poverty is a vital first step. To achieve this she must start by addressing the immediate needs of individuals, thereby gaining the trust of the people she supports and gradually guiding them towards collective issues. This approach is characteristic of the Ekta Parishad operation, which is based on two assumptions: first, that learning about non-violence is a lengthy process; and second that serving the community requires energy, which will only become available once individual needs have been listened to. Activists live amongst the people (in their region of origin or elsewhere, depending on the history of their engagement and the needs of the movement) and they support these communities and show them how to lead a non-violent existence. However, before they can hope to earn the respect of the people, or to encourage others to follow their example, they must establish a relationship based on long-lasting trust between themselves and the local population. This requirement takes time.

Inequalities as structural violence

While Ekta Parishad is rooted in local activism, it does not operate solely at this level. The movement has a global vision and strategy. Its demands are focused on access to three key resources: water, land and forest (*Jal, Jangle and Zameen*). In relation to land, Ekta Parishad calls for a "structural change that consists in a complete land redistribution to enable the marginalized and downtrodden to get out of poverty"[6]. Poverty, which is multidimensional (see illustration), affects a large proportion of the Indian population (the study illustrated here found that 55% of the Indian population lived below the poverty line). P.V. Rajagopal mobilizes people in opposition to a model of development that creates violence through inequality, and the perpetuation of these inequalities.

As one man alone cannot simultaneously be present in all of the places where Ekta Parishad is active, many local leaders and their teams work with P.V. Rajagopal in the field. People committed to the cause of non-violence surround him, but many also come to Ekta Parishad to seek fulfilment of diverse needs or desires (recognition, power, income, network, family...). The understanding of non-violence and the consistency of local initiatives therefore vary according to the skills and the examples set by the local leaders. To address this disparity, Ekta Parishad has organized hundreds of youth camps in recent years, to develop non-violent social action and support the empowerment of the landless[7].

In India, the issue faced by Ekta Parishad is not so much the absence of laws favourable to the poorest, it is rather that they are only partially applied. The movement is concerned that many legal achievements have not been transformed into concrete changes due in particular to corruption and a lingering trace of feudalism within the various levels of government. Ekta Parishad activists regard their mission as corresponding to the definition of

6. www.ektaparishad.com

7. These courses aim to develop the capacity of local people and enable them to better understand and defend their rights. A training manual has also been published: Carr-Harris, J. (2010)

▶ Measuring poverty in India remains a political challenge. Looking at income per capita and per day reveals that only 25% of the population is in a situation of extreme poverty (less than two dollars per day). If we accept a broader definition of poverty, taking into account access to essential services, we arrive at the much higher figure of 55%. Whatever the method, it is the rural populations who bear the greatest material deprivation.

FIGURE1 Persistent poverty in rural India

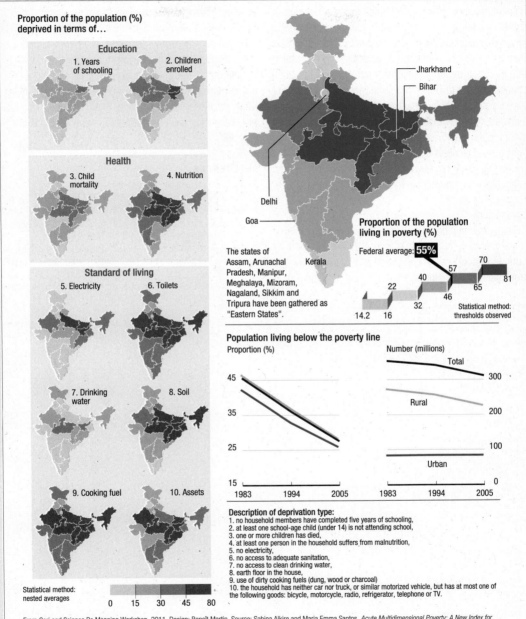

Proportion of the population (%)
deprived in terms of...

Education
1. Years of schooling
2. Children enrolled

Health
3. Child mortality
4. Nutrition

Standard of living
5. Electricity
6. Toilets
7. Drinking water
8. Soil
9. Cooking fuel
10. Assets

Jharkhand
Bihar
Delhi
Goa
Kerala

The states of Assam, Arunachal Pradesh, Manipur, Meghalaya, Mizoram, Nagaland, Sikkim and Tripura have been gathered as "Eastern States".

Proportion of the population living in poverty (%)

Federal average: **55%**

14.2 16 22 32 40 46 57 65 70 81

Statistical method: thresholds observed

Population living below the poverty line

Proportion (%)

45
35
25
15
1983 1994 2005

Number (millions)

Total
300
Rural
200
100
Urban
0
1983 1994 2005

Description of deprivation type:
1. no household members have completed five years of schooling,
2. at least one school-age child (under 14) is not attending school,
3. one or more children has died,
4. at least one person in the household suffers from malnutrition,
5. no electricity,
6. no access to adequate sanitation,
7. no access to clean drinking water,
8. earth floor in the house,
9. use of dirty cooking fuels (dung, wood or charcoal)
10. the household has neither car nor truck, or similar motorized vehicle, but has at most one of the following goods: bicycle, motorcycle, radio, refrigerator, telephone or TV.

Statistical method: nested averages
0 15 30 45 80

From Ceri and Science Po Mapping Workshop, 2011. Design: Benoît Martin. Source: Sabina Alkire and Maria Emma Santos, *Acute Multidimensional Poverty: A New Index for Developing Countries*, 2010, Oxford Poverty & Human Development Initiative (OPHI), University of Oxford, www.ophi.org.uk; World Bank, *Perspectives on Poverty in India*, 2011, p. 5, based on surveys from the National Sample Survey (NSS).

democracy given by the philosopher Alain: "continuous and effective regulation that the ruled apply to the rulers"[8]. At present, the movement is sounding the alarm because of a gradual change in the political discourse from the *right to land for all* moving towards the *right to food for all*. To Ekta Parishad, this subtle change of vocabulary is something that needs to be fought against: namely the devaluation of agriculture in favour of industrialization. For a family, to have land means being able to feed itself; but also to have a place to live, to be able take root in a community, to be autonomous... Conversely, placing the emphasis onto the right to food enables the dependency relationship of the poorest vis-à-vis landowners to persist, and will not lead to a long-term reduction in inequality.

Conclusion

Ekta Parishad firmly believes that a more equitable sharing of natural resources can only be achieved by working in cooperation on several levels. In parallel, the movement has developed a type of local activism that is rooted in the contrasting situations on the ground, and which aims for greater local resilience and a more traditional activism with claims of access to resources made at various levels of government. As a whole, Ekta Parishad is an ideal space for experimentation, using every opportunity available to support the transformation of the individual, to give them control over their own lives and to function as non-violent leaders in service to their communities. While not quite saints perhaps, Ekta Parishad's activists are doing their level best and learning every step of the way. ■

REFERENCES

ALAIN, 1985, Propos sur les pouvoirs, Eléments d'éthique politique, propos choisis et classés par Françis Kaplan. Paris.

BENASAYAG M. and AUBENAS F., 2002, Résister c'est créer. Paris.

CARR-HARRIS J., 2010, A Pedagogy of Non-Violent Social Action. Based on the work of Ekta Parishad. New Delhi.

CHINNAPPAN N., 2010, Accès et contrôle de la terre en Inde, un défi pour les communautés paysannes. Alternatives Sud 17-2010/79,

SHIVA V., 2004, "The future of food: countering globalisation and recolonisation of Indian agriculture." Futures 36 (6-7): 715-732.

SINGLETON M., 2004, "Le World Forum de Mumbai (janvier 2004): foire, foutoir ou foutaise?" Mauss 2004/2(24): 428-440.

---

8. *"True democracy will not come by a few people seizing power, but by the power that everyone has to oppose the abuse of power"* Gandhi, M. K. (1969). Tous les hommes sont frères, Paris, p. 239.

CHAPTER 13

To meet the challenges of sustainable development, attendees at the 2012 Rio+20 Conference – marking the twentieth anniversary of the Earth Summit in Rio de Janeiro – agreed to negotiate Sustainable Development Goals, aiming to strengthen existing accords and conventions. These objectives would be few in number, simple to understand, universal in application and adaptable to each country beginning in 2015. Global inequalities will be a crucial topic of discussion for this new development agenda.

Defining sustainable development goals for 2030

The chapters in this volume document the rise in inequality in many parts of the world, a trend that seems to represent a complex combination of technological forces, globalization, and domestic politics to a varying degree. Whatever the causes, the consequences of high inequality can be severe, not only societies that are less fair, but also societies that are less healthy, politically stable and economically efficient. The goal of greater economic equality is therefore not just a moral one, but also a practical one. It is no accident that "social inclusion" is one of the main pillars of sustainable development, together with economic growth and environmental sustainability.

Xue Lan, Jeffrey D. Sachs, Guido Schmidt-Traub, Laurence Tubiana

and the members of the Leadership Council of the Sustainable Development Solutions Network

Inequality is also not simply a fait accompli. Societies can take measures to make their economies more equal as well as more efficient. The social democracies of Scandinavia, for example, are marked by very low levels of inequality, combined with a high degree of social trust, quality of government, public health and overall economic well-being. The key, it would appear, is universal access to investment in human capital, meaning in essence that every child in a society, whether born in a rich or poor family, has the opportunity to develop his or her skills and physical well-being to the full potential. Societies that invest heavily in public health, children's nutrition, quality day care and pre-school, and quality public education and job training, end up with greater social and economic equality, as well as lower unemployment and higher average economic prosperity.

While the challenges of sustainable development are reasonably well understood the world is not making sufficient progress in ending poverty and promoting economic development, maintaining social inclusion and ensuring environmental sustainability. To accelerate practical problem solving at local, national, regional and global levels, UN Secretary-General Ban Ki-Moon has launched the Sustainable Development Solutions Network. The Network has recently prepared a draft framework for sustainable development, which synthesizes the challenges faced by countries around the world – rich and poor alike, including the challenges of economic and social inequality, and social inclusion.

Below we reproduce an abridged version of this framework. The framework touches on all aspects of sustainable development, including poverty elimination, social inclusion, protection of the Earth's ecosystems and the good governance of public and private institutions needed for success in sustainable development. The Solutions Network invites interested organizations to join the network and to help promote practical problem solving and innovative solutions for addressing the integrated challenges of sustainable development in all parts of the world.

Global sustainable development challenges

The scale of the global sustainable development challenge is difficult to exaggerate. The fight against poverty has made great progress, but more than 1 billion people continue to live in extreme poverty. Inequality and social exclusion are widening within many countries, rich and poor alike. With the world at 7 billion people and an annual GDP of US$70 trillion, human impacts on the environment have reached dangerous levels and are already exceeding some planetary boundaries. By 2050 there may be anywhere from 8.1 billion to 10.6 billion people and a global GDP of more than US$250 trillion.

If this growth occurs on the business-as-usual trajectory, without drastically reducing the resource intensity as well as the pollution caused per dollar of economic output, the consequences will include catastrophic environmental threats. Current growth patterns are also not providing enough decent jobs, and are exacerbating inequalities within our societies. The bottom line is that we need a new global growth framework, one that is compatible with social and environmental objectives.

Even at today's global population and economic output, many key ecosystems are being threatened or destroyed. Climate change is not a distant threat but a stark reality in rich and poor countries alike. Global temperatures are rising; extreme weather events are becoming commonplace; the ocean is acidifying; fisheries are being fished to exhaustion; many fossil resources including oil and groundwater are being rapidly depleted; and the earth is in the midst of an unprecedented mass extinction of species. These problems will expand dangerously and rapidly unless the world changes course urgently.

Fortunately, rapid positive change has become eminently feasible thanks to rising incomes, unprecedented scientific and technological progress, a growing political awareness of the need for sustainable development pathways, and the recognition of the importance of strengthened global partnerships. The world has at its disposal the tools to end extreme poverty in all its forms, promote economic growth and advance environmental sustainability. Where improved tools are needed, particularly to decouple economic progress from the use of environmental resources, these can be developed through concerted action and practical problem solving by governments, business, civil society, science and academia.

No country can tackle the sustainable development challenges alone. Integrated solutions must be developed at local, national, regional and global levels. Every country must rise to the challenge since the traditional distinctions between developed and developing countries or between donors and recipients no longer describe the complex world in which we live. Likewise, businesses and civil society must work towards achieving sustainable development. A compelling framework for sustainable development is needed to mobilize all stakeholders, explain the challenges, focus operational action at the right scale, and form a basis for a true international partnership.

The Sustainable Development Solutions Network (SDSN or the Solutions Network) has been commissioned by UN Secretary-General Ban Ki-Moon to engage scientists, engineers, business and civil society leaders, and development practitioners for practical, evidence-based problem solving.

The framework for sustainable development

We are moving from a development period defined by the Millennium Development Goals[1] (MDGs), which are to be attained by 2015, to one defined by goals that recognize the full economic, social and environmental dimensions of sustainable development. The Rio+20 Conference endorsed the concept of Sustainable Development Goals for this purpose.

The MDGs have successfully focused world attention on ending extreme poverty in all its forms and reducing gender inequality. They have accelerated progress towards these objectives and have become a normative framework for development. The discussion around a post-2015 framework must not detract attention away from achieving the MDGs by the end of 2015 or from the core priority of ending extreme poverty. Yet, today's challenges of sustainable development are broader than the scope of the MDGs. They affect all countries, and all countries must contribute to solutions. In addition to national and local governments, businesses and civil society organizations must also be called upon to contribute to meeting the challenges of sustainable development.

The framework for sustainable development describes society's commitment to four interconnected objectives: economic development (including the end of extreme poverty), social inclusion, environmental sustainability and good governance (including security). Each of these four dimensions of sustainable development contributes to the other three, and all four are therefore necessary for individual

---

1. Many other internationally agreed goals exist that together cover much of sustainable development, but these goals have been far less successful than the MDGs in mobilizing public attention and stimulating action.

and societal well-being. Sustainable development is sometimes described by the first three dimensions: economic, social, and environmental. We add good governance and personal security as a fourth dimension to highlight several enabling conditions for sustainable development, including transparency, effective institutions, the rule of law, participation and personal security, accountability and adequate financing for public goods. These standards of good governance apply to the public sector, the private sector and civil society.

ECONOMIC DEVELOPMENT AND ENDING POVERTY A central task of sustainable development is to complete the job of ending extreme poverty in all its forms and promoting economic development. A billion people or so remain in extreme poverty, lacking adequate incomes, food security, education, basic infrastructure, and access to healthcare as well as being amongst the most vulnerable to disaster risk. Within the coming generation, i.e. by 2030, it should be possible to ensure that all households have access to basic needs through adequate household income, decent nutrition, food security, and universal access to primary health services including the prevention and treatment of certain non-communicable diseases. Likewise, they should have access to early childhood development, adequate education for professional life skills, and access to basic infrastructure services including, safe water and sanitation, clean energy and broadband connectivity.

While most countries of the world have the domestic resource base to achieve sustainable development, some 50 or so low-income or otherwise fragile countries do not. They are too poor, too remote, too conflict-ridden, too bereft of natural resources, or too burdened by other challenges to meet the goals for sustainable development on their own. Often they experience insecurity and armed conflict. These countries, including many in the Horn of Africa, the Sahel, Central Asia and many landlocked and small-island economies, need special international support to break the vicious cycle of lack of economic development, environmental degradation, insecurity and conflict.

Population growth remains very high in some parts of the world. To enable sustainable development, countries where population growth is still high because of high fertility should accelerate the reduction of fertility rates by expanding access to voluntary family planning and reproductive healthcare, investing in child survival, promoting an understanding of the benefits of small families, investing in girls' education and adopting a holistic approach to the empowerment of women. Accelerating the reduction of fertility has the potential of ushering in a period where the age distribution of the population is beneficial for economic growth, as the number of potential workers rises in relation to that of children and older persons. Many middle-income countries have benefitted from those changes. For low-income countries to have similar experiences, action to promote the voluntary reduction of fertility should be expanded.

Through broad-based and environmentally sustainable economic growth, all low-income countries can reach the per-capita income threshold of middle-income countries by 2030. Today's middle-income countries can end extreme poverty and become upper-middle-income or high-income countries, depending on their starting point.

SOCIAL INCLUSION Labour markets around the world are undergoing unprecedented changes driven in large part by globalization and technical change. Workers with low educational attainments increasingly find themselves without marketable skills, left unemployed or with wages at poverty levels. Good jobs now require more schooling and more specialized training than before. Those with the skills, good education and social connections, often enjoy huge gains in income. As a result, inequalities of earnings in many countries, rich and poor, have soared in the past two decades, undermining the fairness, justice and even basic human rights in these societies. Of particular concern is the high youth unemployment in many countries, except in a few where targeted institutions of vocational training and apprenticeships seem to support the school-to-work transition.

Despite major progress, gender inequality persists in many societies and violence against women remains widespread. In addition, discrimination against ethnic minority groups, indigenous peoples and geographically isolated populations still exists in many contexts. Gender inequality and other forms of discrimination rob societies of the full productive potential of large shares of their populations. Realizing the economic and social rights of all members of society and reducing inequalities are therefore important elements of a framework for sustainable development.

Another challenge of social inclusion is to maintain or enhance the quality of social interactions, which sociologists call "social capital". This term has many interconnected meanings. It may signify the extent of trust in the society, a scarce resource that contributes to economic productivity and human well-being. Social capital may refer to cultural rights and practices that enable people to feel pride in their identities. It also refers to the honesty and accountability of governments and companies. Social capital also covers the ability of people to assert their points of view and pursue their interests in shared public decision-making processes, which are critical to poor people's access to resources and opportunities and to the realization of their rights. Finally, social capital refers to the resiliency of civil-society organizations – such as charities, self-help groups and not-for-profit "social companies" that address social needs beyond the profit motive. In many countries research suggests a decline in social capital. Trust is falling, corruption (or the perception of it) is on the rise vis-à-vis both the government and corporate sector, and civil-society organizations may be stymied.

To ensure sustainable development economic gains must be socially inclusive, and the quality of social interactions – culture, trust, honesty, voluntarism and altruism – needs to be enhanced through the promotion of social ethics and the observance of human rights for all. Pathways towards addressing inequalities, overcoming discrimination, and improving other forms of social capital are complex and uncertain. Yet, there is strong evidence that policies and investments can play an important role in lowering inequalities and promoting equal opportunities for all. These include improved education and on-the-job-training, particularly for the poor; smart policies to promote new industries; administrative reforms and measures to combat corruption; affirmative action for the poor and marginalized; and social safety nets to better manage the risk of sickness and the consequences of old age.

ENVIRONMENTAL SUSTAINABILITY Sustainable development cannot be attained without ensuring environmental sustainability and pursuing a green economy, meaning a decoupling of economic progress from human-induced environmental damage. In spite of growing public awareness, the dire environmental challenges have worsened considerably during the twenty years between the Rio Earth Summit in 1992 and Rio+20 in 2012: climate change, pollution and unsound chemicals management, unsustainable water use, unsustainable agriculture, unhealthy cities, massive biodiversity loss, emerging diseases, deforestation, desertification and the depletion and degradation of oceans. It is necessary and possible to reverse these trends, but countries lack long-term strategies to address these deep challenges, and there remains far too little environmental understanding and problem solving at local, national and global scales.

The poor often depend heavily on natural resources for their livelihoods and survival and are most vulnerable to environmental change, so extreme poverty can only be ended if environmental degradation is halted and reversed. This will require inter alia a drastic reduction in key dimensions of primary resource intensity of production and consumption in high-income and middle-income countries.

Of particular urgency is the need to decarbonize the economy by 2050. The world economy is built on fossil fuels, which constitute over 80% of primary energy use globally. In order to safeguard the world from runaway climate change, we need to achieve a decarbonized energy and industrial system by 2050, meaning one that emits far less carbon dioxide, or that captures and sequesters the carbon dioxide that is emitted. Yet even with advances in renewable energy technology, fossil fuels remain cheaper on a market basis than most low-carbon energy sources, and carbon emissions have consequently continued to rise steeply. The crux of the problem is that the market prices of fossil fuels do not reflect their true social and environmental costs, including the costs of climate change and pollution. A "social price on carbon" must be added to the market cost to reflect the true costs of fossil fuels, and thereby induce a shift to low-carbon energy.

Even under the most optimistic scenarios, some severe climate change has by now become unavoidable. For example, in the coming decades the frequency and severity of extreme weather events will increase, putting pressure on agriculture, cities and infrastructure; some coastal areas will likely be flooded and some fragile regions may become uninhabitable; many more coral reefs will bleach and biodiversity loss will accelerate. As a result, strategies to achieve economic, social, environmental, governance and personal security objectives must be "climate resilient" and promote adaption to climate change.

Another central challenge is sustainable agriculture and food security. Food production is often environmentally destructive, causing groundwater depletion, topsoil loss, greenhouse gas emissions, pollution from fertilizers and pesticides, loss of habitat, and declining biodiversity. While, on average, there is enough food today to feed all 7 billion people on Earth, under-nutrition among billions coexists with over-nutrition (excess caloric intake) of another billion or so. Too much food is wasted. Regions experiencing widespread malnutrition and growing food scarcity today will tend to expand and remain vulnerable to food insecurity over the foreseeable future, especially because of climate change, depletion of fresh water supplies, and land erosion. The rising world population and per capita food demands will exacerbate these problems. These challenges must be addressed by pursuing an environmentally sustainable intensification of agriculture – particularly among smallholder farmers, investments in the resilience to climate change, drastically reduced losses in the food production chain, and promoting the rapid, voluntary reduction of fertility.

Cities and urban development constitute another priority challenge. Cities are often growing at unmanageable rates; are unhealthy for their residents; comprise large and growing slum areas; rely on outmoded transportation and energy technologies; are threatened by severe environmental disasters; and fail to generate the number of jobs needed to employ their often young populations. Since urban infrastructure is very long-lived, investment decisions made today risk locking cities into unsustainable resource use and unhealthy environments for a long time. Yet, cities also offer tremendous potential for positive change and are often at the forefront of innovation in technologies and policies. Cities are increasingly the fulcrum of economic development and poverty eradication, social inclusion, environmental sustainability and good governance.

Policymakers are generally not familiar enough with the scale of environmental challenges, are too focused on short-term objectives and are excessively influenced by vested interests that resist the transition to sustainability. Often environmental policies are compromised by the belief that one should go for economic growth now, and then clean up later. But the experiences of many countries show that the cost of "cleaning up later" can be prohibitive. Even more critically, the fact that the world is meeting or exceeding many planetary boundaries makes it impossible to sustain growth-first policies. Alternative development pathways are available, but governments in many parts of the world doubt their feasibility, overestimate costs and lack trust in each other's real intentions to address sustainability.

GOOD GOVERNANCE AND PERSONAL SECURITY Good governance is required of all sectors of society: governments, businesses and civil-society organizations. National and local governments need to build effective institutions and pursue sustainable development with transparency, accountability, clear metrics and openness to the participation of all key stakeholders. They should uphold and promote the rule of law as well as basic economic and social rights. Governments must design financing strategies, help mobilize the necessary resources and provide the public goods needed for sustainable development. Public policy decisions must be made on the basis of scientific evidence.

The most important public good is peace and security, including personal security. Development cannot thrive without safety from personal and psychological violence. When conflict is flaring development becomes impossible and hard-fought gains are quickly reversed, as evidenced by the fact that no conflict countries are achieving the MDGs. Ending conflict often requires international support in the form of mediation, peacekeeping and assistance to address the underlying economic and social needs that drive conflict. Personal security, ending conflict and peace building are therefore essential components of good governance for sustainable development.

The private sector is the principal engine for economic growth and job creation. It will develop and deliver many of the new technologies, organizational models and management systems that are needed for sustainable development. Good corporate governance therefore calls for all companies, especially the major multinational companies, to adopt transparent goals for sustainable development, and to hold themselves accountable for those goals vis-à-vis their investors, customers, suppliers and society at large. We should acknowledge that companies are often more powerful than governments in determining the fate of sustainable development and that they have unrivalled technologies, organizational skills and means. Yet their incentives are often not aligned with the public objectives of sustainable development. There can hence be no sustainable development without good corporate governance and accountability. In particular companies should work responsibly and constructively with governments to address market failures, help mobilize the needed resources and ensure that private incentives become more fully aligned with public objectives. They must be accountable for the environmental and social consequences of their actions, along the lines of the "polluter pays" principle. All of this may require fundamental changes to some business models.

There also can be no sustainable development without civil society doing its part. This includes voluntary organizations that hold both government and business to account in terms of performance and honesty, organize and mobilize communities, deliver services, keep neighbourhoods pleasant and safe, and promote cultural activities. It includes philanthropies that support science, research, education and help for the poor. It includes civil society organizations that defend the environment against pollution and other externalities arising from the economy. And it includes "social enterprises," often with distinct legal status, that work on a business model yet do not pursue profit as their sole or main motive.

A central challenge for governments at all levels, the private sector and civil society is to fulfil the promise of new technologies for sustainable development. Substantial progress on any of the four dimensions of sustainable development will require the large-scale adoption of advanced technologies already available. Many more sustainable technologies will need to be developed. Universities and research institutions therefore play an important role in sustainable development. They are engines of basic scientific and technological research. They train future generations of leaders who will have to resolve many of the sustainable development challenges left by previous generations. They conduct much of the operational research that is needed to better understand the challenges, devise solutions, monitor and evaluate progress. And they can be an important partner in diagnosing local challenges and devising pathways towards sustainability.

SYNERGIES AND TRADE-OFFS – INTEGRATING ACROSS THE FOUR DIMENSIONS OF SUSTAIN-ABLE DEVELOPMENT Strategies for sustainable development must be integrated and address the interconnections across the four dimensions. For example, a food security strategy must address the special needs of the extreme poor in rural and urban areas and address gender disparities so that women and young girls have equal access to food. Just as importantly, it must ensure sustainable use of water resources, preserve soil nutrients, protect biodiversity hotspots, and promote resilience as well as adaptation to climate change. Likewise, such a strategy needs to develop effective institutions, ensure adequate financing in the context of limited resources, and much more.

The interdependencies across the four dimensions of sustainable development vary from country to country, from city to city, and from region to region. Therefore, public and private actors at local, national, and regional levels need to diagnose the interdependencies across sectors, identify strategies for exploiting synergies or "win-wins", and determine how to manage trade-offs across policy areas.

Setting goals for sustainable development for 2030

Addressing the challenges of sustainable development requires a shared focus on ending extreme poverty in all its forms and a fundamental transformation in the way our economies are organized. The necessary focus and collaboration across actors and countries can only be achieved through shared global objectives. For this reason the world needs effective and widely shared goals for sustainable development to follow-up on where the MDGs will leave off in 2015. Of course setting global goals will have little impact unless followed up by concerted action, but it is difficult to imagine a pathway towards global sustainability without an ambitious set of shared goals for sustainable development.

Well-crafted post-2015 goals will guide public understanding of complex long-term challenges, inspire public and private action, and promote accountability. Children will learn the goals at school as a shorthand definition of sustainable development. The goals will also promote integrated thinking and put to rest the futile debates that pit one dimension of sustainable development against another. They will mobilize governments and the international system to strengthen measurement and monitoring for sustainable development.

If our sustainable development framework is a good description of the challenges the world faces, then a new set of post-2015 goals till the year 2030 should apply to all countries – rich and poor – for the four dimensions of sustainable development. This does not mean that every goal must be a "stretch goal" for every country. Rich countries, for instance, are likely to have met most goals relating to economic development, but many still lag behind on goals relating to social inclusion, environmental sustainability and governance. Countries that cannot meet the goals on their own should receive international support to do so.

The General Assembly of the United Nations will adopt the post-2015 goals following an intergovernmental process of negotiation. While that process is just starting, there is a reasonable chance that the post-2015 goals might comprise the components below: Ending extreme poverty and promoting sustainable growth; Promoting healthy lives and sustainable fertility; Promoting quality education, job skills and decent work; Promoting gender equality, personal security and well-being; Averting dangerous climate change and industrial pollution; Ensuring food security and sustainable food supplies; Protecting biodiversity and ecosystem services; Building smart, healthy and resilient cities; Fulfilling the promise of technologies for sustainable development; Ensuring good governance and accountability.

These goals may seem utopian. They are not. Indeed the world has considerable wind in its sails to achieve them. Extreme poverty in developing countries was halved between 1990 and 2010, from 43% to around 22%. Child mortality rates have come down, from 97/1,000 to 63/1,000. Enrolment in primary education has risen from 82% to 90% of the number of children of primary-school age. Access to safe water has increased from 76% to 89% of the population. And the technological revolution is spreading everywhere, with mobile phone subscriptions worldwide exceeding 6 billion, including 250 million in sub-Saharan Africa. By 2017, more than 80% of the world will have access to wireless broadband internet. The impetus of technology, management and global awareness all make it possible to be ambitious regarding sustainable development.

One of the lessons of the MDGs is the need for better data systems to track progress towards the international goals, and to support management efforts aimed at achieving the goals. Therefore, the new set of goals for sustainable development must be bolstered by a massive improvement in local, national, and global data collection and processing, using new tools (GIS, satellite, social networking, etc.) as well as existing tools. We will need real-time, complex, place-based and sub-national data to support the sustainable development efforts.

Applying the framework: Integrated pathways to sustainable development

A framework for sustainable development must be applied at global, regional, national and local scales. Each region, each country, each city, and each rural locality will need to make its own situation analysis, asking questions such as: How can we end extreme poverty in all its forms? How can we reduce youth unemployment? How can we reduce disparities across gender and socio-economic groups? What are the locally and regionally available renewable energy resources? What are the local vulnerabilities of food production and food security? How do prevailing fertility rates and population trends affect prospects for sustainable development? And so forth.

Feasible pathways are of course highly complex, subject to great technological uncertainty, and likely to require substantial financial resources. They often require changes in behaviour and involve complex interactions across objectives, across time and across actors. The sections below identify a few questions that will need to be addressed in applying the framework. This list is not complete and is designed as a starting point to trigger discussion and elicit practical problem solving.

(I) THE IMPORTANCE OF DECOUPLING Pathways to sustainable development need to "decouple" economic growth from the rising use of primary resources, thereby reducing the resource-intensity of production. At a time when high-income economies are looking to maintain living standards and re-start growth, and middle and low-income economies want to achieve economic convergence, decoupling is a fundamental condition of sustainable development.

Decoupling requires a holistic approach to the transformation of the entire economy in regard to the use of energy and to the use of resources and materials. Important areas of decoupling include:

– Energy efficiency measures and low-carbon energy systems (renewables, nuclear, carbon capture and storage) can decouple rising energy use from carbon dioxide emissions;

– Precision farming, improved crop varieties, efficient water management and no-till farm practices can decouple rising food yields from unsustainable utilization of water, chemicals, fertilizers and land;

– Green buildings, smart grids, and improved transportation systems can decouple urbanization from rising urban energy use and ensure effective land use;

Market signals are not currently adequate to achieve decoupling, since the market does not compel polluters[2] to bear the full cost of pollution and does not establish prices for ecosystem services. This is particularly the case when pollution is global or at long distances from impacted areas, since political systems then have great difficulty in internalizing externalities, either through laws, economic incentives or social norms. For this reason, successful decoupling will require corrections to faulty market signals, increased political cooperation regionally and globally, strategies to promote research and development on sustainable technologies, and increased public awareness and understanding of the key challenges.

Investments in sustainable infrastructure will cost money and put a burden on low-income countries. At the core of sustainable development, therefore, must be a *financing strategy* that is deemed to be fair and practical. There will need to be at least three components of such a strategy. First, polluters should pay to clean up after themselves and compensate those bearing the burden of the pollution. Second, ecosystem services need to be priced. Third, rich countries should help poor countries to cover the incremental costs of investment.

---

2. The term 'polluter' includes inter alia low-efficiency producers and wasteful consumers that squander resources with detrimental spillover to society at large.

Finally, decoupling requires clear strategies for managing non-sustainable "stranded assets" such as fossil fuel deposits that should not be exploited or coal-fired power plants that become uneconomical once the price for carbon emissions rises. Such strategies need to address deep political, legal and financial issues, which would otherwise delay or hinder the decoupling of economic growth from resource use and pollution.

(II) THE NEED TO CHANGE BEHAVIOUR AND ARTICULATE THE BUSINESS CASE FOR SUSTAINABLE DEVELOPMENT Putting the world rapidly onto a long-term path towards sustainable development requires very large numbers of individuals to change behaviour and make different choices with regards to business management, ethics, politics, healthy lifestyles and personal consumption, resource use, fertility, education and so forth. In some instances public policies create the incentives that guide behaviour (through corrective pricing for example). Often the behaviour is conditioned by factors outside the direct control of public policies and economic incentives. When government leaders are accountable to their people, changing people's understanding and even behaviours becomes a necessary prerequisite for changing policies.

Operationalizing the framework for sustainable development therefore requires clear diagnoses of the needed changes in professional and personal behaviour as well as explicit strategies for bringing about such changes. Such strategies can draw on successful examples from public health, education, politics and other fields. Changing the behaviour of private corporations requires inter alia a clear articulation of the business case for sustainable development. In some instances companies

BOX 1 ECONOMIC GROWTH AND RESOURCE CHALLENGES.

Using the World Bank's definitions of income groups, the world is divided between low-income, middle-income and high-income categories as follows:

	Population 2011 (billion)	Mean Income 2011 ($US PPP)	Total Income ($US PPP trillions)
Low-Income	0.8	1,383	1.1
Lower Middle-Income	2.5	3,833	9.7
Upper Middle-Income	2.5	10,705	26.6
High-Income	1.1	38,572	43.8
World	7.0	11,574	81.3

As this table shows, raising the low-income countries to at least lower-middle-income status would not by itself lead to a large increase in global income. If today's low-income countries, with average incomes per capita of $1,383, were to become lower-middle-income countries at $3,833 per capita, the increment of income would be $2 trillion, or just 2.5% of today's world income. If today's lower-middle-income countries were to become upper-middle income countries, the increment to world income would be 21% of the world income. If today's upper-middle-income countries were to achieve high-income status, the increment would be 85% of today's world income.

Since resource use remains directly related to income, the main conclusion is that raising average incomes in the poorest countries is not by itself a major resource challenge or burden on the planet. The much greater resource challenge is accommodating the rise of today's middle-income countries to high-income conditions. The latter can only be accomplished sustainably if the world succeeds in decoupling economic growth, primary resource use and environmental degradation.

are beholden to "old ways of doing things" and fail to explore new business opportunities that increase profitability by reducing material use, lowering pollution, and increasing acceptance by their customers. The Sustainable Development Solutions Network will work with private sector networks to help articulate the business case for sustainable development with a particular focus on overcoming the perceived first-mover disadvantage.

(III) QUANTIFYING THE CHALLENGES OF SUSTAINABLE DEVELOPMENT Sustainable development requires quantification. At what pace should de-carbonization occur? How much water use for agriculture is feasible in a particular location? How should fertilizer use be moderated to protect crops and waterways at the same time? What are the implications of the growth of cities? What do different demographic pathways imply for countries' sustainable development prospects? Which are the most effective techniques for reducing and managing disaster risks? These questions, and many others like them, require a quantitative assessment that combines Earth systems with human systems, and does so at many scales, from local to global. As one example, we illustrate the resource challenges emanating from economic growth (box 1).

Conclusion

The post-2015 development framework will be devised and adopted by UN member states over the coming two years. In comparison to the MDGs it seems necessary to broaden the agenda and give greater prominence to issues of inequality and social inclusion, the special needs of fragile states, natural resource use and planetary boundaries, etc. The world has also become more interconnected and is pushing hard against many planetary boundaries, so the post-2015 framework will need to apply to all countries – rich and poor alike.

Adopting a bold and broad post-2015 framework will not guarantee that countries successfully address the four dimensions of sustainable development. Yet, it seems difficult to imagine how meaningful progress can be made in eradicating poverty, promoting economic development, enhancing social inclusion, and promoting environmental sustainability without a shared international framework. For this reason the successful adoption of a bold, operational set of goals is so important.

The Sustainable Development Solutions Network will help mobilize universities, research institutes, business and civil society organizations through an open process to accelerate practical problem solving for sustainable development. In particular the network will identify and promote solution initiatives that can have a transformational impact on sustainable development. In this way we hope to make a contribution towards moving the world onto a sustainable development pathway. ∎

Goal-setting in an era of multilateral mistrust

Mark Halle, International Institute for Sustainable Development, Geneva, Switzerland

The decision by governments at the Rio+20 conference in June to articulate and adopt a comprehensive set of Sustainable Development Goals (SDGs) was then – and is still – hailed as one of the most positive outcomes of the conference. With very few genuinely new commitments emerging from Rio, the sustainable development community has pinned its hopes on the adoption of binding and shared goals covering the period from 2015 forward and addressing the range of sustainability challenges facing humanity. The process for making this aspiration a reality, including the creation of an Open Working Group (OWG) with heavy input from civil society and the private sector, has begun at the UN General Assembly in New York.

As we all know, however, the UN in New York has become a highly vexed forum in which to seek international consensus. What chance do the SDGs have of seeing the light of day, and how can they go beyond the simply aspirational and actually serve as a framework for global development efforts? And what chance does the SDG process have of crossing the mosquito-ridden marsh without sinking irrevocably into the mud?

The most recent proximate experience is that of the Millennium Development Goals (MDGs). Adopted at the Millennium Summit in 2000, the general consensus is that they have proved useful in focusing development effort and available funding on a handful of achievable targets and that, by the time their period of implementation has elapsed, at least some of them will have been met while others will have progressed considerably. Indeed, setting the initiation date of the SDGs in 2015 is intended not only to give space for consensus-building around the new goals, but to provide no excuse whatsoever for distracting attention from the completion of MDG obligations.

By 2015, the UN also aims to adopt a new development agenda, drawing not only on all the intergovernmental undertakings over the two decades since the Earth Summit in 1992 but also very much on the outcomes of the Rio+20 conference. Further, it has established a High-Level Panel of Eminent Persons to advise it on this agenda. The interplay between the development agenda, the Panel and the OWG for the SDGs is clearly important, and the years until 2015 will allow the optimal synergy between the different processes to be achieved – or for one to dominate the others.

But, as so often happens in the intergovernmental world, we have entrusted the realization of our lofty intentions to one of the world's most politically-captured institutions, one with a long track record of sending initiative after initiative into the quicksand. Will the momentum from Rio carry the SDGs across the swamp to dry land on the other side? And how can we organize, run and support the process to maximize our chances for real success?

It is instructive to look at the experience of the MDGs to see what lessons can be learned for the SDG process. On the plus side, despite a slow start, the MDGs achieved a snowball effect throughout the development community and well beyond into civil society and the private sector. Here were – finally – eight goals and an accompanying set of targets that were politically, financially and logistically achievable; in fact the greatest criticism was that they lacked ambition, that in 15 years we should be able to accomplish even more. Indeed, suggesting that we could arrive at 2015 with over a billion still poor and hungry was not easy for many to accept, especially knowing that the resources exist to feed everyone on the planet. Similarly, halving the proportion of people without access to safe drinking water and decent sanitation is a modest goal, especially given that it could leave more people without safe water in 2015 than there were in 2000.

Nevertheless the MDGs, built as they are on existing programmes, served to concentrate and structure international effort and offered a clear and for the most part numerically monitorable pathway to progress and final achievement. The wide acceptance and high profile that the MDGs eventually achieved certainly led to new resources being mobilized and exerted moral pressure on countries to demonstrate what they were doing to favour their successful achievement. As a result, the MDGs rose to the top of the development agenda and stayed there for much of the decade since their adoption. That in itself explains more than any other factor why the MDGs have been regarded as a success, and why the SDGs are expected to meet the same high standard.

The choice to focus on the successes of the MDGs cannot be allowed to mask the much bleaker reality: in most cases the goals will not be met – the majority will not even be approached. Public discourse around the goals focuses on the poverty alleviation targets – regarded as the greatest MDG success story. But even if, as seems possible, these targets are met, it will largely be thanks to the rapid emergence of a middle class in China and India. If we subtract these two factors from the equation, the arrow not only fails to hit the bull's eye, it falls well short of the target itself. And it would be a stretch to claim that the relative success of China and India is the result of actions taken in response to the MDGs.

Some of the MDGs should have been doable with readily available technology and with existing levels of institutional organization and funding – e.g. the targets on drinking water and sanitation, HIV/AIDS or improving the lives of slum dwellers. Others were included because their absence would have made the package seem imbalanced, even if not many observers felt they were achievable in the time period. Ending gender discrimination throughout the planet or ensuring that all girls receive primary education, while worthy and urgent, was not likely to be achieved,

even with the most earnest of efforts.

Further, MDG success should not simply be judged on the differential between 2000 and 2015, but on the differential between 2015 and the likely 2015 scenario if the MDGs had not been adopted. After all, development was proceeding before 2000 and it would have continued even if the MDGs had not been set. It should be possible to project the trends in evidence in 1999 forward to 2015 and determine whether or not the MDGs have caused a major increase in development achievement.

So what will happen in 2015? In all likelihood, we will celebrate the MDGs as a major triumph for development and urge governments not to let up in their efforts to achieve the goals finally and fully. Those goals that were not met will no doubt find their place in one form or another in the newly-minted SDGs; those that were met will be tightened and similarly included. And a new horizon, probably 2030, will be fixed, elegantly kicking the can down the road well beyond the political mandates of any who might be blamed for failure.

How, then, can we build on the successes of the MDGs, and how can we avoid repeating their failures?

One criticism of the MDGs is that they were cooked up in the UN Secretary General's office and sprung on Heads of State at the Millennium Summit with inadequate consultation. Whether or not it is justified, this criticism has stuck; the halls of Rio echoed with warnings not to make the same mistake with the SDGs. This is one of the reasons why a comprehensive set of draft goals was not tabled in Rio, and why a three-year period has been booked for their elaboration. The SDG process not only allows for the OWG and for eventual approval by the General Assembly but also for input from the Secretary-General's new high-level panel and a still-to-be-defined process for collecting ideas from civil society and the private sector. Ideas abound, as do visions for how the process should be organized. The Secretariat will gather, sift and organize these proposals but, in the end, they will feed into a political process that will not necessarily assess them on their merits alone. Recent examples of the broad trawl for ideas, including the commendable process set up by the Brazilians for Rio, while inclusive and welcoming of a wide range of approaches, have had little effect on negotiated outcomes.

FIGURE 1 First MDG reached: water

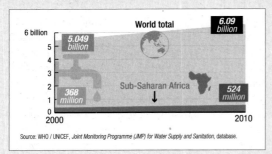

Source: WHO / UNICEF, *Joint Monitoring Programme (JMP) for Water Supply and Sanitation,* database.

FIGURE 2 Sanitation, an almost forgotten MDG?

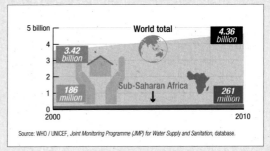

Source: WHO / UNICEF, *Joint Monitoring Programme (JMP) for Water Supply and Sanitation,* database.

Access to water has significantly improved worldwide over the last decade, and is approaching universal provision. It can be said that in 2010, five years before the deadline, the goal of having halved the number of people without access to water compared to the 1990 level was achieved. Sub-Saharan Africa however remains below the overall growth rate, with only 61% of the population having access to water in 2010.

Conversely, five years before the deadline, access to sanitation is one of the goals where least has been achieved. 2.5 billion people have no access to any form of sanitation. Coverage should reach 67% of the world population in 2015 instead of the 75% expected. In sub-Saharan Africa, but also in many Asian countries, investment in this area is virtually non-existent.

Second, the SDGs must avoid the accountability failures of the MDG process. At the intergovernmental level it is easy to make promises, in large part because there is no price to be paid for not fulfilling them. It is all very well to promise to "Reduce Biodiversity Loss, achieving, by 2010, a significant reduction in the rate of loss" (MDG target 7B). The real questions are: who will take what actions to reduce this loss, by when, with what means, and with what consequences if the actions are not taken? In the absence of clear answers to these questions, nobody can be held to account except the elusive "global community" that is, in any event, exempt from punishment. So what happens in such cases? We sit back and hope that somebody, somewhere, will take steps to stem the global haemorrhage of biodiversity because they were inspired by the loftiness and global acceptability of the goal. To pin our hopes on this approach is to suffer from life-threatening naivety.

In fact, what was expected was that the goal would lead governments to beef up existing programmes on biodiversity conservation in FAO, UNEP and others, to launch new initiatives (such as REDD and REDD+) and place biodiversity loss higher up the political agenda. Did that happen? Yes, all of it happened, but in proportions entirely inadequate to the challenge. Who, then, was sent to the corner sporting a tall cone-shaped hat? Nobody, of course. Even when binding, most international undertakings are in reality voluntary, and the will is not there, or at least not powerful enough, to set in motion the game-changing decisions without which we will inexorably fall short of our goals.

The SDG process must take this lesson solidly on board. Without a clear and robust accountability framework, the goals will not be achieved, even if there is a strong intention at the outset to succeed. Each goal adopted should specify who will take what action, against what timetable. The funding needed to reach the targets must be identified and committed, and there must be a genuine link between failure and sanction – or between success and reward.

This is important. We are too inclined to think that accountability means punishment, but accountability can also be positive. How much more successful would we be if full implementation of agreed actions led to economic or political reward? Is it inconceivable that African countries might be rewarded with trade preferences for reaching their targets? Or that they receive an increased quota of scholarships to universities in the OECD countries? Or funding for the next stage of effort?

Finally, and equally important, the MDGs are falling short of our aspirations in part because we have counted on governments to take the bulk of the action. If the SDGs are to draw on the ingenuity and sense of innovation evident in the broader sustainable development community, they must be structured so that each component of that community has a role in achieving the goals. Of particular importance is the private sector which, more so even than governments and civil society, has the financial, institutional, logistical and human capacity to take the lead in turning the goals into achievements. It is idle to suppose that the private sector will be inspired by the kind of insipid soup that is dished out these days by intergovernmental process. It follows that the process around the OWG must be constructed with a good deal of imagination, so that the energy and spirit of enterprise that abound in civil society and the private sector are harnessed to build a bridge across the fetid swamp into which too many good international intentions tend to subside.

In the end, it may be better to set a limited number of SDGs, and to adopt only those to which we are prepared to commit and to whose achievements we are prepared to hold ourselves accountable and for which we have significant buy-in from both the corporate sector and the wider organizations of civil society. ■